Learning R Programming

Become an efficient data scientist with R

Kun Ren

BIRMINGHAM - MUMBAI

Learning R Programming

First published: October 2016

Production reference: 2211016

Published by Packt Publishing Ltd.

Livery Place

35 Livery Street

Birmingham B3 2PB, UK.

ISBN 978-1-78588-977-6

www.packtpub.com

Credits

Author

Kun Ren

Reviewer

Kelly Black

Commissioning Editor

Akram Hussain

Acquisition Editor

Denim Pinto

Content Development Editor

Rohit Kumar Singh

Technical Editor

Vivek Pala

Copy Editor

Karuna Narayanan

Project Coordinator

Izzat Contractor

Proofreader

Safis Editing

Indexer

Tejal Daruwale Soni

Graphics
Kirk D'Penha
Disha Haria
Jason Monteiro

Production Coordinator

Melwyn D'sa

About the Author

Kun Ren has used R for nearly 4 years in quantitative trading, along with C++ and C#, and he has worked very intensively (more than 8-10 hours every day) on useful R packages that the community does not offer yet. He contributes to packages developed by other authors and reports issues to make things work better. He is also a frequent speaker at R conferences in China and has given multiple talks. Kun also has a great social media presence. Additionally, he has substantially contributed to various projects, which is evident from his GitHub account:

- https://github.com/renkun-ken
- https://cn.linkedin.com/in/kun-ren-76027530
- http://renkun.me/
- http://renkun.me/formattable/
- http://renkun.me/pipeR/
- http://renkun.me/rlist/

I would like to thank my wife, who encouraged me to start working on this book a year ago, and my parents, who support me with unconditional love. I would also like to express my gratitude to the editors, Rohit Kumar Singh, Vivek Pala, and those who also worked hard on this book. They did a great job making the writing and publishing smooth.

About the Reviewer

Kelly Black is a member of the department of mathematics at the University of Georgia. His focus is stochastic differential equations, and he makes use of statistical software in a wide range of contexts, ranging from data analysis from Monte Carlo simulations to educational assessment.

I am grateful for the kindness and patience of Izzat Contractor, who helped guide the final production of this book.

www.PacktPub.com

For support files and downloads related to your book, please visit www.PacktPub.com.

Did you know that Packt offers eBook versions of every book published, with PDF and ePub files available? You can upgrade to the eBook version at www.PacktPub.com and as a print book customer, you are entitled to a discount on the eBook copy. Get in touch with us at service@packtpub.com for more details.

At www.PacktPub.com, you can also read a collection of free technical articles, sign up for a range of free newsletters and receive exclusive discounts and offers on Packt books and eBooks.

https://www.packtpub.com/mapt

Get the most in-demand software skills with Mapt. Mapt gives you full access to all Packt books and video courses, as well as industry-leading tools to help you plan your personal development and advance your career.

Why subscribe?

- Fully searchable across every book published by Packt
- Copy and paste, print, and bookmark content
- On demand and accessible via a web browser

Table of Contents

Preface

R is designed for statistical computing, data analysis, and visualization. In recent years, it has become the most popular language for data science and statistics. R programming heavily involves data processing and it can be a challenge to program in R for those who are unfamiliar with the behaviors of the R language.

As a dynamic language, R allows extremely flexible use of data structures that are not as strict as compiled languages, such as C++, Java, and C#. When I started using R to process and analyze data, I found R's behavior quirky, unpredictable, and sometimes very inconsistent.

In those data analysis projects, most effort was not spent running models. Instead, data cleaning, wrangling, and visualization took a major part of my time. In fact, it is most time consuming to find what's wrong with the code that produced weird results or died in unexpected errors. Dealing with programming rather than field problems can be frustrating, especially when you have fought against bugs for hours without a clue.

However, as I work on more projects and gain more experience, I gradually know more about the behavior of objects and functions, and find that R is much more beautiful and consistent than I thought. That's why I've written this book—to share my perspective on programming in R.

Through this book, you will develop a universal and consistent understanding of R as a programming language along with its vast set of tools. You will learn the best practices to boost your productivity, develop a deeper understanding of working with data, and become more confident about programming in R and solving problems with the right techniques.

What this book covers

Chapter 1, *Quick Start*, discusses a few basic facts about R, how to deploy an R environment, and how to code in RStudio.

Chapter 2, *Basic Objects*, introduces basic R objects and their behaviors.

Chapter 3, *Managing Your Workspace*, introduces the methods of managing the working directory, R environment, and the library of extension packages.

Chapter 4, *Basic Expressions*, covers the basic expressions of the R language: assignment, condition, and loop.

Chapter 5, *Working with Basic Objects*, discusses the basic functions each analyst should know in order to work with basic objects in R.

Chapter 6, *Working with Strings*, talks about R objects related with strings, and a number of string manipulation techniques.

Chapter 7, *Working with Data*, explains simple read/write data functions with some practical examples on various topics using basic objects and functions.

Chapter 8, *Inside R*, discusses R's evaluation model by introducing what lazy evaluation, environment, function, and lexical scoping work is.

Chapter 9, *Metaprogramming*, introduces the metaprogramming techniques to help understand language objects and nonstandard evaluation.

Chapter 10, *Object-Oriented Programming*, describes the numerous object-oriented programming systems in R: S3, S4, RefClass, and community-provided R6.

Chapter 11, *Working with Databases*, shows how R works with popular relational databases such as SQLite and MySQL, and non-relational databases such as MongoDB and Redis.

Chapter 12, *Data Manipulation*, introduces techniques of manipulating relational data using data.table and dplyr, and non-relational data using rlist.

Chapter 13, *High Performance Computing*, discusses performance issues in R and several methods to boost computing performance.

Chapter 14, *Web Scraping*, talks about the basic structure of web pages, CSS, and XPath selectors and how to use the rvest package to scrape data from simple web pages.

Chapter 15, *Boosting Productivity*, demonstrates how R Markdown and shiny app, combined with interactive graphics, can boost productivity in the reporting and presentation of data analysis.

What you need for this book

To run the example code in this book, you will need to install R 3.3.0 or newer. RStudio is the recommended development environment.

For Chapter 11, *Working with Databases,* a working MongoDB server and a Redis instance is required to run examples.

For Chapter 13, *High Performance Computing,* Rtools 3.3 is required to build an Rcpp code under Windows, and a gcc toolchain is required under Linux or macOS.

Who this book is for

This book targets those who work on data-related projects and want to boost productivity but may not be familiar with the programming language and related tools.

This book also targets professional data analysts who want to systematically learn the R programming language, related techniques, and recommended packages and practices.

Although several chapters are a bit advanced for beginners, you don't have to be a computer expert or a professional data analyst to read those chapters, but I assume you will have a general idea of basic programming concepts and a basic experience of data processing.

Conventions

In this book, you will find a number of text styles that distinguish between different kinds of information. Here are some examples of these styles and an explanation of their meaning.

Code words in text, database table names, folder names, filenames, file extensions, pathnames, dummy URLs, user input, and Twitter handles are shown as follows: "The apply function also supports array input and matrix output."

The style of inline code words (variables and function names) and code blocks is set as follows:

```
x <- c(1, 2, 3)
class(x)
## [1] "numeric"
typeof(x)
## [1] "double"
str(x)
##  num [1:3] 1 2 3
```

There will be a highlight on certain areas of the code whenever a point is being pointed out:

```
x <- rnorm(100)
y <- 2 * x + rnorm(100) * 0.5
m <- lm(y ~ x)
coef(m)
```

New terms and **important words** are shown in bold.

 Warnings or important notes appear in a box like this.

 Tips and tricks appear like this.

Reader feedback

Feedback from our readers is always welcome. Let us know what you think about this book—what you liked or disliked. Reader feedback is important for us as it helps us develop titles that you will really get the most out of.

To send us general feedback, simply e-mail feedback@packtpub.com, and mention the book's title in the subject of your message.

If there is a topic that you have expertise in and you are interested in either writing or contributing to a book, see our author guide at www.packtpub.com/authors.

Customer support

Now that you are the proud owner of a Packt book, we have a number of things to help you to get the most from your purchase.

Downloading the example code

You can download the example code files for this book from your account at `http://www.packtpub.com`. If you purchased this book elsewhere, you can visit `http://www.packtpub.com/support` and register to have the files e-mailed directly to you.

You can download the code files by following these steps:

1. Log in or register to our website using your e-mail address and password.
2. Hover the mouse pointer on the **SUPPORT** tab at the top.
3. Click on **Code Downloads & Errata**.
4. Enter the name of the book in the **Search** box.
5. Select the book for which you're looking to download the code files.
6. Choose from the drop-down menu where you purchased this book from.
7. Click on **Code Download**.

You can also download the code files by clicking on the **Code Files** button on the book's webpage at the Packt Publishing website. This page can be accessed by entering the book's name in the Search box. Please note that you need to be logged in to your Packt account.

Once the file is downloaded, please make sure that you unzip or extract the folder using the latest version of:

- WinRAR / 7-Zip for Windows
- Zipeg / iZip / UnRarX for Mac
- 7-Zip / PeaZip for Linux

The code bundle for the book is also hosted on GitHub at `https://github.com/PacktPublishing/learningrprogramming`. We also have other code bundles from our rich catalog of books and videos available at `https://github.com/PacktPublishing/`. Check them out!

Errata

Although we have taken every care to ensure the accuracy of our content, mistakes do happen. If you find a mistake in one of our books—maybe a mistake in the text or the code—we would be grateful if you could report this to us. By doing so, you can save other readers from frustration and help us improve subsequent versions of this book. If you find any errata, please report them by visiting http://www.packtpub.com/submit-errata, selecting your book, clicking on the Errata Submission Form link, and entering the details of your errata. Once your errata are verified, your submission will be accepted and the errata will be uploaded to our website or added to any list of existing errata under the Errata section of that title.

To view the previously submitted errata, go to https://www.packtpub.com/books/content/support and enter the name of the book in the search field. The required information will appear under the Errata section.

Piracy

Piracy of copyrighted material on the Internet is an ongoing problem across all media. At Packt, we take the protection of our copyright and licenses very seriously. If you come across any illegal copies of our works in any form on the Internet, please provide us with the location address or website name immediately so that we can pursue a remedy.

Please contact us at copyright@packtpub.com with a link to the suspected pirated material.

We appreciate your help in protecting our authors and our ability to bring you valuable content.

Questions

If you have a problem with any aspect of this book, you can contact us at questions@packtpub.com, and we will do our best to address the problem.

1
Quick Start

Data analysis is difficult without the proper tools. It is almost impossible to extract patterns directly from a large set of numbers aligned in rows and columns and draw any conclusion, even for experts. A suitable tool, such as R, will remarkably boost your productivity in working with data. From my experience, learning a programming language is somehow like learning a human language. It is probably not a good idea to jump right into the details of vocabulary and grammar before looking at the big picture, getting motivated, and starting small. This chapter gives you a quick start by taking an overview of the R programming language in depth.

In this chapter, we will cover the following topics:

- Introducing R
- The need for R
- Installing R
- Tools required to write R code

As soon as the software and tools are ready to go, you will write a simple R program to experience how it basically works. Once this is done, the R journey will unfold from the basics to advanced techniques and applications.

Introducing R

R is a powerful programming language and environment for statistical computing, data exploration, analysis, and visualization. It is free, open source, and has a strong, rapidly growing community where users and developers share their experience and actively contribute to the development of more than 7,500 packages, so that R can deal with problems in a wide range of fields (refer to `https://cran.r-project.org/web/views/`).

Although the origin of the R programming language dates back to 1993, its general adoption in R programming language data-related research industry has grown rapidly in the last decade and has become the lingua franca of data science.

In general, R should be viewed as more than just a programming language; it is a comprehensive computing environment, a strong and active community, and a rapidly growing and expanding ecosystem.

R as a programming language

R, as a programming language, has been evolving and developing over the last 20 years. Its goal is quite clear to make it easy and flexible to perform comprehensive statistical computing, data exploration, and visualization.

However, ease of use and flexibility usually create conflicts. It can be very easy to click a few buttons to finish a variety of tasks in statistical analysis, but it won't be flexible if you need customization, automation, and your work needs to be reproducible. It can be very flexible to use tens of functions to transform data and make complicated graphics, but it won't be easy to learn and combine these functions correctly. R stands out for its well-positioned balance.

R as a computing environment

R, as a computing environment, is lightweight and ready to use. Compared to some other famous statistical software, for example, Matlab and SAS, R is much smaller and easier to deploy.

In this book, we will use RStudio to handle almost all our work in R. This integrated development environment provides rich features such as syntax-highlighting, auto-completion, package management, graphics viewer, help viewer, environment viewer, and debugging. These features hugely boost your productivity.

R as a community

R, as a community, is strong and active. You can visit Try R (`http://tryr.codeschool.com/`) immediately and get a first impression of R basics through an interactive tutorial. In practice, when you are coding, you probably won't solve every problem by yourself. You may google an R question and find that it almost always has answers in StackOverflow (`http://stackoverflow.com/questions/tagged/r`). If your question is not fully addressed, you can ask it and probably get an answer in a couple of minutes.

If you need to use a package but also want to see how it works in detail, you can visit the source code at its online repository (or repo). Many repos are hosted by GitHub (`https://www.github.com`). In GitHub, you can do much more. When you find that a package is not working correctly, you can report a bug by filing an issue on the problem. If you need a feature that fits the purpose of the package, you can request a feature also by filing an issue for your demand. If you are interested in contributing to the package by resolving bugs and implementing features, you can fork the project, edit the code, and send merge requests so that your changes can be accepted by the owner. If your changes are accepted, congratulations, you have become a contributor to the package! Amazingly, R and its thousands of packages are built by contributors all over the world.

R as an ecosystem

R, as an ecosystem, is rapidly growing and expanding in all data-related areas beyond the IT industry. The majority of its users are not professional developers but data analysts and statisticians. These users may not write the best-quality code, but they may contribute cutting-edge tools to the ecosystem in R language, and everyone else has free access to these tools without having to reinvent the wheels.

For example, let's say an econometrician writes an extension package that includes a new method to detect a category of time series patterns; it may attract several users who find it interesting and useful. Some professional users may improve the original code to make it faster and more general-purpose. A while later, a quantitative investor may find it helpful to incorporate this method into a trading strategy because it can detect patterns that usually causes risks in his/her portfolio. At the end of the day, the econometrician's tool is applied in a real-world industry, and the investor finds the portfolio less risky.

That is how the ecosystem works. And that is one of the reasons why R rocks in these areas: it has the ability to quickly adapt cutting-edge knowledge outside the IT industry (usually data science, Academia, and Industry) to generally available and applicable tools in the ecosystem. In other words, it facilitates conversion from the field knowledge and data science to productivity and value.

The need for R

R stands out from a wide variety of statistical software for the following reasons:

- **Free of charge**: R is totally free. You don't need to buy a license, so there is no financial entry barrier to use it and most of its extension packages.
- **Open-source**: R and most of its packages are fully open source. Thousands of developers are constantly reviewing the source code of the packages to check whether there are bugs to fix or things to improve. If you encounter exceptions, you can even dig into the source code, find where the problem is, and contribute to fixing it.
- **Popular**: R is a very popular, if not the most popular, statistical programming language and platform to perform data mining, analysis, and visualization. High popularity often means easier communication between you and other users because you "speak" the same language.
- **Flexible**: R is a dynamic script language. It is highly flexible to allow programming styles in multiple paradigms, including functionality programming and object-oriented programming. It also supports flexible metaprogramming. Its flexibility enables you to perform highly customized and comprehensive data transformation and visualization.
- **Reproducible**: When using software based on a graphical user interface, you only need to choose from menus and click buttons. However, it is hard to accurately reproduce what you have done automatically without writing scripts.

    In most scientific research areas and many industrial applications, reproducibility is necessary for many reasons. R scripts can precisely describe what you do with the computing environment and data so that it is fully reproducible from scratch.

- **Rich resources**: R has a huge, rapidly increasing number of online resources. One type of resource is extension packages. There are, at the time of writing this, more than 7,500 packages available at **CRAN** (short for **Comprehensive R Archive Network**), a world-wide network of mirror servers from which you can get identical, up-to-date, R distributions and packages.

These packages are created and maintained by more than 4,500 package developers in almost all data-related areas, such as multivariate analysis, time series analysis, econometrics, Bayesian inference, optimization, finance, genetics, chemometrics, computational physics, and many others. Take a look at CRAN Task View (`https://cran.r-project.org/web/views/`) for a good summary.

In addition to the enormous number of packages, there are also a great number of authors who regularly write personal blogs and Stack Overflow answers and share their thoughts, experiences, and recommended practices. Plus, there are a lot of websites specializing in R, such as R-bloggers (`http://www.r-bloggers.com/`), R documentation (`http://www.rdocumentation.org/`), and METACRAN (`http://www.r-pkg.org/`).

- **Strong community**: The community of R consists of not only R developers but also, (the majority), R users from a wide range of backgrounds such as statistics, econometrics, finance, bioinformatics, mechanical engineering, physics, medicine, and so on.

    A great number of R developers actively contribute to open source projects or packages written in R. The goal of the community is to make data analysis, exploration, and visualization easier and more interesting.

    If you are stuck in a problem in R, just google what puzzles you; probably, there are already some answers to your question. If not, just ask a question on Stack Overflow and you will get a response in a very short time.

- **Cutting-edge:** Many R users are professional researchers in statistics, econometrics, or other disciplines. Quite often, authors publish their new papers along with a new package that includes the cutting-edge techniques presented in the paper. Maybe it's a new statistical test, a pattern recognition method, or a better-tuned optimization algorithm.

    No matter what it is, the R community has the privilege of applying cutting-edge data science knowledge in the real world often ahead of everyone else, improving its functionality and revealing its potential.

Installing R

To install R, you need to visit R's official website (https://www.r-project.org/), download R (https://cran.r-project.org/mirrors.html), choose a nearby mirror, and download a version for your operating system. At the time of writing, the latest version is 3.2.3. The examples in this book are created and run under this version in Windows and Linux, but there should not be significant differences between the output in previous versions or other supported operating systems.

If you are using Windows, just download an installer for the latest version. To install R, run the Windows installer that you just downloaded. The installation process is easy to handle, but many users may still face problems with several steps.

In the Windows drop-down, when choosing the components to install, the installer lists four components. Here, **Core files** means the core libraries of R, and the **Message translations** component provides many versions of translations of warning and error messages in a list of supported languages. However, what may confuse you is the **32-bit files** and 64-bit files options. Just don't worry; you only need to know that 64-bit R can handle much more data in a single process than its 32-bit counterpart. If you are using a modern computer purchased in recent years, it is most likely to support 64-bit programs and should be running a 64-bit operating system, so the default option will be 64-bit files. If you are using a 32-bit operating system, unfortunately, you cannot use 64-bit R unless you install a 64-bit system if your hardware supports it.

Anyway, I recommend that you install the default options, as shown in the following screenshot:

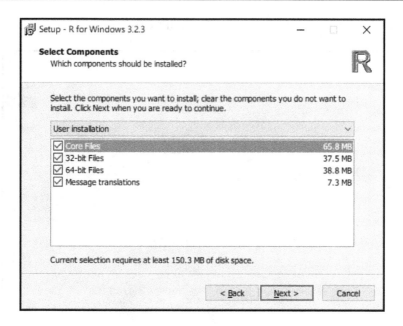

Another option you may feel confused about is whether to save the R version number in the registry. Checking these options makes it easier for other programs to detect which R version is installed. If you are sure you only use R in its own, just go ahead with the defaults.

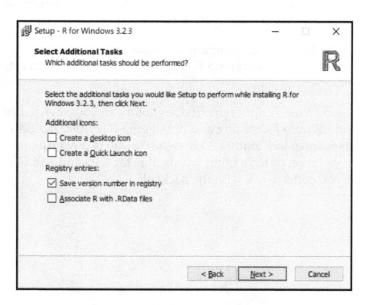

Then, the installation starts copying files to your hard drive.

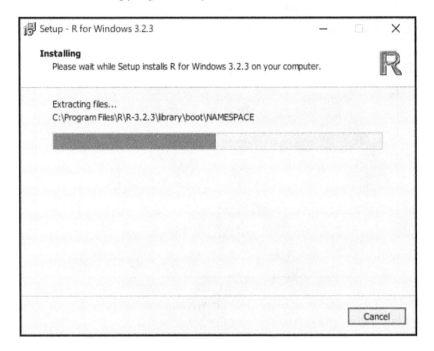

Finally, R is deployed to your computer. At the moment, you only have two ways to use R: In a command prompt (or terminal) or in the R GUI.

If you allowed the installer to create program shortcuts on your desktop, you will find two R shortcuts there. R runs in the Command Prompt and RGUI runs in an extremely simple GUI.

Although you can start to use R right now, it does not mean you have to use it in this way. I strongly recommend RStudio for editing and debugging R scripts. Actually, this book is also written in R Markdown in RStudio. Although RStudio is powerful, it does not work without a proper installation of R. In other words, R is the backend and RStudio is a frontend that helps you better work with the backend.

If you are using Windows, you may also install Rtools (`http://cran.rstudio.com/bin/windows/Rtools/`) so that you can write C++ code, compile it, and call it in R, and you can install and compile packages that contain C/C++ code from their sources.

RStudio

RStudio is a powerful user interface for R programming. It's free, open source, and works on multiple platforms including Windows, Mac, and Linux.

RStudio has very powerful features that hugely boost your productivity in data analysis and visualization. It supports syntax highlighting, autocompletion, multi-tabbed views, file management, graphics viewport, package management, integrated help viewer, code formatting, version control, interactive debugging, and many more features.

You can download the latest release of RStudio at `https://www.rstudio.com/products/rstudio/download`. If you want to try the preview version with new features, download it from `https://www.rstudio.com/products/rstudio/download/preview`. Note that RStudio does not include R, so you need to make sure that you have R installed while working in RStudio.

In followings sections, I'll give you a brief introduction to the user interface of RStudio.

RStudio's user interface

The following screenshot shows the RStudio user interface in the Windows operating system. If you are using Mac OS X or a supported version of Linux, the screen should look almost the same.

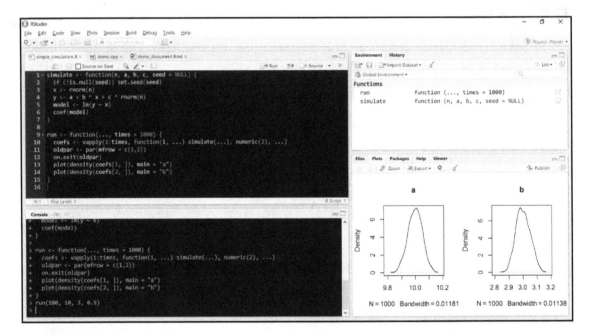

You may notice that the main window consists of several parts. Each part is called a pane and performs different functions. These panes are well designed for data analysts to work with data.

The console

The following screenshot shows the R console embedded in RStudio. In most cases, the console works exactly like a Command Prompt or terminal. In fact, when you type in a command at the console, RStudio will submit the request to the R engine. It is the R engine that executes all the commands. The role of RStudio is to stand in the middle, take inputs from user to the R engine, and present the results it returns.

```
Console ~/R/
+   model <- lm(y ~ x)
+     coef(model)
+ }
>
> run <- function(..., times = 1000) {
+     coefs <- vapply(1:times, function(i, ...) simulate(...), numeric(2), ...)
+     oldpar <- par(mfrow = c(1,2))
+     on.exit(oldpar)
+     plot(density(coefs[1, ]), main = "a")
+     plot(density(coefs[2, ]), main = "b")
+ }
> sim1 <- run(200, 2, 3, 0.2)
> |
```

Using the console, you can easily execute a command, define a variable, or evaluate an expression interactively to compute a statistical measure, transform data, or produce charts.

The editor

Typing in commands at the console is not the usual way we work with data. Instead, we write scripts, a set of commands representing a logic flow that can be read from a file and executed by the R engine. The editor is useful for editing R scripts, markdown documents, web pages, many types of configuration files, and even C++ source code.

```
simple_simulation.R ×   demo.cpp ×   demo_document.Rmd ×
          Source on Save                                        Run      Source
 1 ▾ simulate <- function(n, a, b, c, seed = NULL) {
 2       if (!is.null(seed)) set.seed(seed)
 3       x <- rnorm(n)
 4       y <- a + b * x + c * rnorm(n)
 5       model <- lm(y ~ x)
 6       coef(model)
 7   }
 8
 9 ▾ run <- function(..., times = 1000) {
10       coefs <- vapply(1:times, function(i, ...) simulate(...), numeric(2), ...)
11       oldpar <- par(mfrow = c(1,2))
12       on.exit(oldpar)
13       plot(density(coefs[1, ]), main = "a")
14       plot(density(coefs[2, ]), main = "b")
15   }
16   |
16:1   (Top Level) ≑                                                  R Script ≑
```

The functionality of the code editor is much more than a plain text editor: it supports syntax highlighting, autocompletion of R code, debugging with breakpoints, and so on. More specifically, when editing R scripts you can use the following shortcut keys:

- Press *Ctrl* + *Enter* to execute the selected lines
- Press *Ctrl* + *Shift* + *S* to source the current document, that is, to evaluate all the expressions sequentially in the current document
- Press *Tab* or *Ctrl* + *Space* to show an autocompletion list of variables and functions that match your current typing
- Click on the left margin of a line number and set a breakpoint; now, the next time this line is executed, the program will pause and wait for you to check

The Environment pane

The **Environment** pane shows the variables and functions that you have created and are available for repeated use. By default, it shows the variables in the global environment, that is, the user workspace in which you are working.

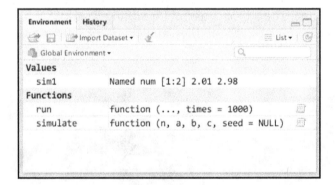

Each time you create a new object (a variable or function), a new entry will appear in the **Environment** pane. The entry shows the variable name and a short description of its value. When you change the value of a symbol or even remove that symbol, you actually modify the environment so that the environment pane reflects your change.

The History pane

The **History** pane shows the previous expressions evaluated in the console. You can repeat the task performed previously by simply pressing up in the console.

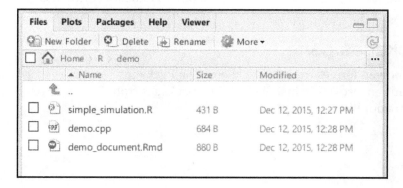

The history may be stored in the `.Rhistory` file in the working directory.

The File pane

The File pane shows the files in the folder. You can navigate between folders, create new folders, delete or rename folders or files, and so on.

If you are working on an RStudio project, the **File** pane is handy for viewing and organizing project files.

The Plots pane

The **Plots** pane is used to show graphics produced by R code. If you produce more than one plot, the previous ones are stored and you can navigate back and forth to view all plots (until you clear them).

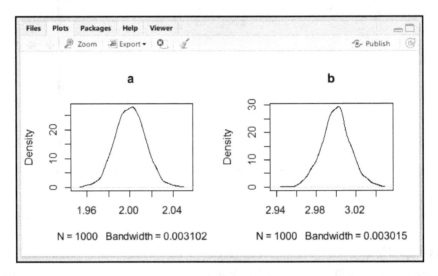

When you resize the plot pane, graphics will adapt to its size so that they look as nice as they did before resizing. You can also export a plot to a file for future use.

The Packages pane

Much of R's power derives from its packages. The **Packages** pane shows all installed packages. You can also easily install or update packages from CRAN or remove an existing package from your library.

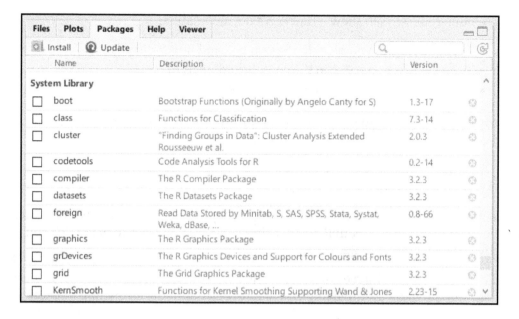

The Help pane

A lot of R's power also derives from its detailed documentation. The **Help** pane shows the documentation so that you can easily learn how to use functions.

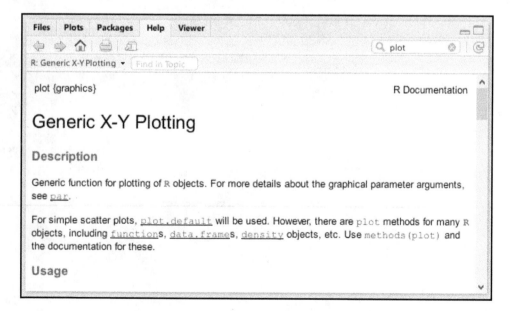

There are numerous ways to View a function's documentation:

- Type the function name in the Search box and find it directly
- Type the function name in the console and press *F1*
- Type ? before the function name and execute it

In practice, you don't have to remember all of R's functions; you only need to remember how to get help with a function you are not familiar with.

The Viewer pane

The **Viewer** pane is a new feature; it was introduced as an increasing number of R packages combine the functionality of both R and existing JavaScript libraries to make rich and interactive presentations of data.

The following screenshot is an example of my formattable (http://renkun.me/formattable) package that provides a simple implementation of conditional formatting in Excel with data frames in R:

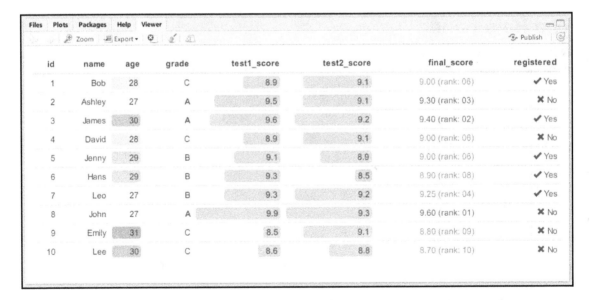

RStudio Server

If you are using a supported version of Linux, you can easily set up a server version of RStudio, or RStudio Server. It runs on a host server (probably much more powerful and stable than your laptop) and you can run an R session in RStudio in your web browser. The user interface is mostly the same but you have access to the computing and memory resources of the server, as if you were using a local computer.

A quick example

In this section, I will demonstrate a simple example of computing, model fitting, and producing graphics by typing in commands in the console.

First, let's create vector x of 100 normally distributed random numbers. Then, create another vector y of 100 numbers, each of which is 3 times the corresponding element in x plus 2 and some random noise. Note that <- is the assignment operator, which we will cover later. I use str() to print the structure of the vectors:

```
x <- rnorm(100) y <- 2 + 3 * x + rnorm(100) * 0.5 str(x)
##   num [1:100] -0.4458 -1.2059 0.0411 0.6394 -0.7866 ...
str(y)
##   num [1:100] -0.022 -1.536 2.067 4.348 -0.295 ...
```

Since we know that the true relationship between X and Y is $Y = 3X + 2 + \epsilon$, we can run a simple linear regression on the sample X and Y and see how the linear model recovers the linear parameters (that is, 2 and 3) of the model. We call *lm(y ~ x)* to fit such a model:

```
model1 <- lm(y ~ x)
```

The result of the model fitting is stored in an object named model1. We can view the model fit by simply typing model1 or explicitly typing print(model1):

```
model1
##  ## Call: ## lm(formula = y ~ x) ##  ## Coefficients: ## (Intercept)
x
##          2.051            2.973
```

If you want to see more details, call summary() with model1:

```
summary(model1)
##
## Call:
## lm(formula = y ~ x)
##
```

```
## Residuals:
##      Min       1Q     Median       3Q       Max
## -1.14529 -0.30477   0.03154   0.30042   0.98045
##
## Coefficients:
##             Estimate Std. Error t value Pr(>|t|)
## (Intercept)  2.05065    0.04533   45.24   <2e-16 ***
## x            2.97343    0.04525   65.71   <2e-16 ***
## ---
## Signif. codes:  0 '***' 0.001 '**' 0.01 '*' 0.05 '.' 0.1 ' ' 1
##
## Residual standard error: 0.4532 on 98 degrees of freedom
## Multiple R-squared:  0.9778, Adjusted R-squared:  0.9776
## F-statistic:  4318 on 1 and 98 DF,  p-value: < 2.2e-16
```

We can plot the points and the fitted model together:

```
plot(x, y, main = "Simple linear regression")
abline(model1$coefficients, col = "blue")
```

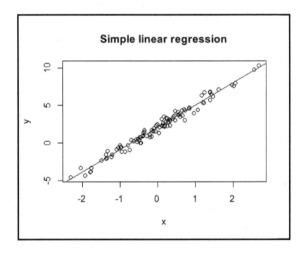

The preceding screenshot demonstrates some simple functions so that you can get a first impression of working with R. If you are not familiar with the symbols and functions in the example, don't worry: the next few chapters will cover the basic objects and functions you need to know.

Summary

In this chapter, you learned some basic facts about R and its major strengths. We learned how to install R in a Windows operating system. To make R programming easier, we chose to use RStudio and went through the user interface of RStudio, and you learned that the functionality of each pane is its main window. Finally, we ran several R commands to fit a model and to plot simple graphics, getting an initial impression of the way we work with R.

In the next chapter, we will go through the basic concepts and data structures in R to help you get familiar with the behavior of basic R objects. Only then can you easily represent, manipulate, and work with a wide variety of data.

2
Basic Objects

The first step of learning R programming is getting familiar with basic R objects and their behavior. In this chapter, you will learn the following topics:

- Creating and subsetting atomic vectors (for example, numeric vectors, character vectors, and logical vectors), matrices, arrays, lists, and data frames.
- Defining and working with functions

"Everything that exists is an object. Everything that happens is a function." — John Chambers

For example, in statistical analysis, we often feed a set of data to a linear regression model and obtain a group of linear coefficients.

Provided that there are different types of objects in R, when we do this, what basically happens in R is that we provide a data frame object that holds the set of data, carry it to the linear model function and get a list object consisting of the properties of the regression results, and finally extract a numeric vector, which is another type of object, from the list to represent the linear coefficients.

Every task involves various different types of objects. Each object has a different goal and behavior. It's important to understand how a basic object works in order to solve real-world problems, especially with more elegant code and fewer steps. More importantly, a more concrete understanding of object behavior allows you to spend more time on working out the solution to your problem than on getting stuck by countless minor problems while producing the right code.

In the following sections, we will see a variety of basic objects in R that represent different types of data and make it easy to analyze and visualize datasets. You will have a basic understanding of how these objects work and how they interact with each other.

Vector

A vector is a group of primitive values of the same type. It can be a group of numbers, true/false values, texts, and values of some other type. It is one of the building blocks of all R objects.

There are several types of vectors in R. They are distinct from each other in the type of elements they store. In the following sections, we will see the most commonly used types of vectors including numeric vectors, logical vectors, and character vectors.

Numeric vector

A numeric vector is a vector of numeric values. A scalar number is the simplest numeric vector. An example is shown as follows:

```
1.5
## [1] 1.5
```

A numeric vector is the most frequently used data type and is the foundation of nearly all kinds of data analysis. In other popular programming languages, there are some scalar types such as integer, double, and string, and these scalar types are the building blocks of the container types such as vectors. In R, however, there is no formal definition of scalar types. A scalar number is only a special case of numeric vector, and it's special only because its length is 1.

When we create a value, it is natural to think of how to store it for future use. To store the value, we can use <- to assign the value to a symbol. In other words, we create a variable named x of the value 1.5:

```
x <- 1.5
```

Then, the value is assigned to symbol x, and we can use x to represent the value from now on:

```
x
## [1] 1.5
```

There are multiple ways to create a numeric vector. We can call `numeric()` to create a zero vector of a given length:

```
numeric (10)
## [1] 0 0 0 0 0 0 0 0 0 0
```

We can also use `c()` to combine several vectors to make one vector. The simplest case is, for example, to combine several single-element vectors to be a multi-element vector:

```
c(1, 2, 3, 4, 5)
## [1] 1 2 3 4 5
```

We can also combine a mixture of single-element vectors and multi-element vectors and obtain a vector with the same elements as we previously created:

```
c(1, 2, c(3, 4, 5))
## [1] 1 2 3 4 5
```

To create a series of consecutive integers, the `:` operator will easily do the trick.

```
1:5
## [1] 1 2 3 4 5
```

Precisely speaking, the preceding code produces an integer vector instead of a numeric vector. In many cases, their difference is not that important. We will cover this topic later.

A more general way to produce a numeric sequence is `seq()`. For example, the following code produces a numeric vector of a sequence from 1 to 10 by increment 2:

```
seq(1, 10, 2)
## [1] 1 3 5 7 9
```

Functions like `seq()` have many arguments. We can call such a function by supplying all the arguments, but it is not necessary in most cases. Most functions provide reasonable default values for some arguments, which makes it easier for us to call them. In this case, we only need to specify the argument that we would like to modify from its default value.

For example, we can create another numeric vector that starts from 3 with the length 10 by specifying the `length.out` argument:

```
seq(3, length.out = 10)
## [1] 3 4 5 6 7 8 9 10 11 12
```

A function call like the above uses a named argument `length.out` so that other arguments are kept default and only this argument is modified.

There are many ways in which we can define numeric vectors, but we should always be careful when we use :, an example is shown as follows:

```
1 + 1:5
## [1] 2 3 4 5 6
```

As the result shows, `1 + 1:5` does not mean a sequence from 2 to 5, but from 2 to 6. It is because : has higher priority than +, which results in evaluating `1:5` first and adding 1 to each entry, yielding the sequence you see in the result. We will cover the priority of operators later.

Logical vector

In contrast to numeric vectors, a logical vector stores a group of TRUE or FALSE values. They are basically yes or no to denote the answers to a group of logical questions.

The simplest logical vectors are TRUE and FALSE themselves:

```
TRUE
## [1] TRUE
```

A more usual way to obtain a logical vector is to ask logical questions about R objects. For example, we can ask R whether 1 is greater than 2:

```
1 > 2
## [1] FALSE
```

The answer is yes, represented by TRUE. Sometimes, it is verbose to write TRUE and FALSE; so, we can use T as an abbreviation for TRUE and F for FALSE. If we want to perform multiple comparisons at the same time, we can directly use numeric vectors in the question:

```
c(1, 2) > 2
## [1] FALSE FALSE
```

R interprets this expression as the element-wise comparison between c(1, 2) and 2. In other words, it is equivalent to c(1 > 2, 2 > 2).

We can compare two multi-element numeric vectors as long as the length of the longer vector is a multiple of that of the shorter one:

```
c(1, 2) > c(2, 1)
## [1] FALSE TRUE
```

The preceding code is equivalent to `c(1 > 2, 2 > 1)`. To demonstrate how two vectors of different lengths are compared, see the following example::

```
c(2, 3) > c(1, 2, -1, 3)
## [1] TRUE TRUE TRUE FALSE
```

This may confuse you a bit. The computing mechanism recycles the shorter vector and works like `c(2 > 1, 3 > 2, 2 > -1, 3 > 3)`. More specifically, the shorter vector will by recycled to finish all the comparisons for each element in the longer vector.

In R, several logical binary operators are defined, such as == to denote equality, > for greater-than, >= for greater-or-equals-to, < for less-than, and <= for less-than-or-equals-to. Moreover, R provides some other additional logical operators like %in% to tell whether each element in the left-hand side vector is contained by the right-hand side vector:

```
1 %in% c(1, 2, 3)
## [1] TRUE
c(1, 4) %in% c(1, 2, 3)
## [1] TRUE FALSE
```

You may notice that all the equality operators perform recycling but %in% does not. Instead, it always works by iterating over the vector on the left and works like `c(1 %in% c(1, 2, 3), 4 %in% c(1, 2, 3))` in the preceding example.

Character vector

A character vector is a group of strings. Here, a character does not mean literally a single letter or symbol in a language, but it means a string like `this is a string`. Both double quotation marks and single quotation mark, can be used to create a character vector, as follows:

```
"hello, world!"
## [1] "hello, world!"
'hello, world!'
## [1] "hello, world!"
```

We can also use the combine function `c()` to construct a multi-element character vector:

```
c("Hello", "World")
## [1] "Hello" "World"
```

We can use `==` to tell whether two vectors have equal values in corresponding positions; this applies to character vectors too:

```
c("Hello", "World") == c('Hello', 'World')
## [1] TRUE TRUE
```

The character vectors are equal because `"` and `'` both work to create a string and do not affect its value:

```
c("Hello", "World") == "Hello, World"
## [1] FALSE FALSE
```

The previous expression yields both `FALSE` because neither `Hello` nor `World` equals `Hello, World`. The only difference between the two quotation marks is the behavior when you create a string containing quotation marks.

If you use `"` to create a string (a single-element character vector) containing `"` itself, you need to type `"` to escape `"` inside the string to prevent the interpreter from regarding `"` in the string as the close quotation mark of the string.

The following examples demonstrate the escaping of quotation marks. The code uses `cat ()` to print the given text:

```
cat("Is "You" a Chinese name?")
## Is "You" a Chinese name?
```

If you feel that this is not easy to read, you may well use `'` to create the string, which can be easier:

```
cat('Is "You" a Chinese name?')
## Is "You" a Chinese name?
```

In other words, `"` allows `'` in the string without escaping, and `'` allows `"` in the string without escaping.

Now we know the basic things about creating numeric vectors, logical vectors, and character vectors. In fact, we also have complex vectors and raw vectors in R. Complex vectors are vectors of complex values, such as `c(1 + 2i, 2 + 3i)`. Raw vectors basically store raw binary data that is represented in the hexadecimal form. These two types of vectors are much less frequently used, but they share many behaviors with the three types of vectors we have covered.

In the next section, you will learn several ways to access part of a vector. By subsetting vectors, you should begin to understand how different types of vectors can be related to each other.

Subsetting vectors

If we want to access some specific entries or a subset of a vector, subsetting a vector means accessing some specific entries or a subset of the vector. In this section, we'll demonstrate various ways to subset a vector.

First, we create a simple numeric vector and assign it to `v1`:

```
v1 <- c(1, 2, 3, 4)
```

Each of the following lines gets a specific subset of `v1`.

For example, we can get the second element:

```
v1[2]
## [1] 2
```

We can get the second to fourth elements:

```
v1[2:4]
## [1] 2 3 4
```

We can get all elements except the third one:

```
v1[-3]
## [1] 1 2 4
```

The patterns are clear—we can put any numeric vector inside the square brackets after the vector to extract a corresponding subset:

```
a <- c(1, 3)
v1[a]
## [1] 1 3
```

All the preceding examples perform subsetting by position, that is, we get a subset of a vector by specifying the positions of elements. Using negative numbers will exclude those elements. One thing to notice is that you can't use positive numbers and negative numbers together:

```
v1[c(1, 2, -3)]
## Error in v1[c(1, 2, -3)]: only 0's may be mixed with negative subscripts
```

What if we subset the vector using positions beyond the range of the vector? The following example tries to get a subset of `v1` from the third element to the nonexisting sixth element:

```
v1[3:6]
## [1] 3 4 NA NA
```

As we can see, the nonexisting positions end up in missing values represented by NA. In real-world data, missing values are common. The good part is that all arithmetic calculations with NA also result in NA for consistency. On the other hand, however, it takes extra effort to deal with data because it may not be safe to assume that the data contains no missing values.

Another way to subset a vector is using logical vectors. We can supply an equal-length logical vector to determine whether each entry should be extracted:

```
v1[c(TRUE, FALSE, TRUE, FALSE)]
## [1] 1 3
```

More than subsetting, we can overwrite a specific subset of a vector like this:

```
v1[2] <-
```

In this case, `v1` becomes the following:

```
v1
## [1] 1 0 3 4
```

We can also overwrite multiple elements at different positions at the same time:

```
v1[2:4] <- c(, 1, 3)
```

Now, `v1` becomes the following:

```
v1
## [1] 1 0 1 3
```

Like subsetting, logical selectors are also accepted for overwriting:

```
v1[c(TRUE, FALSE, TRUE, FALSE)] <- c(3, 2)
```

As you may expect, `v1` becomes the following:

```
v1
## [1] 3 0 2 3
```

A useful implication of this operation is selecting entries by logical criterion. For example, the following code picks out all elements that are not greater than 2 in v1:

```
v1[v1 <= 2]
## [1] 0 2
```

A more complex selection criterion also works. The following example picks out all elements of v1 that satisfy $x^2 - x + 1 \geq 0$:

```
v1[v1 ^ 2 - v1 + 1 >= ]
## [1] 3 0 2 3
```

To replace all entries that satisfy x <= 2 with , we can call the following:

```
v1[v1 <= 2] <-
```

As you may expect, v1 becomes the following:

```
v1
## [1] 3 0 0 3
```

If we overwrite the vector at a nonexisting entry, the vector will automatically expand with the unassigned value being NA as missing values:

```
v1[10] <- 8
v1
## [1] 3 0 0 3 NA NA NA NA NA 8
```

Named vectors

A named vector is not a specific type of vector parallel to a numeric or logical vector. It is a vector with names corresponding to the elements. We can give names to a vector when we create it:

```
x <- c(a = 1, b = 2, c = 3)
x
## a b c
## 1 2 3
```

Then, we can access the elements with a single-valued character vector:

```
x["a"]
## a
## 1
```

We can also get multiple elements with a character vector:

```
x[c("a", "c")]
## a c
## 1 3
```

If the character vector has duplicate elements, the selection will result in selecting duplicate elements:

```
x[c("a", "a", "c")]
## a a c
## 1 1 3
```

In addition to this, all other operations to a vector also perfectly work for named vectors.

We can get the names of a vector with `names()`:

```
names(x)
## [1] "a" "b" "c"
```

The names of a vector are not fixed. We can change the names of a vector by assigning another character vector to its names.

```
names(x) <- c("x", "y", "z")
x["z"]
## z
## 3
```

If the names are no longer needed, we can simply remove the vector's names using NULL, a special object that represents undefined value:

```
names(x) <- NULL
x
## [1] 1 2 3
```

You may wonder what happens when the name does not exist at all. Let's experiment with the original x value:

```
x <- c(a = 1, b = 2, c = 3)
x["d"]
## <NA>
## NA
```

By intuition, accessing a nonexisting element should produce an error. However, the result is not an error but a vector of a single missing value with a missing name:

```
names(x["d"])
## [1] NA
```

If you provide a character vector in which some names exist but others do not, the resulting vector will preserve the length of the selection vector:

```
x[c("a", "d")]
## a <NA>
## 1 NA
```

Extracting an element

While `[]` creates a subset of a vector, `[[]]` extracts an element from a vector. A vector is like ten boxes of candy, `[]` gets you three boxes of candy, but `[[]]` opens a box and gets you a candy from it.

For simple vectors, using `[]` and `[[]]` to get one element will produce the same result. However, in some cases, they have different behaviors. For example, subsetting a named vector using one entry and extracting an element from it will produce different results:

```
x <- c(a =  1, b = 2, c = 3)
x["a"]
## a
## 1
x[["a"]]
## [1] 1
```

The metaphor of candy boxes makes it easier to understand. The `x["a"]` argument gives you the box of candy labeled `"a"`, while `x[["a"]]` gives you the candy in the box labeled `"a"`.

Since `[[]]` only extracts one element, it does not work with vectors of more than one element:

```
x[[c(1, 2)]]
## Error in x[[c(1, 2)]]: attempt to select more than one element
```

Also, it does not work with negative integers meaning excluding elements at certain positions:

```
x[[-1]]
## Error in x[[-1]]: attempt to select more than one element
```

We already know that subsetting a vector with a nonexisting position or name will produce missing values. However, `[[]]` simply does not work when we extract an element with a position beyond the range, nor does it work with a nonexisting name:

```
x[["d"]]
## Error in x[["d"]]: subscript out of bounds
```

For many beginners, it may be confusing to see both `[[]]` and `[]` used in the code and it is easy to misuse them. Just remember the metaphor of the candy boxes.

Telling the class of vectors

Sometimes we need to tell which kind of vector we are dealing with before taking an action. The `class()` function tells us the class of any R object:

```
class(c(1, 2, 3))
## [1] "numeric"
class(c(TRUE, TRUE, FALSE))
## [1] "logical"
class(c("Hello", "World"))
## [1] "character"
```

If we need to ensure that an object is indeed a vector of a specific class, we can use `is.numeric`, `is.logical`, `is.character`, and some other functions with similar names:

```
is.numeric(c(1, 2, 3))
## [1] TRUE
is.numeric(c(TRUE, TRUE, FALSE))
## [1] FALSE
is.numeric(c("Hello", "World"))
## [1] FALSE
```

Converting vectors

Different classes of vectors can be coerced to a specific class of vector. For example, some data are string representation of numbers, such as 1 and 20. If we leave these strings as they are, we won't be able to perform numeric calculations with them. Fortunately, these two strings can be converted to numeric vectors. This will make R regard them as numbers rather than strings so that we can do the math with them.

To demonstrate a typical conversion, we first create a character vector:

```
strings <- c("1", "2", "3")
class(strings)
## [1] "character"
```

As I mentioned, strings cannot be used to do maths directly:

```
strings + 10
## Error in strings + 10: non-numeric argument to binary operator
```

We can use as.numeric() to convert the character vector to a numeric vector:

```
numbers <- as.numeric(strings)
numbers
## [1] 1 2 3
class(numbers)
## [1] "numeric"
```

Now we can do maths with numbers:

```
numbers + 10
## [1] 11 12 13
```

Similar to is.* functions (for example, is.numeric, is.logical, and is.character) that check the class of a given object, we can use the as.* function family to convert a vector from its original class to another:

```
as.numeric(c("1", "2", "3", "a"))
## Warning: NAs introduced by coercion
## [1] 1 2 3 NA
as.logical(c(-1, , 1, 2))
## [1] TRUE FALSE TRUE TRUE
as.character(c(1, 2, 3))
## [1] "1" "2" "3"
as.character(c(TRUE, FALSE))
## [1] "TRUE" "FALSE"
```

It seems that each type of vector can be somehow converted to all other types. However, the conversion follows a set of rules.

The first line in the preceding block of code attempts to convert the character vector to a numeric vector, just as we did in the previous example. Obviously, the last element a cannot be converted to a number. The conversion is done except for the last element, so a missing value is produced instead.

As for converting a numeric vector to a logical vector, the rule is that only corresponds to `FALSE` and all non-zero numbers will produce `TRUE`.

Each kind of vector can be converted to a character vector since everything has a character representation. However, if a numeric vector or a logical vector is coerced to a character vector, it cannot be directly involved in the arithmetic operations with other numeric or logical vectors unless it is converted back. That is why the following code does not work, as I have just mentioned:

```
c(2, 3) + as.character(c(1, 2))
## Error in c(2, 3) + as.character(c(1, 2)): non-numeric argument to binary
operator
```

From the preceding examples, I have stressed that although R does not impose strong typing rules, it does not mean that R is smart enough to do exactly what you want it to do automatically. In most cases, it is better to ensure that the type of vectors are correct in computations; otherwise, an unexpected error will occur. In other words, only when you get the right type of data objects can you do the right math.

Arithmetic operators for numeric vectors

The arithmetic operations of numeric vectors are very simple. They basically follow two rules: Computing in an element-wise manner and recycling the shorter vector. The following examples demonstrate the behavior of the operators working with numeric vectors:

```
c(1, 2, 3, 4) + 2
## [1] 3 4 5 6
c(1, 2, 3) - c(2, 3, 4)
## [1] -1 -1 -1
c(1, 2, 3) * c(2, 3, 4)
## [1] 2 6 12
c(1, 2, 3) / c(2, 3, 4)
## [1] 0.5000000 0.6666667 0.7500000
c(1, 2, 3) ^ 2
## [1] 1 4 9
c(1, 2, 3) ^ c(2, 3, 4)
## [1] 1 8 81
c(1, 2, 3, 14) %% 2
## [1] 1 0 1 0
```

Although vectors can have names, the operations do not function with corresponding names. Only the names of vectors on the left-hand side will remain and the names of those on the right-hand side will be ignored:

```
c(a = 1, b = 2, c = 3) + c(b = 2, c = 3, d = 4)
## a b c
## 3 5 7
c(a = 1, b = 2, 3) + c(b = 2, c = 3, d = 4)
## a b
## 3 5 7
```

We saw some basic behaviors of numeric vectors, logical vectors, and character vectors. They are the most commonly used data structures and are the building blocks of a wide variety of other useful objects. One of them is matrix, which is intensively used in the formulation of statistical and econometric theories, and it is very useful in representing two-dimensional data and solving linear systems. In the next chapter, we will see how we can create a matrix in R and how it is deeply rooted in vectors.

Matrix

A matrix is a vector represented and accessible in two dimensions. Therefore, what applies to vectors is most likely to apply to a matrix. For example, each type of vector (for example, numeric vector or logical vectors) has its matrix version, that is, there are numeric matrices, logical matrices, and so on.

Creating a matrix

We can call `matrix()` to create a matrix from a vector by setting up one of its two dimensions:

```
matrix(c(1, 2, 3, 2, 3, 4, 3, 4, 5), ncol = 3)
##      [,1] [,2] [,3]
## [1,]    1    2    3
## [2,]    2    3    4
## [3,]    3    4    5
```

By specifying `ncol = 3`, we mean that the provided vector should be regarded as a matrix with 3 columns (and 3 rows automatically). You may feel the original vector is not as straightforward as its representation. To make the code more user-friendly, we can write the vector in multiple lines:

```
matrix(c(1, 2, 3,  4, 5, 6,  7, 8, 9), nrow = 3, byrow = FALSE)
##      [,1] [,2] [,3]
## [1,]    1    4    7
## [2,]    2    5    8
## [3,]    3    6    9
```

```
matrix(c(1, 2, 3, 4, 5, 6, 7, 8, 9), nrow = 3, byrow = TRUE)
##      [,1] [,2] [,3]
## [1,]   1    2    3
## [2,]   4    5    6
## [3,]   7    8    9
```

Often, we may need to create a diagonal matrix. Here, `diag()` is the most handy way to do this:

```
diag(1, nrow = 5)
##      [,1] [,2] [,3] [,4] [,5]
## [1,]   1    0    0    0    0
## [2,]   0    1    0    0    0
## [3,]   0    0    1    0    0
## [4,]   0    0    0    1    0
## [5,]   0    0    0    0    1
```

Naming rows and columns

By default, creating a matrix does not automatically give names to its rows and columns. Sometimes, it is useful and straightforward to do so when different rows and columns have different meanings. We can give row names and/or column names when creating the matrix:

```
matrix(c(1, 2, 3, 4, 5, 6, 7, 8, 9), nrow = 3, byrow = TRUE, dimnames
= list(c("r1", "r2", "r3"), c("c1", "c2", "c3")))
##    c1 c2 c3
## r1  1  2  3
## r2  4  5  6
## r3  7  8  9
```

Alternatively, we can use row names and/or columnnames after the matrix is created:

```
m1 <- matrix(c(1, 2, 3, 4, 5, 6, 7, 8, 9), ncol = 3)
rownames(m1) <- c("r1", "r2", "r3")
colnames(m1) <- c("c1", "c2", "c3")
```

Here, we encounter two new things: a list and a type of function, such as `rownames(x) <-`. We will discuss them later in this chapter.

Subsetting a matrix

Just as we deal with vectors, we need not only create matrices but also extract data from a matrix. This is called **matrix subsetting**.

Note that a matrix is a vector that is represented and accessible in two dimensions; we not only view a matrix in two dimensions, but also access it with a two-dimensional accessor [,], which is quite similar to the one-dimensional accessor, [] , for subsetting vectors.

To use it, we can supply two vectors for each dimension to determine a subset of a matrix. The first argument in the square bracket is the row selector, and the second is the column selector. As we tried in subsetting vectors, we can use numeric vectors, logical vectors, and character vectors in the two dimensions.

The following code demonstrates the various ways to subset the following matrix:

```
m1
##      c1 c2 c3
## r1    1  4  7
## r2    2  5  8
## r3    3  6  9
```

We can extract only one element in the first row and the second column:

```
m1[1, 2]
## [1] 4
```

We can subset it with a range of positions:

```
m1[1:2, 2:3]
##      c2 c3
## r1   4  7
## r2   5  8
```

If one dimension is left blank, all the values in that dimension will be selected:

```
m1[1,]
## c1 c2 c3
##  1  4  7
m1[,2]
## r1 r2 r3
##  4  5  6
m1[1:2,]
##      c1 c2 c3
## r1    1  4  7
## r2    2  5  8
m1[, 2:3]
##      c2 c3
## r1   4  7
## r2   5  8
## r3   6  9
```

Negative numbers exclude positions in a subsetting matrix, which is exactly the same as working with vectors:

```
m1[-1,]
##      c1 c2 c3
## r2 2   5  8
## r3 3   6  9
m1[,-2]
##      c1 c3
## r1   1  7
## r2   2  8
## r3   3  9
```

Note that the matrix has row names and column names, and we can use character vectors to subset it:

```
m1[c("r1", "r3"), c("c1", "c3")]
##      c1 c3
## r1   1  7
## r3   3  9
```

Note again that a matrix is a vector represented and accessible in two dimensions; however, it is still a vector in its nature. This allows us to use a one-dimensional accessor for vectors to subset a matrix:

```
m1[1]
## [1] 1
m1[9]
## [1] 9
m1[3:7]
## [1] 3 4 5 6 7
```

Since a vector only contains entries of the same type, so does a matrix. Therefore, their operations are quite similar. If you type an inequality, it will return another logical matrix of equal size:

```
m1 > 3
##         c1    c2    c3
## r1 FALSE  TRUE  TRUE
## r2 FALSE  TRUE  TRUE
## r3 FALSE  TRUE  TRUE
```

We can use an equal-sized logical matrix for subsetting as if it is a vector:

```
m1[m1 > 3]
## [1] 4 5 6 7 8 9
```

Using matrix operators

All arithmetic operators for vectors also work with matrices as if they were vectors. These operators perform calculations element-wise, except for matrix-only operators, such as matrix product, `%*%`:

```
m1 + m1
##     c1 c2 c3
## r1   2  8 14
## r2   4 10 16
## r3   6 12 18
m1 - 2 * m1
##     c1 c2 c3
## r1 -1 -4 -7
## r2 -2 -5 -8
## r3 -3 -6 -9
m1 * m1
##    c1 c2 c3
## r1 1 16 49
## r2 4 25 64
## r3 9 36 81
m1 / m1
##     c1 c2 c3
## r1 1  1  1
## r2 1  1  1
## r3 1  1  1
m1 ^ 2
##    c1 c2 c3
## r1  1 16 49
## r2  4 25 64
## r3  9 36 81
m1 %*% m1
##     c1 c2 c3
## r1  30 66 102
## r2  36 81 126
## r3  42 96 150
```

We can also transpose a matrix using `t()`:

```
t(m1)
##    r1 r2 r3
## c1 1  2  3
## c2 4  5  6
## c3 7  8  9
```

Vectors and matrices are sufficient for many use cases. However, some particular problems need a data structure with even higher dimensions. In this next section, we will briefly introduce arrays and you will see how these data structures share similar behaviors.

Array

An array is a natural extension to a matrix in its number of dimensions. More specifically, an array is a vector that is represented and accessible in a given number of dimensions (mostly more than two dimensions).

If you are already familiar with vectors and matrices, you won't be surprised to see how arrays behave.

Creating an array

To create an array, we call `array()` by supplying a vector of data, how this data is arranged in different dimensions, and sometimes the names of the rows and columns of these dimensions.

Suppose we have some data (10 integers from 0 to 9) and we need to arrange them in three dimensions: 1 for the first dimension, 5 for the second, and 2 for the third:

```
a1 <- array(c(, 1, 2, 3, 4, 5, 6, 7, 8, 9), dim = c(1, 5, 2))
a1
## , , 1
##
##      [,1] [,2] [,3] [,4] [,5]
## [1,]   0    1    2    3    4
##
## , , 2
##
##      [,1] [,2] [,3] [,4] [,5]
## [1,]   5    6    7    8    9
```

We can clearly see how we can access these entries by looking at the notations around them.

Moreover, we can add names for these dimensions when we create the array:

```
a1 <- array(c(, 1, 2, 3, 4, 5, 6, 7, 8, 9), dim = c(1, 5, 2), dimnames
= list(c("r1"), c("c1", "c2", "c3", "c4", "c5"), c("k1", "k2")))
a1
## , , k1
##
```

```
##      c1  c2  c3  c4  c5
## r1   0   1   2   3   4
##
## , , k2
##
##      c1  c2  c3  c4  c5
## r1   5   6   7   8   9
```

Alternatively, for an array that is already created, we can call `dimnames(x) <-` to setup the names for each dimension by supplying a list of several character vectors:

```
a0 <- array(c(, 1, 2, 3, 4, 5, 6, 7, 8, 9, 10), dim = c(1, 5, 2))
dimnames(a0) <- list(c("r1"), c("c1", "c2", "c3", "c4", "c5"), c("k1",
"k2"))
a0
## , , k1
##
##    c1 c2 c3 c4 c5
## r1 0  1  2  3  4
##
## , , k2
##
##    c1 c2 c3 c4 c5
## r1 5  6  7  8  9
```

Subsetting an array

The principle of subsetting an array is exactly the same as subsetting a matrix. Here, we can supply a vector for each dimension to extract a subset of an array:

```
a1[1,,]
##     k1 k2
## c1   0 5
## c2   1 6
## c3   2 7
## c4   3 8
## c5   4 9
a1[, 2,]
## k1 k2
## 1 6
a1[,,1]
## c1 c2 c3 c4 c5
## 0  1  2  3  4
a1[1, 1, 1]
## [1] 0
a1[1, 2:4, 1:2]
```

```
##      k1  k2
## c2  1    6
## c3  2    7
## c4  3    8
a1[c("r1"), c("c1", "c3"), "k1"]
## c1 c3
## 0   2
```

As you may notice, atomic vectors, matrices, and arrays share almost the same set of behaviors. A fundamental common feature they share is that they are all **homogeneous data types**, that is, the type of elements they store must be the same. However, there are also **heterogeneous data types** in R, that is, they can store different types of elements, which makes them much more flexible but they are less memory efficient and slower to operate.

Lists

A list is a generic vector that is allowed to include different types of objects, even other lists.

It is useful for its flexibility. For example, the result of a linear model fit in R is basically a list object that contains rich results of a linear regression such as linear coefficients (numeric vectors), residuals (numeric vectors), QR decomposition (a list containing a matrix and other objects), and so on.

It is very handy to extract the information without calling different functions each time because these results are all packed into a list.

Creating a list

We can use `list()` to create a list, as the function name suggests. Different types of objects can be put into one list. For example, the following code creates a list that contains a single-element numeric vector, a two-entry logical vector, and a character vector of three values:

```
l0 <- list(1, c(TRUE, FALSE), c("a", "b", "c"))
l0
## [[1]]
## [1] 1
##
## [[2]]
## [1] TRUE FALSE
##
## [[3]]
## [1] "a" "b" "c"
```

We can assign names to each list entry using named arguments:

```
l1 <- list(x = 1, y = c(TRUE, FALSE), z = c("a", "b", "c"))
l1
## $x
## [1] 1
##
## $y
## [1] TRUE FALSE
##
## $z
## [1] "a" "b" "c"
```

Extracting an element from a list

There are various ways to access the elements of a list. The most common way is to use a dollar-sign $ to extract the value of a list element by name:

```
l1 <- list(x = 1, y = c(TRUE, FALSE), z = c("a", "b", "c"), m = NULL)
l1$x
## [1] 1
l1$y
## [1] TRUE FALSE
l1$z
## [1] "a" "b" "c"
l1$m
## NULL
```

Note that if we ask for a non-existing element m, NULL will be returned.

Alternatively, we can supply a number in double square brackets to extract the value of the nth list member. For example, we can extract the value of the second member of list l1, as follows:

```
l1[[2]]
## [1] TRUE FALSE
```

With the same notation, we can also supply a name to extract the value of the list member with that name, just like using a dollar sign:

```
l1[["y"]]
## [1] TRUE FALSE
```

It can be more flexible to use double square brackets for value extraction from a list because, sometimes, we might not know which member we need to extract before a computation:

```
member <- "z" # you can dynamically determine which member to extract
l1[[member]]
## [1] "a" "b" "c"
```

Here, we supply a runtime-evaluated, single-element character vector to the brackets. But why should we use double brackets here? Where are the single brackets?

Subsetting a list

In many cases, we need to extract multiple elements from a list. These multiple members also construct a list as a subset of the original list.

To subset a list, we can use single-square-bracket notation, just like what we use for vectors and matrices. We can extract some elements of a list and put them into a new list.

The notation is very much consistent with how it works for vectors. We can extract elements from a list by name using a character vector, or by position using a numeric vector, or by criterion using a logical vector:

```
l1["x"]
## $x
## [1] 1
l1[c("x", "y")]
## $x
## [1] 1
##
## $y
## [1] TRUE FALSE
l1[1]
## $x
## [1] 1
l1[c(1, 2)]
## $x
## [1] 1
##
## $y
## [1] TRUE FALSE
l1[c(TRUE, FALSE, TRUE)]
## $x
## [1] 1
##
## $z
```

```
## [1] "a" "b" "c"
```

To summarize, we can say that `[[` means extracting one element from a vector or list, and `[` means subsetting a vector or list. Subsetting a vector will result in a vector. Likewise, subsetting a list will result in a list.

Named lists

Irrespective of whether the list members have already got names when the list is created, we can always name or rename the members of a list, by simply naming a vector:

```
names(l1) <- c("A","B","C")
l1
## $A
## [1] 1
##
## $B
## [1] TRUE FALSE
##
## $C
## [1] "a" "b" "c"
```

To remove their names, we replace the names of `l1` with `NULL`:

```
names(l1) <- NULL
l1
## [[1]]
## [1] 1
##
## [[2]]
## [1] TRUE FALSE
##
## [[3]]
## [1] "a" "b" "c"
```

Once the names of list members are removed, we can no longer access the list members by name but by position and logical criterion.

Setting values

Setting the values in a list is as straightforward as working with vectors:

```
l1 <- list(x = 1, y = c(TRUE, FALSE), z = c("a", "b", "c"))
l1$x <-
```

If we assign a value to a nonexisting member, we will add a new member to the list with the given name or position:

```
l1$m <- 4
l1
## $x
## [1]  0
##
## $y
## [1]  TRUE FALSE
##
## $z
## [1]  "a" "b" "c"
##
## $m
## [1]  4
```

Also, we can set multiple values at the same time:

```
l1[c("y", "z")] <- list(y = "new value for y", z = c(1, 2))
l1
## $x
## [1]  0
##
## $y
## [1]  "new value for y"
##
## $z
## [1]  1 2
##
## $m
## [1]  4
```

If we need to remove some of the members in a list, just assign the NULL value to them:

```
l1$x <- NULL
l1
## $y
## [1]  "new value for y"
##
## $z
## [1]  1 2
##
## $m
## [1]  4
```

We can remove more than one member from a list altogether:

```
l1[c("z", "m")] <- NULL
l1
## $y
## [1] "new value for y"
```

Other functions

Many functions in R are related to lists. For example, if we are not sure whether an object is a list or not, we can call `is.list()` to find out:

```
l2 <- list(a = c(1, 2, 3), b = c("x", "y", "z", "w"))
is.list(l2)
## [1] TRUE
is.list(l2$a)
## [1] FALSE
```

Here, `l2` is a list, and but `l2$a` is a numeric vector rather than a list.

We can also convert a vector to a list using `as.list()`:

```
l3 <- as.list(c(a = 1, b =2, c = 3))
l3
## $a
## [1] 1
##
## $b
## [1] 2
##
## $c
## [1] 3
```

It is also easy to coerce a list to a vector by calling `unlist` that basically converts all list members and puts them to a vector of a compatible type:

```
l4 <- list(a = 1, b = 2, c = 3)
unlist(l4)
## a b c
## 1 2 3
```

If we unlist a list of numbers and texts in mixture, all members will be converted to the closest type that each one can be converted to:

```
l4 <- list(a = 1, b = 2, c = "hello")
unlist(l4)
```

```
## a b c
## "1" "2" "hello"
```

Here, `l4$a` and `l4$b` are numbers and can be converted to a character; however, `butl4$c` is a character vector and cannot be converted to numeric values. Therefore, their closest type that is compatible with all elements is a character vector.

Data frames

A data frame represents a set of data with a number of rows and columns. It looks like a matrix but its columns are not necessarily of the same type. This is consistent with the most commonly seen formats of datasets: each row, or data record, is described by multiple columns of various types.

The following table is an example that can be fully characterized by a data frame.

Name	Gender	Age	Major
Ken	Male	24	Finance
Ashley	Female	25	Statistics
Jennifer	Female	23	Computer Science

Creating a data frame

To create a data frame, we can call `data.frame()` and supply the data of each column by a vector of the corresponding type:

```
persons <- data.frame(Name = c("Ken", "Ashley", "Jennifer"),
  Gender = c("Male", "Female", "Female"),
  Age = c(24, 25, 23),
  Major = c("Finance", "Statistics", "Computer Science"))
persons
##     Name    Gender  Age  Major
## 1 Ken       Male    24   Finance
## 2 Ashley    Female  25   Statistics
## 3 Jennifer  Female  23   Computer Science
```

Note that creating a data frame is exactly the same as creating a list. This is because, in essence, a data frame is a list in which each element is a vector and represents a table column and has the same number of elements.

Other than creating a data frame from raw data, we can also create it from a list by calling either data.frame directly or as.data.frame:

```
l1 <- list(x = c(1, 2, 3), y = c("a", "b", "c"))
data.frame(l1)
##   x y
## 1 1 a
## 2 2 b
## 3 3 c
as.data.frame(l1)
##   x y
## 1 1 a
## 2 2 b
## 3 3 c
```

We can also create a data frame from a matrix with the same method:

```
m1 <- matrix(c(1, 2, 3, 4, 5, 6, 7, 8, 9), nrow = 3, byrow = FALSE)
data.frame(m1)
##   X1 X2 X3
## 1 1  4  7
## 2 2  5  8
## 3 3  6  9
as.data.frame(m1)
##   V1 V2 V3
## 1 1  4  7
## 2 2  5  8
## 3 3  6  9
```

Note that the conversion also automatically assigns column names to the new data frame. In fact, as you may verify, if the matrix already has column names or row names, they will be preserved in the conversion.

Naming rows and columns

Since a data frame is a list but also looks like a matrix, the ways we access these two types of objects both apply to a data frame:

```
df1 <- data.frame(id = 1:5, x = c(, 2, 1, -1, -3), y = c(0.5, 0.2, 0.1,
0.5, 0.9))
df1
##   id x    y
## 1 1  0  0.5
## 2 2  2  0.2
## 3 3  1  0.1
## 4 4 -1  0.5
```

```
## 5  5 -3  0.9
```

We can rename the columns and rows just like we do with a matrix:

```
colnames(df1) <- c("id", "level", "score")
rownames(df1) <- letters[1:5]
df1
##    id level score
## a  1    0    0.5
## b  2    2    0.2
## c  3    1    0.1
## d  4   -1    0.5
## e  5   -3    0.9
```

Subsetting a data frame

Since a data frame is a matrix-like list of column vectors, we can use both sets of notations to access the elements and subsets in a data frame.

Subsetting a data frame as a list

If we would like to regard a data frame as a list of vectors, we can use list notations to extract a value or perform subsetting.

For example, we can use $ to extract the values of one column by name, or use [[to do so by position:

```
df1$id
## [1] 1 2 3 4 5
df1[[1]]
## [1] 1 2 3 4 5
```

List subsetting perfectly applies to a data frame and also yields a new data frame. The subsetting operator ([) allows us to use a numeric vector to extract columns by position, a character vector to extract columns by name, or a logical vector to extract columns by TRUE and FALSE selection:

```
df1[1]
##    id
## a 1
## b 2
## c 3
## d 4
## e 5
```

```
df1[1:2]
##   id level
## a 1   0
## b 2   2
## c 3   1
## d 4  -1
## e 5  -3
df1["level"]
##   level
## a   0
## b   2
## c   1
## d  -1
## e  -3
df1[c("id", "score")]
##   id score
## a 1   0.5
## b 2   0.2
## c 3   0.1
## d 4   0.5
## e 5   0.9
df1[c(TRUE, FALSE, TRUE)]
##    id score
## a 1   0.5
## b 2   0.2
## c 3   0.1
## d 4   0.5
## e 5   0.9
```

Subsetting a data frame as a matrix

However, the list notation does not support row selection. In contrast, the matrix notation provides more flexibility. If we view a data frame as a matrix, the two-dimensional accessor enables us to easily access an entry of a subset, which supports both column selection and row selection.

In other words, we can use the [row, column] notation to subset a data frame by specifying the row selector and column selector, which can be numeric vectors, character vectors, and/or logical vectors.

For example, we can specify the column selector:

```
df1[, "level"]
## [1] 0 2 1 -1 -3
df1[, c("id", "level")]
##   id level
```

```
## a 1   0
## b 2   2
## c 3   1
## d 4  -1
## e 5  -3
df1[, 1:2]
##  id level
## a 1   0
## b 2   2
## c 3   1
## d 4  -1
## e 5  -3
```

Alternatively, we can specify the row selector:

```
df1[1:4,]
##   id level score
## a  1   0    0.5
## b  2   2    0.2
## c  3   1    0.1
## d  4  -1    0.5
df1[c("c", "e"),]
##   id level score
## c  3   1    0.1
## e  5  -3    0.9
```

We can even specify both selectors at the same time:

```
df1[1:4, "id"]
## [1] 1 2 3 4
df1[1:3, c("id", "score")]
##   id score
## a  1  0.5
## b  2  0.2
## c  3  0.1
```

Note that the matrix notation automatically simplifies the output. That is, if only one column is selected, the result won't be a data frame but the values of that column. To always keep the result as a data frame, even if it only has a single column, we can use both notations together:

```
df1[1:4,]["id"]
##    id
## a 1
## b 2
## c 3
## d 4
```

Here, the first group of brackets subsets the data frame as a matrix with the first four rows and all columns selected. The second group of brackets subsets the resultant data frame as a list with only the `id` column selected, which results in a data frame.

Another way is to specify `drop = FALSE` to avoid simplifying the results:

```
df1[1:4, "id", drop = FALSE]
##    id
## a 1
## b 2
## c 3
## d 4
```

If you expect the output of a data frame subsetting to always be a data frame, you should always set `drop = FALSE`; otherwise, some edge cases (like a user input selecting only one column) may end up in unexpected behaviors if you assume that you will get a data frame but actually get a vector.

Filtering data

The following code filters the rows of `df1` by `criterionscore >= 0.5` and selects the `id` and `level` columns:

```
df1$score >= 0.5
## [1] TRUE FALSE FALSE TRUE TRUE
df1[df1$score >= 0.5, c("id", "level")]
##    id level
## a  1    0
## d  4   -1
## e  5   -3
```

The following code filters the rows of `df1` by a criterion that the row name must be among a, d, or e, and selects the `id` and `score` columns:

```
rownames(df1) %in% c("a", "d", "e")
## [1] TRUE FALSE FALSE TRUE TRUE
df1[rownames(df1) %in% c("a", "d", "e"), c("id", "score")]
##    id score
## a  1   0.5
## d  4   0.5
## e  5   0.9
```

Both of these examples basically use matrix notation to select rows by a logical vector and select columns by a character vector.

Setting values

Setting the values of a subset of a data frame allows both methods working with a list and a matrix.

Setting values as a list

We can assign new values to a list member using $ and <- together:

```
df1$score <- c(0.6, 0.3, 0.2, 0.4, 0.8)
df1
##   id level score
## a 1     0   0.6
## b 2     2   0.3
## c 3     1   0.2
## d 4    -1   0.4
## e 5    -3   0.8
```

Alternatively, [works too, and it also allows multiple changes in one expression in contrast to [[, which only allows modifying one column at a time:

```
df1["score"] <- c(0.8, 0.5, 0.2, 0.4, 0.8)
df1
##   id level score
## a 1     0   0.8
## b 2     2   0.5
## c 3     1   0.2
## d 4    -1   0.4
## e 5    -3   0.8
df1[["score"]] <- c(0.4, 0.5, 0.2, 0.8, 0.4)
df1
##   id level score
## a 1     0   0.4
## b 2     2   0.5
## c 3     1   0.2
## d 4    -1   0.8
## e 5    -3   0.4
df1[c("level", "score")] <- list(level = c(1, 2, 1, , ), score = c(0.1,
0.2, 0.3, 0.4, 0.5))
df1,
##   id level score
## a 1     1   0.1
## b 2     2   0.2
## c 3     1   0.3
## d 4     0   0.4
## e 5     0   0.5
```

Setting values as a matrix

Using list notations to set values of a data frame has the same problem as subsetting–we can only access the columns. If we need to set values with more flexibility, we can use matrix notations:

```
df1[1:3, "level"] <- c(-1, , 1)
df1
##    id level score
## a  1    -1    0.1
## b  2     0    0.2
## c  3     1    0.3
## d  4     0    0.4
## e  5     0    0.5
df1[1:2, c("level", "score")] <- list(level = c(, ), score = c(0.9, 1.0))
df1
##    id level score
## a  1     0    0.9
## b  2     0    1.0
## c  3     1    0.3
## d  4     0    0.4
## e  5     0    0.5
```

Factors

One thing to notice is that the default behavior of a data frame tries to use memory more efficiently. Sometimes, this behavior might silently lead to unexpected problems.

For example, when we create a data frame by supplying a character vector as a column, it will by default convert the character vector to a factor that only stores the same value once so that repetitions will not cost much memory. In fact, a factor is essentially an integer vector with a pre-specified set of possible values called levels to represent values of limited possibilities.

We can verify this by calling str() on the data frame persons we created in the beginning:

```
str(persons)
## 'data.frame': 3 obs. of 4 variables:
## $ Name  : Factor w/ 3 levels "Ashley","Jennifer",..: 3 1 2
## $ Gender: Factor w/ 2 levels "Female","Male": 2 1 1
## $ Age   : num 24 25 23
## $ Major : Factor w/ 3 levels "Computer Science",..: 2 3 1
```

As we can clearly find out that `Name`, `Gender`, and `Major` are not character vectors but factor objects. It is reasonable that `Gender` is represented by a factor because it may only be either `Female` or `Male`, so using two integers to represent these two values is more efficient than using a character vector to store all the values regardless of the repetition.

However, it may induce problems for other columns not limited to taking several possible values. For example, if we want to set a name in `persons`:

```
persons[1, "Name"] <- "John"
## Warning in `[<-.factor`(`*tmp*`, iseq, value = "John"): invalid factor
## level, NA generated
persons
##      Name    Gender Age  Major
## 1 <NA>       Male   24   Finance
## 2 Ashley    Female 25   Statistics
## 3 Jennifer Female 23   Computer Science
```

A warning message appears. This happens because in the initial `Name` dictionary, there is no word called `John`, therefore we cannot set the name of the first person to be such a non-existing value. The same thing happens when we set any `Gender` to be `Unknown`. The reason is exactly the same: when the column is initially created from a character vector when we define a data frame, the column will by default be a factor whose value must be taken from the dictionary created from the unique values in that character vector.

This behavior is sometimes very annoying and does not really help much, especially as memory is cheap today. The simplest way to avoid this behavior is to set `stringsAsFactors = FALSE` when we create a data frame using `data.frame()`:

```
persons <- data.frame(Name = c("Ken", "Ashley", "Jennifer"),
  Gender = factor(c("Male", "Female", "Female")),
  Age = c(24, 25, 23),
  Major = c("Finance", "Statistics", "Computer Science"),
  stringsAsFactors = FALSE)
str(persons)
## 'data.frame': 3 obs. of 4 variables:
## $ Name : chr "Ken" "Ashley" "Jennifer"
## $ Gender: Factor w/ 2 levels "Female","Male": 2 1 1
## $ Age : num 24 25 23
## $ Major : chr "Finance" "Statistics" "Computer Science"
```

If we really want a factor object to play its role, we can explicitly call `factor()` at specific columns, just like we did previously for the `Gender` column.

Useful functions for data frames

There are many useful functions for a data frame. Here we only introduce a few but the most commonly used ones.

The `summary()` function works with a data frame by generating a table that shows the summary statistics of each column:

```
summary(persons)
## Name Gender Age Major
## Length:3 Female:2 Min. :23.0 Length:3
## Class :character Male :1 1st Qu.:23.5 Class :character
## Mode :character Median :24.0 Mode :character
## Mean :24.0
## 3rd Qu.:24.5
## Max. :25.0
```

For a factor `Gender`, the summary counts the number of rows taking each value, or level. For a numeric vector, the summary shows the important quantiles of the numbers. For other types of columns, it shows the length, class, and mode of them. Another common demand is binding multiple data frames together by either row or column. For this purpose, we can use `rbind()` and `cbind()` which, as their names suggest, perform row binding and column binding respectively.

If we want to append some rows to a data frame, in this case, add a new record of a person, we can use `rbind()`:

```
rbind(persons, data.frame(Name = "John", Gender = "Male", Age = 25, Major
= "Statistics"))
##    Name    Gender Age Major
## 1 Ken      Male    24 Finance
## 2 Ashley   Female  25 Statistics
## 3 Jennifer Female  23 Computer Science
## 4 John     Male    25 Statistics
```

If we want to append some columns to a data frame, in this case, add two new columns to indicate whether each person is registered and the number of projects in hand, we can use `cbind()`:

```
cbind(persons, Registered = c(TRUE, TRUE, FALSE), Projects = c(3, 2, 3))
##    Name    Gender Age Major            Registered Projects
## 1 Ken      Male    24 Finance          TRUE       3
## 2 Ashley   Female  25 Statistics       TRUE       2
## 3 Jennifer Female  23 Computer Science FALSE      3
```

Note that `rbind()` and `cbind()` do not modify the original data but create a new data frame with given rows or columns appended.

Another useful function is `expand.grid()`. This generates a data frame that includes all combinations of the values in the columns:

```
expand.grid(type = c("A", "B"), class = c("M", "L", "XL"))
##   type class
## 1  A     M
## 2  B     M
## 3  A     L
## 4  B     L
## 5  A    XL
## 6  B    XL
```

There are many other useful functions working with data frames. We will discuss these functions in data manipulation chapters.

Loading and writing data on disk

In practice, data is usually stored in files. R provides a number of functions to read a table from a file or write a data frame to a file. If a file stores a table, it is often well organized and follows some convention that specifies how rows and columns are arranged. In most cases, we don't have to read a file byte to byte but call functions such as `read.table()` or `read.csv()`.

The most popular software-neutral data format is **CSV (Comma-Separated Values)**. The format is basically organized in a way that values in different columns are separated by a comma and the first row is by default regarded as the header. For example, persons may be represented in the following CSV format:

```
Name,Gender,Age,Major
Ken,Male,24,Finance
Ashley,Female,25,Statistics
Jennifer,Female,23,Computer Science
```

To read the data into the R environment, we only need to call `read.csv(file)` where the file is the path of the file. To ensure that the data file can be found, please place the `data` folder directly in your working directory, call `getwd()` to find out. We'll talk about this in detail in the next chapter:

```
read.csv("data/persons.csv")
##   Name   Gender Age Major
## 1 Ken    Male   24  Finance
```

```
## 2 Ashley    Female 25   Statistics
## 3 Jennifer Female 23   Computer Science
```

If we need to save a data frame to a CSV file, we may call `write.csv(file)` with some additional arguments:

```
write.csv(persons, "data/persons.csv", row.names = FALSE, quote = FALSE)
```

The argument `row.names = FALSE` avoids storing the row names which are not necessary, and the `argument quote = FALSE` avoids quoting text in the output, both of which in most cases are not necessary.

There are a number of built-in functions and several packages related to reading and writing data in different formats. We will cover this topic in later chapters.

Functions

A function is an object you can call. Basically, it is a machine with internal logic that takes a group of inputs (parameters or arguments) and returns a value as output.

In the previous sections, we encountered some built-in functions of R. For example, `is.numeric()` takes an argument that can be any R object and returns a logical value that indicates whether the object is a numeric vector. Similarly, `is.function()` can tell whether a given R object is a function object.

In fact, in R environment, everything we use is an object, everything we do is a function, and, maybe to your surprise, all functions are still objects. Even <- and + are both functions that take two arguments. Although they are called binary operators, they are essentially functions.

When we do casual, interactive data analysis, at times, we won't have to write any function on our own since the built-in functions and those provided by thousands of packages are usually enough.

However, if you need to repeat your logic or a process in data manipulation or analysis, those functions may not fully serve your purpose because they are not designed to meet the specific needs of a task or the format of a particular dataset. Then, you need to create your own functions targeting a specific set of demands.

Creating a function

It is easy to create a function in R. Suppose we define a function called add that simply adds two numbers x and y, respectively:

```
add <- function(x, y) {
  x + y
}
```

The syntax function (x, y) specifies the arguments of the function. In other words, the function takes two arguments named x and y. The { x + y } is the function body that contains a series of expressions expressed in terms of x, y and other symbols available. The value of the last expression determines the value returned by the function unless return() is called inside the function. Finally, the function is assigned to add so that we can call this function using add later on.

Creating such a simple function, or any more complicated functions, does not impose any difference on evaluating a vector. The function in R just acts like another object. To see what object add refers to, just type add at the console:

```
add
## function(x, y) {
## x + y
## }
```

Calling a function

Once the function is defined, we can call the function just as we do in math. The calling requires the same syntax: name (arg1, arg2, …). Take a look at the following:

```
add(2, 3)
## [1] 5
```

The call is quite transparent. When we evaluate such a call, R will find out if there is a function named add in the environment. Then, it will figure out that add refers to the function we just created and creates a local environment in which x takes 2 and y takes 3. The expression in the function body is then evaluated given the values of the arguments. Finally, the function returns the value of that expression, 5.

Dynamic typing

Functions in R can be very flexible since it is not strongly typed. In other words, the type of inputs are not fixed prior to the calling. Even if the function is originally designed to work for scalar numbers, it is automatically generalized to also work with all vectors as long as + works with them. For example, we can run the following code without any change in the function:

```
add(c(2, 3), 4)
## [1] 6 7
```

The preceding example does not really demonstrate the flexibility of dynamic typing because scalar is also a vector in R. A more qualified example is:

```
add(as.Date("2014-06-01"), 1)
## [1] "2014-06-02"
```

The function put the two arguments into the expression without any type checking. `as.Date()` creates a `Date` object, which has a date representation. Without changing any code of `add`, it works with `Date` perfectly. The function fails only when + is not well-defined for the two arguments:

```
add(list(a = 1), list(a = 2))
## Error in x + y: non-numeric argument to binary operator
```

Generalizing a function

Functions are a well-defined abstraction of a particular set of logic or process intended for solving some particular problem. Developers often want a function to be general enough to adapt to a wide range of use cases so that we can easily use it to solve similar problems without writing too many specialized functions for each problem.

To make a function more widely applicable is called **generalization**. It is very handy to generalize a function in a weakly-typed programming language like R, but it can be error-prone if it is incorrectly implemented.

To make `add()` more general so that it can handle various primitive algebraic operations, we can define another function called `calc`. This new function accepts three arguments where x and y are the two vectors, and `type` accepts a character vector which is the kind of algebraic operation the user wants to perform.

The following code implements such a function using **flow control**, which we will cover soon, but it should be easy to understand at first look. In this code, the choice of expression to be evaluated depends on the value of `type`:

```
calc <- function(x, y, type) {
  if (type == "add") {
    x + y
  } else if (type == "minus") {
    x - y
  } else if (type == "multiply") {
    x * y
  } else if (type == "divide") {
    x / y
  } else {
    stop("Unknown type of operation")
  }
}
```

Once the function is defined, we can call it by supplying appropriate arguments:

```
calc(2, 3, "minus")
## [1] -1
```

The function automatically works with numeric vectors:

```
calc(c(2, 5), c(3, 6), "divide")
## [1] 0.6666667 0.8333333
```

The function is also generalized to work with non-numeric vectors for which + is well-defined:

```
calc(as.Date("2014-06-01"), 3, "add")
## [1] "2014-06-04"
```

Consider supplying some invalid arguments:

```
calc(1, 2, "what")
## Error in calc(1, 2, "what"): Unknown type of operation
```

In this case, no conditions are satisfied, so the expression in the last else block will be evaluated. The `stop()` call yields an error message and terminates the whole evaluation immediately.

The functions seem to work fine and consider all possible situations with invalid arguments. However, it is not true:

```
calc(1, 2, c("add", "minue"))
## Warning in if (type == "add") {: the condition has length > 1 and only
the
## first element will be used
## [1] 3
```

Here, we didn't consider the case where type is given as a multi-element vector. The problem is: when such a vector is compared with another vector, it will also result in a multi-element logical vector, it will also result in a mult-element logical vector which makes an ambiguous condition for if. Consider what it means by if(c(TRUE, FALSE))?

To avoid such ambiguity explicitly, we need to refine the function so that the error will be more informative and transparent. To proceed, we just need to check whether the vector has the length 1:

```
calc <- function(x, y, type) {
  if (length(type) > 1L) stop("Only a single type is accepted")
  if (type == "add") {
    x + y
  } else if (type == "minus") {
    x - y
  } else if (type == "multiply") {
    x * y
  } else if (type == "divide") {
    x / y
  } else {
    stop("Unknown type of operation")
  }
}
```

Then, we retry the trouble-making call and see how the exception is handled by pre-checking of arguments:

```
calc(1, 2, c("add", "minue"))
## Error in calc(1, 2, c("add", "minue")): Only a single type is accepted
```

Default value for function arguments

Some functions are very flexible because they accept a wide range of input and meet a variety of demands. In many cases, more flexibility means an increasing number of arguments.

If we have to specify tens of arguments each time using a very flexible function, it would certainly be a mess to look at the code. In this case, reasonable default values for arguments will largely simplify the code to call a function.

To set the default value of an argument, use `arg = value`. This will make the argument optional. The following example creates a function with an optional argument:

```
increase <- function(x, y = 1) {
  x + y
}
```

The new function `increase()` allows us to call it with only x. In this case, y automatically takes 1 unless it is explictly specified.

```
increase(1)
## [1] 2
increase(c(1, 2, 3))
## [1] 2 3 4
```

Many R functions have multiple arguments and some of them are given default values. Sometimes, it is tricky to determine the default values of arguments because it heavily relies on the intention of most users.

Summary

In this chapter, you learned the basic behaviors of numeric vectors, logical vectors, and character vectors. These vectors are homogeneous data types that can only store elements of the same type. By contrast, lists and data frames are more flexible since they store elements of different types. You learned how to subset these data structures and extract an element from them. Finally, you learned about creating and calling functions.

Now you know the rules of the game, you need to get familiar with the playground. In the next chapter, we will cover some basic yet important things about managing the workspace. I will show you some common practices of managing the working directory, the environment, and the library of packages.

3

Managing Your Workspace

If the behavior of R objects is compared to game rules, then the workspace can be compared to the playground. To play the game well, you need to familiarize yourself not only with the rules, but also with the playground. In this chapter, I will introduce to you some basic but important skills to manage your workspace. These skills include:

- Using the working directory
- Inspecting the working environment
- Modifying global options
- Managing the library of packages

R's working directory

An R session always starts in a directory, no matter whether it is launched as an R terminal or in RStudio. The directory in which R is running is called the **working directory** of the R session. When you access other files on your hard drive, you can use either absolute paths (for example, `D:\Workspaces\test-project\data\2015.csv`) in most cases or relative paths (for example, `data\2015.csv`) with the right working directory (in this case, `D:\Workspaces\test-project`).

The use of relative paths to the working directory does not change the file paths, but the way you specify them is shorter. It also makes your scripts more portable. Imagine you are writing some R scripts to produce graphics according to a bunch of data files in a directory. If you write the directory as an absolute path, then anyone else who wants to run your script on their own computer would have to modify the paths in your code to the location of the data in their hard drives. However, if you write the directory as a relative path, then if the data is kept in the same relative location, the script will work without any modification.

In an R terminal, you can get the current working directory of the running R session using `getwd()`. By default, commandR starts a new R session from your user directory, and RStudio runs an R session in the background from your user documents directory.

Apart from the defaults, you can choose a directory and create an R project in RStudio. Then, every time you open that project, the working directory is the location of the project, which makes it super easy to access files in the project directory using relative paths, which improves the portability of the project.

Creating an R project in RStudio

To create a new project, simply go to **File** | **New Project** or click the Project drop-down menu in the top-right corner of the main window and choose **New Project**. A window will appear, and you can create a new directory or choose an existing directory on your hard drive as the project directory:

Once you choose a local directory, the project will be created there. An R project is nothing but a `.Rproj` file that stores some settings. If you open such a project file in RStudio, the settings in it will be applied, and the working directory will be set to the directory in which the project file is located.

Another useful point in using RStudio to work in a project is that auto-completion makes writing file paths much more efficient. When you are typing a string of either an absolute or relative file path, press *Tab* and RStudio will list the files in that directory:

Comparing absolute and relative paths

Since I'm writing this book with RMarkdown in RStudio, the working directory is the directory of my book project:

```
getwd()
## [1] "D:/Workspaces/learn-r-programming"
```

You may notice that the working directory mentioned earlier uses / instead of \. In Windows operating systems, \ is the default path separator, but this symbol is already used to make special characters. For example, when you create a character vector, you can use \n to represent a new line:

```
"Hello\nWorld"
## [1] "Hello\nWorld"
```

Special characters are preserved when the character vector is directly printed as a representation of the string. However, if you add cat() to it, the string will be written in the console with the escape characters translated to the characters they represent:

```
cat("Hello\nWorld")
## Hello ## World
```

The second word starts by a new line (\n) as normal. However, if \ is so special, how should we write \ itself? Just use \\:

```
cat("The string with '' is translated")
## The string with '' is translated
```

That is why we should use \\ or / in paths in Windows operating systems since both are supported. In Unix-like operating systems, such as macOS and Linux, things are easier: always use /. If you are using Windows and misuse \ to refer to a file, an error will occur:

```
filename <- "d:\data\test.csv"
## Error: '\d' is an unrecognized escape in character string starting
## ""d:\d"
```

Instead, you need to write it like this:

```
filename <- "d:\\data\\test.csv"
```

Fortunately, we can use / in Windows in most cases, which makes the same code runnable in nearly all popular operating systems using relative paths:

```
absolute_filename <- "d:/data/test.csv"
relative_filename <- "data/test.csv"
```

Instead of getting the working directory using `getwd()`, we can also set the working directory of the current R session using `setwd()`. However, this is almost always not recommended because it can direct all relative paths in a script to another directory and make everything go wrong.

Therefore, a good practice is to create an R project to start your work.

Managing project files

Once we create a project in RStudio, a `.Rproj` file is also created in the project directory in which there is no other file at the moment. Since R is related to statistical computing and data visualization, an R project mainly contains R scripts that do statistical computing (or other programming tasks), data files (such as `.csv` files), documents (such as Markdown files), and sometimes output graphics.

If different types of file are mixed up in the project directory, it will be increasingly more difficult to manage these project files, especially as input data accumulates or output data and graphics clutter the directory.

A recommended practice is to create subdirectories to contain different types of files resulting from different types of tasks.

For example, the following directory structure is plain, with all files together:

```
project/
- household.csv
- population.csv
- national-income.png
- popluation-density.png
- utils.R
- import-data.R
- check-data.R
- plot.R
- README.md
- NOTES.md
```

By contrast, the following directory structure is much cleaner and nicer to work with:

```
project/
- data/
   - household.csv
   - population.csv
- graphics/
   - national-income.png
   - popluation-density.png
- R/
   - utils.R
   - import-data.R
   - check-data.R
   - plot.R
- README.md
- NOTES.md
```

In the preceding directory structures, directories are represented in the form of `directory/` and files in the form of `file-name.ext`. In most cases, the second structure is recommended because, as project needs and tasks become more complex, the first structure will end up in a mess while the second structure will remain tidy.

Apart from the structure issue, it is common to write the project introduction in `README.md` and put additional notes in `NOTES.md`. These two documents are Markdown documents (`.md`), and it is worth becoming familiar with its extremely simple syntax. Read *Daring Fireball: Markdown Syntax Documentation* (`https://daringfireball.net/projects/markdown/syntax`) and *GitHub Help: Markdown Basics* (`https://help.github.com/articles/markdown-basics/`) for details. We will cover the topic of combining R and Markdown in `Chapter 15`, *Boosting Productivity*.

Now the working directory is ready. In the next section, you will learn various methods to inspect the working environment in an R session.

Inspecting the environment

In R, every expression is evaluated within a specific environment. An environment is a collection of symbols and their bindings. When we bind a value to a symbol, call a function, or refer to a name, R will find the symbols in the current environment. If you type commands in the RStudio console, your commands are evaluated in the **Global Environment**.

For example, when we start a fresh R session in a terminal or RStudio, we start working within an empty global environment. In other words, there is no symbol defined in this environment. If we run x <- c(1, 2, 3), the numeric vector c(1, 2, 3) is bound to symbol x in the global environment. Then, the global environment has one binding that maps x to the vector c(1, 2, 3). In other words, if you evaluate x, then you will get its value.

Inspecting existing symbols

In addition to manipulating vectors and lists as we did in the previous chapter, we need to know some basic functions to inspect and manipulate our working environment. The most basic but useful function to inspect the collection of objects we are working with is objects(). The function returns a character vector of the names of existing objects in the current environment.

In a fresh R session, there should not be any symbol in the current environment:

```
objects()
## character(0)
```

Let's assume we create the following objects:

```
x <- c(1, 2, 3)
y <- c("a", "b", "c")
z <- list(m = 1:5, n = c("x", "y", "z"))
```

Then, you will get a character vector of the existing object names:

```
objects()
## [1] "x" "y" "z"
```

Many developers prefer ls() as an alias of objects():

```
ls()
## [1] "x" "y" "z"
```

In most cases, especially when you are working in RStudio, you don't have to use objects() or ls() to see what symbols have been created because the **Environment** pane shows all symbols available in the global environment:

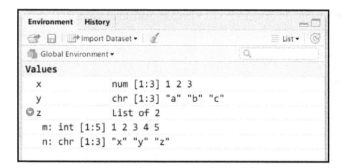

The **Environment** pane shows symbols and their values in a compact representation. You can interact with objects in it by expanding a list or data frame and viewing the vectors inside.

In addition to the list view, the **Environment** pane also provides an alternative grid view. The grid view shows not only the names, types, and the value structures of existing objects, but also their object sizes:

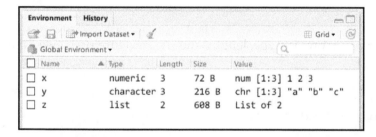

Although the **Environment** pane in RStudio makes it straightforward to inspect all existing variables, objects() or ls() can be still useful when RStudio is not available, when you write a function to work with their names, or the objects are provided dynamically in different manners.

Viewing the structure of an object

In the **Environment** pane, the compact representation of an object comes from the str() function, which prints the structure of a given object.

For example, when `str()` is applied to a simple numeric vector, it shows its type, positions, and a preview of its values:

```
x
## [1] 1 2 3
str(x)
## num [1:3] 1 2 3
```

If the vector has more than 10 elements, `str()` will only show the first 10:

```
str(1:30)
## int [1:30] 1 2 3 4 5 6 7 8 9 10 ...
```

For a list, directly evaluating it in the console or using `print()` will show the elements in a verbose form:

```
z
## $m
## [1] 1 2 3 4 5
##
## $n
## [1] "x" "y" "z"
```

Alternatively, `str()` shows its type, length, and the structure preview of the elements:

```
str(z)
## List of 2
## $ m: int [1:5] 1 2 3 4 5
## $ n: chr [1:3] "x" "y" "z"
```

Let's assume we created the following nested list:

```
nested_list <- list(m = 1:15, n = list("a", c(1, 2, 3)),
    p = list(x = 1:10, y = c("a", "b")),
    q = list(x = :9, y = c("c", "d")))
```

Directly printing will show all its elements and tell us how we can access them which can be long and unnecessary in most cases:

```
nested_list
## $m
## [1] 1 2 3 4 5 6 7 8 9 10 11 12 13 14 15
##
## $n
## $n[[1]]
## [1] "a"
##
## $n[[2]]
```

```
## [1] 1 2 3
##
##
## $p
## $p$x
## [1] 1 2 3 4 5 6 7 8 9 10
##
## $p$y
## [1] "a" "b"
##
##
## $q
## $q$x
## [1] 0 1 2 3 4 5 6 7 8 9
##
## $q$y
## [1] "c" "d"
```

To get a compact representation that is easier to view and work with, call str() with a list:

```
str(nested_list)
## List of 4
## $ m: int [1:15] 1 2 3 4 5 6 7 8 9 10 ...
## $ n:List of 2
## ..$ : chr "a"
## ..$ : num [1:3] 1 2 3
## $ p:List of 2
## ..$ x: int [1:10] 1 2 3 4 5 6 7 8 9 10
## ..$ y: chr [1:2] "a" "b"
## $ q:List of 2
## ..$ x: int [1:10] 0 1 2 3 4 5 6 7 8 9
## ..$ y: chr [1:2] "c" "d"
```

While str() shows the structure of an object, ls.str() shows the structure of the current environment:

```
ls.str()
## nested_list : List of 4
## $ m: int [1:15] 1 2 3 4 5 6 7 8 9 10 ...
## $ n:List of 2
## $ p:List of 2
## $ q:List of 2
## x : num [1:3] 1 2 3
## y : chr [1:3] "a" "b" "c"
## z : List of 2
## $ m: int [1:5] 1 2 3 4 5
## $ n: chr [1:3] "x" "y" "z"
```

Its functionality is similar to that of the **Environment** pane in RStudio and can be useful when you need to inspect a customized environment or only show the structures of some particular variables.

One filter for `ls.str()` is the mode argument. You can show the structures of all values that are list objects:

```
ls.str(mode = "list")
## nested_list : List of 4
## $ m: int [1:15] 1 2 3 4 5 6 7 8 9 10 ...
## $ n:List of 2
## $ p:List of 2
## $ q:List of 2
## z : List of 2
## $ m: int [1:5] 1 2 3 4 5
## $ n: chr [1:3] "x" "y" "z"
```

The other filter is the pattern argument, which specifies the pattern of the names to match. The pattern is expressed in a **regular expression**. If you want to show the structures of all variables whose names contain only one character, you can run the following command:

```
ls.str(pattern = "^\\w$")
## x : num [1:3] 1 2 3
## y : chr [1:3] "a" "b" "c"
## z : List of 2
## $ m: int [1:5] 1 2 3 4 5
## $ n: chr [1:3] "x" "y" "z"
```

If you want to show the structures of all list objects whose names contain only one character, you can use both pattern and mode at the same time:

```
ls.str(pattern = "^\\w$", mode = "list")
## z : List of 2
## $ m: int [1:5] 1 2 3 4 5
## $ n: chr [1:3] "x" "y" "z"
```

If you're put off by commands such as `^\\w$`, don't worry. This pattern matches all strings in the form of `(string begin)(any one word character like a, b, c)(string end)`. We will cover this powerful tool in `Chapter 6`, *Working with Strings*.

Removing symbols

So far, we have only created symbols. Sometimes, it can be useful to remove them. The `remove()` function, or equivalently `rm()`, removes existing symbols from the environment.

Before removing x, the symbols in the environment are as follows:

```
ls()
## [1] "nested_list" "x" "y" "z"
```

Then, we will use `rm()` to remove x from the environment:

```
rm(x)
ls()
## [1] "nested_list" "y" "z"
```

Note that the function also works with variable names in strings. Therefore, `rm("x")` has exactly the same effect. We can also remove multiple symbols in one function call:

```
rm(y, z)
ls()
## [1] "nested_list"
```

If the symbol to be removed does not exist in the environment, a warning will appear:

```
rm(x)
## Warning in rm(x): object 'x' not found
```

The `rm()` function can also remove all symbols specified by a character vector of symbol names:

```
p <- 1:10
q <- seq(1, 20, 5)
v <- c("p", "q")
rm(list = v)
## [1] "nested_list" "v"
```

If we want to clear all the bindings in an environment, we can combine `rm()` and `ls()` and call the function like this:

```
rm(list = ls())
ls()
## character(0)
```

Now there's no symbol in the environment.

In many cases, removing symbols is not necessary, but it can be useful to remove very large objects that occupy a big area of memory. If R feels memory pressure, it will clean up unused objects with no bindings.

Modifying global options

Instead of creating, inspecting, and removing objects in the working environment, R options have effects in the global scale of the current R session. We can call `getOption()` to see the value of a given option and call `options()` to modify one.

Modifying the number of digits to print

In RStudio, when you type `getOption(<Tab>)`, you can see a list of available options and their descriptions. A commonly used option, for instance, is the number of digits to display. Sometimes, it is not sufficient when we deal with numbers requiring higher precision. In an R session, the number of digits printed on screen is entirely managed by digits. We can call `getOption()` to see the current value of digits and call `options()` to set `digits` to a larger number:

When an R session starts, the default value of digits is 7. To demonstrate its effect, run the following code:

```
123.12345678
## [1] 123.1235
```

It is obvious that the 11-digit number is only shown with 7 digits. This means the last few decimal digits are gone; the printer only displays the number with 7 digits. To verify no precision is lost because of `digits = 7`, see the output of the following code:

```
0.10000002
## [1] 0.1
0.10000002 -0.1
## [1] 2e-08
```

If the numbers are rounded to the seventh decimal place by default, then `0.10000002` should be rounded to `0.1` and the second expression should result in . However, apparently, this does not happen because `digits = 7` only means the number of numeric digits to be displayed rather than rounded up.

However, in some cases, the number before the decimal point can be large, and we don't want to ignore digits following the decimal point. Without modifying digits, the following number will only display the integer part:

```
1234567.12345678
## [1] 1234567
```

If we want to see more digits printed, we need to increase digits from the default value 7 to a higher number:

```
getOption("digits")
## [1] 7
1e10 + 0.5
## [1] 1e + 10
options(digits = 15)
1e10 + 0.5
## [1] 10000000000.5
```

Note that once, `options()` is called, the modified options take effect immediately and may affect the behavior of all subsequent commands. To reset options, use this command:

```
options(digits = 7)
1e10 + 0.5
## [1] 1e + 10
```

Modifying the warning level

Another options example managing the warning level by specifying the value of the `warn` option:

```
getOption("warn")
## [1] 0
```

By default, the warning level is , which means a warning is a warning and an error is an error. In this state, a warning will be displayed but will not stop the code, while an error terminates the code immediately. If multiple warnings occur, they will be combined and displayed together. For example, the following conversion from a string to a numeric vector will produce a warning and result in a missing value:

```
as.numeric("hello")
## Warning: NAs introduced by coercion
## [1] NA
```

We can make it completely silent and still get a missing value from the unsuccessful conversion:

```
options(warn = -1)
as.numeric("hello")
## [1] NA
```

Then, the warning is gone. Making the warning messages disappear is almost always a bad idea. It will make potential errors silent. You can (or cannot) realize something is wrong from the final result. The recommendation is to be strict in your code and save a lot of time debugging it.

Setting warn to 1 or 2 will make buggy code fail fast. When `warn = 0`, the default behavior for evaluating a function call is to first return the value and then show all the warning messages together, if any. To demonstrate this behavior, the following function is called with two strings:

```
f <- function(x, y) {
  as.numeric(x) + as.numeric(y)
}
```

At the default warning level, all warning messages are shown after the function returns:

```
options(warn = )
f("hello", "world")
## [1] NA
## Warning messages:
## 1: In f("hello", "world") : NAs introduced by coercion
## 2: In f("hello", "world") : NAs introduced by coercion
```

The function coerces two input arguments to numeric vectors. As the input arguments are both strings, two warnings will be produced, but will only appear after the function returns. If the preceding function does some heavy work and takes a considerable period of time, you won't see any warning before you get the final result but in fact the intermediate computing has been way off the correct results for quite a while.

This prompts the use of `warn = 1`, which forces the warning message to be printed as soon as a warning is produced:

```
options(warn = 1)
f("hello", "world")
## Warning in f("hello", "world") : NAs introduced by coercion
## Warning in f("hello", "world") : NAs introduced by coercion
## [1] NA
```

The result is the same, but the warning messages appear ahead of the result. If the function is time-consuming, we should be able to see the warning messages first. So, we can choose to stop the code and check whether something is wrong.

A warning level is even stricter. The `warn = 2` argument directly regards any warning as an error.

```
options(warn = 2)
f("hello", "world")
## Error in f("hello", "world") :
## (converted from warning) NAs introduced by coercion
```

These options have effects in the global scale. Therefore, it is convenient to manage common aspects of an R session, but it can also be dangerous to change options. Just like changing the working directory may invalidate all relative paths in the script from running, changing global options may break all subsequent code that is based on incompatible assumptions of the global options.

In general, it is not recommended to modify global options unless absolutely necessary.

Managing the library of packages

In R, packages play an indispensable role in data analysis and visualization. In fact, R itself is only a tiny core and is built on several basic packages. A package is a container of predefined functions, which are often designed to be general enough to solve a certain range of problems. Using a well-designed package, we don't have to reinvent the wheel again and again, which allows us to focus more on the problem we are trying to solve.

R is powerful not only because of its rich source of packages, but also because of the well-maintained package archive system called *The Comprehensive R Archive Network*, or CRAN (http://cran.r-project.org/). The source code of R and thousands of packages is archived in this system. At the time of writing, there are 7,750 active packages on CRAN maintained by more than 4,500 package maintainers around the world. Every week, more than 100 packages will be updated and more than 2 million package downloads happen. You can check out the table of packages at https://cran.rstudio.com/web/packages/ in which all the packages currently available are listed.

Just don't panic when you hear the number of packages on CRAN! The number is large and the coverage is wide, but you only have to learn a small fraction of them. If you focus on the work of a specific field, it is very likely that there are no more than 10 packages that are heavily related to your work and field. Therefore, there's absolutely no need for you to know all the packages (nobody can or even need to), but only the most useful and field-related ones.

Instead of finding packages in the table, which is not that informative, I recommend that you visit CRAN Task Views (`https://cran.rstudio.com/web/views/`) and METACRAN `http://www.r-pkg.org/`, and get started by learning about the packages that are most commonly used or closely related to your working field. Before learning how to use a specific package, we need to have a general idea about installing packages from different sources and understand how a package basically works.

Getting to know a package

A package is a collection of functions to solve a certain range of problems. It can be an implementation of a family of statistical estimators, data-mining methods, database interfaces, or optimization tools. To know more about a package, for example, ggplot2, a super powerful graphics package, several information sources are useful:

- **Package description page**
  (`https://cran.rstudio.com/web/packages/ggplot2/`): The page contains the basic information about the package, including the name, description, version, publishing date, authors, related websites, reference manuals, vignettes, relationship to other packages, and so on. The description page of a package is provided not only by CRAN, but by some other third-party package information websites. METACRAN also provides a description of ggplot2
  at `http://www.r-pkg.org/pkg/ggplot2`.

- **Package website (**`http://ggplot2.org/`**)**: The webpage contains a description and related resources for the package, such as blogs, tutorials, and books. Not every package has a website, but if one does the website is the official starting point for learning about the package.

- **Package source code** (`https://github.com/hadley/ggplot2`): The authors host the source code of the package on GitHub (`https://github.com`), and the page is the source code the package. If you are interested in the implementation of the package functions, you can check out the source code and take a look. If you find some unexpected behavior that looks like a bug, you can report it
  at `https://github.com/hadley/ggplot2/issues`. Also, you can file an issue at the same place to request a new feature.

After reading the package description, you can try it by installing the package to the R library.

Installing packages from CRAN

CRAN archives R packages and distributes them to more than 120 mirrors around the world. You can visit CRAN Mirrors (`https://cran.r-project.org/mirrors.html`) and check out a nearby mirror. If you find one, you can go to **Tools | Global Options** and open the following dialog:

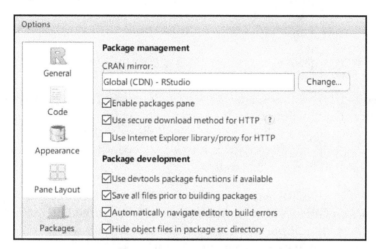

You can change the CRAN mirror to a nearby one or simply use the default mirror. In general, you will experience very fast downloading if you use a nearby mirror. In recent months, some mirrors have started using HTTPS to secure data transfers. If **Use secure download method for HTTP** is checked, then you can only view HTTPS mirrors.

Once a mirror is chosen, to download and install a package in R becomes extremely easy. Just call `install.packages("ggplot2")`, and R will automatically download the package, install it, and sometimes compile it.

RStudio also provides an easy way to install packages. Just go to the Packages pane and click on **Install**. The following dialog appears:

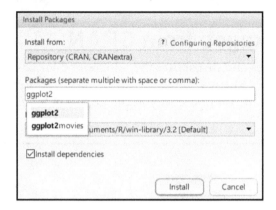

As the package description shows, a package may depend on other packages. In other words, when you call a function in the package, the function also calls some functions in other packages, which requires that you also install those packages as well. Fortunately, `install.packages()` is smart enough to know the dependency structure of the package to install and will install those packages first.

In the main page of METACRAN (`http://www.r-pkg.org/`), featured packages are those with the most stars on GitHub. That is, these packages are marked by many GitHub users. You may want to install multiple featured packages in one call, which is naturally allowed if you write the package names as a character vector:

```
install.packages(c("ggplot2", "shiny", "knitr", "dplyr", "data.table"))
```

Then the `install.packages()` function automatically resolves the joint dependency structure of all these packages and installs them.

Updating packages from CRAN

By default, the `install.packages()` function installs the latest version of the specified packages. Once they are installed, the package version stays fixed. However, the packages may be updated to fix bugs or add new features. Sometimes, an updated version of a package may deprecate functions in older versions with warnings. In these cases, we may keep the package out-of-date, or update it after reading the `NEWS` package, which can be found in the package description (for example, `https://cran.r-project.org/web/packages/ggplot2/news.html`; see this for details about the new version in the case of breaking changes).

RStudio provides an **Update** button next to **Install** in the package pane. We can also use the following function and choose which packages are going to be updated:

```
update.packages()
```

Both RStudio and the preceding function scan newer versions of packages and install these packages along with dependencies if necessary.

Installing packages from online repositories

Nowadays, many package authors host their work on GitHub because version control and community development are very easy, thanks to the well-designed issue-tracking systems and merge request system. Some authors do not release their work to CRAN, and others only release the stable versions to CRAN and keep new versions under development on GitHub.

If you want to try the latest development version, which often has new features or has fixed some bugs, you can directly install the package from the online repository using the devtools package.

First, install the devtools package if it does not appear in your library:

```
install.packages("devtools")
```

Then, use `install_github()` in the devtools package to install the latest development version of ggplot2:

```
library(devtools)
install_github("hadley/ggplot2")
```

The devtools package will download the source code from GitHub and makes it a package in your library. If your library has already got the package, the installation will replace it without asking. If you want to revert the development version to the latest CRAN version, you can run the CRAN installing code again:

```
install.packages("ggplot2")
```

Then, the local version (GitHub version) is replaced by the CRAN version.

Using package functions

There are two ways to use the functions in a package. First, we can call `library()` to attach the package so that the functions in it can be directly called. Second, we can call `package::function()` to only use the function without attaching the whole package to the environment.

For example, some statistical estimators are not implemented as built-in functions in base R but in other packages. One instance is skewness; the statistical function is provided by the moments package.

To calculate the skewness of numeric vector x, we can attach the package first and directly call the function:

```
library(moments)
skewness(x)
```

Alternatively, we can call package functions without attaching the package, using `:::`

```
moments::skewness(x)
```

The two methods return the same result, but they work in different ways and have a different impact on the environment. More specifically, the first method (using `library()`) modifies the search path of symbols, whereas the second method (using `::`) does not. When you call `library(moments)`, the package is attached and added to the search path so that the package functions are directly available in subsequent code.

Sometimes, it is useful to see what packages we are using by calling `sessionInfo()`:

```
sessionInfo()
## R version 3.2.3 (2015-12-10)
## Platform: x86_64-w64-mingw32/x64 (64-bit)
## Running under: Windows 10 x64 (build 10586)
##
## locale:
## [1] LC_COLLATE=English_UnitedStates.1252
## [2] LC_CTYPE=English_UnitedStates.1252
## [3] LC_MONETARY=English_UnitedStates.1252
## [4] LC_NUMERIC=C
## [5] LC_TIME=English_UnitedStates.1252
##
## attached base packages:
## [1] stats graphics grDevicesutils datasets
## [6] methods base
##
## loaded via a namespace (and not attached):
```

```
## [1]  magrittr_1.5formatR_1.2.1tools_3.2.3
## [4]  htmltools_0.3yaml_2.1.13stringi_1.0-1
## [7]  rmarkdown_0.9.2knitr_1.12stringr_1.0.0
## [10] digest_0.6.8evaluate_0.8
```

The session info shows the R version and lists the attached packages and loaded packages.
When we use : : to access a function in a package, the package is not attached but loaded in
memory. In this case, other functions in the package are still not directly available:

```
moments::skewness(c(1, 2, 3, 2, 1))
## [1] 0.3436216
sessionInfo()
## R version 3.2.3 (2015-12-10)
## Platform: x86_64-w64-mingw32/x64 (64-bit)
## Running under: Windows 10 x64 (build 10586)
##
## locale:
## [1] LC_COLLATE=English_UnitedStates.1252
## [2] LC_CTYPE=English_UnitedStates.1252
## [3] LC_MONETARY=English_UnitedStates.1252
## [4] LC_NUMERIC=C
## [5] LC_TIME=English_UnitedStates.1252
##
## attached base packages:
## [1] stats graphics grDevicesutils datasets
## [6] methods base
##
## loaded via a namespace (and not attached):
## [1]  magrittr_1.5formatR_1.2.1tools_3.2.3
## [4]  htmltools_0.3yaml_2.1.13stringi_1.0-1
## [7]  rmarkdown_0.9.2knitr_1.12stringr_1.0.0
## [10] digest_0.6.8moments_0.14evaluate_0.8
```

This shows that the moments package is loaded but not attached. When we
call library(moments), the package will be attached:

```
library(moments)
sessionInfo()
## R version 3.2.3 (2015-12-10)
## Platform: x86_64-w64-mingw32/x64 (64-bit)
## Running under: Windows 10 x64 (build 10586)
##
## locale:
## [1] LC_COLLATE=English_UnitedStates.1252
## [2] LC_CTYPE=English_UnitedStates.1252
## [3] LC_MONETARY=English_UnitedStates.1252
## [4] LC_NUMERIC=C
## [5] LC_TIME=English_UnitedStates.1252
```

```
##
## attached base packages:
## [1] stats graphics grDevicesutils datasets
## [6] methods base
##
## other attached packages:
## [1] moments_0.14
##
## loaded via a namespace (and not attached):
## [1] magrittr_1.5formatR_1.2.1tools_3.2.3
## [4] htmltools_0.3yaml_2.1.13stringi_1.0-1
## [7] rmarkdown_0.9.2knitr_1.12stringr_1.0.0
## [10] digest_0.6.8evaluate_0.8
skewness(c(1, 2, 3, 2, 1))
## [1] 0.3436216
```

Then, `skewness()` as well as other package functions in moments are directly available.

An easier way to see attached packages is `search()`:

```
search()
## [1] ".GlobalEnv" "package:moments"
## [3] "package:stats" "package:graphics"
## [5] "package:grDevices" "package:utils"
## [7] "package:datasets" "package:methods"
## [9] "Autoloads" "package:base"
```

The function returns the current search path of symbols. When you evaluate a function call that uses skewness, it finds a skewness symbol in the current environment first. Then, it goes to `package:moment` and the symbol is found. If the package is not attached, the symbol will not be found, so an error will occur. We will cover this symbol-finding mechanism in later chapters.

To attach a package, `require()` is similar to `library()`, but it returns a logical value to indicate whether the package is successfully attached:

```
loaded <- require(moments)
## Loading required package: moments
loaded
## [1] TRUE
```

This feature allows the following code to attach a package if it is installed or install it if it is not yet installed:

```
if (!require(moments)) {
  install.packages("moments")
  library(moments)
}
```

However, most uses of the `require()` function in user code are not like this. The following is typical:

```
require(moments)
```

This looks equivalent to using `library()` but has a silent drawback:

```
require(testPkg)
## Loading required package: testPkg
## Warning in library(package, lib.loc = lib.loc,
## character.only = TRUE, logical.return = TRUE, : there is no
## package called 'testPkg'
```

If the package to attach is not installed or even does not exist at all (maybe a typo), `require()` only produces a warning instead of an error like that produced by `library()`:

```
library(testPkg)
## Error in library(testPkg): there is no package called 'testPkg'
```

Imagine you are running a long and time-consuming R script that depends on several packages. If you use `require()` and unfortunately the computer running your script does not happen to have installed the required packages, the script will only fail later, when the package function is being called and the function is not found. However, if you use `library()` instead, the script will stop immediately if the packages do not exist on the running computer. Yihui Xie wrote a blog (http://yihui.name/en/2014/07/library-vs-require/) on this issue and proposes the *fail fast* principle: if the task has to fail, it is better to fail fast.

Masking and name conflicts

A fresh R session starts with basic packages automatically attached. The basic packages refer to base, stats, graphics, and so on. With these packages attached, you can calculate the average of a numeric vector using `mean()` and the median of it using `median()`, without using `base::mean()` and `stats::median()` or having to manually attach base and stats packages.

In fact, thousands of functions are immediately available from automatically attached packages, and each package defines a number of functions for a particular purpose. Therefore, it is likely that the functions in two packages conflict with each other. For example, suppose two packages A and B both have a function named X. If you attach A and then attach B, the function A::X will be masked by the function B::X. In other words, when you attach A and you call X(), then A's X is called. Then, you attach B and call X(); it is now B's X that is called. This mechanism is known as **masking**. The following example shows what happens when masking occurs.

The powerful data manipulation package dplyr defines a family of functions that make it easier to manipulate tabular data. When we attach the package, some messages are printed to show you that some existing functions are masked by the package functions with the same names:

```
library(dplyr)
##
## Attaching package: 'dplyr'
## The following objects are masked from 'package:stats':
##
## filter, lag
## The following objects are masked from 'package:base':
##
## intersect, setdiff, setequal, union
```

Fortunately, the implementation of these functions in `dplyr` does not change the meaning and usage, but generalizes them. These functions are compatible with the masked version. Therefore, you don't have to worry that the masked functions are broken and no longer work.

Package functions that mask basic functions almost always generalize rather than replace. However, if you have to use two packages in which some functions share the same names, you had better not attach either package; instead, extract the functions from both packages you need, as shown here:

```
fun1 <- package1::some_function
fun2 <- pacakge2::some_function
```

If you happen to attach one package and want to detach it, you can call `unloadNamespace()`. For example, we have attached moments and we can detach it:

```
unloadNamespace("moments")
```

As soon as the package is detached, the package functions are no longer directly available:

```
skewness(c(1, 2, 3, 2, 1))
## Error in eval(expr, envir, enclos): could not find function "skewness"
```

However, you can still use : : to call the function:

```
moments::skewness(c(1, 2, 3, 2, 1))
## [1] 0.3436216
```

Checking whether a package is installed

It is useful to know that `install.packages()` performs the installation, while `installed.packages()` shows information about the installed packages, which is a matrix of 16 columns that covers a wide range of information:

```
pkgs <- installed.packages()
colnames(pkgs)
## [1] "Package" "LibPath"
## [3] "Version" "Priority"
## [5] "Depends" "Imports"
## [7] "LinkingTo" "Suggests"
## [9] "Enhances" "License"
## [11] "License_is_FOSS" "License_restricts_use"
## [13] "OS_type" "MD5sum"
## [15] "NeedsCompilation" "Built"
```

This can be useful when you need to check whether a package is installed:

```
c("moments", "testPkg") %in% installed.packages()[, "Package"]
## [1] TRUE FALSE
```

Sometimes, you need to check the version of a package:

```
installed.packages()["moments", "Version"]
## [1] "0.14"
```

A simpler way to get the package version is using the following command:

```
packageVersion("moments")
## [1] '0.14'
```

We can compare two package versions so that we can check whether a package is newer than a given version:

```
packageVersion("moments") >= package_version("0.14")
## [1] TRUE
```

In fact, we can directly use a string version to perform the comparison:

```
packageVersion("moments") >= "0.14"
## [1] TRUE
```

Checking package versions can be useful if your scripts depend on some packages that must be equal to or newer than, a specific version. This can be true if your scripts rely on some of the new features introduced in that version. In addition, `packageVersion()` will produce an error if a package is not installed, which also makes it check the package installation status.

Summary

In this chapter, you learned about the working-directory concept and tools dealing with it. You also explored functions to inspect the working environment, modify global options, and manage the library of packages. Now, you have the basic knowledge to manage your workspace.

In this next chapter, you will learn several basic expressions, including assignment, condition, and loop. These expressions are the building blocks of program logic. I will show you how to write efficient and robust control-flow expressions in the next chapter.

4
Basic Expressions

Expressions are the building blocks of a function. R has a very clear syntax that suggests that an expression is either a symbol or a function call.

Although everything we do is in essence implemented by functions, R gives some functions a special syntax so that it is more friendly to write readable R code.

In the next few sections, we will see the following fundamental expressions that are given a special syntax:

- Assignment expressions
- Conditional expressions
- Loop expressions

Assignment expressions

Assignment may be one of the most fundamental expressions in all programming languages. What it does is assign or bind a value to a symbol so that we can refer to the value by that symbol later.

Despite the similarity, R adopts the <- operator to perform assignment. This is a bit different from many other languages using = although this is also allowed in R:

```
x <- 1
y <- c(1, 2, 3)
z <- list(x, y)
```

We don't have to declare the symbol and its type before assigning a value to it. If a symbol does not exist in the environment, the assignment will create that symbol. If a symbol already exists, the assignment will not end up in conflict, but will rebind the new value to that symbol.

Alternative assignment operators

There are some alternate yet equivalent operators we can use. Compared to x <- f(z), which binds the value of f(z) to symbol x, we can also use -> to perform assignment in the opposite direction:

```
2 -> x1
```

We can even chain the assignment operators so that a set of symbols all take the same value:

```
x3 <- x2 <- x1 <- 0
```

The expression is evaluated only once so that the same value is assigned to the three symbols. To verify how it works, we can change to a random number generator:

```
x3 <- x2 <- x1 <- rnorm(1)
c(x1, x2, x3)
## [1] 1.585697 1.585697 1.585697
```

The rnorm(1) method generates a random number following the standard normal distribution. If each assignment re-invokes the random number generator, each symbol will have different values. In fact, however, it does not happen. Later, I will explain what really happens and you will have a better understanding of it.

Like other programming languages, = also can perform assignment:

```
x2 = c(1, 2, 3)
```

If you are familiar with other popular programming languages such as Python, Java, and C#, you may find it almost an industry standard to use = as the assignment operator and may feel uncomfortable using <-, which requires more typing. However, Google's *R Style Guide* (https://google.github.io/styleguide/Rguide.xml#assignment) suggests the usage of <- instead of =, even though both are allowed and have exactly the same effect when they are used as assignment operators.

Here, I will provide a simple explanation to the subtle difference between <- and =. Let's first create a f() function that takes two arguments:

```
f <- function(input, data = NULL) {
  cat("input:\n")
  print(input)
  cat("data:\n")
  print(data)
}
```

The function basically prints the value of the two arguments. Then, let's use this function to demonstrate the difference between the two operators:

```
x <- c(1, 2, 3)
y <- c("some", "text")
f(input = x)
## input:
## [1] 1 2 3
## data:
## NULL
```

The preceding code uses both <- and = operators but they play different roles. The <- operator in the first two lines is used as an assignment operator, while = in the third line specifies a named argument input for the f() method.

More specifically, the <- operator evaluates the expression on its right-hand side c(1, 2, 3) and assigns the evaluated value to the symbol (variable) on the left-hand side x. The = operator is not used as an assignment operator but to match the function argument by name.

We know that the <- and = operators are interchangeable when they are used as assignment operators. Therefore, the preceding code is equivalent to the following code:

```
x = c(1, 2, 3)
y = c("some", "text")
f(input = x)
## input:
## [1] 1 2 3
## data:
## NULL
```

Here, we only use the = operator but for two different purposes: in the first two lines, = performs an assignment, while in the third line = specifies the named argument.

Now, let's see what happens if we change every = to <-:

```
x <- c(1, 2, 3)
y <- c("some", "text")
f(input <- x)
## input:
## [1] 1 2 3
## data:
## NULL
```

If you run this code, you will find that the outputs are similar. However, if you inspect the environment, you will observe the difference: a new `input` variable is now created in the environment and gains the value of `c(1, 2, 3)`:

```
input
## [1] 1 2 3
```

So, what happened? Actually, in the third line, two things happened: First, the assignment, `input <- x`, introduces a new `input` symbol to the environment and results in x. Then, the value of `input` is provided to the first argument of function `f()`. In other words, the first function argument is not matched by name but by position.

To elaborate, we will conduct more experiments. The standard usage of the function is as follows:

```
f(input = x, data = y)
## input:
## [1] 1 2 3
## data:
## [1] "some" "text"
```

If we replace both = with <-, the result looks the same:

```
f(input <- x, data <- y)
## input:
## [1] 1 2 3
## data:
## [1] "some" "text"
```

For the code using =, we can exchange the two named arguments without changing the result:

```
f(data = y, input = x)
## input:
## [1] 1 2 3
## data:
## [1] "some" "text"
```

In this case, however, if we exchange = for <-, the values of `input` and `data` are also exchanged:

```
f(data <- y, input <- x)
## input:
## [1] "some" "text"
## data:
## [1] 1 2 3
```

The following code has the same effect as that of the preceding code:

```
data <- y
input <- x
f(y, x)
## input:
## [1] "some" "text"
## data:
## [1] 1 2 3
```

This code not only results in `f(y, x)`, but unnecessarily creates additional `data` and `input` variables in the current environment.

From the preceding examples and experiments, the bottom line is clear. To reduce ambiguity, it is allowed to use either <- or = as the assignment operator and only use = to specify the named argument for functions. In conclusion, for better readability of R code, as the Google Style Guide suggests, only use <- for assignment and = to specify named arguments.

Using backticks with non-standard names

Assignment operators allow us to assign a value to a variable (or a symbol or name). However, direct assignment limits the format of the name. It contains only letters from a to z, A to Z (R is case-sensitive), the underscore(_), and dot(.), and it should not contain spaces or start with an underscore(_).

The following are some valid names:

```
students <- data.frame()
us_population <- data.frame()
sales.2015 <- data.frame()
```

The following are invalid names due to violating naming rules:

```
some data <- data.frame()
## Error: unexpected symbol in "some data"
```

```
_data <- data.frame()
## Error: unexpected input in "_"
Population(Millions) <- data.frame()
## Error in Population(Millions) <- data.frame() :
##   object 'Millions' not found
```

The preceding names violate the rules in different ways. The `some data` variable name contains a space, `_data` starts with `_`, and `Population(Millions)` is not a symbol name but a function call. In practice, it is quite likely that some invalid names might indeed be column names in a data table, such as the third name.

To walk around, we need to use back-ticks to quote the invalid names to make them valid:

```
`some data` <- c(1, 2, 3)
`_data` <- c(4, 5, 6)
`Population(Millions)` <- c(city1 = 50, city2 = 60)
```

To refer to these variables, also use backticks; otherwise, they will still be regarded as invalid:

```
`some data`
## [1] 1 2 3
`_data`
## [1] 4 5 6
`Population(Millions)`
## city1city2
##    50    60
```

Backticks can be used wherever we create a symbol, irrespective of whether it is a function:

```
`Tom's secret function` <- function(a, d) {
  (a ^ 2 - d ^ 2) / (a ^ 2 + d ^ 2)
}
```

It does not even matter if it is a list:

```
l1 <- list(`Group(A)` = rnorm(10), `Group(B)` = rnorm(10))
```

If the symbol name cannot be validly referred to directly, we also need to use quotation marks to refer to the symbol:

```
`Tom's secret function`(1,2)
## [1] -0.6
l1$`Group(A)`
##  [1] -0.8255922 -1.1508127 -0.7093875  0.5977409 -0.5503219 -1.0826915
##  [7]  2.8866138  0.6323885 -1.5265957  0.9926590
```

An exception is `data.frame()`:

```
results <- data.frame(`Group(A)` = rnorm(10), `Group(B)` = rnorm(10))
results
##          Group.A.     Group.B.
## 1     -1.14318956    1.66262403
## 2     -0.54348588    0.08932864
## 3      0.95958053   -0.45835235
## 4      0.05661183   -1.01670316
## 5     -0.03076004    0.11008584
## 6     -0.05672594   -2.16722176
## 7     -1.31293264    1.69768806
## 8     -0.98761119   -0.71073080
## 9      2.04856454   -1.41284611
## 10     0.09207977   -1.16899586
```

Unfortunately, even if we use backticks around a name with unusual symbols, the resulting `data.frame` variable will replace those symbols with the dots or using `make.names()`, a method that can be confirmed by looking at the column names of the resulting `data.frame`:

```
colnames(results)
## [1] "Group.A." "Group.B."
```

This often happens when you import a table such as the following CSV data resulted from an experiment:

```
ID,Category,Population(before),Population(after)
0,A,10,12
1,A,12,13
2,A,13,16
3,B,11,12
4,C,13,12
```

When you read the CSV data using `read.csv()`, the `Population(before)` and `Population(after)` variable will not preserve their original names, but will change them to valid names in R using the `make.names()` method. To know what names we will get, we can run the following command:

```
make.names(c("Population(before)", "Population(after)"))
## [1] "Population.before." "Population.after."
```

Sometimes, this behavior is undesirable. To disable it, set `check.names = FALSE` when you call either `read.csv()` or `data.frame()`:

```
results <- data.frame(
ID = c(0, 1, 2, 3, 4),
```

```
Category = c("A", "A", "A", "B", "C"),
`Population(before)` = c(10, 12, 13, 11, 13),
`Population(after)` = c(12, 13, 16, 12, 12),
stringsAsFactors = FALSE,
check.names = FALSE)
results
##     ID Category Population(before) Population(after)
## 1   0     A            10                 12
## 2   1     A            12                 13
## 3   2     A            13                 16
## 4   3     B            11                 12
## 5   4     C            13                 12
colnames(results)
## [1] "ID"       "Category"      "Population(before)"
## [4] "Population(after)"
```

In the preceding call, `stringAsFactors = FALSE` avoids converting character vectors to factors and `check.names = FALSE` avoids applying `make.names()` on the column names. With these two arguments, the `data.frame` variable created will preserve most aspects of the input data.

Just as I mentioned, to access the column with special symbols, use backticks to quote the name:

```
results$`Population(before)`
## [1] 10 12 13 11 13
```

Backticks make it possible to create and access variables, with symbols not allowed in direct assignment. This does not mean using such names is recommended. Rather, it can make the code harder to read and more error-prone, and it makes it more difficult to work with external tools that impose strict naming rules.

In conclusion, using backticks to create special variable names should be avoided unless absolutely necessary.

Conditional expressions

It is common that the logic of a program is not perfectly sequential but contains several branches dependent on certain conditions. Therefore, one of the most basic constructs of a typical programming language is its conditional expressions. In R, `if` can be used to branch the logic flow by logical conditions.

Using if as a statement

Like many other programming languages, the `if` expression works with a logical condition. In R, a logical condition is represented by an expression producing a single-element logical vector. For example, we can write a simple function `check_positive` that returns 1 if a positive number is provided and nothing otherwise:

```
check_positive <- function(x) {
  if (x > 0) {
    return(1)
  }
}
```

In the preceding function, `x > 0` is the condition to check. If the condition is satisfied, then the function returns 1. Let's verify the function with various inputs:

```
check_positive(1)
## [1] 1
check_positive(0)
```

It seems that the function works as expected. If we add some `else if` and `else` branches, the function can be generalized as the sign function that returns **1** for positive input, −1 for negative input, and for 0:

```
check_sign <- function(x) {
  if (x > 0) {
    return(1)
  } else if (x < 0) {
    return(-1)
  } else {
    return(0)
  }
}
```

The preceding function has the same functionality as the built-in function `sign()`. To verify its logic, just call it with different inputs with full coverage of the conditional branches:

```
check_sign(15)
## [1] 1
check_sign(-3.5)
## [1] -1
check_sign(0)
## [1] 0
```

The function does not need to return anything. We can also perform actions that return nothing (more accurately, NULL) depending on various conditions. The following function always does not explicitly return a value, but it sends a message in the console. The kind of message depends on the sign of the input number:

```
say_sign <- function(x) {
  if (x > 0) {
    cat("The number is greater than 0")
  } else if (x < 0) {
    cat("The number is less than 0")
  } else {
    cat("The number is 0")
  }
}
```

We can use a similar method, that is say_sign(), to test its logic:

```
say_sign(0)
## The number is 0
say_sign(3)
## The number is greater than 0
say_sign(-9)
## The number is less than 0
```

The workflow for evaluating if statement branches is quite straightforward:

1. First, evaluate cond1 in the first if (cond1) { expr1 }.
2. If cond1 is TRUE, then evaluate its corresponding expression { expr1 }. Otherwise, evaluate the cond2 condition in the next else if (cond2) branch and so forth.
3. If the conditions in all if and else if branches are violated, then evaluate the expression in the else branch, if any.

According to the workflow, an if statement can be more flexible than you might think. For example, an if statement can be in one of the following forms.

The simplest form is a simple if statement branch:

```
if (cond1) {
  # do something
}
```

A more complete form is with an `else` branch that deals with situations where `cond1` is not TRUE:

```
if (cond1) {
  # do something
} else {
  # do something else
}
```

An even more complex form is with one or more `else if` branches:

```
if (cond1) {
  expr1
} else if (cond2) {
  expr2
} else if (cond3) {
  expr3
} else {
  expr4
}
```

In the preceding conditional branches, the branch conditions (`cond1`, `cond2`, and `cond3`) may or may not be related. For example, the simple grading policy perfectly fits the branching logic in the preceding template in which each branch condition is a slice of the score range:

```
grade <- function(score) {
  if (score >= 90) {
    return("A")
  } else if (score >= 80) {
    return("B")
  } else if (score >= 70) {
    return("C")
  } else if (score >= 60) {
    return("D")
  } else {
    return("F")
  }
}
c(grade(65), grade(59), grade(87), grade(96))
## [1] "D" "F" "B" "A"
```

In this case, each branch condition in `else if` actually implicitly assumes that the previous condition does not hold; that is, `score >= 80` actually means `score < 90` and `score >= 80`, which is dependent on previous conditions. As a result, we cannot switch the order of these branches without explicitly stating the assumptions and making all branches independent.

Let's assume we switch some of the branches:

```
grade2 <- function(score) {
  if (score >= 60) {
    return("D")
  } else if (score >= 70) {
    return("C")
  } else if (score >= 80) {
    return("B")
  } else if (score >= 90) {
    return("A")
  } else {
    return("F")
  }
}
c(grade2(65), grade2(59), grade2(87), grade2(96))
## [1] "D" "F" "D" "D"
```

It is obvious that only `grade(59)` got the right grade and all others are broken. To fix the function without reordering the conditions, we need to rewrite the condition so that they do not depend on the order of evaluation:

```
grade2 <- function(score) {
  if (score >= 60 && score < 70) {
    return("D")
  } else if (score >= 70 && score < 80) {
    return("C")
  } else if (score >= 80 && score < 90) {
    return("B")
  } else if (score >= 90) {
    return("A")
  } else {
    return("F")
  }
}
c(grade2(65), grade2(59), grade2(87), grade2(96))
## [1] "D" "F" "B" "A"
```

This makes the function much more verbose than the first correct version. Therefore, it is important to figure out the correct order for branch conditions and be careful of the dependency of each branch.

Fortunately, R provides convenient functions such as `cut()`, which does exactly the same thing. Read the documentation by typing in `?cut` for more details.

Using if as an expression

Since `if` is in essence a primitive function, its returned value is the value of the expression in the branch whose condition is satisfied. Therefore, `if` can be used as an inline expression too. Take the `check_positive()` method for example. Rather than writing `return()` in the conditional expression, we can also return the value of the `if` statement expression in the function body to achieve the same goal:

```
check_positive <- function(x) {
  return(if (x > 0) {
    1
  })
}
```

In fact, the expression syntax can to be simplified to merely one line:

```
check_positive <- function(x) {
  return(if (x > 0) 1)
}
```

Since the return value of a function is the value of its last expression in the function body, `return()` can be removed in this case:

```
check_positive <- function(x) {
  if (x > 0) 1
}
```

The same principle also applies to the `check_sign()` method. A simpler form of `check_sign()` is as follows:

```
check_sign <- function(x) {
  if (x > 0) 1 else if (x < 0) -1 else 0
}
```

To explicitly get the value of the `if` expression, we can implement a grade reporting function that mentions the grade of a student, given the student name and their score:

```
say_grade <- function(name, score) {
  grade <- if (score >= 90) "A"
    else if (score >= 80) "B"
    else if (score >= 70) "C"
    else if (score >= 60) "D"
    else "F"
  cat("The grade of", name, "is", grade)
}
say_grade("Betty", 86)
## The grade of Betty is B
```

Using the `if` statement as an expression seems more compact and less verbose. However, in practice, it is rarely the case that all conditions are simple numeric comparisons and return simple values. For more complex conditions and branching, I suggest that you use `if` as a statement to clearly state different branches and do not omit `{}` to avoid unnecessary mistakes. The following function is a bad example:

```
say_grade <- function(name, score) {
  if (score >= 90) grade <- "A"
  cat("Congratulations!\n")
  else if (score >= 80) grade <- "B"
  else if (score >= 70) grade <- "C"
  else if (score >= 60) grade <- "D"
  else grade <- "F"
  cat("What a pity!\n")
  cat("The grade of", name, "is", grade)
}
```

The function author wants to add something to say to some branches. Without `{}` brackets around the branch expression, you are very likely to write code with syntax errors when you add more behaviors to conditional branches. If you evaluate the preceding code in the console, you will get enough errors to confuse you for a while:

```
>say_grade <- function(name, score) {
+   if (score >= 90) grade <- "A"
+   cat("Congratulations!\n")
+   else if (score >= 80) grade <- "B"
Error: unexpected 'else' in:
"  cat("Congratulations!\n")
  else"
>   else if (score >= 70) grade <- "C"
Error: unexpected 'else' in "  else"
>   else if (score >= 60) grade <- "D"
Error: unexpected 'else' in "  else"
>   else grade <- "F"
Error: unexpected 'else' in "  else"
>   cat("What a pity!\n")
What a pity!
>   cat("The grade of", name, "is", grade)
Error in cat("The grade of", name, "is", grade) : object 'name' not found
> }
Error: unexpected '}' in "}"
```

A better form of the function that avoids such potential pitfalls is as follows:

```
say_grade <- function(name, score) {
  if (score >= 90) {
    grade <- "A"
```

```
    cat("Congratulations!\n")
  } else if (score >= 80) {
    grade <- "B"
  }
  else if (score >= 70) {
    grade <- "C"
  }
  else if (score >= 60) {
    grade <- "D"
  } else {
    grade <- "F"
    cat("What a pity!\n")
  }
  cat("The grade of", name, "is", grade)
}
say_grade("James", 93)
## Congratulations!
## The grade of James is A
```

The function seems a bit more verbose, but it is more robust to changes and clearer in its logic. Remember, it is always better to be correct than short.

Using if with vectors

All the example functions created earlier only work with a single-value input. If we provide a vector, the functions will produce warnings because if does not work with multi-element vectors:

```
check_positive(c(1, -1, 0))
## Warning in if (x > 0) 1: the condition has length > 1 and only the first
## element will be used
## [1] 1
```

From the preceding output, we can see that the `if` statement ignores all but the first element, if a multi-element logical vector is supplied:

```
num <- c(1, 2, 3)
if (num > 2) {
cat("num > 2!")
}
## Warning in if (num > 2) {: the condition has length > 1 and only the
first
## element will be used
```

The expression throws a warning saying that only the first element (1 > 2) will be used. In fact, its logic is unclear when we try to condition an expression on a logical vector since its values can be mixed up with TRUE and FALSE values.

Some logical functions are useful to avoid such ambiguity. For example, the any() method returns TRUE if at least one element in the given vector is TRUE:

```
any(c(TRUE, FALSE, FALSE))
## [1] TRUE
any(c(FALSE, FALSE))
## [1] FALSE
```

Therefore, if what we really mean is to print the message if any single value is greater than 2, we should call the any() method in the condition:

```
if (any(num > 2)) {
  cat("num > 2!")
}
## num > 2!
```

If we mean to print the first message if all values are greater than 2, we should instead call the all() method:

```
if (all(num > 2)) {
  cat("num > 2!")
} else {
  cat("Not all values are greater than 2!")
}
## Not all values are greater than 2!
```

Therefore, every time we use an if expression to branch the workflow, we should ensure that the condition is a single-value logical vector. Otherwise, something unexpected may happen.

Another exception is NA, which is also a single-value logical vector but can cause an error as an if condition without notice:

```
check <- function(x) {
  if (all(x > 0)) {
    cat("All input values are positive!")
  } else {
    cat("Some values are not positive!")
  }
}
```

The `check()` function works perfectly for typical numeric vectors with no missing values. However, if argument x contains a missing value, the function may end up in an error:

```
check(c(1, 2, 3))
## All input values are positive!
check(c(1, 2, NA, -1))
## Some values are not positive!
check(c(1, 2, NA))
## Error in if (all(x > 0)) {: missing value where TRUE/FALSE needed
```

From this example, we should be careful of missing values when we write `if` conditions. If the logic is complicated and the input data is diverse, you cannot easily walk around handling missing values in appropriate ways. Note that the `any()` and `all()` methods both accept `na.rm` to handle missing values. We should take this into account too when writing conditions.

One way to simplify condition checking is to use `isTRUE(x)`, which calls `identical(TRUE, x)` internally. In this case, only a single `TRUE` value will meet the condition and all other values will not.

Using vectorized if: ifelse

An alternate method to branch a computation is `ifelse()`. This function accepts a logical vector as the test condition and returns a vector. For each element in the logical test condition, if the value is `TRUE`, then the corresponding element in the second argument `yes` will be chosen. If the value is `FALSE`, then the corresponding element in the third argument `no` will be chosen. In other words, `ifelse()` is the vectorized version of `if`, as demonstrated here:

```
ifelse(c(TRUE, FALSE, FALSE), c(1, 2, 3), c(4, 5, 6))
## [1] 1 5 6
```

Since the `yes` and `no` arguments can be recycled, we can rewrite `check_positive()` using `ifelse()`:

```
check_positive2 <- function(x) {
  ifelse(x, 1, 0)
}
```

One difference between `check_positive()` (using the `if` statement) and `check_positive2()` (using `ifelse`) is subtle: `check_positive(-1)` does not return values explicitly, but `chek_positive2(-1)` returns 0. The `if` statement does not necessarily return a value explicitly by using only one `if` but not `else`. By contrast, `ifelse()` always returns a vector because you have to specify the values in both `yes` and `no` arguments.

Another reminder is that `ifelse()` and `if` are not always able to achieve the same goal if you simply replace one with the other. For example, imagine you want to return a two-element vector according to a condition. Let's assume we use `ifelse()`:

```
ifelse(TRUE, c(1,2), c(2,3))
## [1] 1
```

Only the first element of the `yes` argument is returned. If you want to return the `yes` argument, you need to modify the condition to `c(TRUE, TRUE)`, which looks a bit unnatural.

If we use `if`, then the expression looks much more natural:

```
if (TRUE) c(1,2) else c(2,3)
## [1] 1 2
```

If the demand is a vectorized input and output, then another problem is that, if the `yes` argument is a numeric vector and the `no` argument is a character vector, a condition with mixed `TRUE` and `FALSE` values will coerce all elements in the output vector to be able to represent all values. Thus, a character vector is produced:

```
ifelse(c(TRUE, FALSE), c(1, 2), c("a", "b"))
## [1] "1" "b"
```

Using switch to branch values

In contrast with if, which deals with `TRUE` and `FALSE` conditions, `switch` works with a number or a string and chooses a branch to return according to the input.

Suppose the input is an integer n. The `switch` keyword works in a way that returns the value of the nth arguments in following the first argument:

```
switch(1, "x", "y")
## [1] "x"
switch(2, "x", "y")
## [1] "y"
```

If the input integer is out of bounds and does not match any given argument, no visible value is explicitly returned (in fact, an invisible NULL is returned):

```
switch(3, "x", "y")
```

The `switch()` method has a different behavior when working with string input. It returns the value of the first argument that matches its name with the input:

```
switch("a", a = 1, b = 2)
## [1] 1
switch("b", a = 1, b = 2)
## [1] 2
```

For the first `switch, a = 1` matches the variable a. For the second, `b = 2` matches the variable b. If no argument matches the input, an invisible NULL value will be returned:

```
switch("c", a = 1, b = 2)
```

To cover all possibilities, we can add a last argument (without argument name) that captures all other inputs:

```
switch("c", a = 1, b = 2, 3)
## [1] 3
```

Compared to the `ifelse()` method, `switch()` behaves more like `if()` method. It only accepts a single value input (number of string) but it can return anything:

```
switch_test <- function(x) {
   switch(x,
      a = c(1, 2, 3),
      b = list(x = 0, y = 1),
      c = {
         cat("You choose c!\n")
         list(name = "c", value = "something")
      })
}
switch_test("a")
## [1] 1 2 3
switch_test("b")
## $x
## [1] 0
##
## $y
## [1] 1
switch_test("c")
## You choose c!
## $name
## [1] "c"
```

```
##
## $value
## [1] "something"
```

In conclusion, `if`, `ifelse()`, and `switch()` have slightly different behaviors. You should apply them in different situations accordingly.

Loop expressions

Loop (or iteration) evaluates an expression repeatedly by either iterating over a vector (`for`) or checking whether a condition is violated (while).

Such language constructs largely reduce the redundancy of the code if the same task is run over and over again each time with some changes in input.

Using the for loop

The `for` loop evaluates an expression by iterating over a given vector or list. The syntax of a `for` loop is as follows:

```
for (var in vector) {
  expr
}
```

Then, `expr` will be evaluated iteratively, with `var` taking the value of each element of `vector` in turn. If `vector` has n elements, then the preceding loop is equivalent to evaluating:

```
var <- vector[[1]]
expr
var <- vector[[2]]
expr
...
var <- vector[[n]]
expr
```

For example, we can create a loop to iterate over `1:3` with iterator variable `i`. In each iteration, we will show text on the screen to indicate the value of `i`:

```
for (i in 1:3) {
cat("The value of i is", i, "\n")
}
## The value of i is 1
```

```
## The value of i is 2
## The value of i is 3
```

The iterator works with not only numeric vectors but all vectors. For example, we can replace the integer vector $1:3$ with a character vector:

```
for (word in c("hello","new", "world")) {
cat("The current word is", word, "\n")
}
## The current word is hello
## The current word is new
## The current word is world
```

We can also replace it with a list:

```
loop_list <- list(
  a = c(1, 2, 3),
  b = c("a", "b", "c", "d"))
for (item in loop_list) {
  cat("item:\n length:", length(item),
    "\n class: ", class(item), "\n")
}
## item:
##    length: 3
##    class:  numeric
## item:
##    length: 4
##    class:  character
```

Alternatively, we can replace it with a data frame:

```
df <- data.frame(
   x = c(1, 2, 3),
   y = c("A", "B", "C"),
stringsAsFactors = FALSE)
for (col in df) {
  str(col)
}
##   num [1:3] 1 2 3
##   chr [1:3] "A" "B" "C"
```

Previously, we mentioned that a data frame is a list in which each element (column) must have the same length. Therefore, the preceding loop iterates over the columns rather than rows, which is consistent with the behavior of `for` when it iterates over an ordinary list.

However, in many cases, we want to iterate over a data frame row by row. We can do this using `for`, but over an integer sequence from 1 to the number of rows of the data frame.

As long as `i` gets a row number, we can single out that particular row from the data frame and do something with it. The following code iterates over a data frame row by row and prints the structure of each row using `str()`:

```
for (i in 1:nrow(df)) {
    row <- df[i,]
    cat("row", i, "\n")
    str(row)
    cat("\n")
}
## row 1
## 'data.frame':    1 obs. of   2 variables:
##  $ x: num 1
##  $ y: chr "A"
##
## row 2
## 'data.frame':    1 obs. of   2 variables:
##  $ x: num 2
##  $ y: chr "B"
##
## row 3
## 'data.frame':    1 obs. of   2 variables:
##  $ x: num 3
##  $ y: chr "C"
```

I should give a little warning here that iterating over a data frame row by row is generally not a good idea because it can be slow and verbose. A better way is to use either the apply family functions covered in Chapter 5, *Working with Basic Objects,* or more powerful yet advanced package functions covered in Chapter 12, *Data Manipulation.*

In the preceding examples, each iteration of the `for` loops is independent. In some cases, however, the iterations alter variables outside the loop to keep track of certain states or keep a record of an accumulation. The simplest example is counting the sum from 1 to 100:

```
s <- 0
for (i in 1:100) {
    s <- s + i
}
s
## [1] 5050
```

The preceding example demonstrates an accumulation using the `for` loop. The following example produces a simple realization of a random walk using a random number generator that samples from normal distribution `rnorm()`:

```
set.seed(123)
x <- numeric(1000)
for (t in 1:(length(x) - 1)) {
  x[[t + 1]] <- x[[t]] + rnorm(1, 0, 0.1)
}
plot(x, type = "s", main = "Random walk", xlab = "t")
```

The plot generated is as shown:

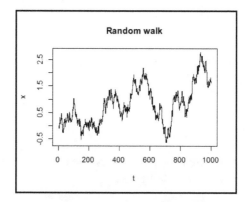

Although the `for` loops in the preceding two examples have a one-step dependency on the previous result, they can be simplified using existing functions such as the `sum()` method and `cumsum()`:

```
sum100 <- sum(1:100)
random_walk <- cumsum(rnorm(1000, 0, 0.1))
```

The basic idea in the implementation of these functions is similar to the preceding `for` loops, but they are vectorized and implemented in C so that they can be a lot faster than a `for` loop in R. Therefore, you should first consider using these built-in functions if possible.

Managing the flow of a for loop

Sometimes, it is useful to intervene in a `for` loop. In each iteration, we can choose to interrupt the `for` loop, to skip the current iteration, or do nothing and finish the loop.

We can use break to terminate a `for` loop:

```
for (i in 1:5) {
  if (i == 3) break
  cat("message ", i, "\n")
}
## message 1
## message 2
```

This can be used, for example, to find a solution to a problem. The following code attempts to find the numbers between 1,000 and 1,100 that satisfy `(i ^ 2) %% 11` equals `(i ^ 3) %% 17`, where `^` is the power operator and `%%` is the modulo operator that returns the remainder of a division:

```
m <- integer()
for (i in 1000:1100) {
  if ((i ^ 2) %% 11 == (i ^ 3) %% 17) {
    m <- c(m, i)
  }
}
m
## [1] 1055 1061 1082 1086 1095
```

If you only need one number in the range to satisfy the condition, you can replace the record tracking expression with a simple break:

```
for (i in 1000:1100) {
  if ((i ^ 2) %% 11 == (i ^ 3) %% 17) break
}
i
## [1] 1055
```

Once a solution is found, the `for` loop breaks and the last value of `i` is preserved in the current environment so that you know the solution that satisfies the condition.

In some other cases, skipping an iteration in a `for` loop is also useful. We can use the `next` keyword to skip the rest expressions in the current iteration and directly jump to the next iteration of the loop:

```
for (i in 1:5) {
  if (i == 3) next
  cat("message ", i, "\n")
}
## message  1
## message  2
## message  4
## message  5
```

Creating nested for loops

The expression in a `for` loop can be anything, including another `for` loop. For example, if we want to exhaust all permutations of the elements in a vector, we can write a two-level nested `for` loop to solve the problem:

```
x <- c("a", "b", "c")
combx <- character()
for (c1 in x) {
  for (c2 in x) {
    combx <- c(combx, paste(c1, c2, sep = ",", collapse = ""))
  }
}
combx
## [1] "a,a" "a,b" "a,c" "b,a" "b,b" "b,c" "c,a" "c,b" "c,c"
```

If you only need permutations that contain distinct elements, you can add a test condition in the inner `for` loop:

```
combx2 <- character()
for (c1 in x) {
  for (c2 in x) {
    if (c1 == c2) next
    combx2 <- c(combx2, paste(c1, c2, sep = ",", collapse = ""))
  }
}
combx2
## [1] "a,b" "a,c" "b,a" "b,c" "c,a" "c,b"
```

Alternatively, you can just negate the condition and replace the expression in the inner `for` loop with the following code to get exactly the same result:

```
if (c1 != c2) {
combx2 <- c(combx2, paste(c1, c2, sep = ",", collapse = ""))
}
```

The preceding code demonstrates how nested loops work, but it is not optimal to solve the problem. Some built-in functions help generate combinations or permutations of vector elements. The `combn()` method produces a matrix of combinations of vector elements, given an atomic vector and the number of elements in each combination:

```
combn(c("a", "b", "c"), 2)
##      [,1] [,2] [,3]
## [1,] "a"  "a"  "b"
## [2,] "b"  "c"  "c"
```

Similar to the preceding examples implemented using the for loop, expand.grid() produces a data frame containing all permutations of elements in multiple vectors:

```
expand.grid(n = c(1, 2, 3), x = c("a", "b"))
##   n x
## 1 1 a
## 2 2 a
## 3 3 a
## 4 1 b
## 5 2 b
## 6 3 b
```

Although the for loop can be powerful, there are functions designed for certain tasks. It is better to consider using built-in functions than directly putting everything in a for loop. In the following chapter, I will introduce lapply() and related functions to replace many for loops, which makes code easier to write and understand.

Using the while loop

In contrast to the for loop, the while loop does not stop running until the given condition is violated.

For example, the following while loop starts with x = 0. Each time, the loop checks whether x <= 10 holds. If so, the inner expressions are evaluated; otherwise, the while loop terminates:

```
x <- 0
while (x <= 5) {
  cat(x, " ", sep = "")
  x <- x + 1
}
## 0 1 2 3 4 5
```

If we remove x <- x + 1 so that x no longer gains any increment, the code will run forever (until R is terminated by force). Therefore, the while loop can sometimes be dangerous if not properly implemented.

Like the for loop, flow control statements (break and next) are also applicable in while:

```
x <- 0
while (TRUE) {
  x <- x + 1
  if (x == 4) break
  else if (x == 2) next
  else cat(x, '\n')
```

```
}
## 1
## 3
```

In practice, the `while` loop is often used where the number of iterations is unknown. This usually happens when we fetch rows chunk-by-chunk from the result set of a database query. The code may look as follows:

```
res <- dbSendQuery(con, "SELECT * FROM table1 WHERE type = 1")
while (!dbHasCompleted(res)) {
  chunk <- dbFetch(res, 10000)
  process(chunk)
}
```

First, we query all records whose type is 1 from a database through the con connection. Once the database returns a result set, `res`, we can fetch data from the result set chunk by chunk and process one chunk each time. Since the number of records is unknown prior to the query, we need to use a while loop that breaks when all data is completely fetched, which is indicated by `dbHasCompleted()`.

In this way, we avoid fetching a (perhaps huge) data frame to memory. Instead, we work with small chunks. This allows us to process a large amount of data with only a small working set in memory. However, the major premise is that the algorithm `process()` must support processing data chunk by chunk.

You may not be familiar with the preceding code example or the terminologies, but don't worry. We will cover database topics in detail in a later chapter.

In addition to the `for` loop and the `while` loop, R also provides the `repeat` loop. Like `while (TRUE)`, the `repeat` keyword is also a real loop, because it does not require an explicit termination condition or boundary unless `break` is hit:

```
x <- 0
repeat {
  x <- x + 1
  if (x == 4) break
  else if (x == 2) next
  else cat(x, '\n')
}
## 1
## 3
```

However, the `repeat` keyword can be very dangerous and is not recommended in practice.

Summary

In this chapter, you learned the syntax of assignment, conditional expressions, and loops. In the section on assignment, you got to know the naming rules of variables and how to walk around. In the section on conditional expressions, you learned how to use the `if` statement as either a statement or an expression, and how `ifelse()` is distinct from `if` when dealing with vectors. In the section on loops, you learned about the similarities and differences between `for` loops and `while` loops. Now, we are equipped with the basic expressions to control the logic flow of an R program.

In the next chapter, you will use what you learned in the previous chapters and see what you can do with the basic objects representing data and basic expressions representing our logic. You will learn about basic functions in various categories as the building blocks of data transformation and statistical analysis.

5
Working with Basic Objects

In the previous chapters, you learned how to create several basic types of objects, including atomic vectors, lists, and data frames to store data. You learned how to create functions to store logic. Given these building blocks of R script, you learned about different types of expressions to control the flow of logic involving basic objects. Now, we are getting familiar with the basic grammar and syntax of the R programming language. It's time to build a vocabulary of R using built-in functions to work with basic objects.

The real power of R lies in the enormous amount of functions it provides. Getting to know a variety of basic functions is extremely useful, and it will save you time and boost your productivity.

Although R is mainly a statistical computing environment, many basic functions are not related to any statistics but to more fundamental tasks such as inspecting the environment, converting texts to numbers, and performing logical operations.

In this chapter, you will get to know a wide range of basic yet most useful functions in R, including:

- Object functions
- Logical functions
- Math functions
- Numeric methods
- Statistical functions
- Apply-family functions

Using object functions

In the previous chapter, you learned about some functions that work with the environment and packages. In this section, we will get to know some basic functions that deal with objects in general. More specifically, I will introduce you to more functions to access the type and dimensions of a data object. You will get an impression of how these concepts can be combined and how they work together.

Testing object types

Although everything in R is an object, objects have different types.

Suppose the object we are dealing with is user-defined. We will create a function that behaves in different ways according to the type of the input object. For example, we need to create a function named `take_it` that returns the first element if the input object as an atomic vector (for example, numeric vector, character vector, or logical vector), but returns a user-defined element if the input object is a list of data and index.

For example, if the input is a numeric vector such as `c(1, 2, 3)`, then the function should return its first element `1`. If the input is a character vector such as `c("a", "b", "c")`, then the function should return `a`. However, if the input is a list `list(data = c("a", "b", "c"), index = 3)`, then the function should return the third element (`index = 3`) of `data`, that is, `c`.

To create such a function, we can imagine the functions and logic flow that might appear in it. First, as the output of the function depends on the type of input, we need to use one of the `is.*` functions to tell whether the input is of a certain type. Second, as the function behaves differently due to the type of input, we need to use conditional expressions such as `if else` to branch the logic. Finally, if the function basically takes out an element from the input, we need to use an element-extraction operator. Now, the implementation of the function becomes pretty clear:

```
take_it <- function(x) {
  if (is.atomic(x)) {
    x[[1]]
  } else if (is.list(x)) {
    x$data[[x$index]]
  } else {
    stop("Not supported input type")
  }
}
```

The preceding function behaves differently as x takes different types. When x takes an atomic vector (for example, a numeric vector), the function extracts its first element. When x takes a list of data and index, the function extracts the element with the index of index from x$data:

```
take_it(c(1, 2, 3))
## [1] 1
take_it(list(data = c("a", "b", "c"), index = 3))
## [1] "c"
```

For unsupported input types, the function is supposed to stop with an error message rather than return any value. For example, take_it cannot handle the function input. Note that we can pass any function around to other functions as an argument, just like any other object. However, in this case, if mean as a function is passed to it, then it will turn to the else condition and stop:

```
take_it(mean)
## Error in take_it(mean): Not supported input type
```

What if the input is indeed a list but does not contain any of the expected elements, data and index? Just do an experiment with a list of input (instead of data), without any index element:

```
take_it(list(input = c("a", "b", "c")))
## NULL
```

It might surprise you that the function does not produce an error. The output is NULL because x$data is NULL and extracting any value from NULL is also NULL:

```
NULL[[1]]
## NULL
NULL[[NULL]]
## NULL
```

However, if the list only contains data but misses index, the function will end up in an error:

```
take_it(list(data = c("a", "b", "c")))
## Error in x$data[[x$index]]: attempt to select less than one element
```

The error occurs because x$index turns out to be NULL, and extracting value from a vector by NULL produces an error:

```
c("a", "b", "c")[[NULL]]
## Error in c("a", "b", "c")[[NULL]]: attempt to select less than one
element
```

The third possibility is a bit similar to the first case in which NULL[[2]] returns NULL:

```
take_it(list(index = 2))
## NULL
```

From the earlier exceptions, it is normal to see that the error message is not so informative if you are not very familiar with these edge cases in which NULL is involved in the computation. For more complicated cases, if those errors do happen, you probably won't be able to find out the exact causes in a short period of time. One good solution is to check the input yourself in the implementation of the function and reflect the assumptions made to the arguments.

To handle the preceding cases of misuse, the following implementation takes into account whether the type of each argument is desired:

```
take_it2 <- function(x) {
  if (is.atomic(x)) {
    x[[1]]
  } else if (is.list(x)) {
    if (!is.null(x$data) && is.atomic(x$data)) {
      if (is.numeric(x$index) && length(x) == 1) {
        x$data[[x$index]]
      } else {
        stop("Invalid index")
      }
    } else {
      stop("Invalid data")
    }
  } else {
    stop("Not supported input type")
  }
}
```

For the case where x is a list, we check whether x$data is not null and is an atomic vector. If so, then we check if x$index is properly specified as a single-element numeric vector, or a scalar. If any of the conditions is violated, the function stops with an informative error message telling the user what is wrong with the input.

There are also quirky behaviors of the built-in checker functions. For example, is.atomic(NULL) returns TRUE. Therefore, if list x does not contain an element called data, the positive branch of if (is.atomic(x$data)) can still be triggered, which also leads to NULL. With some argument checking, the code is now more robust and can produce more informative error messages when the assumptions are violated:

```
take_it2(list(data = c("a", "b", "c")))
## Error in take_it2(list(data = c("a", "b", "c"))): Invalid index
```

```
take_it2(list(index = 2))
## Error in take_it2(list(index = 2)): Invalid data
```

Another possible implementation of this function is using the S3 dispatch, which will be covered in a later chapter on object-oriented programming.

Accessing object classes and types

Apart from using is.* functions, we can also use class() or typeof() to implement this function. Before directly accessing the type of an object, it is useful to know how these two functions differ from each other.

The following examples demonstrate the difference between the output of class() and typeof() when they are called upon different types of objects.

For each object x, class() and typeof() are called and then str() is called to show its structure.

For a numeric vector:

```
x <- c(1, 2, 3)
class(x)
## [1] "numeric"
typeof(x)
## [1] "double"
str(x)
##  num [1:3] 1 2 3
```

For an integer vector:

```
x <- 1:3
class(x)
## [1] "integer"
typeof(x)
## [1] "integer"
str(x)
##  int [1:3] 1 2 3
```

For a character vector:

```
x <- c("a", "b", "c")
class(x)
## [1] "character"
typeof(x)
## [1] "character"
str(x)
```

```
##  chr [1:3] "a" "b" "c"
```

For a list:

```
x <- list(a = c(1, 2), b = c(TRUE, FALSE))
class(x)
## [1] "list"
typeof(x)
## [1] "list"
str(x)
## List of 2
## $ a: num [1:2] 1 2
##  $ b: logi [1:2] TRUE FALSE
```

For a data frame:

```
x <- data.frame(a = c(1, 2), b = c(TRUE, FALSE))
class(x)
## [1] "data.frame"
typeof(x)
## [1] "list"
str(x)
## 'data.frame': 2 obs. of 2 variables:
## $ a: num 1 2
##  $ b: logi  TRUE FALSE
```

We can see that `typeof()` returns the low-level internal type of an object, while `class()` returns the high-level class of an object. One contrast we have mentioned before is that `data.frame` is in essence a `list` with equal-length list elements. Therefore, a data frame has the class of `data.frame` for data frame related functions to recognize, but `typeof()` still tells it is a `list` internally.

The topic is related to the S3 object-oriented programming mechanism and will be covered in detail in a later chapter. However, it is still useful to mention the difference between `class()` and `typeof()` here.

From the preceding output, it is also clear that `str()`, which we introduced in the previous chapter, shows the structure of an object. For vectors in the object, it usually shows their internal type (`typeof()`).

Accessing data dimensions

Matrices, arrays, and data frames have the property of dimensions in addition to classes and types.

Getting data dimensions

In R, a vector is by construction a one-dimensional data structure:

```
vec <- c(1, 2, 3, 2, 3, 4, 3, 4, 5, 4, 5, 6)
class(vec)
## [1] "numeric"
typeof(vec)
## [1] "double"
```

The same underlying data can be represented with more dimensions, which can be accessed via dim(), nrow(), or ncol():

```
sample_matrix <- matrix(vec, ncol = 4)
sample_matrix
## [,1] [,2] [,3] [,4]
## [1,] 1 2 3 4
## [2,] 2 3 4 5
## [3,] 3 4 5 6
class(sample_matrix)
## [1] "matrix"
typeof(sample_matrix)
## [1] "double"
dim(sample_matrix)
## [1] 3 4
nrow(sample_matrix)
## [1] 3
ncol(sample_matrix)
## [1] 4
```

The first preceding expression creates a four-column matrix from numeric vector vec. The matrix has the class of matrix, while typoef() preserves double from vec. Since a matrix is a dimensional data structure, dim() shows its dimensions in vector form. The nrow() and ncol() functions are shortcuts to access its number of rows and columns. If you read the source code of these two shortcuts, you will find that they are nothing special, but they return the first and second elements of dim() of the same input, respectively.

Higher dimensional data is usually represented by an array. For example, the same data vec can also be represented in three dimensions, that is, to access one element, you need to specify three positions in the three dimensions in turn:

```
sample_array <- array(vec, dim = c(2, 3, 2))
sample_array
## , , 1
##
## [,1] [,2] [,3]
## [1,] 1 3 3
```

```
## [2,] 2 2 4
##
## , , 2
##
## [,1] [,2] [,3]
## [1,] 3 5 5
## [2,] 4 4 6
class(sample_array)
## [1] "array"
typeof(sample_array)
## [1] "double"
dim(sample_array)
## [1] 2 3 2
nrow(sample_array)
## [1] 2
ncol(sample_array)
## [1] 3
```

Similar to matrix, an array has a class of array but still preserves the type of the underlying data. The length of the output of dim() is the number of dimensions needed to represent the data.

Another data structure that has a notion of dimensions is a data frame. However, a data frame is fundamentally different from a matrix. A matrix is derived from a vector but adds a dimensional property. On the other hand, a data frame is derived from a list but adds a constraint that each list element must have the same length:

```
sample_data_frame <- data.frame(a = c(1, 2, 3), b = c(2, 3, 4))
class(sample_data_frame)
## [1] "data.frame"
typeof(sample_data_frame)
## [1] "list"
dim(sample_data_frame)
## [1] 3 2
nrow(sample_data_frame)
## [1] 3
ncol(sample_data_frame)
## [1] 2
```

However, dim(), nrow(), and ncol() are still useful for data frames.

Reshaping data structures

The syntax of dim(x) <- y means change the value of dimensions of x to y.

For a plain vector, the expression converts the vector to a matrix with the specified dimensions:

```
sample_data <- vec
dim(sample_data) <- c(3, 4)
sample_data
## [,1] [,2] [,3] [,4]
## [1,] 1 2 3 4
## [2,] 2 3 4 5
## [3,] 3 4 5 6
class(sample_data)
## [1] "matrix"
typeof(sample_data)
## [1] "double"
```

You can see that the class of the object changes from `numeric` to `matrix`, and the type of the object remains unchanged.

For a matrix, the expression reshapes the matrix:

```
dim(sample_data) <- c(4, 3)
sample_data
## [,1] [,2] [,3]
## [1,] 1 3 5
## [2,] 2 4 4
## [3,] 3 3 5
## [4,]    2    4    6
```

It is useful to understand that changing the dimension of a vector, matrix, or array only alters the representation and accessing methods of the object and does not change the underlying data stored in memory. Therefore, it should be no surprise that a matrix is reshaped to an array as follows:

```
dim(sample_data) <- c(3, 2, 2)
sample_data
## , , 1
##
## [,1] [,2]
## [1,] 1 2
## [2,] 2 3
## [3,] 3 4
##
## , , 2
##
## [,1] [,2]
## [1,] 3 4
## [2,] 4 5
```

```
## [3,] 5 6
class(sample_data)
## [1] "array"
```

It should be obvious that `dim(x) <- y` works only if `prod(y)` equals `length(x)`, that is, the product of all dimensions must be equal to the length of the data elements. Otherwise, an error will occur:

```
dim(sample_data) <- c(2, 3, 4)
## Error in dim(sample_data) <- c(2, 3, 4): dims [product 24] do not match
the length of object [12]
```

Iterating over one dimension

A data frame is often a collection of records, and each row represents a record. It is common to iterate over all records stored in a data frame. Let's look at the following data frame:

```
sample_data_frame
## a b
## 1 1 2
## 2 2 3
## 3 3 4
```

For this data frame, we can iterate over the rows by printing the values of the variables using a `for` loop over `1:nrow(x)`:

```
for (i in 1:nrow(sample_data_frame)) {
  # sample text:
  # row #1, a: 1, b: 2
  cat("row #", i, ", ",
    "a: ", sample_data_frame[i, "a"],
    ", b: ", sample_data_frame[i, "b"],
    "\n", sep = "")
}
## row #1, a: 1, b: 2
## row #2, a: 2, b: 3
## row #3, a: 3, b: 4
```

Using logical functions

A logical vector only takes TRUE or FALSE and is mostly used to filter data. In practice, it is common to create joint conditions by multiple logical vectors where a number of logical operators and functions may involve.

Logical operators

Like many other programming languages, R enables a few operators to do basic logical calculations. The following table demonstrates what they do:

Symbol	Description	Example	Result
&	Vectorized AND	`c(T, T) & c(T, F)`	`c(TRUE, FALSE)`
|	Vectorized OR	`c(T, T) | c(T, F)`	`c(TRUE, TRUE)`
&&	Univariate AND	`c(T, T) && c(F, T)`	`FALSE`
||	Univariate OR	`c(T, T) || c(F, T)`	`TRUE`
!	Vectorized NOT	`!c(T, F)`	`c(FALSE, TRUE)`
%in%	Vectorized IN	`c(1, 2) %in% c(1, 3, 4, 5)`	`c(TRUE, FALSE)`

Note that in an `if` expression, `&&` and `||` are often used to perform logical calculations that are only needed to yield a single-element logical vector. However, the potential risk of using `&&` is that if it is made to work with multi-element vectors, it will silently ignore all but the first element of the vectors on both sides. The following example demonstrates the difference in behavior of using either `&&` or `&` in conditional statements.

The following code creates a `test_direction` function that tells the monotonicity of supplied argument values. We'll build on this example through the next section. If the values of x, y, and z are monotonically increasing, the function returns 1; if they are monotonically decreasing, the function returns −1. Otherwise, it returns . Note that the function uses `&` to perform a vectorized AND operation:

```
test_direction <- function(x, y, z) {
  if (x < y & y < z) 1
  else if (x > y & y > z) -1
  else 0
}
```

If the arguments are supplied scalar numbers, the function works perfectly:

```
test_direction(1, 2, 3)
## [1] 1
```

Note that & performs a vectorized calculation and thus returns a multi-element vector if one argument has more than one element. However, if only works with a single-value logical vector; otherwise, it would produce a warning:

```
test_direction(c(1, 2), c(2, 3), c(3, 4))
## Warning in if (x < y & y < z) 1 else if (x > y & y > z)
## -1 else 0: the condition has length > 1 and only the first
## element will be used
## [1] 1
```

If we replace both & operators present in `test_direction2` with && and create a new function `test_direction2`, the function would look as follows:

```
test_direction2 <- function(x, y, z) {
  if (x < y && y < z) 1
  else if (x > y && y > z) -1
  else 0
}
```

Then, the two example test cases may have different behaviors. For scalar input, the behavior of the two versions are exactly the same:

```
test_direction2(1, 2, 3)
## [1] 1
```

However, for multi-element input, `test_direction2` silently ignores the second element of each input vector and thus does not produce any warnings:

```
test_direction2(c(1, 2), c(2, 3), c(3, 4))
## [1] 1
```

Finally, which is the correct use, & or &&? It all depends on your demand. What behavior do you expect under all circumstances? What do you expect if the input is scalar values or multi-element vectors? If you expect the function to tell you whether all elements in the same position of each input vector have monotonicity, then both uses are incorrect in part and require the use of logical aggregation functions, to be introduced in the next section.

Logical functions

In this section, we will look at aggregating logical vectors and finding the true elements.

Aggregating logical vectors

In addition to the binary logical operators, a few logical aggregation functions are very useful, as we mentioned earlier.

The most commonly used two logical aggregation functions are `any()` and `all()`. The `any()` function returns TRUE if any (for example, at least one) element of the given logical vector is TRUE; otherwise, it will return FALSE. The `all()` function returns TRUE if all elements of the given logical vector are TRUE; otherwise, it will return FALSE:

```
x <- c(-2, -3, 2, 3, 1, 0, 0, 1, 2)
any(x > 1)
## [1] TRUE
all(x <= 1)
## [1] FALSE
```

One common point of the two functions is that they only return a single TRUE or FALSE value and never return a multi-element logical vector. Therefore, to implement a function that meets the demand in the previous section, use `all()` and `&` together in the `if` conditions:

```
test_all_direction <- function(x, y, z) {
  if (all(x < y & y < z)) 1
  else if (all(x > y & y > z)) -1
  else 0
}
```

For scalar input, `test_all_direction()` behaves exactly the same with the `test_direction()` and `test_direction2()` functions:

```
test_all_direction(1, 2, 3)
## [1] 1
```

For vector input, the function tests whether `c(1, 2, 3)` and `c(2, 3, 4)` have (the same) monotonicity:

```
test_all_direction(c(1, 2), c(2, 3), c(3, 4))
## [1] 1
```

The following code is a counterexample in which the elements at position 2, that is, `c(2, 4, 4)`, have no monotonicity:

```
test_all_direction(c(1, 2), c(2, 4), c(3, 4))
## [1] 0
```

The value returned by the function is thus meaningful because it correctly implements the demand of testing whether all elements at each position in the three input vectors have monotonicity.

The function has several possible variations that instead uses `any()` or `&&`. You may try to figure out the underlying demand (what are these functions trying to do?) of each of the following versions:

```
test_any_direction <- function(x, y, z) {
  if (any(x < y & y < z)) 1
  else if (any(x > y & y > z)) -1
  else 0
}
test_all_direction2 <- function(x, y, z) {
  if (all(x < y) && all(y < z)) 1
  else if (all(x > y) && all(y > z)) -1
  else 0
}
test_any_direction2 <- function(x, y, z) {
  if (any(x < y) && any(y < z)) 1
  else if (any(x > y) && any(y > z)) -1
  else 0
}
```

Asking which elements are TRUE

The logical operations we introduced earlier usually return a logical vector to indicate whether a certain condition is TRUE or FALSE. It is also useful to know which elements satisfy those conditions. The `which()` function returns the positions (or indices) of TRUE elements in a logical vector:

```
x
## [1] -2 -3 2 3 1 0 0 1 2
abs(x) >= 1.5
## [1] TRUE TRUE TRUE TRUE FALSE FALSE FALSE FALSE TRUE
which(abs(x) >= 1.5)
## [1] 1 2 3 4 9
```

If we take a closer look at what happens, it should be clear that at first, `abs(x) >= 1.5` is evaluated to be a logical vector, and then, `which()` returns the positions of those TRUE elements in that logical vector.

The mechanism is quite similar when we use a logical condition to filter elements from a vector or list:

```
x[x >= 1.5]
## [1] 2 3 2
```

In the preceding example, x >= 1.5 is evaluated to be a logical vector. Then, it is used to select elements in x corresponding to TRUE values.

A special case is that we can even use a logical vector with all FALSE values. A zero-length numeric vector is returned since the logical vector only contains FALSE values, and thus, no element in x is singled out:

```
x[x >= 100]
## numeric(0)
```

Dealing with missing values

Real-world data often contains missing values represented by NA. The following numeric vector is a simple example:

```
x <- c(-2, -3, NA, 2, 3, 1, NA, 0, 1, NA, 2)
```

Arithmetic calculations with missing values also produce missing values:

```
x + 2
## [1]  0 -1 NA  4  5  3 NA  2  3 NA  4
```

To take this into account, a logical vector has to accept not only TRUE and FALSE values but also NA values to represent unknown truthfulness:

```
x > 2
## [1] FALSE FALSE NA FALSE TRUE FALSE NA FALSE FALSE
## [10]    NA FALSE
```

As a consequence, logical aggregation functions such as any() and all() have to deal with missing values too:

```
x
## [1] -2 -3 NA 2 3 1 NA 0 1 NA 2
any(x > 2)
## [1] TRUE
any(x < -2)
## [1] TRUE
any(x < -3)
## [1] NA
```

The preceding output demonstrates the default behavior of `any()` when it deals with a logical vector that contains missing values. More specifically, if any element in the input vector is TRUE, then the function will return TRUE. If no element in the input vector is TRUE in which any missing value is present, then the function will return NA. Otherwise, if the input vector contains only FALSE, then the function will return FALSE. To verify the preceding logic, just run the following code:

```
any(c(TRUE, FALSE, NA))
## [1] TRUE
any(c(FALSE, FALSE, NA))
## [1] NA
any(c(FALSE, FALSE))
## [1] FALSE
```

To directly ignore all missing values, just specify `na.rm = TRUE` in the call:

```
any(x < -3, na.rm = TRUE)
## [1] FALSE
```

A similar but somehow opposite logic applies to `all()`:

```
x
## [1] -2 -3 NA 2 3 1 NA 0 1 NA 2
all(x > -3)
## [1] FALSE
all(x >= -3)
## [1] NA
all(x < 4)
## [1] NA
```

If any element in the input vector is FALSE, then the function will return FALSE. If no element in the input vector is FALSE in which any missing value is present, then the function will return NA. Otherwise, if the input vector contains only TRUE, then it will return TRUE. To verify the logic, just run the following code:

```
all(c(TRUE, FALSE, NA))
## [1] FALSE
all(c(TRUE, TRUE, NA))
## [1] NA
all(c(TRUE, TRUE))
## [1] TRUE
```

Similarly, `na.rm = TRUE` forces the function to directly ignore all missing values:

```
all(x >= -3, na.rm = TRUE)
## [1] TRUE
```

Apart from logical aggregation functions, data filtering also behaves differently when missing values involve. For example, the following code will preserve the missing values at corresponding positions of the logical vector produced by x >= 0:

```
x
## [1] -2 -3 NA 2 3 1 NA 0 1 NA 2
x[x >= 0]
## [1] NA 2 3 1 NA 0 1 NA 2
```

By contrast, which() does not preserve the missing values present in the input logical vector:

```
which(x >= 0)
## [1]  4  5  6  8  9 11
```

Therefore, the vector subsetted by the indices does not contain missing values in the following case:

```
x[which(x >= 0)]
## [1] 2 3 1 0 1 2
```

Logical coercion

Some functions that are supposed to take logical input also accept non-logical vectors such as numeric vectors. However, the behavior of the function may not be different from what they do with logical vectors. This is because the non-logical vectors are coerced to logical values.

For example, if we put a numeric vector in the if condition, it will be coerced:

```
if (2) 3
## [1] 3
if (0) 0 else 1
## [1] 1
```

In R, all non-zero values in a numeric vector or integer vector can be coerced to TRUE, only zero values will be coerced to FALSE, and string values cannot be coerced to logical values:

```
if ("a") 1 else 2
## Error in if ("a") 1 else 2: argument is not interpretable as logical
```

Using math functions

Mathematical functions are an essential part in all computing environments. R provides several groups of basic math functions.

Basic functions

The basic functions include square root, and exponential and logarithm functions as the following table shows:

Symbol	Example	Value
$\sqrt{x}$	sqrt(2)	1.4142136
e^x	exp(1)	2.7182818
$\ln(x)$	log(1)	0
$\log_{10}(x)$	log10(10)	1
$\log_2(x)$	log2(8)	3

Note that sqrt() only works with real numbers. If a negative number is supplied, NaN will be produced:

```
sqrt(-1)
## Warning in sqrt(-1): NaNs produced
## [1] NaN
```

In R, numeric values can be finite, infinite (Inf and -Inf), and NaN values. The following code will produce infinite values.

First, produce a positively infinite value:

```
1 / 0
## [1] Inf
```

Then, produce a negatively infinite value:

```
log(0)
## [1] -Inf
```

There are several test functions to check whether a numeric value is finite, infinite, or NaN:

```
is.finite(1 / 0)
## [1] FALSE
```

```
is.infinite(log(0))
## [1] TRUE
```

Using `is.infinite()`, how can we check whether a numeric value is `-Inf`? Inequality still works with infinite values in R:

```
1 / 0 < 0
## [1] FALSE
1 / 0 > 0
## [1] TRUE
log(0) < 0
## [1] TRUE
log(0) > 0
## [1] FALSE
```

Therefore, we can test the number with `is.infinite()` and compare the elements to 0 at the same time:

```
is.pos.infinite <- function(x) {
  is.infinite(x) & x > 0
}
is.neg.infinite <- function(x) {
  is.infinite(x) & x < 0
}
is.pos.infinite(1/0)
## [1] TRUE
is.neg.infinite(log(0))
## [1] TRUE
```

Like `sqrt()`, if the input value goes beyond the domain of `log` function, that is, $x > 0$, then the function returns NaN with a warning:

```
log(-1)
## Warning in log(-1): NaNs produced
## [1] NaN
```

Number rounding functions

The following functions are used to round numbers in different ways:

Symbol	Example	Value
[x] log	`ceiling(10.6)`	11
[x] log	`floor(9.5)`	9

truncate	`trunc(1.5)`	1
round	`round(pi,3)`	3.142
significant numbers	`signif(pi, 3)`	3.14

Previously, we showed that using `options(digits =)` can modify the number of digits to display, but this does not change the actual number of digits to remember. The preceding functions round the numbers and may cause potential loss of information.

For example, if the input number `1.50021` is already precise, then rounding it to `1` digit will result in `1.5` and the other digits (information) are lost. Therefore, you should make sure if the digits to drop are indeed ignorable due to imprecision or noise before performing any rounding.

Trigonometric functions

The following table lists the most commonly used trigonometric functions:

Symbol	Example	Value
`sin (x)`	`sin(0)`	0
`cos (x)`	`cos(0)`	1
`tan (x)`	`tan(0)`	0
`arcsin (x)`	`asin(1)`	1.5707963
`arcos (x)`	`acos(1)`	0
`arctan (x)`	`atan(1)`	0.7853982

R also provides a numeric version of π:

```
pi
## [1] 3.141593
```

In maths, equation *sin (π) = 0* strictly holds. However, the same formula does not lead to 0 in R or any other typical numeric computing software due to some precision issues of floating numbers:

```
sin(pi)
## [1] 1.224606e-16
```

To compare numbers with near equality, use `all.equal()` instead. While `sin(pi) == 0` returns `FALSE`, `all.equal(sin(pi), 0)` returns `TRUE` with the default tolerance of `1.5e-8`.

Another three functions are provided to make it precise when the input is a multiple of π:

Symbol	Example	Value
sin (πx)	sinpi(1)	0
cos (πx)	cospi(0)	1
tan (πx)	tanpi(1)	0

Hyperbolic functions

Similar to other computing software, hyperbolic functions are provided as shown in the following table:

Symbol	Example	Value
sinh (x)	sinh(1)	1.1752012
cosh (x)	cosh(1)	1.5430806
tanh (x)	tanh(1)	0.7615942
arcsinh (x)	asinh(1)	0.8813736
arccosh (x)	acosh(1)	0
arctanh (x)	atanh(0)	0

Extreme functions

It is common to calculate the maximum or minimum values of some numbers. The following table lists and demonstrates the simple use of `max()` and `min()`:

Symbol	Example	Value
max(...)	max(1, 2, 3)	3
min(...)	min(1, 2, 3)	1

These two functions work not only with multiple scalar arguments but also with a vector input:

```
max(c(1, 2, 3))
## [1] 3
```

Also, they work with multiple vector input:

```
max(c(1, 2, 3),
    c(2, 1, 2),
    c(1, 3, 4))
## [1] 4
min(c(1, 2, 3),
    c(2, 1, 2),
    c(1, 3, 4))
## [1] 1
```

The output demonstrates that `max()` returns the maximal value among all values of all input vectors and `min()` returns vice versa.

What if we want to obtain maximal or minimal values of each position among all vectors? Look at the following lines of code:

```
pmax(c(1, 2, 3),
     c(2, 1, 2),
     c(1, 3, 4))
## [1] 2 3 4
```

This basically finds the maximal value among all numbers at position 1, then at position 2, and so on, which has the same output as the following code:

```
x <- list(c(1, 2, 3),
          c(2, 1, 2),
          c(1, 3, 4))
c(max(x[[1]][[1]], x[[2]][[1]], x[[3]][[1]]),
```

```
  max(x[[1]][[2]], x[[2]][[2]], x[[3]][[2]]),
   max(x[[1]][[3]], x[[2]][[3]], x[[3]][[3]]))
## [1] 2 3 4
```

This is called the **parallel maxima**. The twin function `pmin()` works to find the **parallel minima**:

```
pmin(c(1, 2, 3),
     c(2, 1, 2),
     c(1, 3, 4))
## [1] 1 1 2
```

These two functions can be very useful to quickly compose a vectorized function with specific functions as floor and/or ceiling. For example, suppose `spread()` is a piecewise function. If the input is less than –5, the value is –5. If the input is between –5 to 5, the value is input. If the input is greater than 5, then the value is 5.

A naive implementation uses `if` to branch the pieces:

```
spread <- function(x) {
  if (x < -5) -5
  else if (x > 5) 5
  else x
}
```

The function works with scalar input, but it is not automatically vectorized:

```
spread(1)
## [1] 1
spread(seq(-8, 8))
## Warning in if (x < -5) -5 else if (x > 5) 5 else x: the
## condition has length > 1 and only the first element will be
## used
## [1] -5
```

One method is to use `pmin()` and `pmax()`, and the function will be automatically vectorized:

```
spread2 <- function(x) {
  pmin(5, pmax(-5, x))
}
spread2(seq(-8, 8))
##  [1] -5 -5 -5 -5 -4 -3 -2 -1  0  1  2  3  4  5  5  5  5
```

Another method is to use `ifelse()`:

```
spread3 <- function(x) {
  ifelse(x < -5, -5, ifelse(x > 5, 5, x))
```

```
}
spread3(seq(-8, 8))
##  [1] -5 -5 -5 -5 -4 -3 -2 -1  0  1  2  3  4  5  5  5  5
```

The previous two functions, spread2() and spread3(), both have the same graphics:

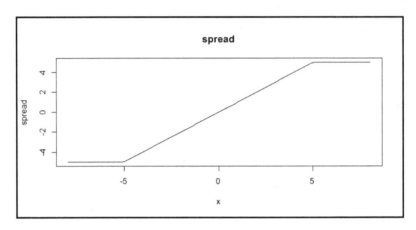

Applying numeric methods

In the previous sections, you learned about a number of functions that range from inspecting data structures to math and logical operations. These functions are fundamental to solving problems such as root finding and doing calculus. As a computing environment, R already implements various tools of good performance so that users do not have to reinvent the wheel. In the following sections, you will learn the built-in functions designed for root finding and calculus.

Root finding

Root finding is a commonly encountered task. Suppose we want to find the roots of the following equation:

$x2 + x - 2 = 0$

To manually find the roots, we can transform the preceding equation in product terms:

$(x+2)(x-1) = 0$

Therefore, the roots of the equation are $x1 = -2$ and $x_2 = 1$.

In R, `polyroot()` can find roots of a polynomial equation in the form of:

$$p(x) = z_1 + z_2 x + \cdots + z_n x^{n-1}$$

For the preceding problem, we need to specify the polynomial coefficient vector from zero order to the term of the highest order present in the equation. In this case, the vector is `c(-2, 1, 1)` to represent the coefficients in the increasing order of power:

```
polyroot(c(-2, 1, 1))
## [1]  1-0i -2+0i
```

The function always returns a complex vector in which each element is a complex number in the form of `a + bi`. On the one hand, if the function surely has only real roots, you can use `Re()` to extract the real parts of the complex roots:

```
Re(polyroot(c(-2, 1, 1)))
## [1]  1 -2
```

On the other hand, the type of output implies that `polyroot()` has the capability to find complex roots of a polynomial equation. The simplest one is as follows:

$$x^2 + 1 = 0$$

To find its complex roots, just specify a polynomial coefficient vector:

```
polyroot(c(1, 0, 1))
## [1] 0+1i 0-1i
```

A slightly more complex example is to find the roots of the following equation:

$$x^3 - x^2 - 2x - 1$$

```
r <- polyroot(c(-1, -2, -1, 1))
r
## [1] -0.5739495+0.3689894i -0.5739495-0.3689894i
## [3]  2.1478990-0.0000000i
```

Note that all complex roots are found. To verify, just replace x with `r`:

```
r ^ 3 - r ^ 2 - 2 * r - 1
## [1] 8.881784e-16+1.110223e-16i 8.881784e-16+2.220446e-16i
## [3] 8.881784e-16-4.188101e-16i
```

Due to some numeric computing issues, the preceding expression does not strictly go to zero, but it gets extremely near. If you only care about 8 digits of the error, use the `round()` function, and you will find that the roots are valid:

```
round(r ^ 3 - r ^ 2 - 2 * r - 1, 8)
## [1] 0+0i 0+0i 0+0i
```

As for general numeric root finding for equation *f(x)=0*, the `uniroot ()` function, as its name suggests, can be useful to find one root. A simple example is to find the root of the following equation:

$$x^2 - e^x = 0$$

Within the following range:

$$x \in [-2,1]$$

The plot generated is as shown:

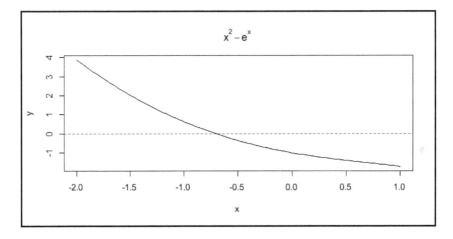

The curve of the function shows that the root lies in **[-1.0,0.5]**. Using `uniroot ()` with the function and interval will return a list containing the approximate root, the function value at that point, the number of iteration it takes, and the estimated precision of the root:

```
uniroot (function (x) x ^ 2 - exp (x), c(-2, 1))
## $root
## [1] -0.7034583
##
## $f.root
## [1] -1.738305e-05
##
```

```
## $iter
## [1] 6
##
## $init.it
## [1] NA
##
## $estim.prec
## [1] 6.103516e-05
```

A more complex example is to find a root of the following equation:

$$e^x - 3e^{-x^2+x} + 1$$

Within the following range:

$$x \in [-2,2]$$

The plot generated is as shown:

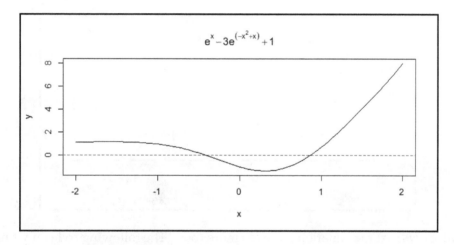

It is obvious that the equation has two roots from **-2** to **2**. However, `uniroot()` is only capable of finding one root at a time, and it's best that the function is monotonic in the interval to search. If we directly let it find a root in the **[-2,2]** interval, the function produces an error:

```
f <- function(x) exp(x) - 3 * exp(-x ^ 2 + x) + 1
uniroot(f, c(-2, 2))
## Error in uniroot(f, c(-2, 2)): f() values at end points not of opposite
sign
```

We have to make sure that the function values of both ends of the interval have opposite signs. We can separate the interval into two smaller ones and find roots in a separate manner:

```
uniroot(f, c(-2, 0))$root
## [1] -0.4180424
uniroot(f, c(0, 2))$root
## [1] 0.8643009
```

An even more complex equation is as follows:

$$x^2 - 2x + 3\cos(x^2) - 4$$

Within the following range:

$$x \in [-5,5]$$

The plot generated is as shown:

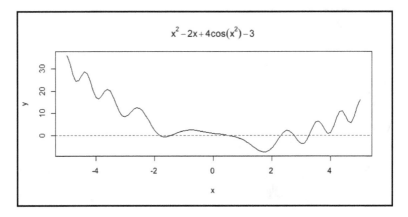

The curve shows that the equation has even more roots. The following code only finds one in the **[0,1]** interval:

```
uniroot(function(x) x ^ 2 - 2 * x + 4 * cos(x ^ 2) - 3, c(0, 1))$root
## [1] 0.5593558
```

In some of the preceding root-finding function calls, we directly pass a function to `uniroot()` without giving the function a name. They are called **anonymous functions**. We will cover this concept in detail in later chapters.

Calculus

In addition to root finding, numeric methods in base R also include computing basic calculus.

Derivatives

`D()` computes the derivative of a function symbolically with respect to given variables.

For example, derive dx^2/dx:

```
D(quote (x ^ 2), "x")
## 2 * x
```

Derive $dsin(x)cos(xy)/dx$:

```
D(quote(sin(x) * cos(x * y)), "x")
## cos(x) * cos(x * y) - sin(x) * (sin(x * y) * y)
```

Thanks to the `quote()` function, it keeps the expression unevaluated so that the symbols are directly accessible as they are written.

Since the derivative is also an unevaluated expression, we can evaluate it, given all necessary symbols by calling `eval()`:

```
z <- D(quote(sin(x) * cos(x * y)), "x")
z
## cos(x) * cos(x * y) - sin(x) * (sin(x * y) * y)
eval(z, list(x = 1, y = 2))
## [1] -1.75514
```

In the preceding example, `quote()` creates an expression object and `eval()` evaluates a given expression with specified symbols. Expression object gives R the power of meta programming. We will cover this topic in `Chapter 9`, *Metaprogramming*.

Integration

R also supports numeric integration. Here, we do not have to write the expression but provide a function since it is not symbolic computation. For instance, the following formula is a problem of definite integral. It basically calculates the area below the sine curve from to *pi/2*. R provides built-in function, `integrate()`, to solve such problems with great flexibility as long as the mathematical function can be represented by an R function:

$$\int_0^{\frac{\pi}{2}} \sin(x)\, dx$$

```
result <- integrate(function(x) sin(x), 0, pi / 2)
result
## 1 with absolute error < 1.1e-14
```

The result looks like a numeric value, but it seems to take some other information. In fact, it is a list:

```
str(result)
## List of 5
## $ value : num 1
## $ abs.error : num 1.11e-14
## $ subdivisions: int 1
## $ message : chr "OK"
## $ call : language integrate(f = function(x) sin(x), lower = 0, upper =
pi/2)
##  - attr(*, "class")= chr "integrate"
```

Since it is a numerical computation, it inherits all the pros and cons of such computing techniques.

Using statistical functions

R is highly productive in doing statistical computing and modeling since it provides a good variety of functions ranging from random sampling to statistical testing. The functions in the same category share a common interface. In this section, I will demonstrate a number of examples so that you can draw inferences about the usage of other similar functions.

Sampling from a vector

In statistics, the study of a population often begins with a random sample of it. The `sample()` function is designed for drawing a random sample from a given vector or list. In default, `sample()` draws a sample without replacement. For example, the following code draws a sample of five from a numeric vector without replacement:

```
sample(1:6, size = 5)
## [1] 2 6 3 1 4
```

With `replace = TRUE`, the sampling is done with replacement:

```
sample(1:6, size = 5, replace = TRUE)
## [1] 3 5 3 4 2
```

Although `sample()` is often used to draw samples from a numeric vector, it also works with other types of vectors:

```
sample(letters, size = 3)
## [1] "q" "w" "g"
```

It even works with lists:

```
sample(list(a = 1, b = c(2, 3), c = c(3, 4, 5)), size = 2)
## $b
## [1] 2 3
##
## $c
## [1] 3 4 5
```

In fact, `sample()` is capable of sampling from any object that supports subsetting with brackets (`[]`). In addition, it supports weighted sampling, that is, you can specify a probability for each element:

```
grades <- sample(c("A", "B", "C"), size = 20, replace = TRUE,
prob = c(0.25, 0.5, 0.25))
grades
## [1] "C" "B" "B" "B" "C" "C" "C" "C" "C" "B" "B" "A" "A" "C"
## [15] "B" "B" "A" "B" "A" "C"
```

We can use `table()` to see the number of occurrences of each value:

```
table(grades)
## grades
## A B C
## 4 8 8
```

Working with random distributions

In numeric simulations, it is more often the case that we need to draw samples from a random distribution rather than from a given vector. R provides a good variety of built-in functions to work with popular probability distributions. In this section, we will see how R provides basic statistical tools to work with R objects that represent sample data. These tools can be used to work mainly with numeric vectors.

In R, it is very easy to generate random numbers following a statistical distribution. The most commonly used two distributions are uniform distribution and normal distribution.

In a statistical sense, it is equally probable to draw any value from a uniform distribution within a given range. We can call `runif(n)` to generate n random numbers from a uniform distribution over **[0,1]**:

```
runif(5)
## [1] 0.8894535 0.1804072 0.6293909 0.9895641 0.1302889
```

To generate random numbers within a non-default interval, specify `min` and `max`:

```
runif(5, min = -1, max = 1)
## [1] -0.3386789  0.7302411  0.5551689  0.6546069  0.2066487
```

If we generate 1000 random numbers using `runif(1000)` and draw the points, we will get a scatter plot (a plot to show X-Y points) as follows:

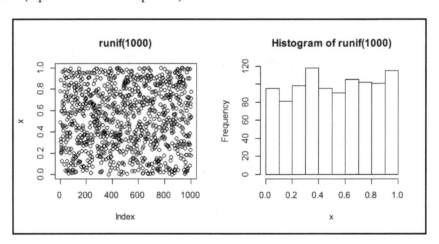

The histogram shows that the random numbers we generated distribute almost evenly across each interval from 0 to 1, which is consistent with uniform distribution.

Another distribution that is most commonly seen in the real world is the normal distribution. Similar to `runif()`, we can use `rnorm()` to generate random numbers following a standard normal distribution:

```
rnorm(5)
## [1]  0.7857579  1.1820321 -0.9558760 -1.0316165  0.4336838
```

You may notice that the random generator functions share the same interface. The first argument of both `runif()` and `rnorm()` is n, the number of values to generate, and the rest of the arguments are the parameters of the random distribution itself. As for a normal distribution, its parameters are `mean` and standard deviation (`sd`):

```
rnorm(5, mean = 2, sd = 0.5)
## [1] 1.597106 1.971534 2.374846 3.023233 2.033357
```

The plot generated is as shown:

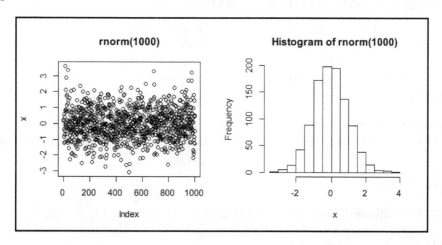

From the preceding graphics, it is obvious that the points are not evenly distributed but concentrate on the mean instead. As we know, statistical distributions can be described by certain formulas. To access these formulas in theory, R provides a family of functions for each built-in random distribution. More specifically, for uniform distribution, R provides its probability density function `dunif()`, cumulative density function `punif()`, quantile function `qunif()`, and random generator `runif()`. For normal distribution, the corresponding names are `dnorm()`, `pnorm()`, and `qnorm()`. The same naming scheme of density function, cumulative density function, quantile function, as well as random generator also applies to other distributions R supports.

In addition to these two most commonly used statistical distributions, R also provides functions for discrete distributions, such as binomial distribution, and continuous distributions, such as exponential distribution. You can run `?Distributions` to see a full list of supported distributions. The features of those distributions are beyond the scope of this book. If you are not familiar with them but are interested in the features of these distributions, you may read any textbook
on probability theory or visit Wikipedia
(`https://en.wikipedia.org/wiki/Probability_distribution`) for more details.

R supports many distributions, and each of them has corresponding functions. Fortunately we don't need to remember a lot of different function names because they all follow the same naming convention.

Computing summary statistics

For a given dataset, we often need some summary statistics to get an initial impression on it. R provides a set of functions to compute summary statistics for a numeric vector, including mean, median, standard deviation, variance, maximum, minimum, range, and quantiles. For multiple numeric vectors, we can compute the covariance matrix and correlation matrix.

The following examples show how we use the built-in functions to compute these summary statistics. First, we generate a random numeric vector of length 50 from standard normal distribution:

```
x <- rnorm(50)
```

To compute the arithmetic sample mean value of x, we call `mean()`:

```
mean(x)
## [1] -0.1051295
```

This is equivalent to:

```
sum(x) / length(x)
## [1] -0.1051295
```

However, `mean()` supports trimming a fraction of observations from each end of the input data:

```
mean(x, trim = 0.05)
## [1] -0.141455
```

If x contains a few outliers far from other values, the mean value obtained from the preceding equation should be more robust since the outliers are omitted from the input.

An alternative measure of the representative location of a sample data is the sample median. For a given sample, half of the observations are higher than the median, and the other half are lower than the median. The median can be a robust measure if there are a few extreme values in the data. For x, the sample median is:

```
median(x)
## [1] -0.2312157
```

In addition to location measures such as mean and median, variation measures are important too. To compute the standard deviation of a numeric vector, we use sd():

```
sd(x)
## [1] 0.8477752
```

To compute the variance, we use var():

```
var(x)
## [1] 0.7187228
```

To simply get the extreme values in the data, we use min() and max():

```
c(min = min(x), max = max(x))
## min max
## -1.753655  2.587579
```

Alternatively, you can use range() to directly get both:

```
range(x)
## [1] -1.753655  2.587579
```

Sometimes, the data is not regularly distributed. In this case, the location measures and variation measures suffer from such irregularity and may produce misleading results. Here, we should probably take a look at the values at critical quantiles of the data:

```
quantile(x)
## 0% 25% 50% 75% 100%
## -1.7536547 -0.6774037 -0.2312157  0.2974412  2.5875789
```

To see more quantiles, specify more values for the probs argument:

```
quantile(x, probs = seq(0, 1, 0.1))
## 0% 10% 20% 30%
## -1.753654706 -1.116231750 -0.891186551 -0.504630513
## 40% 50% 60% 70%
```

```
## -0.412239924 -0.231215699 0.009806393 0.177344522
## 80% 90% 100%
##   0.550510144   0.968607716   2.587578887
```

If the data is not regularly distributed, the gap of values between two quantiles can be very large or small, compared to others. A shortcut for this is to use `summary()`, which directly gives the most commonly used summary statistics, including four quantiles, median, and mean:

```
summary(x)
## Min. 1st Qu. Median Mean 3rd Qu. Max.
## -1.7540 -0.6774 -0.2312 -0.1051  0.2974  2.5880
```

Note that the minimum values and the maximum values are the 0 percent quantile and 100 percent quantile, respectively.

In fact, `summary()` is a generic function that works for many types of objects and has different behaviors. For example, `summary()` works with data frames too:

```
df <- data.frame(score = round(rnorm(100, 80, 10)),
grade = sample(letters[1:3], 100, replace = TRUE))
summary(df)
##  score grade
## Min.  : 60.00 a:34
## 1st Qu.: 73.00 b:38
## Median : 79.00 c:28
## Mean : 79.65
## 3rd Qu.: 86.00
##  Max.   :107.00
```

It can be seen that for a numeric column, `summary()` shows the summary statistics. For columns of other types, it may just simply show a table of value occurrences.

Computing covariance and correlation matrix

The preceding examples introduced the most commonly used summary statistics for one vector. For two or more vectors, we can compute the covariance matrix and the correlation matrix.

The following code generates another vector that is correlated with x:

```
y <- 2 * x + 0.5 * rnorm(length(x))
```

We can compute the covariance between x and y:

```
cov(x, y)
## [1] 1.419859
```

We can also compute the correlation coefficient:

```
cor(x, y)
## [1] 0.9625964
```

These two functions also work with more than two vectors. If we need to compute the covariance and correlation matrix of more than two vectors, we need to input a matrix or a data frame. In the following example, we generate another random vector z of the same length of x. This time, z follows a uniform distribution and does not depend on either x or y. We use cbind() to create a three-column matrix and compute the covariance matrix of them:

```
z <- runif(length(x))
m1 <- cbind(x, y, z)
cov(m1)
##            x          y          z
## x 0.7187228 1.41985899 0.04229950
## y 1.4198590 3.02719645 0.07299981
## z 0.0422995 0.07299981 0.08005535
```

Similarly, we can call cor() directly with the matrix to compute the correlation matrix.

```
cor(m1)
##            x          y          z
## x 1.0000000 0.9625964 0.1763434
## y 0.9625964 1.0000000 0.1482881
## z 0.1763434 0.1482881 1.0000000
```

Since y is generated by a linear relationship with x, plus some noise, we should expect that x and y are highly correlated, but the same thing should not happen with z. The correlation matrix looks consistent with our expectation. To draw such a conclusion in a statistical sense, we need to perform rigorous statistical tests, which is beyond the scope of this book.

Using apply-family functions

Previously, we talked about using a `for` loop to repeat evaluating an expression with an iterator on a vector or list. In practice, however, the `for` loop is almost the last choice because an alternative way is much cleaner and easier to write and read when each iteration is independent of each other.

For example, the following code uses `for` to create a list of three independent, normally distributed random vectors whose length is specified by vector `len`:

```
len <- c(3, 4, 5)
# first, create a list in the environment.
x <- list()
# then use `for` to generate the random vector for each length
for (i in 1:3) {
  x[[i]] <- rnorm(len[i])
}
x
## [[1]]
## [1] 1.4572245 0.1434679 -0.4228897
##
## [[2]]
## [1] -1.4202269 -0.7162066 -1.6006179 -1.2985130
##
## [[3]]
## [1] -0.6318412  1.6784430  0.1155478  0.2905479 -0.7363817
```

The preceding example is simple, but the code is quite redundant compared to the implementation with `lapply`:

```
lapply(len, rnorm)
## [[1]]
## [1] -0.3258354 -1.4658116 -0.1461097
##
## [[2]]
## [1] -0.1715198 0.5215857 -0.3178271 -0.3967798
##
## [[3]]
## [1] -0.2047106 -1.2009772  1.4859955  0.1940920  0.3758798
```

The `lapply` version is much simpler. It applies `rnorm()` on each element in `len` and puts each result into a list.

From the preceding example, we should realize that it is only possible if R allows us to pass functions as ordinary objects. Fortunately, it is true. Functions in R are treated just like objects and can be passed around as arguments, just as we showed in the section on numeric methods. This feature largely boosts the flexibility of coding.

Each apply-family function is a so-called **higher-order function** that accepts a function as an argument. We will introduce this concept in detail later.

lapply

The `lapply()` function, as we previously demonstrated, takes a vector and a function as its arguments. It simply applies the function to each element in the given vector and finally returns a list that contains all the results.

This function is useful when each iteration is independent of the other. In this case, we don't have to explicitly create an iterator.

It works not only with vectors but also with lists. Suppose we have a list of students:

```
students <- list(
  a1 = list(name = "James", age = 25,
    gender = "M", interest = c("reading", "writing")),
  a2 = list(name = "Jenny", age = 23,
    gender = "F", interest = c("cooking")),
  a3 = list(name = "David", age = 24,
    gender = "M", interest = c("running", "basketball")))
```

Now, we need to create a character vector in which each element is formatted as follows:

```
James, 25 year-old man, loves reading, writing.
```

Note that `sprintf()` is useful to format text by replacing the placeholders (for example, `%s` for string, `%d` for integer) with corresponding input arguments. Here is an example:

```
sprintf("Hello, %s! Your number is %d.", "Tom", 3)
## [1] "Hello, Tom! Your number is 3."
```

Now, first, we are sure that an iteration is working on `students`, and each is independent. In other words, the computation for James has nothing to do with that for Jenny, and so on. Therefore, we can use `lapply` to do the work:

```
lapply(students, function(s) {
  type <- switch(s$gender, "M" = "man", "F" = "woman")
  interest <- paste(s$interest, collapse = ", ")
  sprintf("%s, %d year-old %s, loves %s.", s$name, s$age, type, interest)
```

```
})
## $a1
## [1] "James, 25 year-old man, loves reading, writing."
##
## $a2
## [1] "Jenny, 23 year-old woman, loves cooking."
##
## $a3
## [1] "David, 24 year-old man, loves running, basketball."
```

The preceding code uses an anonymous function which is a function that is not assigned to a symbol. In other words, the function is only temporal and has no name. Of course, we can explicitly bind the function to a symbol, that is, give it a name, and use that name in `lapply`.

Despite this, the code is quite straightforward. For each element s in `students`, the function decides the type of the student and pastes their interests together, separated by commas. It then puts the information in a format we want.

Fortunately, a major part of how we use `lapply` also works with other apply-family functions, but their iterating mechanism or the type of results may be different.

sapply

List is not always a favorable container for the results. Sometimes, we want them to be put in a simple vector or a matrix. The `sapply` function simplifies the result according to its structure.

Suppose we apply a square on each element of `1:10`. If we do it with `lapply`, we will have a list of squared numbers. This result looks a bit heavy and redundant because the resulted list is actually a list of single-valued numeric vectors. However, we might want to keep the results still as a vector:

```
sapply(1:10, function(i) i ^ 2)
##  [1]   1   4   9  16  25  36  49  64  81 100
```

If the applying function returns a multi-element vector each time, `sapply` will put the results into a matrix in which each returned vector occupies a column:

```
sapply(1:10, function(i) c(i, i ^ 2))
##      [,1] [,2] [,3] [,4] [,5] [,6] [,7] [,8] [,9] [,10]
## [1,]    1    2    3    4    5    6    7    8    9    10
## [2,]    1    4    9   16   25   36   49   64   81   100
```

vapply

Although `sapply` is very handy and smart, the smartness may sometimes become a risk. Suppose we have a list of input numbers:

```
x <- list(c(1, 2), c(2, 3), c(1, 3))
```

If we want to get a numeric vector of the squared numbers for each number in `x`, `sapply` can be easy to use because it automatically tries to simplify the data structure of the result:

```
sapply(x, function(x) x ^ 2)
##  [,1] [,2] [,3]
## [1,]  1   4   1
## [2,]  4   9   9
```

However, if the input data has some mistakes or corruption, `sapply()` will silently accept the input and may return an unexpected value. For example, let's assume that the third element of x has mistakenly got an additional element:

```
x1 <- list(c(1, 2), c(2, 3), c(1, 3, 3))
```

Then, `sapply()` finds that it can no longer be simplified to a matrix and thus returns a list:

```
sapply(x1, function(x) x ^ 2)
## [[1]]
## [1] 1 4
##
## [[2]]
## [1] 4 9
##
## [[3]]
## [1] 1 9 9
```

If we use `vapply()` in the first place, the mistake will be spotted very soon. The `vapply()` function has an additional argument that specifies the template of the returned value from each iteration. In the following code, the template is `numeric(2)`, which means each iteration should return a numeric vector of two elements. If the template is violated, the function will end up in an error:

```
vapply(x1, function(x) x ^ 2, numeric(2))
## Error in vapply(x1, function(x) x^2, numeric(2)): values must be length
2,
##  but FUN(X[[3]]) result is length 3
```

For the original and correct input, `vapply()` returns exactly the same matrix as `sapply()` did:

```
vapply(x, function(x) x ^ 2, numeric(2))
## [,1] [,2] [,3]
## [1,] 1 4 1
## [2,] 4 9 9
```

In conclusion, `vapply` is the safer version of `sapply` as it performs additional template checking. In practical use, if the template can be determined, it is better to use `vapply()` than `sapply()`.

mapply

While `lappy()` and `sapply()` both iterate over one vector, `mapply()` iterates over multiple vectors. In other words, `mapply` is a multivariate version of `sapply`:

```
mapply(function(a, b, c) a * b + b * c + a * c,
a = c(1, 2, 3), b = c(5, 6, 7), c = c(-1, -2, -3))
## [1] -1 -4 -9
```

The iterating function is allowed to return not only scalar values but multi-element vectors. Then, `mapply()` will simplify the result, just like `sapply()` does:

```
df <- data.frame(x = c(1, 2, 3), y = c(3, 4, 5))
df
## x y
## 1 1 3
## 2 2 4
## 3 3 5
mapply(function(xi, yi) c(xi, yi, xi + yi), df$x, df$y)
## [,1] [,2] [,3]
## [1,] 1 2 3
## [2,] 3 4 5
## [3,]    4    6    8
```

`Map` is the multivariate version of `lapply` and hence, always returns a list:

```
Map(function(xi, yi) c(xi, yi, xi + yi), df$x, df$y)
## [[1]]
## [1] 1 3 4
##
## [[2]]
## [1] 2 4 6
##
```

```
## [[3]]
## [1] 3 5 8
```

apply

The `apply` function applies a function on a given margin or dimension of a given matrix or array. For example, to calculate the sum of each row, which is the first dimension, we need to specify `MARGIN = 1` so that `sum` is applied to a row (numeric vector) sliced from the matrix in each iteration:

```
mat <- matrix(c(1, 2, 3, 4), nrow = 2)
mat
## [,1] [,2]
## [1,] 1 3
## [2,] 2 4
apply(mat, 1, sum)
## [1] 4 6
```

To calculate the sum of each column, which is the second dimension, we need to specify `MARGIN=2` so that `sum` is applied to a column sliced from `mat` in each iteration:

```
apply(mat, 2, sum)
## [1] 3 7
```

The `apply` function also supports array input and matrix output:

```
mat2 <- matrix(1:16, nrow = 4)
mat2
## [,1] [,2] [,3] [,4]
## [1,] 1 5 9 13
## [2,] 2 6 10 14
## [3,] 3 7 11 15
## [4,] 4 8 12 16
```

To build a matrix that shows the max and min value for each column, run the following code:

```
apply(mat2, 2, function(col) c(min = min(col), max = max(col)))
## [,1] [,2] [,3] [,4]
## min 1 5 9 13
## max 4 8 12 16
```

To build a matrix that shows the max and min value for each row, run the following code:

```
apply(mat2, 1, function(col) c(min = min(col), max = max(col)))
## [,1] [,2] [,3] [,4]
## min 1 2 3 4
## max 13 14 15 16
```

Summary

In this chapter, you learned how to work basic objects by demonstrating the use of built-in functions. They are the vocabulary of R in practice. You learned some basic functions to test and get object types and to access and reshape data dimensions. You learned about a number of logical operators and functions to filter data.

To work with numeric data structures, you learned basic math functions, built-in numeric methods to find roots and do calculus, and some statistical functions to perform random sampling and make summaries of data. You also understood the apply-family functions that make it easier to iterate and collect results.

Another important category of data is string, which is represented by character vectors. In the next chapter, you will learn string-manipulation techniques to facilitate text analysis.

6

Working with Strings

In the previous chapter, you learned many built-in functions in several categories to work with basic objects. You learned how to access object classes, types, and dimensions; how to do logical, math, and basic statistical calculations; and how to perform simple analytic tasks such as root solving. These functions are the building blocks of our solution to specific problems.

String-related functions are a very important category of functions. They will be introduced in this chapter. In R, texts are stored in character vectors, and a good number of functions and techniques are useful to manipulate and analyze texts. In this chapter, you will learn the basics and useful techniques of working with strings, including the following topics:

- Basic manipulation of character vectors
- Converting between date/time objects and their string representations
- Using regular expressions to extract information from texts

Getting started with strings

Character vectors in R are used to store text data. You previously learned that in contrast with many other programming languages, a character vector is not a vector of single characters, letters, or alphabet symbols such as a, b, c. Rather, it is a vector of strings.

R also provides a variety of built-in functions to deal with character vectors. Many of them also perform vectorized operations so they can process numerous string values in one step.

In this section, you will learn more about printing, combining, and transforming texts stored in character vectors.

Printing texts

Perhaps the most basic thing we can do with texts is to view them. R provides several ways to view texts in the console.

The simplest way is to directly type the string in quotation marks:

```
"Hello"
## [1] "Hello"
```

Like a numeric vector of floating numbers, a character vector is a vector of character values, or strings. Hello is in the first position and is the only element of the character vector we created earlier.

We can also print a string value stored in a variable by simply evaluating it:

```
str1 <- "Hello"
str1
## [1] "Hello"
```

However, simply writing a character value in a loop does not print it iteratively. It does not print anything at all:

```
for (i in 1:3) {
  "Hello"
}
```

That's because R only automatically prints the *value* of an expression as it is being typed in the console. A for loop does not explicitly return a value. This behavior also explains the difference between the printing behaviors when the following two functions are called, respectively:

```
test1 <- function(x) {
  "Hello"
  x
}
test1("World")
## [1] "World"
```

In the preceding output, test1 does not print Hello, but it prints World because test1("World") returns the value of the last expression x, which is given as World, the value of the function call and R automatically prints this value. Let's assume we remove x from the function as follows:

```
test2 <- function(x) {
  "Hello"
```

```
}
test2("World")
## [1] "Hello"
```

Then, `test2` always returns `Hello`, no matter what value x takes. As a result, R automatically prints the value of expression `test2("World")`, that is, `Hello`.

If we want to explicitly print an object, we should use `print()`:

```
print(str1)
## [1] "Hello"
```

Then, the character vector is printed with a position `[1]`. This works in a loop too:

```
for (i in 1:3) {
  print(str1)
}
## [1] "Hello"
## [1] "Hello"
## [1] "Hello"
```

It also works in a function:

```
test3 <- function(x) {
  print("Hello")
  x
}
test3("World")
## [1] "Hello"
## [1] "World"
```

In some cases, we want the texts to appear as a message rather than a character vector with indices. In such cases, we can call `cat()` or `message()`:

```
cat("Hello")
## Hello
```

We can construct the message in a more flexible way:

```
name <- "Ken"
language <- "R"
cat("Hello,", name, "- a user of", language)
## Hello, Ken - a user of R
```

We change the input to print a more formal sentence:

```
cat("Hello, ", name, ", a user of ", language, ".")
## Hello, Ken , a user of R .
```

It looks like the concatenated string appears to use unnecessary spaces between different arguments. It is because the space character is used by default as the separator between the input strings. We can change it by specifying the sep= argument. In the following example, we will avoid the default space separator and manually write spaces in the input strings to create a correct version:

```
cat ("Hello, ", name, ", a user of ", language, ".", sep = "")
## Hello, Ken, a user of R.
```

An alternative function is message(), which is often used in serious situations such as an important event. The output text has a more conspicuous appearance. It is distinct from cat(), in that, it does not automatically use space separators to concatenate input strings:

```
message ("Hello, ", name, ", a user of ", language, ".")
## Hello, Ken, a user of R.
```

Using message(), we need to write the separators manually in order to show the same text as earlier.

Another difference in the behavior between cat() and message() is that message() automatically ends the text with a new line while cat() does not.

The following two examples demonstrate the difference. We want to print the same contents but get different results:

```
for (i in 1:3) {
  cat (letters[[i]])
}
## abc
for (i in 1:3) {
  message (letters[[i]])
}
## a
## b
## c
```

It is obvious that each time cat() is called, it prints the input string without a new line appended. The effect is that the three letters show in the same line. By contrast, each time message() is called, it appends a new line to the input string. As a result, the three letters show in three lines. To print each letter in a new line using cat(), we need to explicitly add a new line character in the input. The following code prints exactly the same contents as message() did in the previous example:

```
for (i in 1:3) {
```

```
  cat(letters[[i]], "\n", sep = "")
}
## a
## b
## c
```

Concatenating strings

In practice, we often need to concatenate several strings to build a new one. The `paste()` function is used to concatenate several character vectors together. This function also uses space as the default separator:

```
paste("Hello", "world")
## [1] "Hello world"
paste("Hello", "world", sep = "-")
## [1] "Hello-world"
```

If we don't want the separator, we can set `sep=""` or alternatively call `paste0()`:

```
paste0("Hello", "world")
## [1] "Helloworld"
```

Maybe you are confused by `paste()` and `cat()` because they both are capable of concatenating strings. But what's the difference? Although both functions concatenate strings, the difference is that `cat()` only prints the string to the console, but `paste()` returns the string for further uses. The following code demonstrates that `cat()` prints the concatenated string but returns `NULL`:

```
value1 <- cat("Hello", "world")
## Hello world
value1
## NULL
```

In other words, `cat()` only prints strings, but `paste()` creates a new character vector.

The previous examples show the behavior of `paste()` working with single-element character vectors. What about working with multi-element ones? Let's see how this is done:

```
paste(c("A", "B"), c("C", "D"))
## [1] "A C" "B D"
```

We can see that `paste()` works element-wise, that is, `paste("A", "C")` first, then `paste("B", "D")`, and finally, the results are collected to build a character vector of two elements.

If we want the results to be put together in one string, we can specify how these two elements are again concatenated by setting `collapse=`:

```
paste(c("A", "B"), c("C", "D"),collapse = ", ")
## [1] "A C, B D"
```

If we want to put them in two lines, we can set `collapse` to be `\n` (new line):

```
result <- paste(c("A", "B"), c("C", "D"), collapse = "\n") result
## [1] "A C\nB D"
```

The new character vector `result` is a two-lined string, but the text representation of it is still written in one line. The new line is represented by `\n` as we specified. To view the text we created, we need to call `cat()`:

```
cat(result)
## A C ## B D
```

Now, the two-lined string is printed to the console in its intended format. The same thing also works with `paste0()`.

Transforming texts

Turning texts into another form is useful in many cases. It is easy to perform a number of basic types of transformation on texts.

Changing cases

When we process data with texts, the input may not comply with our standard as supposed. For example, we expect all products to be graded in capital letters, from A to F, but the actual input may consist of these letters in both cases. Changing cases is useful to ensure that the input strings are consistent in cases.

The `tolower()` function changes the texts to lowercase letters, while `toupper()` does the opposite:

```
tolower("Hello")
## [1] "hello"
toupper("Hello")
## [1] "HELLO"
```

This is particularly useful when a function accepts character input. For example, we can define a function that returns x + y when type is add in all possible cases. It returns x * y when type is times in all possible cases. The best way to do it is to always convert type to lowercase or uppercase, no matter what the input value is:

```
calc <- function(type, x, y) {
  type <- tolower(type)
  if (type == "add") {
    x + y
  }else if (type == "times") {
    x * y
  } else {
    stop("Not supported type of command")
  }
}
c(calc("add", 2, 3), calc("Add", 2, 3), calc("TIMES", 2, 3))
## [1] 5 5 6
```

This gives more tolerance to similar inputs only in different cases so that type is case-insensitive.

In addition, the two functions are vectorized, that is, it changes the cases of each string element of the given character vector:

```
toupper(c("Hello", "world"))
## [1] "HELLO" "WORLD"
```

Counting characters

Another useful function is nchar(), which simply counts the number of characters of each element of a character vector:

```
nchar("Hello")
## [1] 5
```

Like toupper() and tolower(), nchar() is also vectorized:

```
nchar(c("Hello", "R", "User"))
## [1] 5 1 4
```

This function is often used to check whether an argument is supplied a valid string. For example, the following function takes some personal information of a student and stores it in the database:

```
store_student <- function(name, age) {
  stopifnot(length(name) == 1, nchar(name) >= 2,
```

```
    is.numeric(age), age > 0)
  # store the information in the database
}
```

Before storing the information in the database, the function uses stopifnot() to check whether name and age are provided valid values. If the user does not provide a meaningful name (for example, no less than two letters), the function would stop with an error:

```
store_student("James", 20)
store_student("P", 23)
## Error: nchar(name) >= 2 is not TRUE
```

Note that nchar(x) == 0 is equivalent to x == "". To check against an empty string, both methods work.

Trimming leading and trailing whitespaces

In the previous example, we used nchar() to check whether name is valid. However, sometimes, the input data comes with useless whitespaces. This adds more noise to the data and requires a careful checking of string arguments. For example, store_student() in the previous section makes pass of a name such as " P", which is as invalid as a straight "P" argument, but nchar(" P") returns 3:

```
store_student(" P", 23)
```

To take the possibility into account, we need to refine store_student. In R 3.2.0, trimws() is introduced to trim leading and/or trailing whitespaces of given strings:

```
store_student2 <- function(name, age) {
  stopifnot(length(name) == 1, nchar(trimws(name)) >= 2,
    is.numeric(age), age > 0)
  # store the information in the database
}
```

Now, the function is more robust to noisy data:

```
store_student2(" P", 23)
## Error: nchar(trimws(name)) >= 2 is not TRUE
```

The function, by default, trims both the leading and trailing whitespaces, which can be spaces and tabs. You can specify whether "left" or "right" to only trim one side of the strings:

```
trimws(c(" Hello", "World "), which = "left")
## [1] "Hello" "World "
```

Substring

In previous chapters, you learned how to subset vectors and lists. We can also subset the texts in a character vector by calling `substr()`. Suppose we have several dates in the following form:

```
dates <- c("Jan 3", "Feb 10", "Nov 15")
```

All the months are represented by three-letter abbreviations. We can use `substr()` to extract the months:

```
substr(dates, 1, 3)
## [1] "Jan" "Feb" "Nov"
```

To extract the day, we need to use `substr()` and `nchar()` together:

```
substr(dates, 5, nchar(dates))
## [1] "3" "10" "15"
```

Now that we can extract both months and days in the input strings, it is useful to write a function to transform the strings in such format to numeric values to represent the same date. The following function uses many functions and ideas you learned previously:

```
get_month_day <- function(x) {
  months <- vapply(substr(tolower(x), 1, 3), function(md) {
    switch(md, jan = 1, feb = 2, mar = 3, apr = 4, may = 5,
    jun = 6, jul = 7, aug = 8, sep = 9, oct = 10, nov = 11, dec = 12)
  }, numeric(1), USE.NAMES = FALSE)
  days <- as.numeric(substr(x, 5, nchar(x)))
  data.frame(month = months, day = days)
}
get_month_day(dates)
##    month day
## 1     1    3
## 2     2   10
## 3    11   15
```

The `substr()` function also has a counterpart function to replace the substrings with a given character vector:

```
substr(dates, 1, 3) <- c("Feb", "Dec", "Mar") dates
## [1] "Feb 3" "Dec 10" "Mar 15"
```

Splitting texts

In many cases, the lengths of string parts to extract are not fixed. For example, person names such as "Mary Johnson" or "Jack Smiths" have no fixed lengths for the first names and last names. It is more difficult to use `substr()`, as you learned in the previous section, to separate and extract both parts. Texts in such format have a regular separator such as space or a comma. To extract the useful parts, we need to split the texts and make each part accessible. The `strsplit()` function is used to split texts by specific separators given as a character vector:

```
strsplit("a,bb,ccc", split = ",")
## [[1]]
## [1] "a" "bb" "ccc"
```

The function returns a list. Each element in the list is a character vector produced from splitting that element in the original character vector. It is because `strsplit()`, like all previous string functions we have introduced, is also vectorized, that is, it returns a list of character vectors as a result of the splitting:

```
students <- strsplit(c("Tony, 26, Physics", "James, 25, Economics"),
split = ", ")
students
## [[1]]
## [1] "Tony" "26" "Physics"
##
## [[2]]
## [1] "James" "25" "Economics"
```

The `strsplit()` function returns a list of character vectors containing split parts by working element-wise. In practice, splitting is only the first step to extract or reorganize data. To continue, we can use `rbind` to put the data into a matrix and give appropriate names to the columns:

```
students_matrix <- do.call(rbind, students)
colnames(students_matrix) <- c("name", "age", "major")
students_matrix
##        name    age   major
## [1,] "Tony"  "26"  "Physics"
## [2,] "James" "25"  "Economics"
```

Then, we will convert the matrix to a data frame so that we can transform each column to more proper types:

```
students_df <- data.frame(students_matrix, stringsAsFactors = FALSE)
students_df$age <- as.numeric(students_df$age)
students_df
```

```
##    name   age major
## 1 Tony   26   Physics
## 2 James  25   Economics
```

Now, raw string input students are transformed into a more organized and more useful data frame `students_df`.

One small trick to split the whole string into single characters is to use an empty `split` argument:

```
strsplit(c("hello", "world"), split = "")
## [[1]]
## [1] "h" "e" "l" "l" "o"
##
## [[2]]
## [1] "w" "o" "r" "l" "d"
```

In fact, `strsplit()` is more powerful than is shown. It also supports *regular expressions,* a very powerful framework to process text data. We will cover this topic in the last section of this chapter.

Formatting texts

Concatenating texts with `paste()` is sometimes not a good idea because the text has to be broken into pieces and it becomes harder to read as the format gets longer.

For example, let's assume we need to print each record in `students_df` in the following format:

```
#1, name: Tony, age: 26, major: Physics
```

In this case, using `paste()` will be a pain:

```
cat(paste("#", 1:nrow(students_df), ", name: ", students_df$name, ", age:
", students_df$age, ", major: ", students_df$major, sep = ""), sep = "\n")
## #1, name: Tony, age: 26, major: Physics
## #2, name: James, age: 25, major: Economics
```

The code looks messy, and it is hard to get the general template at first glance. By contrast, `sprintf()` supports a formatting template and solves the problem in a nice way:

```
cat(sprintf("#%d, name: %s, age: %d, major: %s",
  1:nrow(students_df), students_df$name, students_df$age,
  students_df$major), sep = "\n")
#1, name: Tony, age: 26, major: Physics
## #2, name: James, age: 25, major: Economics
```

In the preceding code, `#%d, name: %s, age: %d, major: %s` is the formatting template in which `%d` and `%s` are placeholders to represent the input arguments to appear in the string. The `sprintf()` function is especially easy to use because it prevents the template string from tearing apart, and each part to replace is specified as a function argument. In fact, this function uses C style formatting rules as described in detail at `https://en.wikipedia.org/wiki/Printf_format_string`.

In the preceding example, `%s` stands for string and `%d` for digits (integers). Moreover, `sprintf()` is also very flexible in formatting numeric values using `%f`. For example, `%.1f` means to round the number to 0.1:

```
sprintf("The length of the line is approximately %.1fmm", 12.295)
## [1] "The length of the line is approximately 12.3mm"
```

In fact, there is a formatting syntax of different types of values. The following table shows the most commonly used syntax:

Format	Output
sprintf("%s", "A")	A
sprintf("%d", 10)	10
sprintf("%04d", 10)	0010
sprintf("%f", pi)	3.141593
sprintf("%.2f", pi)	3.14
sprintf("%1.0f", pi)	3
sprintf("%8.2f", pi)	3.14
sprintf("%08.2f", pi)	00003.14
sprintf("%+f", pi)	+3.141593
sprintf("%e", pi)	3.141593e+00
sprintf("%E", pi)	3.141593E+00

The official documentation
(`https://stat.ethz.ch/R-manual/R-devel/library/base/html/sprintf`
`.html`) gives a full description of the supported formats.

Note that % in the format text is a special character and will be interpreted as the initial character of a place holder. What if we really mean % in the string? To avoid formatting interpretation, we need to use %% to represent a literal %. The following code is an example:

```
sprintf("The ratio is %d%%", 10)
## [1] "The ratio is 10%"
```

Using Python string functions in R

The `sprintf()` function is powerful but not perfect for all use cases. For example, if some parts have to appear multiple times in the template, you will need to write the same arguments multiple times. This often makes the code more redundant and a bit hard to modify:

```
sprintf("%s, %d years old, majors in %s and loves %s.", "James", 25,
"Physics", "Physics")
## [1] "James, 25 years old, majors in Physics and loves Physics."
```

There are other ways to represent the placeholders. The `pystr` package provides the `pystr_format()` function to format strings in Python formatting style using either numeric or named placeholders. The preceding example can be rewritten with this function in two ways:

One is using numeric placeholders:

```
# install.packages("pystr")
library(pystr)
pystr_format("{1}, {2} years old, majors in {3} and loves {3}.", "James",
25, "Physics", "Physics")
## [1] "James, 25 years old, majors in Physics and loves Physics."
```

The other is using named placeholders:

```
pystr_format("{name}, {age} years old, majors in {major} and loves
{major}.",
name = "James", age = 25, major = "Physics")
## [1] "James, 25 years old, majors in Physics and loves Physics."
```

In both cases, no argument has to repeat, and the position the input appears at can be easily moved to other places in the template string.

Formatting date/time

In data analysis, it is common to encounter date and time data types. Perhaps, the simplest functions related with date are `Sys.Date()`, which returns the current date, and `Sys.time()`, which returns the current time.

As the book is being rendered, the date is printed as follows:

```
Sys.Date()
## [1] "2016-02-26"
```

And the time is:

```
Sys.time()
## [1] "2016-02-26 22:12:25 CST"
```

From the output, the date and time look like character vectors, but actually they are not:

```
current_date <- Sys.Date()
as.numeric(current_date)
## [1] 16857
current_time <- Sys.time()
as.numeric(current_time)
## [1] 1456495945
```

They are, in essence, numeric values relative to an origin and have special methods to do date/time calculations. For a date, its numeric value means the number of days passed after 1970-01-01. For a time, its numeric value means the number of seconds passed after 1970-01-01 00:00.00 UTC.

Parsing text as date/time

We can create a date relative to a customized origin:

```
as.Date(1000, "1970-01-01")
## [1] "1972-09-27"
```

However, in more cases, we create date and time from a standard text representation:

```
my_date <- as.Date("2016-02-10")
my_date
## [1] "2016-02-10"
```

But if we can represent time in string such as 2016-02-10, then why do we need to create a `Date` object like we did earlier? It is because a date has more features: we can do date math with them. Suppose we have a date object, we can add or minus a number of days and get a new date:

```
my_date + 3
## [1] "2016-02-13"
my_date + 80
## [1] "2016-04-30"
my_date - 65
## [1] "2015-12-07"
```

We can directly subtract a date from another to get the difference in number of days between two dates:

```
date1 <- as.Date("2014-09-28")
date2 <- as.Date("2015-10-20")
date2 - date1
## Time difference of 387 days
```

The output of `date2 - date1` looks like a message, but it is actually a numeric value. We can make it explicit using `as.numeric()`:

```
as.numeric(date2 - date1)
## [1] 387
```

Time is similar, but there is no function called `as.Time()`. To create a date time from a text representation, we can use either `as.POSIXct()` or `as.POSIXlt()`. These two functions are different implementations of a date/time object under the POSIX standard. In the following example, we use `as.POSIXlt` to create a date/time object:

```
my_time <- as.POSIXlt("2016-02-10 10:25:31")
my_time
## [1] "2016-02-10 10:25:31 CST"
```

This type of object also defines + and − for simple time calculations. Unlike the date object, it works at the unit of seconds rather than days:

```
my_time + 10
## [1] "2016-02-10 10:25:41 CST"
my_time + 12345
## [1] "2016-02-10 13:51:16 CST"
my_time - 1234567
## [1] "2016-01-27 03:29:24 CST"
```

Given a string representation of date or time in data, we have to convert it to date or date/time objects, which enable us to do calculations. Often, however, what we get in raw data is not always the format that can be directly recognized by `as.Date()` or `as.POSIXlt()`. In this case, we need to use a set of special letters as placeholders to represent certain parts of a date or time, just like we did with `sprintf()`.

For example, for the input `2015.07.25`, `as.Date()` will produce an error if no format string is supplied:

```
as.Date("2015.07.25")
## Error in charToDate(x): character string is not in a standard
unambiguous format
```

We can use a format string as a template to tell `as.Date()` how to parse the string to a date:

```
as.Date("2015.07.25", format = "%Y.%m.%d")
## [1] "2015-07-25"
```

Similarly, for a non-standard date/time string, we also need to specify a template string to tell `as.POSIXlt()` how to handle it:

```
as.POSIXlt("7/25/2015 09:30:25", format = "%m/%d/%Y %H:%M:%S")
## [1] "2015-07-25 09:30:25 CST"
```

An alternative (and more direct) function to convert a string to a date/time is `strptime()`:

```
strptime("7/25/2015 09:30:25", "%m/%d/%Y %H:%M:%S")
## [1] "2015-07-25 09:30:25 CST"
```

In fact, `as.POSIXlt()` is only a wrapper of `strptime()` for character input, but `strptime()` always requires that you supply the format string, while `as.POSIXlt()` works for standard formats without a supplied template.

Just like numeric vectors, date and date/time are vectors too. You can supply a character vector to `as.Date()` and get a vector of dates:

```
as.Date(c("2015-05-01", "2016-02-12"))
## [1] "2015-05-01" "2016-02-12"
```

The math is also vectorized. In the following code, we will add some consecutive integers to the date, and we get consecutive dates as expected:

```
as.Date("2015-01-01") + 0:2
## [1] "2015-01-01" "2015-01-02" "2015-01-03"
```

The same feature also applies to date/time objects:

```
strptime("7/25/2015 09:30:25", "%m/%d/%Y %H:%M:%S") + 1:3
## [1] "2015-07-25 09:30:26 CST" "2015-07-25 09:30:27 CST" ## [3]
"2015-07-25 09:30:28 CST"
```

Sometimes, the data uses integer representations of date and time. It makes parsing the date and time trickier. For example, to parse 20150610, we will run the following code:

```
as.Date("20150610", format = "%Y%m%d")
## [1] "2015-06-10"
```

To parse 20150610093215, we can specify the template to describe such a format:

```
strptime("20150610093215", "%Y%m%d%H%M%S")
## [1] "2015-06-10 09:32:15 CST"
```

A trickier example is to parse the date/time in the following data frame:

```
datetimes <- data.frame(
date = c(20150601, 20150603),
time = c(92325, 150621))
```

If we use paste0() on the columns of datetimes and directly call strptime() with the template used in the previous example, we will get a missing value that indicates that the first element is not consistent with the format:

```
dt_text <- paste0(datetimes$date, datetimes$time)
dt_text
## [1] "2015060192325" "20150603150621"
strptime(dt_text, "%Y%m%d%H%M%S")
## [1] NA "2015-06-03 15:06:21 CST"
```

The problem lies in 92325, which should be 092325. We need to use sprintf() to make sure a leading zero is present when necessary:

```
dt_text2 <- paste0(datetimes$date, sprintf("%06d", datetimes$time))
dt_text2
## [1] "20150601092325" "20150603150621"
strptime(dt_text2, "%Y%m%d%H%M%S")
## [1] "2015-06-01 09:23:25 CST" "2015-06-03 15:06:21 CST"
```

Finally, the conversion works as supposed.

Formatting date/time to strings

In the previous section, you learned how to convert strings to date and date/time objects. In this section, you will learn the opposite: converting date and date/time objects back to strings according to a specific template.

Once a date object is created, every time we print it, it is always represented in the standard format:

```
my_date
## [1] "2016-02-10"
```

We can convert the date to a string in a standard representation with `as.character()`:

```
date_text <- as.character(my_date)
date_text
## [1] "2016-02-10"
```

From the output, `my_date` looks the same, but the string is now merely a plain text and no longer supports date calculations:

```
date_text + 1
## Error in date_text + 1: non-numeric argument to binary operator
```

Sometimes, we need to format the date in a non-standard way:

```
as.character(my_date, format = "%Y.%m.%d")
## [1] "2016.02.10"
```

In fact, `as.character()` calls `format()` directly behind the scenes. We will get exactly the same result using `format()`, and this is recommended in most cases:

```
format(my_date, "%Y.%m.%d")
## [1] "2016.02.10"
```

The same thing also applies to a date/time object. We can further customize the template to include more texts other than the placeholders:

```
my_time
## [1] "2016-02-10 10:25:31 CST"
format(my_time, "date: %Y-%m-%d, time: %H:%M:%S")
## [1] "date: 2016-02-10, time: 10:25:31"
```

 The format placeholders are much more than we mentioned. Read the documentation by typing in `?strptime` for detailed information.

There are a number of packages to make dealing with date and time much easier. I recommend the `lubridate` package (`https://cran.r-project.org/web/packages/lubridate`) because it provides almost all the functions you need to work with date and time objects.

In the previous sections, you learned a number of basic functions to deal with strings and date/time objects. These functions are useful but much less flexible than regular expressions. You will learn this very powerful technique in the next section.

Using regular expressions

For research, you may need to download data from open-access websites or authentication-required databases. These data sources provide data in various formats, and most of the data supplied are very likely well-organized. For example, many economic and financial databases provide data in the CSV format, which is a widely supported text format to represent tabular data. A typical CSV format looks like this:

```
id,name,score
1,A,20
2,B,30
3,C,25
```

In R, it is convenient to call `read.csv()` to import a CSV file as a data frame with the right header and data types because the format is a natural representation of a data frame.

However, not all data files are well organized, and dealing with poorly organized data is painstaking. Built-in functions such as `read.table()` and `read.csv()` work in many situations, but they may not help at all for such format-less data.

For example, if you need to analyze raw data (`messages.txt`) organized in a CSV-like format as shown here, you had better be careful when you call `read.csv()`:

```
2014-02-01,09:20:25,James,Ken,Hey, Ken!
2014-02-01,09:20:29,Ken,James,Hey, how are you?
2014-02-01,09:20:41,James,Ken, I'm ok, what about you?
2014-02-01,09:21:03,Ken,James,I'm feeling excited!
2014-02-01,09:21:26,James,Ken,What happens?
```

Suppose you want to import this file as a data frame in the following format which is nicely organized:

```
    Date       Time      Sender   Receiver   Message
1   2014-02-01 09:20:25  James    Ken        Hey, Ken!
2   2014-02-01 09:20:29  Ken      James      Hey, how are you?
```

```
3   2014-02-01  09:20:41   James      Ken        I'm ok, what about you?
4   2014-02-01  09:21:03   Ken        James      I'm feeling excited!
5   2014-02-01  09:21:26   James      Ken        What happens?
```

However, if you blindly call `read.csv()`, then you will see that it does not work out correctly. This dataset is somehow special in the message column. There are extra commas that will be mistakenly interpreted as separators in a CSV file. Here is the data frame translated from the raw text:

```
read.csv("data/messages.txt", header = FALSE)
## V1V2V3V4V5V6
## 1 2014-02-01 09:20:25 James Ken Hey Ken!
## 2 2014-02-01 09:20:29 Ken James Hey how are you?
## 3 2014-02-01 09:20:41 James Ken I'm ok what about you?
## 4 2014-02-01 09:21:03 Ken James I'm feeling excited!
## 5 2014-02-01 09:21:26 James Ken What happens?
```

There are various methods to tackle this problem. You may consider using `strsplit()` for each line and manually take out the first several elements and paste others for each line split into multiple parts. But one of the simplest and most robust ways is to use the so-called Regular Expression (`https://en.wikipedia.org/wiki/Regular_expression`). Don't worry if you feel strange about the terminology. Its usage is very simple: describe the pattern that matches the text and extract the desired part from that text.

Before we apply the technique, we need some basic knowledge. The best way to motivate yourself is look at a simpler problem and consider what is needed to solve the problem.

Suppose we are dealing with the following text (`fruits.txt`) that describes the number or status of some fruits:

```
apple: 20
orange: missing
banana: 30
pear: sent to Jerry
watermelon: 2
blueberry: 12
strawberry: sent to James
```

Now, we want to pick out all fruits with a number rather than with status information. Although we can easily finish the task visually, it is not that easy for a computer. If the number of lines exceeds two thousand, it can be easy for a computer with the appropriate technique applied and, by contrast, be hard, time-consuming, and error prone for a human.

The first thing that should come to our mind is that we need to distinguish fruits with numbers and fruits with no numbers. In general, we need to distinguish texts that match a particular pattern from the ones that do not. Here, regular expression is definitely the right technique to work with.

Regular expressions solve problems using two steps: the first is to find a pattern to match the text and the second is to group the patterns to extract the information in need.

Finding a string pattern

To solve the problem, our computer does not have to understand what fruits actually are. We only need to find out a pattern that describes what we want. Literally, we want to get all lines that start with a word followed by a semicolon and a space, and end with an integer rather than words or other symbols.

Regular expression provides a set of symbols to represent patterns. The preceding pattern can be described with `^\w+:\s\d+$` where meta-symbols are used to represent a class of symbols:

- `^`: This symbol is used at the beginning of the line
- `\w`: This symbol represents a word character
- `\s`: This symbol is a space character
- `\d`: This symbol is a digit character
- `$`: This symbol is used at the end of the line

Moreover, `\w+` means one or more word characters, `:` is exactly the symbol we expect to see after the word, and `\d+` means one or more digit characters. See, this pattern is so magical that it represents all the cases we want and excludes all the cases we don't want.

More specifically, this pattern matches lines such as `abc: 123` but excludes lines otherwise. To pick out the desired cases in R, we use `grep()` to get which strings match the pattern:

```
fruits <- readLines("data/fruits.txt") fruits
## [1] "apple: 20" "orange: missing"
## [3] "banana: 30" "pear: sent to Jerry"
## [5] "watermelon: 2" "blueberry: 12"
## [7] "strawberry: sent to James"
matches <- grep("^\\w+:\\s\\d+$", fruits)
matches
## [1] 1 3 5 6
```

Note that \ in R should be written as \\ to avoid escaping. Then, we can filter fruits by matches:

```
fruits[matches]
## [1] "apple: 20" "banana: 30" "watermelon: 2" "blueberry: 12"
```

Now, we successfully distinguish desirable lines from undesirable ones. The lines that match the pattern are chosen, and those that do not match the pattern are omitted.

Note that we specify a pattern that starts with ^ and ends with $ because we don't want a partial matching. In fact, regular expressions perform partial matching by default, that is, if any part of the string matches the pattern, the whole string is considered to match the pattern. For example, the following code attempts to find out which strings match the two patterns respectively:

```
grep("\\d", c("abc", "a12", "123", "1"))
## [1] 2 3 4
grep("^\\d$", c("abc", "a12", "123", "1"))
## [1] 4
```

The first pattern matches strings that include any digit (partial matching), while the second pattern with ^ and $ matches strings that have only one digit.

Once the pattern works correctly, we go to the next step: using groups to extract the data.

Using groups to extract the data

In the pattern string, we can make marks to identify the parts we want to extract from the texts using parenthesis. In this problem, we can modify the pattern to (\w+):\s(\d+), where two groups are marked: one is the fruit name matched by \w+ and the other is the number of the fruit matched by \d+.

Now, we can use this modified version of the pattern to extract the information we want. Although it is perfectly possible to use built-in functions in R to do the job, I strongly recommend using functions in the stringr package. This package makes it substantially easier to use regular expressions. We call str_match() with the modified pattern with groups:

```
library(stringr)
matches <- str_match(fruits, "^(\\w+):\\s(\\d+)$")
matches
##        [,1]          [,2]       [,3]
## [1,] "apple: 20"    "apple"    "20"
## [2,] NA             NA         NA
```

```
## [3,] "banana: 30"     "banana"     "30"
## [4,] NA               NA           NA
## [5,] "watermelon: 2"  "watermelon" "2"
## [6,] "blueberry: 12"  "blueberry"  "12"
## [7,] NA               NA           NA
```

This time the matches are a matrix with more than one column. The groups in parenthesis are extracted from the text and are put to columns 2 and 3. Now, we can easily transform this character matrix to a data frame with the right header and data types:

```
# transform to data frame
fruits_df <- data.frame(na.omit(matches[, -1]), stringsAsFactors =FALSE)
# add a header
colnames(fruits_df) <- c("fruit","quantity")
# convert type of quantity from character to integer
fruits_df$quantity <- as.integer(fruits_df$quantity)
```

Now, `fruits_df` is a data frame with the right header and data types:

```
fruits_df
##      fruit   quantity
## 1    apple        20
## 2    banana       30
## 3    watermelon   2
## 4    blueberry    12
```

If you are not sure about the intermediate results in the preceding code, you can run the code line by line and see what happens in each step. Finally, this problem is perfectly solved with regular expressions.

From the previous example, we see that the magic of regular expressions is but a group of identifiers used to represent different kinds of characters and symbols. In addition to the meta-symbols we have mentioned, the following are also useful:

- [0-9]: This symbol represents a single integer from 0 to 9
- [a-z]: This symbol represents a single lower capital letter from a to z
- [A-Z]: This symbol represents a single upper capital letter from A to Z
- .: This symbol represents any single symbol
- *: This symbol represents a pattern, which may appear zero, one, or more times
- +: This is a pattern, which appears one or more than one time
- {n}: This is a pattern that appears n times
- {m, n}: This is a pattern that appears at least m times and at most n times

With these meta-symbols, we can easily check or filter string data. For example, suppose we have some telephone numbers from two countries that are mixed together. If the pattern of telephone numbers in one country is different from that of the other, regular expressions can be helpful to split them into two categories:

```
telephone <- readLines("data/telephone.txt")
telephone
## [1] "123-23451" "1225-3123" "121-45672" "1332-1231" "1212-3212"
"123456789"
```

Note that there is an exception in the data. The number has no – in the middle. For unexceptional cases, it should be easy to figure out the pattern of the two types of telephone numbers:

```
telephone[grep("^\\d{3}-\\d{5}$", telephone)]
## [1] "123-23451" "121-45672"
telephone[grep("^\\d{4}-\\d{4}$", telephone)]
## [1] "1225-3123" "1332-1231" "1212-3212"
```

To find out the exceptional cases, grepl() is more useful because it returns a logical vector to indicate whether each element matches the pattern. Therefore, we can use this function to choose all records that do not match the given patterns:

```
telephone[!grepl("^\\d{3}-\\d{5}$", telephone) & !grepl("^\\d{4}-\\d{4}$",
telephone)]
## [1] "123456789"
```

The preceding code basically says that all records that do not match the two patterns are considered exceptional. Imagine we have millions of records to check. Exceptional cases may be in any format, so it is more robust to use this method: excluding all valid records to find out invalid records.

Reading data in customizable ways

Now, let's go back to the problem we faced at the very beginning of this section. The procedure is exactly the same with the fruits example: finding the pattern and making groups.

First, let's look at a typical line of the raw data:

```
2014-02-01,09:20:29,Ken,James,Hey, how are you?
```

It is obvious that all lines are based on the same format, that is, date, time, sender, receiver, and message are separated by commas. The only special thing is that commas may appear in the message, but we don't want our code to interpret it as separators.

Note that regular expressions perfectly works with this purpose as it did in the previous example. To represent one or more symbols that follow the same pattern, just place a plus sign (+) after the symbolic identifier. For example, \d+ represents a string consisting of one or more digital characters between "" and "9". For example,"1","23", and"456" all match this pattern, while"word" does not. There are also situations where a pattern may or may not appear at all. Then, we need to place a * after the symbolic identifier to mark that this particular pattern may appear once or more, or may not appear, in order to match a wide range of texts.

Now, let's go back to our problem. We need to recognize a sufficiently general pattern of a typical line. The following is the pattern with grouping we should figure out:

```
(\d+-\d+-\d+),(\d+:\d+:\d+),(\w+),(\w+),\s*(.+)
```

Now, we need to import the raw texts in exactly the same way as we did in the fruits example using readLines():

```
messages <- readLines("data/messages.txt")
```

Then, we need to work out the pattern that represents the text and the information we want to extract from the text:

```
pattern <- "^(\\d+-\\d+-\\d+),(\\d+:\\d+:\\d+),(\\w+),(\\w+),\\s*(.+)$"
matches <- str_match(messages, pattern)
messages_df <- data.frame(matches[, -1])
colnames(messages_df) <- c("Date", "Time", "Sender", "Receiver", "Message")
```

The pattern here looks like some secret code. Don't worry. That's exactly how regular expression works, and it should make some sense now if you go through the previous examples.

The regular expression works perfectly. The messages_df file looks like the following structure:

```
messages_df
##        Date       Time     Sender   Receiver    Message
## 1 2014-02-01   09:20:25   James    Ken         Hey, Ken!
## 2 2014-02-01   09:20:29   Ken      James       Hey, how are you?
```

```
## 3 2014-02-01   09:20:41   James   Ken      I'm ok, what about you?
## 4 2014-02-01   09:21:03   Ken     James    I'm feeling excited!
## 5 2014-02-01   09:21:26   James   Ken      What happens?
```

The pattern we use is comparable to a key. The hard part of any regular expression application is to find the key. Once we get it, we are able to open the door and extract as much information as we want from the messy texts. Generally speaking, how difficult it is to find that key largely relies on the difference between the positive cases and negative cases. If the difference is quite obvious, a few symbols will solve the problem. If the difference is subtle and many special cases are involved, just like most real-world problems, you need more experience, harder thinking, and many trials and errors to work out the solution.

Through the motivating examples mentioned earlier, you should now grasp the idea of regular expressions. You don't have to understand how it works internally, but it is very useful to become familiar with the related functions, whether they are built in or provided by certain packages.

If you want to learn more, RegexOne (`http://regexone.com/`) is a very good place to learn the basics in an interactive manner. To learn more specific examples and the full set of identifiers, this website (`http://www.regular-expressions.info/`) is a good reference. To find out good patterns to solve your problem, you can visit RegExr (`http://www.regexr.com/`) to test your patterns interactively online.

Summary

In this chapter, you learned about a number of built-in functions for manipulating character vectors and converting between date/time objects and their string representations. You also learned about the basic idea of regular expressions, a very powerful tool to check and filter string data and extract information from raw texts.

With the vocabulary we built in this and previous chapters, we are now able to work with basic data structures. In the next chapter, you will learn about some tools and techniques to work with data. We will get started with reading and writing simple data files, producing graphics of various types, applying basic statistical analysis and data-mining models on simple datasets, and using numeric methods to solve root-solving and optimization problems.

7
Working with Data

In the previous chapters, you learned the most commonly used object types and functions to work in R. We know how to create and modify vectors, lists, and data frames, how to define our own functions and how to use proper expressions to translate our logic in mind to R code in the editor. With these objects, functions, and expressions, we can start working with data.

In this chapter, we will set out on a journey of working with data and cover the following topics:

- Reading and writing data in a file
- Visualizing data with plot functions
- Analyzing data with simple statistical models and data mining tools

Reading and writing data

The first step in any kind of data analysis in R is to load data, that is, to import a dataset into the environment. Before that, we have to figure out the type of data file and choose appropriate tools to read the data.

Reading and writing text-format data in a file

Among all the file types used to store data, perhaps the most widely used one is CSV. In a typical CSV file, the first line is the header of columns, and each subsequent line represents a data record with columns separated by commas. Here is an example of student records written in this format:

```
Name,Gender,Age,Major
Ken,Male,24,Finance
Ashley,Female,25,Statistics
Jennifer,Female,23,Computer Science
```

Importing data via RStudio IDE

RStudio provides an interactive way to import data. You can navigate to **Tools | Import Dataset | From Local File** and choose a local file in a text format, such as `.csv` and `.txt`. Then, you can adjust the parameters and preview the resulting data frame:

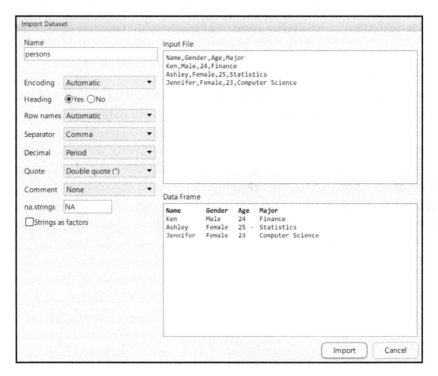

Note that you should check **Strings as factors** only if you intend to convert string columns to factors.

The file importer is not magic, but translates the file path and options to R code. Once you set up the data importing parameters and click on **Import**, it will execute a call to `read.csv()`. Using this interactive tool to import data is very handy and will help you avoid many mistakes when you import a data file for the first time.

Importing data using built-in functions

When you write a script, you can't expect the user to interact with the file importer every time. You can copy the generated code to your script so that it will automatically work each time you run the script. Therefore, it is useful to know how to use built-in functions to import data.

The simplest built-in function to import data is `readLines()`, as we mentioned in previous chapters. This function reads a text file and returns a number of lines as a character vector:

```
readLines("data/persons.csv")
## [1] "Name,Gender,Age,Major"
## [2] "Ken,Male,24,Finance"
## [3] "Ashley,Female,25,Statistics"
## [4] "Jennifer,Female,23,Computer Science"
```

By default, it will read all the lines of the file. To preview the first two lines, run the following code:

```
readLines("data/persons.csv", n = 2)
## [1] "Name,Gender,Age,Major" "Ken,Male,24,Finance"
```

For practical data importing, `readLines()` is too simple in most cases. It works by reading lines as strings rather than parsing them into a data frame. If you want to import data from a CSV file like the preceding code, directly call `read.csv()`:

```
persons1 <- read.csv("data/persons.csv", stringsAsFactors = FALSE)
str(persons1)
## 'data.frame': 3 obs. of 4 variables:
## $ Name  : chr "Ken" "Ashley" "Jennifer"
## $ Gender: chr "Male" "Female" "Female"
## $ Age   : int 24 25 23
## $ Major : chr "Finance" "Statistics" "Computer Science"
```

Note that we want to keep the string value as it is, so we set `stringsAsFactors = FALSE` in the function call to avoid converting the strings to factors.

The function provides many useful arguments to customize importing. For example, we can use `colClasses` to explicitly specify the types of columns and use `col.names` to replace the original column names in the data file:

```
persons2 <- read.csv("data/persons.csv", colClasses = c("character",
"factor", "integer", "character"),
  col.names = c("name", "sex", "age", "major"))
  str(persons2)
## 'data.frame': 3 obs. of 4 variables:
## $ name : chr "Ken" "Ashley" "Jennifer"
## $ sex : Factor w/ 2 levels "Female","Male": 2 1 1
## $ age : int 24 25 23
## $ major: chr "Finance" "Statistics" "Computer Science"
```

Note that CSV is a special case of the delimited data format. Technically, the CSV format is a delimited data format that uses a comma (,) to separate columns and a new line to separate rows. More generally speaking, any character can be the column separator and row separator. Many datasets are stored in the tab-delimited format, that is, they use tab character to separate columns. In this case, you may try using `read.table()`, a more general version, based on which `read.csv()` is implemented.

Importing data using the readr package

For historical reasons, `read.*` functions have some inconsistencies and are not very friendly in some situations. The `readr` package is a good choice to import tabular data in a fast and consistent manner.

To install the package, run `install.packages("readr")`. You can then use a family of `read_*` functions to import tabular data:

```
persons3 <- readr::read_csv("data/persons.csv")
str(persons3)
## Classes 'tbl_df', 'tbl' and 'data.frame': 3 obs. of 4 variables:
## $ Name : chr "Ken" "Ashley" "Jennifer"
## $ Gender: chr "Male" "Female" "Female"
## $ Age : int 24 25 23
## $ Major : chr "Finance" "Statistics" "Computer Science"
```

Here, we use `readr::read_csv` instead of `library(readr)` first and then directly call `read_csv` because it is easy to confuse `read_csv` with the built-in `read.csv` file since they have slightly different behaviors.

Also, note that the default behavior of `read_csv` is smart enough to handle most situations. To make a contrast with built-in functions, let's import a data file (`data/persons.txt`) in an irregular format:

```
Name     Gender Age Major
Ken      Male   24  Finance
Ashley   Female 25  Statistics
Jennifer Female 23  Computer Science
```

The file content looks quite standard and tabular, but the number of spaces between each column is unequal across rows, which fails to let `read.table()` work with `sep = " "`:

```
read.table("data/persons.txt", sep = " ")
## Error in scan(file, what, nmax, sep, dec, quote, skip, nlines,
na.strings, : line 1 did not have 20 elements
```

If you insist on using `read.table()` to import data, you may waste a lot of time trying to figure out the right argument to control the behavior. However, with the same input, the default behavior of `read_table` in `readr` is smart enough and thus helps you save time:

```
readr::read_table("data/persons.txt")
##     Name     Gender Age Major
## 1 Ken      Male   24  Finance
## 2 Ashley   Female 25  Statistics
## 3 Jennifer Female 23  Computer Science
```

That's why I strongly recommend that you use the functions in `readr` to import tabular data into R. The functions in `readr` are fast, smart, and consistent and support the features of the built-in functions which are much easier to use. To learn more about the `readr` package, visit `https://github.com/hadley/readr`.

Writing a data frame to a file

A typical procedure in data analysis is importing data from a data source, transforming the data, applying appropriate tools and models, and finally creating some new data to be stored for decision making. The interface for writing data to file is very similar to that for reading data—we use `write.*` functions to export a data frame to a file.

For example, we can create an arbitrary data frame and store it in a CSV file:

```
some_data <- data.frame(
id = 1:4,
grade = c("A", "A", "B", NA),
width = c(1.51, 1.52, 1.46, NA),
check_date = as.Date(c("2016-03-05", "2016-03-06", "2016-03-10",
```

```
  "2016-03-11")))
some_data
##   id grade width check_date
## 1 1    A   1.51  2016-03-05
## 2 2    A   1.52  2016-03-06
## 3 3    B   1.46  2016-03-10
## 4 4  <NA>   NA   2016-03-11
write.csv(some_data, "data/some_data.csv")
```

To check whether the CSV file correctly preserves the missing values and dates, we can read the output file in raw text:

```
cat(readLines("data/some_data.csv"), sep = "\n")
## "","id","grade","width","check_date"
## "1",1,"A",1.51,2016-03-05
## "2",2,"A",1.52,2016-03-06
## "3",3,"B",1.46,2016-03-10
## "4",4,NA,NA,2016-03-11
```

Although the data is correct, sometimes we may have different standards for storing such data. The `write.csv()` function allows us to modify the writing behavior. From the preceding output, we might think there are some unnecessary components in it. For example, we don't usually want the row names to be exported because they seem a bit redundant, since id already does its job. We don't need the quotation marks around string values. We want the missing values to be represented by – instead of NA. To proceed, we can run the following code to export the same data frame with the behavior and standard we want:

```
write.csv(some_data, "data/some_data.csv", quote =FALSE, na = "-",
row.names = FALSE)
```

Now, the output data is a simplified CSV file:

```
cat(readLines("data/some_data.csv"), sep = "\n")
## id,grade,width,check_date
## 1,A,1.51,2016-03-05
## 2,A,1.52,2016-03-06
## 3,B,1.46,2016-03-10
## 4,-,-,2016-03-11
```

We can use `readr::read_csv()` to import such a CSV file with customized missing values and a date column:

```
readr::read_csv("data/some_data.csv", na = "-")
##   id grade width check_date
## 1 1    A   1.51  2016-03-05
## 2 2    A   1.52  2016-03-06
```

```
## 3 3    B    1.46   2016-03-10
## 4 4  <NA>    NA    2016-03-11
```

Note that – are correctly translated to missing values and the date column is correctly imported as date objects too:

```
## [1] TRUE
```

Reading and writing Excel worksheets

An import advantage of text-format data such as CSV is software neutrality, that is, you don't have to rely on certain software to read the data and the file is directly readable by a human. However, its disadvantage is obvious too—we can't directly perform calculations on the data represented in a text editor because the contents are pure text.

Another popular format for storing tabular data is the Excel workbook. An Excel workbook contains one or more worksheets. Each worksheet is a grid where you can fill in texts and values to make tables. With the tables, you can easily perform calculations within a table, between tables, or even across worksheets. Microsoft Excel is a powerful software, but its data format (.xls for Excel 97-2003 and .xlsx since Excel 2007) is not directly readable.

For example, data/prices.xlsx is a simple Excel workbook as shown in the following screenshot:

⊿	A	B	C	D
1	Date	Price	Growth	
2	3/1/2016	85	#N/A	
3	3/2/2016	88	3.5%	
4	3/3/2016	84	-4.5%	
5	3/4/2016	81	-3.6%	
6	3/5/2016	83	2.5%	
7	3/6/2016	87	4.8%	
8				

Although no built-in function is provided to read an Excel workbook, several R packages are designed to work with it. The simplest one is readxl (https://github.com/hadley/readxl), which makes it much easier to extract the table stored in a single sheet of an Excel workbook. To install the package from CRAN, use install.package("readxl"):

```
readxl::read_excel("data/prices.xlsx")
##    Date       Price Growth
## 1 2016-03-01  85    NA
## 2 2016-03-02  88    0.03529412
```

```
## 3 2016-03-03  84   -0.04545455
## 4 2016-03-04  81   -0.03571429
## 5 2016-03-05  83    0.02469136
## 6 2016-03-06  87    0.04819277
```

From the preceding data frame, it is obvious that `read_excel()` automatically translates the dates in Excel to dates in R and correctly preserves the missing value in the `Growth` column.

Another package for working with an Excel workbook is `openxlsx`. This package can read, write, and edit XLSX files, which is more comprehensive than what `readr` is designed for. To install the package, run `install.package("openxlsx")`.

With `openxlsx`, we can call `read.xlsx` to read data from a specified workbook into a data frame, just like `readr::read_excel()`:

```
openxlsx::read.xlsx("data/prices.xlsx", detectDates = TRUE)
##    Date      Price Growth
## 1 2016-03-01  85   NA
## 2 2016-03-02  88    0.03529412
## 3 2016-03-03  84   -0.04545455
## 4 2016-03-04  81   -0.03571429
## 5 2016-03-05  83    0.02469136
## 6 2016-03-06  87    0.04819277
```

To ensure that the date values are correctly imported, we need to specify `detectDates = TRUE`; otherwise, the dates will be left as numbers as you may try. In addition to reading data, `openxlsx` is also able to create a workbook with an existing data frame:

```
openxlsx::write.xlsx(mtcars, "data/mtcars.xlsx")
```

The package supports more advanced features such as editing an existing workbook by creating styles and inserting plots, but these features are beyond the scope of this book. For more details, please read the documentation of the package.

There are other packages designed for working with Excel workbooks. XLConnect (http://cran.r-project.org/web/packages/XLConnect) is another Excel connector which is cross-platform and does not depend on an existing installation of Microsoft Excel, but it does rely on an existing installation of Java Runtime Environment (JRE). RODBC (http://cran.r-project.org/web/packages/RODBC) is a more general database connector that is able to connect to Access databases and Excel workbooks with properly installed ODBC drivers on Windows. Since these two packages have heavier dependencies, we won't introduce them in this session.

Reading and writing native data files

In the previous sections, we introduced the reader and writer functions of CSV files and Excel workbooks. These are non-native data formats to R, that is, there is a gap between the original data object and the output file.

For example, if we export a data frame with many columns of different types to a CSV file, the information on the column types is discarded. Whether the column is numeric, string, or date, it is always represented in text format This certainly makes it easier for a human to read the data directly from the output file, but we will have to rely on how a computer would guess the type of each column. In other words, it is sometimes hard for the reader functions to recover the data in CSV format to exactly the same data frame as the original one, since the writing process throws the column types away in exchange for portability (for example, other software can read the data too).

If you do not care for portability and only use R to work with the data, you can use the native formats to read and write data. You can no longer uses an arbitrary text editor to read the data, nor can you read the data from other software, but it is easy to write and read a single object or even the whole environment with high efficiency and no data losses. In other words, the native format allows you to save objects in file and recover exactly the same data without worrying about issues like the symbols of missing values and the types, classes and attributes of columns.

Reading and writing a single object in native format

There are two groups of functions related to working with the native data format. One group is designed to write a single object to an RDS file or read a single object from an RDS file, a file format to store a single R object in serialized form. The other group works with multiple R objects, which we will cover in the next section. In the following example, we write `some_data` to an RDS file and read it from the same file and see whether two data frames are exactly identical.

First, we use `saveRDS` to save `some_data` to `data/some_data.rds`:

```
saveRDS(some_data, "data/some_data.rds")
```

Then we read the data from the same file and store the data frame in `some_data2`:

```
some_data2 <- readRDS("data/some_data.rds")
```

Finally, we use `identical()` to test whether two data frames are exactly the same:

```
identical(some_data, some_data2)
## [1] TRUE
```

The two data frames are exactly the same, as supposed.

The native format has two notable advantages: space efficiency and time efficiency. In the following example, we will create a large data frame with 200,000 rows of random data. Then, we time the process for saving the data frame to a CSV file and an RDS file, respectively:

```
rows <- 200000
large_data <- data.frame(id = 1:rows, x = rnorm(rows), y = rnorm(rows))
system.time(write.csv(large_data, "data/large_data.csv"))
## user system elapsed
## 1.33 0.06 1.41
system.time(saveRDS(large_data, "data/large_data.rds"))
## user system elapsed
## 0.23 0.03 0.26
```

It is obvious that `saveRDS` has much higher writing efficiency than `write.csv`.

Then we use `file.info()` to see the size of the two output files:

```
fileinfo <- file.info("data/large_data.csv", "data/large_data.rds")
fileinfo[, "size", drop = FALSE]
## size
## data/large_data.csv 10442030
## data/large_data.rds 3498284
```

The gap between the two file sizes is large—the size of the CSV file is almost three times that of the RDS file, indicating that the native format has higher storage or space efficiency.

Finally, we read the CSV and RDS files and see how much time both formats consume. To read the CSV file, we use both the built-in function `read.csv` and the faster implementation, `read_csv()`, provided by the `readr` package:

```
system.time(read.csv("data/large_data.csv"))
## user system elapsed
## 1.46 0.07 1.53
system.time(readr::read_csv("data/large_data.csv"))
## user system elapsed
## 0.17 0.01 0.19
```

It may be surprising to see that `read_csv()` is almost four times faster than the built-in `read.csv()` in this case. But with the native format, the performance of both CSV reader functions is not comparable:

```
system.time(readRDS("data/large_data.rds"))
## user system elapsed
## 0.03 0.00 0.03
```

The native format clearly has much higher writing efficiency.

In addition, `saveRDS` and `readRDS` work not only with data frames but also with any R object. For example, we create a numeric vector with a missing value and a list with a nested structure. Then, we save them in separate RDS files:

```
nums <- c(1.5, 2.5, NA, 3)
list1 <- list(x = c(1, 2, 3),
    y = list(a =c("a", "b"),
    b = c(NA, 1, 2.5)))
saveRDS(nums, "data/nums.rds")
saveRDS(list1, "data/list1.rds")
```

Now we read the RDS files, and these two objects are exactly recovered, respectively:

```
readRDS("data/nums.rds")
## [1] 1.5 2.5 NA 3.0
readRDS("data/list1.rds")
## $x
## [1] 1 2 3
##
## $y
## $y$a
## [1] "a" "b"
##
## $y$b
## [1] NA 1.0 2.5
```

Saving and restoring the working environment

While the RDS format is used to store a single R object, the RData format is used to store multiple R objects. We can call `save()` to store `some_data`, `nums`, and `list1` together in a single RData file:

```
save(some_data, nums, list1, file = "data/bundle1.RData")
```

To verify that the three objects are stored and can be recovered, we remove them first and call `load()` to recover the objects from the file:

```
rm(some_data, nums, list1)
load("data/bundle1.RData")
```

Now, the three objects are fully recovered:

```
some_data
##   id grade width check_date
## 1 1    A    1.51 2016-03-05
## 2 2    A    1.52 2016-03-06
## 3 3    B    1.46 2016-03-10
## 4 4 <NA>    NA   2016-03-11
nums
## [1] 1.5 2.5 NA 3.0
list1
## $x
## [1] 1 2 3
##
## $y
## $y$a
## [1] "a" "b"
##
## $y$b
## [1] NA 1.0 2.5
## [1] TRUE TRUE TRUE TRUE TRUE TRUE
```

Loading built-in datasets

In R, there are already a great number of built-in datasets. They can be easily loaded and put into use, mostly for demonstration and test purposes. The built-in datasets are mostly data frames and come with detailed specifications.

For example, iris and mtcars are probably among the most famous datasets in R. You can read the description of the datasets with ? iris and ? mtcars, respectively. Typically, the description is quite specific—it not only tells you what is in the data, how was it collected and formatted, and what each column means, but it also provides related sources and references. Reading the description helps you know more about the dataset.

It is extremely handy to conduct experiments on data analysis tools with built-in datasets because these datasets are immediately available once R is ready. For example, you can directly use iris and mtcars without explicitly loading them from somewhere.

The following is the view of the first six rows of iris:

```
head(iris)
##   Sepal.Length Sepal.Width Petal.Length Petal.Width Species
## 1     5.1         3.5          1.4         0.2       setosa
## 2     4.9         3.0          1.4         0.2       setosa
## 3     4.7         3.2          1.3         0.2       setosa
## 4     4.6         3.1          1.5         0.2       setosa
## 5     5.0         3.6          1.4         0.2       setosa
## 6     5.4         3.9          1.7         0.4       setosa
```

The following code shows its structure:

```
str(iris)
## 'data.frame': 150 obs. of 5 variables:
## $ Sepal.Length: num 5.1 4.9 4.7 4.6 5 5.4 4.6 5 4.4 4.9 ...
## $ Sepal.Width : num 3.5 3 3.2 3.1 3.6 3.9 3.4 3.4 2.9 3.1 ...
## $ Petal.Length: num 1.4 1.4 1.3 1.5 1.4 1.7 1.4 1.5 1.4 1.5 ...
## $ Petal.Width : num 0.2 0.2 0.2 0.2 0.2 0.4 0.3 0.2 0.2 0.1 ...
## $ Species : Factor w/ 3 levels "setosa","versicolor",..: 1 1 1 1 1 1 1 1
## 1 1 ...
```

The structure of iris is straightforward. You can either print iris to see the whole data frame in the console or use View(iris) in a grid pane or window.

To view the first six rows of mtcars and see its structure:

```
head(mtcars)
##                    mpg cyl disp  hp drat    wt  qsec vs am
## Mazda RX4         21.0   6  160 110 3.90 2.620 16.46  0  1
## Mazda RX4 Wag     21.0   6  160 110 3.90 2.875 17.02  0  1
## Datsun 710        22.8   4  108  93 3.85 2.320 18.61  1  1
## Hornet 4 Drive    21.4   6  258 110 3.08 3.215 19.44  1  0
## Hornet Sportabout 18.7   8  360 175 3.15 3.440 17.02  0  0
## Valiant           18.1   6  225 105 2.76 3.460 20.22  1  0
##                   gear carb
## Mazda RX4            4    4
## Mazda RX4 Wag        4    4
## Datsun 710           4    1
## Hornet 4 Drive       3    1
## Hornet Sportabout    3    2
## Valiant              3    1
str(mtcars)
## 'data.frame':    32 obs. of  11 variables:
## $ mpg : num  21 21 22.8 21.4 18.7 18.1 14.3 24.4 22.8 19.2 ...
## $ cyl : num  6 6 4 6 8 6 8 4 4 6 ...
## $ disp: num  160 160 108 258 360 ...
## $ hp  : num  110 110 93 110 175 105 245 62 95 123 ...
```

```
##  $ drat: num  3.9 3.9 3.85 3.08 3.15 2.76 3.21 3.69 3.92 3.92 ...
##  $ wt  : num  2.62 2.88 2.32 3.21 3.44 ...
##  $ qsec: num  16.5 17 18.6 19.4 17 ...
##  $ vs  : num  0 0 1 1 0 1 0 1 1 1 ...
##  $ am  : num  1 1 1 0 0 0 0 0 0 0 ...
##  $ gear: num  4 4 4 3 3 3 3 4 4 4 ...
##  $ carb: num  4 4 1 1 2 1 4 2 2 4 ...
```

As you can see, iris and mtcars are small and simple. In fact, most built-in datasets only have tens or hundreds of rows and a few columns. They are often used to demonstrate the usage of particular data analysis tools.

If you want to experiment with larger data, you may turn to some R packages that come along with datasets. For example, the most famous data visualization package, ggplot2, provides a dataset called diamonds, which contains the prices and other attributes of a large number of diamonds. Use?ggplot2::diamonds to know more about the data specification. If you don't have the package installed, run install.package("ggplot2").

To load the data in the package, we can use data():

```
data("diamonds", package = "ggplot2")
dim(diamonds)
## [1] 53940 10
```

The output shows that diamonds has 53940 rows and 10 columns. Here is a preview:

```
head(diamonds)
##    carat       cut color clarity depth table price    x    y
## 1   0.23     Ideal     E     SI2  61.5    55   326 3.95 3.98
## 2   0.21   Premium     E     SI1  59.8    61   326 3.89 3.84
## 3   0.23      Good     E     VS1  56.9    65   327 4.05 4.07
## 4   0.29   Premium     I     VS2  62.4    58   334 4.20 4.23
## 5   0.31      Good     J     SI2  63.3    58   335 4.34 4.35
## 6   0.24 Very Good     J    VVS2  62.8    57   336 3.94 3.96
##       z
## 1  2.43
## 2  2.31
## 3  2.31
## 4  2.63
## 5  2.75
## 6  2.48
```

Besides packages that provide useful functions, there are also packages that only provide datasets. For example, nycflights13 and babynames each only contains several datasets. The method to load the data in them is exactly the same as the previous example. To install the two packages, run `install.package(c("nycflights13", "babynames"))`.

In the next few sections, we will use these datasets to demonstrate basic graphic tools and data analysis tools.

Visualizing data

In the previous section, we introduced a number of functions to import data, the first step in most data analysis. It is usually a good practice to look at the data before pouring it into a model, so that is what we will do in the next step. The reason is simple—different models have different strengths, and no model is universally the best choice for all cases since they have a different set of assumptions. Arbitrarily applying a model without checking the data against its assumptions usually results in misleading conclusions.

An initial way to choose a model and perform such checks is to just visually examine the data by looking at its boundaries and patterns. In other words, we need to visualize the data first. In this section, you will learn the basic graphic functions to produce simple charts to visualize a given dataset.

We will use the datasets in the `nycflights13` and `babynames` packages. If you don't have them installed, run the following code:

```
install.package(c("nycflights13", "babynames"))
```

Creating scatter plots

In R, the basic function to visualize data is `plot()`. If we simply provide a numeric or integer vector to `plot()`, it will produce a scatter plot of value by index. For example, the following code creates a scatter plot of 10 points in the increasing order:

```
plot(1:10)
```

The plot generated is as follows:

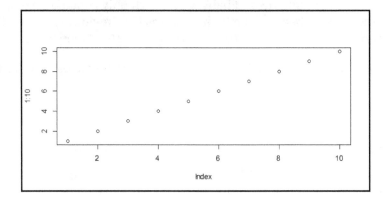

We can create a more realistic scatter plot by generating two linearly correlated random numeric vectors:

```
x <- rnorm(100)
y <- 2 * x + rnorm(100)
plot(x, y)
```

The plot generated is as follows:

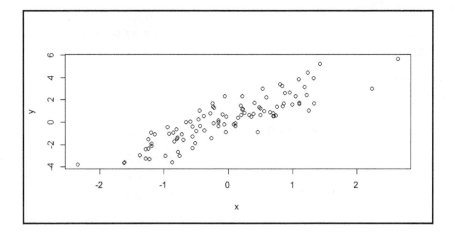

Customizing chart elements

In a plot, there are numerous chart elements that can be customized. The most common elements to be specified are the title (main or `title()`), the label of the *x* axis (`xlab`), the label of the *y* axis (`ylab`), the range of the *x* axis (`xlim`), and the range of the *y* axis (`ylim`):

```
plot(x, y,
  main = "Linearly correlated random numbers",
  xlab = "x", ylab = "2x + noise",
  xlim = c(-4, 4), ylim = c(-4, 4))
```

The plot generated is as follows:

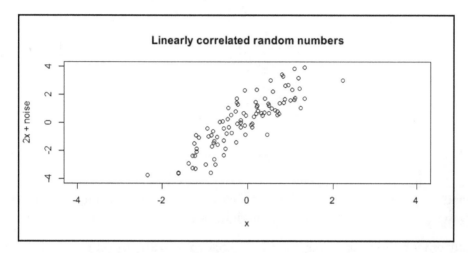

The chart title can be specified by either the main argument or a separate `title()` function call. Therefore, the preceding code is equivalent to the following code:

```
plot(x, y,
  xlim = c(-4, 4), ylim = c(-4, 4),
  xlab = "x", ylab = "2x + noise")
title("Linearly correlated random numbers")
```

Customizing point styles

The default point style of a scatter plot is a circle. By specifying the `pch` argument (plotting character), we can change the point style. There are 26 point styles available:

```
plot(:25, :25, pch = :25,
  xlim = c(-1, 26), ylim = c(-1, 26),
  main = "Point styles (pch)")
```

```
text(:25+1, :25, :25)
```

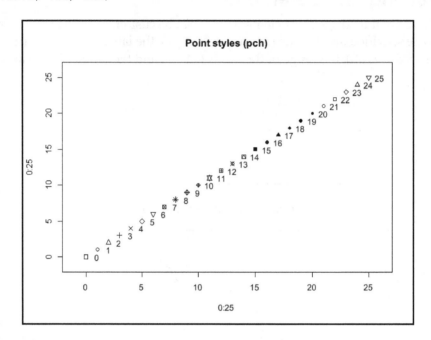

The preceding code produces a scatter plot of all point styles available with the corresponding pch numbers printed beside. First, plot() creates a simple scatter plot, and then text() prints the pch numbers on the right side of each point.

Like many other built-in functions, plot() is vectorized with respect to pch and several other arguments. It makes it possible to customize the style of each point in the scatter plot. For example, the simplest case is that we use only one non-default point style for all points by setting pch = 16:

```
x <- rnorm(100)
y <- 2 * x + rnorm(100)
plot(x, y, pch = 16,
   main = "Scatter plot with customized point style")
```

The plot generated is as follows:

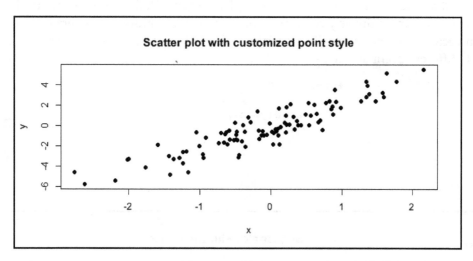

Sometimes, we need to distinguish two groups of points by a logical condition. Knowing that pch is vectorized, we can use ifelse() to specify the point style of each observation by examining whether a point satisfies the condition. In the following example, we want to apply pch = 16 to the points satisfying x * y > 1 otherwise, pch = 1:

```
plot(x, y,
   pch = ifelse(x * y > 1, 16, 1),
   main = "Scatter plot with conditional point styles")
```

The plot generated is as follows:

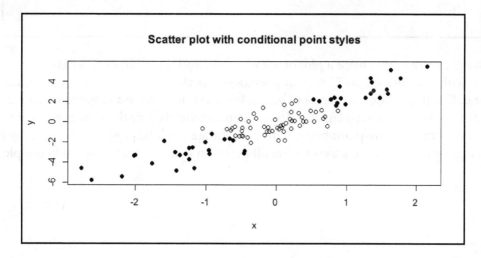

We can also draw the points in two separate datasets that share the same x axis using `plot()` and `points()`. In the previous example, we generated a normally distributed random vector x and a linearly correlated random vector y. Now, we generate another random vector z that has a non-linear relationship with x and plot both y and z against x but with different point styles:

```
z <- sqrt(1 + x ^ 2) + rnorm(100)
plot(x, y, pch = 1,
   xlim = range(x), ylim = range(y, z),
   xlab = "x", ylab = "value")
points(x, z, pch = 17)
title("Scatter plot with two series")
```

The plot generated is as follows:

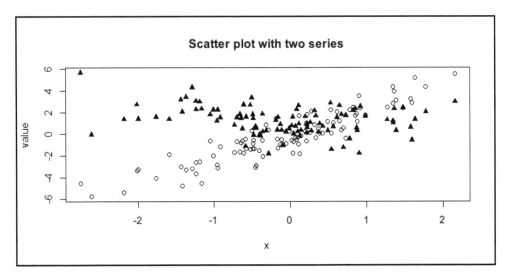

After we generate z, we create a plot of x and y first, and then add another group of points z with a different `pch`. Note that if we don't specify `ylim = range(y, z)`, the plot builder will only consider the range of y, and the y axis may have a range narrower than the range of z. Unfortunately, `points()` does not automatically lengthen the axes created by `plot()`, therefore any point beyond the axes' range will disappear. The preceding code sets an appropriate range of y axis so that all points in y and z can be shown in the plot area.

Customizing point colors

If the graphics are not limited to gray-scale printing, we may also use different point colors by setting the column of `plot()`:

```
plot(x, y, pch = 16, col = "blue",
   main = "Scatter plot with blue points")
```

The plot generated is as follows:

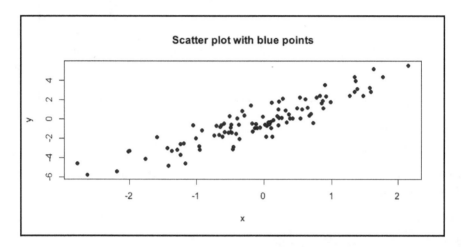

Like `pch`, `col` is also a vectorized argument. With the same method, we can apply different colors to separate points into two different categories depending on whether they satisfy a certain condition:

```
plot(x, y, pch = 16,
   col = ifelse(y >= mean(y), "red", "green"),
   main = "Scatter plot with conditional colors")
```

The plot generated is as follows:

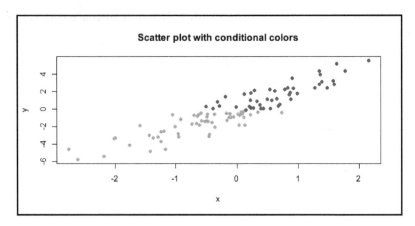

Note that if the scatter plot is printed grayscale, the colors can only be viewed as different intensities of grayness.

Also, we can use `plot()` and `points()` again, but with different `col`to distinguish different groups of points:

```
plot(x, y, col = "blue", pch = ,
   xlim = range(x), ylim = range(y, z),
   xlab = "x", ylab = "value")
points(x, z, col = "red", pch = 1)
title("Scatter plot with two series")
```

The plot generated is as follows:

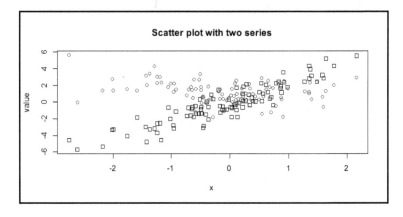

R supports commonly used color names and many others (657 in total). Call `colors()` to get a full list of colors supported by R.

Creating line plots

For time series data, line plots are more useful to demonstrate the trend and variation across time. To create line plots, we only need to set `type = "l"` when calling `plot()`:

```
t <- 1:50
y <- 3 * sin(t * pi / 60) + rnorm(t)
plot(t, y, type = "l",
  main = "Simple line plot")
```

The plot generated is as follows:

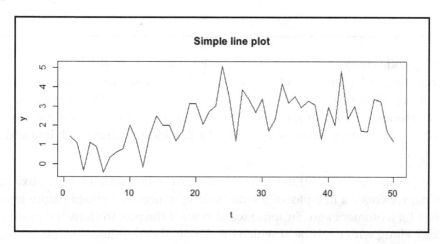

Customizing line type and width

Just like `pch` for scatter plot, `lty` is used to specify the line type of a line plot. The following shows a preview of six line types supported by R:

```
lty_values <- 1:6
plot(lty_values, type = "n", axes = FALSE, ann = FALSE)
abline(h =lty_values, lty = lty_values, lwd = 2)
mtext(lty_values, side = 2, at = lty_values)
title("Line types (lty)")
```

The plot generated is as follows:

The preceding code creates an empty canvas with `type = "n"` with proper axes ranges and turns off axes, and another label `elements.abline()` is used to draw the horizontal lines with different line types but of equal line width (`lwd = 2`). The `mtext()` function is used to draw the text on the margin. Note that `abline()` and `mtext()` are vectorized with respect to their arguments so that we don't need a `for` loop to draw each line and margin text in turn.

The following example demonstrates how `abline()` can be useful to draw auxiliary lines in a plot. First, we create a line plot of `y` with time, `t`, which we defined before we created the first line plot a moment ago. Suppose we also want the plot to show the mean value and the range of `y` along with the time at which the maximal and minimal values appear. With `abline()`, we can easily draw these auxiliary lines with different line types and colors to avoid ambiguity:

```
plot(t, y, type = "l", lwd = 2)
abline(h = mean(y), lty = 2, col = "blue")
abline(h = range(y), lty = 3, col = "red")
abline(v = t[c(which.min(y), which.max(y))], lty = 3, col = "darkgray")
title("Line plot with auxiliary lines")
```

The plot generated is as follows:

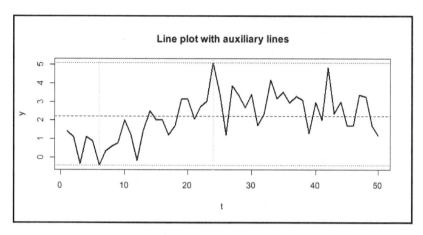

Plotting lines in multiple periods

Another kind of line plot in which different line types are mixed is a multi-period line plot.
A typical form is that the first period is historic data and the second period is predictions.
Suppose the first period of y includes the first 40 observations and the remaining points are
predictions based on the historic data. We want to use solid lines to represent the historic
data and dashed lines for the predictions. Here, we plot the data in the first period and add
dashed `lines()` for the data in the second period of the plot. Note that `lines()` is to a line
plot as `points()` is to a scatter plot:

```
p <- 40
plot(t[t <= p], y[t <= p], type = "l",
  xlim = range(t), xlab = "t")
lines(t[t >= p], y[t >= p], lty = 2)
title("Simple line plot with two periods")
```

The plot generated is as follows:

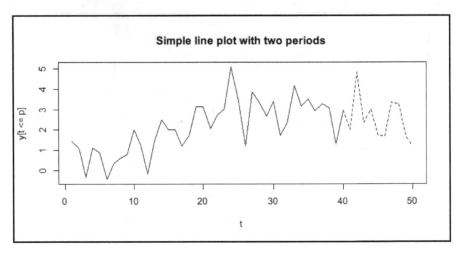

Plotting lines with points

Sometimes, it is useful to plot both lines and points in the same chart to emphasize that the observations are discrete or simply make the chart clearer. The method is simple, just plot a line chart and add `points()` of the same data to the plot again:

```
plot(y, type = "l")
points(y, pch = 16)
title("Lines with points")
```

The plot generated is shown as follows:

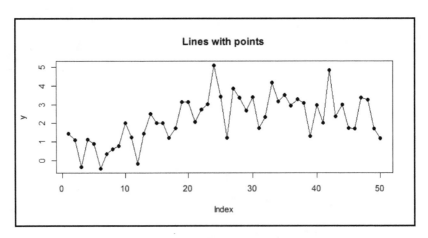

An equivalent way to do this is to plot a scatter chart first using the `plot()` function and then add lines using the `lines()` function of the same data to the plot again. Therefore, the following code should produce exactly the same graphics as the previous example:

```
plot(y, pch = 16)
lines(y)
title("Lines with points")
```

Plotting a multi-series chart with a legend

The full version of a multi-series chart should include multiple series represented by lines and points, and a legend to illustrate the series in the chart.

The following code randomly generates two series, y and z, with time, x, and creates a chart with these put together:

```
x <- 1:30
y <- 2 * x + 6 * rnorm(30)
z <- 3 * sqrt(x) + 8 * rnorm(30)
plot(x, y, type = "l",
   ylim = range(y, z), col = "black")
points(y, pch = 15)
lines(z, lty = 2, col = "blue")
points(z, pch = 16, col = "blue")
title ("Plot of two series")
legend("topleft",
   legend = c("y", "z"),
   col = c("black", "blue"),
   lty = c(1, 2), pch = c(15, 16),
   cex = 0.8, x.intersp = 0.5, y.intersp = 0.8)
```

The plot generated is as follows:

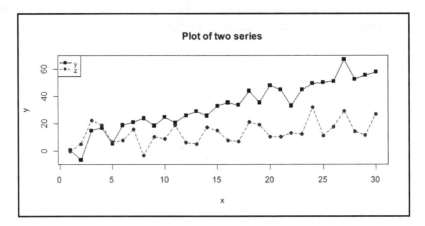

The preceding code uses plot() to create the line-point chart of y and adds the lines() and points() of z. In the end, we add a legend() on the top left to demonstrate the line and point styles of y and z, respectively. Note that cex is used to scale the font sizes of the legend and x.intersp and y.intersp are used for minor adjustments to the legend.

Another useful type of line plot is step-lines. We use type = "s" in plot() and lines() to create a step-line plot:

```
plot(x, y, type = "s",
    main = "A simple step plot")
```

The plot generated is as follows:

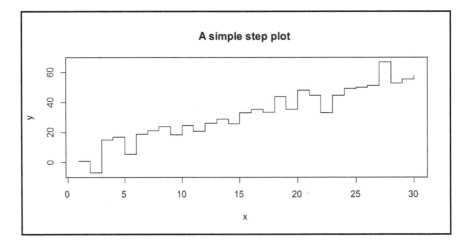

Creating bar charts

In the previous sections, you learned how to create scatter plots and line plots. There are several other types of charts that are useful and worth mentioning. Bar charts are among the most commonly used ones. The height of bars in a bar chart can make a constrast quantitatively between different categories.

The simplest bar chart we can create is the following one. Here, we use `barplot()` instead of `plot()`:

```
barplot(1:10, names.arg = LETTERS[1:10])
```

The plot generated is as follows:

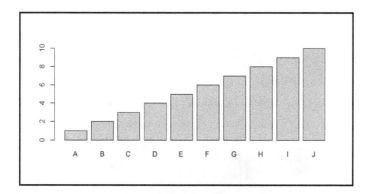

If the numeric vector has names, the names will automatically be the names on the *x* axis. Therefore, the following code will produce exactly the same bar chart as the previous one:

```
ints <- 1:10
names(ints) <- LETTERS[1:10]
barplot(ints)
```

The making of a bar chart looks so easy. Now that we have the flights dataset in `nycflights13`, we can create a bar plot of the top eight carriers with the most flights in the record:

```
data("flights", package = "nycflights13")
carriers <- table(flights$carrier)
carriers
##
##     9E     AA     AS     B6     DL     EV     F9     FL     HA     MQ
## 18460 32729    714  54635  48110  54173    685   3260    342  26397
##     OO     UA     US     VX     WN     YV
##     32  58665  20536   5162  12275    601
```

In the preceding code, `table()` is used to count the number of flights in the record for each carrier:

```
sorted_carriers <- sort(carriers, decreasing = TRUE)
sorted_carriers
##
##    UA    B6    EV    DL    AA    MQ    US    9E    WN    VX
## 58665 54635 54173 48110 32729 26397 20536 18460 12275  5162
##    FL    AS    F9    YV    HA    OO
##  3260   714   685   601   342    32
```

As shown in the preceding code, the carriers are sorted in descending order. We can take the first 8 elements out of the table and make a bar plot:

```
barplot(head(sorted_carriers, 8),
    ylim = c(, max(sorted_carriers) * 1.1),
    xlab = "Carrier", ylab = "Flights",
    main ="Top 8 carriers with the most flights in record")
```

The plot generated is as follows:

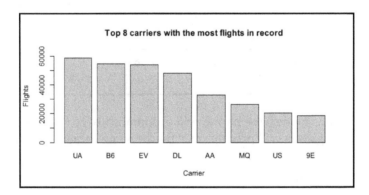

Creating pie charts

Another useful chart is the pie chart. The function to create a pie chart, `pie()`, works in a way similar to `barplot()`. It works with a numeric vector with labels specified; it also works directly with a named numeric vector. The following code is a simple example:

```
grades <- c(A = 2, B = 10, C = 12, D = 8)
pie(grades, main = "Grades", radius = 1)
```

The plot generated is as follows:

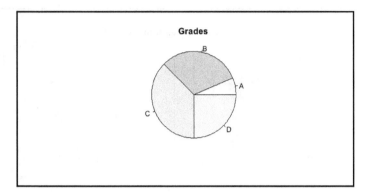

Creating histogram and density plots

Previously, you learned how to create several different types of charts. Scatter plots and line plots are direct illustrations of the observations in a dataset. Bar charts and pie charts are usually used to show a rough summary of data points in different categories.

They are two limitations to plots: scatter plots and line plots convey too much information and are difficult to draw insights from, while bar charts and pie charts drop too much information, so with these too it can be difficult to make a conclusive judgement with confidence.

A histogram shows the distribution of a numeric vector, and it summarizes the information in the data without dropping too much and thus can be easier to make use of. The following example demonstrates how to use hist () to produce a histogram of a normally distributed random numeric vector and the density function of normal distribution:

```
random_normal <- norm(10000)
hist(random_normal)
```

The plot generated is as follows:

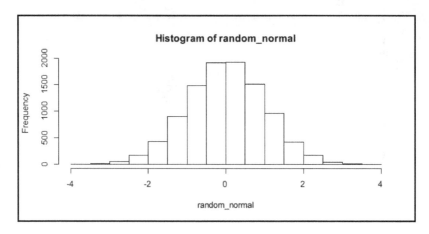

By default, the *y* axis of a histogram is the frequency of the value in the data. We can verify that the histogram is quite close to the standard normal distribution from which `random_normal` was generated. To overlay the curve of a probability density function of the standard normal distribution, `dnorm()`, we need to ensure that the *y* axis of the histogram is a probability and the curve is to be added to the histogram:

```
hist(random_normal, probability = TRUE, col = "lightgray")
curve(dnorm, add = TRUE, lwd = 2, col ="blue")
```

The plot generated is as follows:

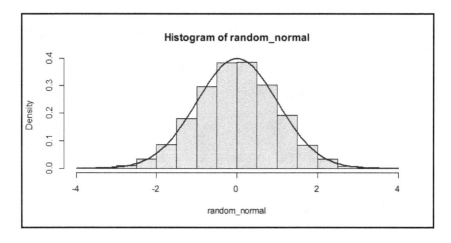

Now, let's make a histogram of the speed of an aircraft in flight. Basically, the average speed of an aircraft in a trip is the distance of the trip (`distance`) divided by the air time (`air_time`):

```
flight_speed <- flights$distance / flights$air_time
hist(flight_speed, main = "Histogram of flight speed")
```

The plot generated is as follows:

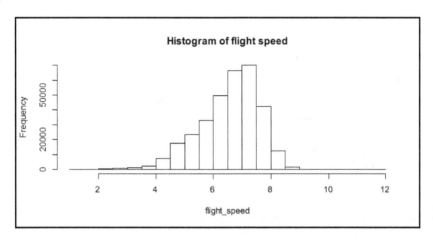

The histogram seems a bit different from a normal distribution. In this case, we use `density()` to estimate an empirical distribution of the speed, plot a pretty smooth probability distribution curve out of it, and add a vertical line to indicate the global average of all observations:

```
plot(density(flight_speed, from = 2, na.rm = TRUE),
   main ="Empirical distribution of flight speed")
abline(v = mean(flight_speed, na.rm = TRUE),
   col = "blue", lty = 2)
```

The plot generated is as follows:

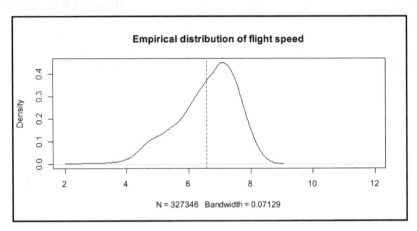

Just like the first histogram and curve example, we can combine the two graphics together to get a better view of the data:

```
hist(flight_speed,
    probability = TRUE, ylim = c(, 0.5),
    main ="Histogram and empirical distribution of flight speed",
    border ="gray", col = "lightgray")
lines(density(flight_speed, from = 2, na.rm = TRUE),
    col ="darkgray", lwd = 2)
abline(v = mean(flight_speed, na.rm = TRUE),
    col ="blue", lty =2)
```

The plot generated is as follows:

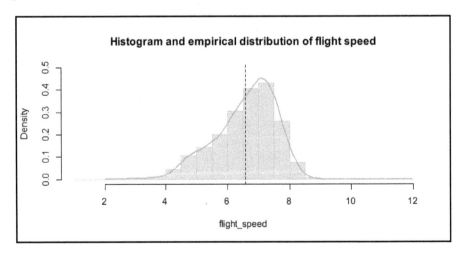

Creating box plots

Histograms and density plots are two ways to demonstrate the distribution of data. Usually, we only need several critical quantiles to get an impression of the whole distribution. The box plot (or box-and-whisker plot) is a simple way to do this. For a randomly generated numeric vector, we can call boxplot() to draw a box plot:

```
x <- rnorm(1000)
boxplot(x)
```

The plot generated is as follows:

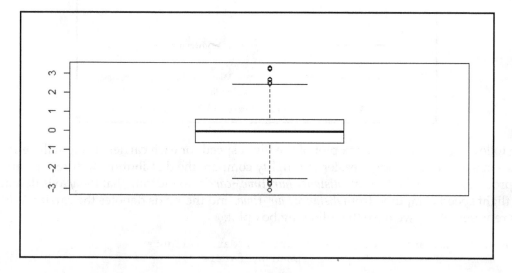

A box plot contains several components to show critical quartile levels of data as well as outliers. The following image clearly explains what a box plot means:

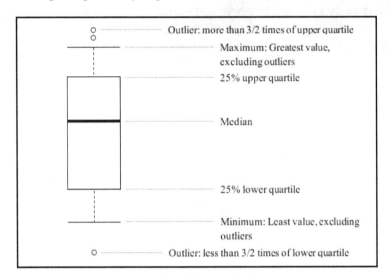

The following code draws a box plot of the flight speed for each carrier. There will be 16 boxes in one chart, making it easier to roughly compare the distribution of different carriers. To proceed, we use the formula *distance /air_time ~carrier* to indicate that the *y* axis denotes the flight speed computed from *distance / air_time*, and the *x* axis denotes the carrier. With this representation, we have the following box plot:

```
boxplot(distance / air_time ~ carrier, data =flights,
    main = "Box plot of flight speed by carrier")
```

The plot generated is as follows:

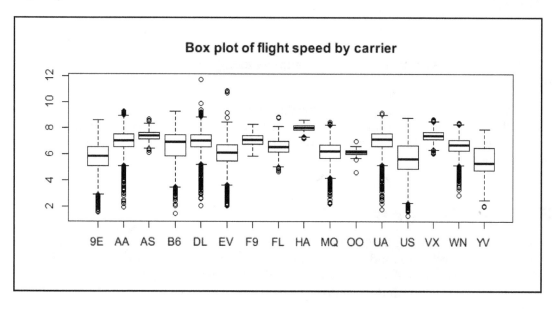

Note that we use the formula interface of creating graphics in boxplot(). Here, *distance / air_time ~ carrier* basically means the *y* axis should represent the values of *distance / air_time*, that is, flight speed, and the *x* axis should represent different carriers. *data = flights* tells *boxplot()* where to find the symbols in the formula we specify. As a result, the box plot of flight speed is created and grouped by carrier.

The formula interface of visualizing and analyzing data is very expressive and powerful. In the next section, we will introduce some basic tools and models to analyze data. Behind the functions that implement these tools and models are not only algorithms but also a user-friendly interface (formula) to make it easier to specify relationships for the model to fit.

There are also other packages that are specially tailored for data visualization. One great example is ggplot2, which implements a very powerful grammar of graphics to create, compose, and customize different types of charts. However, it is beyond the scope of this book. To know more, I recommend that you read *ggplot2: Elegant Graphics for Data Analysis* by Hadley Wickham.

Analyzing data

In practical data analysis, most time is spent on data cleansing, that is, to filter and transform the original data (or raw data) to a form that is easier to analyze. The filtering and transforming process is also called data manipulation. We will dedicate an entire chapter to this topic.

In this section, we directly assume that the data is ready for analysis. We won't go deep into the models, but will apply some simple models to leave you an impression of how to fit a model with data, how to interact with fitted models, and how to apply a fitted model to make predictions.

Fitting a linear model

The simplest model in R is the linear model, that is, we use a linear function to describe the relationship between two random variables under a certain set of assumptions. In the following example, we will create a linear function that maps x to $3 + 2 * x$. Then we generate a normally-distributed random numeric vector x, and generate y by `f(x)` plus some independent noise:

```
f <- function(x) 3 + 2 * x
x <- rnorm(100)
y <- f(x) + 0.5 * rnorm(100)
```

If we pretend not to know how y is generated by x, can we use a linear model to recover their relationship, that is, to recover the coefficient of the linear function? The following code uses `slm()` to fit x and y with a linear model. Note that a formula $y \sim x$ is an accessible representation to tell `m()` that the linear regression is between the dependent variable y and a single regressor x:

```
model1 <- lm(y ~ x)
model1
##
## Call:
## lm(formula = y ~ x)
##
## Coefficients:
## (Intercept)  x
##    2.969    1.972
```

The true coefficients are 3 (intercept) and 2 (slope), and with the sample data x and y, the fitted model has coefficients `2.9692146` (intercept) and `1.9716588` (slope), which are quite close to the true coefficients.

We store the model in `model1`. To access the coefficients of the model, we can use the following code:

```
coef(model1)
## (Intercept)    x
##   2.969215   1.971659
```

Alternatively, we can use the `model1$` coefficients, since `model1` is essentially a list.

Then, we can call `summary()` to know more about the statistical properties of the linear model:

```
summary(model1)
##
## Call:
## lm(formula = y ~ x)
##
## Residuals:
##       Min       1Q   Median       3Q      Max
## -0.96258 -0.31646 -0.04893  0.34962  1.08491
##
## Coefficients:
##               Estimate Std. Error t value Pr(>|t|)
## (Intercept)   2.96921    0.04782    62.1   <2e-16 ***
## x             1.97166    0.05216    37.8   <2e-16 ***
## ---
## Signif. codes:
## 0 '***' 0.001 '**' 0.01 '*' 0.05 '.' 0.1 ' ' 1
##
## Residual standard error: 0.476 on 98 degrees of freedom
## Multiple R-squared:  0.9358, Adjusted R-squared:  0.9352
## F-statistic:  1429 on 1 and 98 DF,  p-value: < 2.2e-16
```

To interpret the summary, you had better review the chapter on linear regression in one or two textbooks of statistics. The following plot puts the data and the fitted model together:

```
plot(x, y, main = "A simple linear regression")
abline(coef(model1), col = "blue")
```

The plot generated is shown as follows:

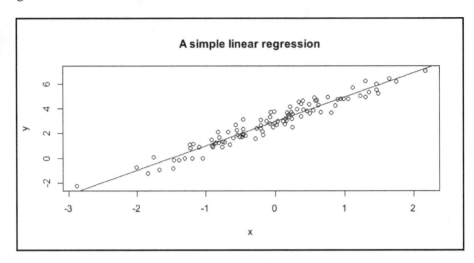

In the preceding code, we directly supply a two-element numeric vector of estimated regression coefficients to abline(), so it smartly draws the regression line as supposed.

Then, we can call predict() to use the fitted model to make predictions. To predict y with standard errors when x = -1 and x = 0.5, run the following code:

```
predict(model1, list(x = c(-1, 0.5)), se.fit = TRUE)
## $fit
## 1          2
## 0.9975559 3.9550440
##
## $se.fit
## 1          2
## 0.06730363 0.05661319
##
## $df
## [1] 98
##
## $residual.scale
## [1] 0.4759621
```

The prediction result is a list of predicted values of y ($fit), the standard errors of the fitted values ($se.fit), the degree of freedom ($df), and $residual.scale.

Now that you know the basics of how to fit a linear model given some data, it is time to look at some real-world data. In the following examples, we try to predict the air time of a flight using linear models of different complexity. The most obvious variable that should be helpful to predict air time is distance.

First, we load the dataset and make a scatter plot of distance and `air_time`. We use `pch = "."` to make each point very small, since the number of records in the dataset is large:

```
data("flights", package = "nycflights13")
plot(air_time ~ distance, data = flights,
  pch = ".",
  main = "flight speed plot")
```

The plot generated is as follows:

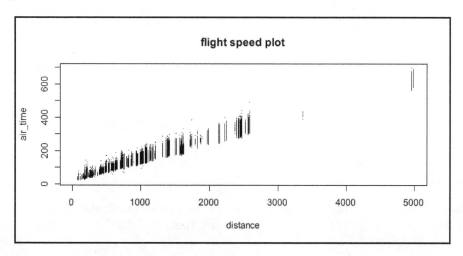

The plot clearly suggests that distance and `air_time` has a positive correlation. So, it is reasonable to fit a linear model between the two variables.

Before pouring the whole dataset into a linear model, we divide the dataset into two parts: a training set and a testing set. The purpose of dividing the dataset is that we want to perform not only sample evaluation but also out-of-sample evaluation of the model. More specifically, we put 75% of the data to the training set, and the remaining 25% of data to the testing set. In the following code, we use `sample()` to draw a random sample of 75% records from the original data and use `setdiff()` to get the rest of the records:

```
rows <- nrow(flights)
rows_id <- 1:rows
sample_id <- sample(rows_id, rows * 0.75, replace = FALSE)
flights_train <- flights[sample_id,]
```

```
flights_test <- flights[setdiff (rows_id, sample_id), ]
```

Note that `setdiff(rows_id, sample_id)` returns the indices in `rows_id` but not in `sample_id`.

Now `flights_train` is the training set and `flights_test` is the testing set. With the divided datasets, the procedure of model fitting and model evaluation is straightforward. First, use the training set to fit the model, then make an in-sample prediction to see the magnitude of the in-sample errors:

```
model2 <- lm(air_time ~ distance, data = flights_train)
predict2_train <- predict(model2, flights_train)
error2_train <- flights_train$air_time - predict2_train
```

To evaluate the magnitude of the errors, we define a function named `evaluate_error()` to calculate the mean absolute errors and the standard deviation of errors:

```
evaluate_error <- function(x) {
  c(abs_err = mean(abs(x), na.rm = TRUE),
    std_dev = sd(x, na.rm = TRUE))
}
```

Using this function, we can evaluate the errors of the in-sample predictions of `model2`:

```
evaluate_error(error2_train)
## abs_err   std_dev
## 9.413836 12.763126
```

The absolute mean errors indicate that on average the prediction deviates from the correct value by around 9.45 minutes in absolute value and has a standard deviation of 12.8 minutes.

Then, we perform a simple out-of-sample evaluation by using the model to predict on the testing set:

```
predict2_test <- predict(model2, flights_test)
error2_test <- flights_test$air_time - predict2_test
evaluate_error(error2_test)
## abs_err std_dev
## 9.482135 12.838225
```

The prediction results in a numeric vector of predicted values. Both the absolute mean errors and the standard deviation of errors go up slightly, which suggests that the quality of the out-of-sample prediction does not get significantly worse, indicating that `model2` does not seem to be a result of overfitting.

Since `model2` has only one regressor, `distance`, it is natural to consider whether more regressors would improve the prediction. The following code fits a new linear model with not only distance but also `carrier`, `month` and departure time (`dep_time`) as regressors:

```
model3 <- lm(air_time ~ carrier + distance + month + dep_time,
   data = flights_train)
predict3_train <- predict(model3, flights_train)
error3_train <- flights_train$air_time - predict3_train
evaluate_error(error3_train)
## abs_err   std_dev
## 9.312961 12.626790
```

The in-sample errors are slightly lower in both magnitude and variation:

```
predict3_test <- predict(model3, flights_test)
error3_test <- flights_test$air_time - predict3_test
evaluate_error(error3_test)
## abs_err std_dev
## 9.38309 12.70168
```

Also, the out-of-sample errors looks slightly better than `model2`. To compare the distribution of out-of-sample errors before and after adding new regressors to the linear model, we overlay the two density curves:

```
plot(density(error2_test, na.rm = TRUE),
   main = "Empirical distributions of out-of-sample errors")
lines(density(error3_test, na.rm = TRUE), lty = 2)
legend("topright", legend = c("model2", "model3"),
   lty = c(1, 2), cex = 0.8,
   x.intersp = 0.6, y.intersp = 0.6)
```

The plot generated is as follows:

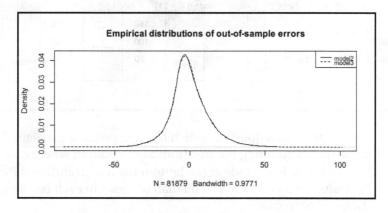

From the preceding density plot, the improvement from `model2` to `model3` is too small to notice, that is, there's no significant improvement at all.

Fitting a regression tree

In this section, we try another model to fit the data. The model is called a **regression tree** (https://en.wikipedia.org/wiki/Decision_tree_learning) and is one of the machine learning models. It is not a simple linear regression, but uses a decision tree to fit the data.

Suppose we want to predict the daily air quality (`Ozone`) according to solar radiation (`Solar.R`), average wind speed (`Wind`), and maximum daily temperature (`Temp`), the built-in dataset `airquality` being the training set. The following graph illustrates how a fitted regression tree works:

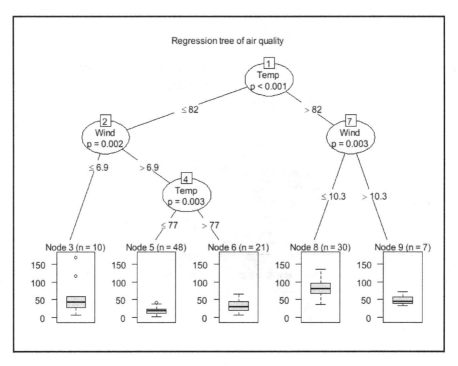

In the tree, each circle represents a question which has two possible answers. To predict `Ozone`, we need to ask questions along the tree from top to bottom where each observation lies in one of the bottom cases. Each node at the bottom has a distribution different from the others, which is illustrated by a box plot. The median or mean in each box should be reasonable predictions for each case.

There are a number of packages that implement decision tree learning algorithms. In this section, we use a simple package called party
(`https://cran.r-project.org/web/packages/party`). If you don't have it installed yet, run `install.package("party")`.

Now we use the same formula and data to train a regression tree model. Note that we took a subset of the data where there is no missing value of `air_time` because `ctree` does not accept missing values in a response variable:

```
model4 <- party::ctree(air_time ~ distance + month + dep_time,
    data = subset(flights_train, !is.na(air_time)))
predict4_train <- predict(model4, flights_train)
error4_train <- flights_train$air_time - predict4_train[, 1]
evaluate_error(error4_train)
## abs_err   std_dev
## 7.418982 10.296528
```

It looks like `model4` performs better than `model3`. Then, we take a look at its out-of-sample performance:

```
predict4_test <- predict(model4, flights_test)
error4_test <- flights_test$air_time - predict4_test[, 1]
evaluate_error(error4_test)
## abs_err   std_dev
## 7.499769 10.391071
```

The preceding output suggests that the regression tree, on average, can make better predictions for this problem. The following density plots make a contrast between the distributions of the out-of-sample prediction errors of `model3` and `model4`:

```
plot(density(error3_test, na.rm = TRUE),
    ylim = range(, 0.06),
    main = "Empirical distributions of out-of-sample errors")
lines(density(error4_test, na.rm = TRUE), lty = 2)
legend("topright", legend = c("model3", "model4"),
    lty = c(1, 2), cex = 0.8,
    x.intersp = 0.6, y.intersp = 0.6)
```

The plot generated is as follows:

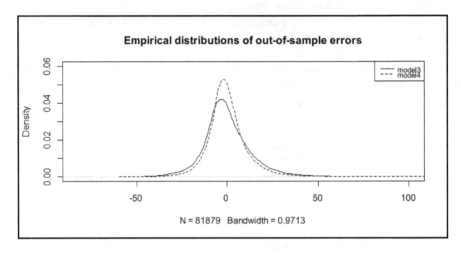

For the preceding plot, we can see that the variance of the prediction errors of `model4` is lower than that of `model3`.

The preceding examples may suffer from many problems because we apply the linear models and machine learning models without any serious checking of the data. The point of these sections is not about the models but to demonstrate a common procedure and interface of fitting models in R. For a real-world problem, you need more careful analysis of the data rather than directly pouring them into an arbitrary model and making conclusions.

Summary

In this chapter, you learned how to read and write data in various formats, how to visualize data with plot functions, and how to apply basic models on the data. Now, you know the basic tools and interface of working with data. However, you may learn more data analysis tools from other sources.

For statistical and econometric models, I recommend that you read not only text books of statistics and econometrics but also R books that focus on statistical analysis. For machine learning models such as artificial neural networks, support vector machines, and random forests, I recommend that you read machine learning books and go to *CRAN Task View: Machine Learning & Statistical Learning* (https://cran.r-project.org/web/views/MachineLearning.html).

Since this book is focused on the R programming language rather than any specific model, we will continue our journey in the next chapter by going deeper into R. If you are not familiar with how R code works, you can hardly predict what will happen, which slows down your coding, and a small issue can waste a lot of your time.

The next few chapters will help you build a concrete understanding of R's evaluation model, metaprogramming facilities, object-oriented systems, and several other mechanisms R chose to facilitate data analysis, which enables you to use more advanced packages of data manipulation and to work on more complicated tasks.

8
Inside R

In the previous chapters, you learned the basics of R programming language, and understood the usage of vectors, matrices, lists, and data frames to represent data in different shapes. You also saw how we can use the built-in functions to solve simple problems. However, simply knowing these features does not help you solve every problem. Real-world data analysis usually involves careful and detailed transformation and aggregation of data, which can be done with a good variety of functions, whether they are built-in or provided by extension packages.

To best use these functions rather than let them confuse you with unexpected results, you need a basic but concrete understanding of how R functions work. In this chapter, we will cover the following topics:

- Lazy evaluation
- Copy-on-modify mechanism
- Lexical scoping
- Environments

If you understand these concepts and their roles in the code, most R code should appear highly predictable to you, which means higher productivity in both finding bugs and writing properly functional code.

Understanding lazy evaluation

A big part of understanding how R works can be done by figuring out how R functions work. After going through the previous chapters, you should know the most commonly used basic functions. However, you may still be confused about their exact behavior. Suppose we create the following function:

```
test0 <- function(x, y) {
   if (x > 0) x else y
}
```

The function is somewhat special because y seems to be needed only when x is greater than zero. What if we only supply a positive number to x and ignore y? Will the function fail because we don't supply every argument in its definition? Let's find out by calling the following function:

```
test0(1)
## [1] 1
```

The function works without y being supplied. It looks like we are not required to supply the values to all arguments when we call a function but only to those that are needed. If we call test0 with a negative number, y is needed:

```
test0(-1)
## Error in test0(-1): argument "y" is missing, with no default
```

Since we did not specify the value of y, the function stopped, reporting that y is missing.

From the preceding examples, you learn that a function does not require all arguments to be specified if they are not needed to return a value. What if we insist on specifying those arguments that are not used in the function? Will they be evaluated before we call the function or not evaluated at all? Let's find out by putting a stop() function in the position of argument y. If the expression is evaluated by any means somewhere, it should stop immediately before x is returned:

```
test0(1, stop("Stop now"))
## [1] 1
```

The output indicates that stop() does not happen, which indicates that it is not evaluated at all. If we change the value of x to a negative number, the function should stop instead:

```
test0(-1, stop("Stop now"))
## Error in test0(-1, stop("Stop now")): Stop now
```

Now, it is very clear that `stop()` is evaluated in this case. The mechanism becomes quite transparent. In a function call, the expression of an argument is evaluated only when the value of the argument is needed. This mechanism is called **lazy evaluation**, and therefore, we can also say that the arguments of a function call are lazily evaluated, that is, evaluated only when needed.

If you are not aware of the lazy evaluation mechanism, you may think that the following function call must be extremely time consuming and may exhaust all your computer memory. However, lazy evaluation prevents it from happening because `rnorm(1000000)` is never evaluated. This is because it is never needed when evaluating `if (x > 0) x else y`, which can be verified by timing the function calls in turn using `system.time()`:

```
system.time(rnorm(10000000))
## user system elapsed
## 0.91  0.01   0.92
```

Generating 10 million random numbers is not an easy job. It takes more than a second. By contrast, evaluating a number should be the easiest thing R can do, and it is so fast that the timer itself can't tell:

```
system.time(1)
## user system elapsed
##  0     0     0
```

If we time the following expression, given the logic of `test0` and the knowledge of lazy evaluation, at an educated guess it should be zero:

```
system.time(test0(1, rnorm(10000000)))
## user system elapsed
##  0     0     0
```

Another lazy evaluation scenario that could happen is the default values of arguments. More precisely, the default values of function arguments should really be default expressions because the value is not available until the expression is actually evaluated. Consider the following function:

```
test1 <- function(x, y = stop("Stop now")) {
  if (x > 0) x else y
}
```

We give y a default value that calls `stop()`. If lazy evaluation does not apply here, that is, if y is evaluated irrespective of whether it is needed, we should receive an error as long as we call `test1()` without supplying y. However, if lazy evaluation applies, calling `test1()` with a positive x argument should not cause an error since the `stop()` expression of y is never evaluated.

Let's do an experiment to find out which is true. First, we will call `test1()` with a positive `x` argument:

```
test1(1)
## [1] 1
```

The output implies that lazy evaluation also works here. The function only uses `x`, and the default expression of `y` is not evaluated at all. If we supply a negative `x` argument instead, the function should stop as supposed:

```
test1(-1)
## Error in test1(-1): Stop now
```

The preceding examples demonstrate an advantage of lazy evaluation: it makes it possible to save time and avoid unnecessary evaluation of expressions. Besides, it also allows more flexible specification of default values of function arguments. For example, you can use other arguments in the expression of a function argument:

```
test2 <- function(x, n = floor(length(x) / 2)) {
  x[1:n]
}
```

This allows you to set up the default behavior of a function in a more reasonable or desirable way, while the function arguments are still as customizable as they were without those default values.

If we call `test2` without specifying n, the default behavior takes out the first half elements of x:

```
test2(1:10)
## [1] 1 2 3 4 5
```

The function remains flexible because you can always override its default behavior by specifying another value of n:

```
test2(1:10, 3)
## [1] 1 2 3
```

Like all other features, lazy evaluation also has its pros and cons. Since the arguments of a function are only parsed but not evaluated when the function is called, we can only make sure that the expressions supplied to the arguments are syntactically correct. It is hard to ensure that the arguments are going to work.

For example, if an undefined variable appears in the default value of an argument, there will be no warning or error the moment we create the function. In the following example, we create a `test3` function, which is exactly the same as `test2`, except that x in n is mistakenly written as an undefined variable m.

```
test3 <- function(x, n = floor(length(m) / 2)) {
    x[1:n]
}
```

When we create `test3`, there's no warning or error because `floor(length(m) / 2)` is never evaluated before `test3` is called, and the value of n is demanded by `1:n`. The function will stop only when we actually call it:

```
test3(1:10)
## Error in test3(1:10): object 'm' not found
```

If we have m defined before `test3` is called, the function works, but in an unexpected way:

```
m <- c(1, 2, 3)
test3(1:10)
## [1] 1
```

Another example that makes how lazy evaluation works more explicit is as follows:

```
test4 <- function(x, y = p) {
    p <- x + 1
    c(x, y)
}
```

Note that the default value of y is p, which is not defined before the function is called, just like the previous example. A notable difference between these two examples is when the missing symbol in the default value of the second argument is supplied. In the previous example, p is defined before the function is called. However, in this example, p is defined inside the function before y is used.

Let's see what happens when we call the function:

```
test4(1)
## [1] 1 2
```

It looks like the function works rather than ending up in an error. It will become easier to understand if we go through the detailed process of how `test4(1)` is executed:

1. Find a function named `test4`.
2. Match the given arguments, but both x and y are unevaluated.
3. `p <- x + 1` evaluates `x + 1` and assigns the value to a new variable p.

4. `c(x, y)` evaluates both x and y, where x takes 1 and y takes p, which just happens to get the value of `x + 1`, which is 2.
5. The function returns a numeric vector `c(1, 2)`.

Therefore, in the whole evaluation process of `test4(1)`, no warning or error occurs because no rules are violated. The most important trick here is that p is just defined before y is used.

The preceding example helps exaplain how lazy evaluation works, but it is indeed a bad practice. I won't recommend writing a function in this way because such a trick only makes the behavior of the function less transparent. A good practice is to simplify the arguments and avoid using undefined symbols outside the function. Otherwise, it can be hard to predict its behavior or debug the function due to its dependency on the outer environment.

Despite this, there is some wise use of lazy evaluation too. For example, `stop()` can be used along with `switch()` in the last argument to make the function stop when no cases are matched. The following function `check_input()` uses `switch()` to regulate the input of x so that it only accepts y or n and stops when other strings are supplied:

```
check_input <- function(x) {
  switch(x,
    y = message("yes"),
    n = message("no"),
    stop("Invalid input"))
}
```

When x takes y, a message saying yes shows:

```
check_input("y")
## yes
```

When x takes n, a message saying no shows:

```
check_input("n")
## no
```

Otherwise, the function stops:

```
check_input("what")
## Error in check_input("what"): Invalid input
```

The example works because `stop()` is lazily evaluated as an argument of `switch()`.

As a summary of the examples, the reminder here is that you cannot rely too much on the parser to check the code. It only checks the code in its syntax, and it does not tell you whether the code is written with good practice. To avoid the potential pitfalls caused by lazy evaluation, do necessary checking in the function to make sure that the input can be handled correctly.

Understanding the copy-on-modify mechanism

In the previous section, we showed how lazy evaluation works and how it may help save computing time and working memory by avoiding unnecessary evaluation of function arguments. In this section, I will show you an important feature of R that makes it safer to work with data. Suppose we create a simple numeric vector x1:

```
x1 <- c(1, 2, 3)
```

Then, we assign the value of x1 to x2:

```
x2 <- x1
```

Now, x1 and x2 have exactly the same value. What if we modify an element in one of the two vectors? Will both vectors change?

```
x1[1] <- 0
x1
## [1] 0 2 3
x2
## [1] 1 2 3
```

The output shows that when x1 is changed, x2 will remain unchanged. You may guess that the assignment automatically copies the value and makes the new variable point to the copy of the data instead of the original data. Let's use tracemem() to track the footprint of the data in memory.

Let's reset the vectors and conduct an experiment by tracing the memory addresses of x1 and x2:

```
x1 <- c(1, 2, 3)
x2 <- x1
```

As we call `tracemem()` on the two vectors, it shows the current memory address of the data. If the memory address being traced changes, a text will show up with the original address and the new address, indicating that the data is copied:

```
tracemem(x1)
## [1] "<0000000013597028>"
tracemem(x2)
## [1] "<0000000013597028>"
```

Now, both vectors have the same value, and x1 and x2 share the same address, which implies that they point to exactly the same piece of data in memory and that the assignment operation does not copy the data automatically. But when is the data copied?

Now, we will modify the first element of x1 to :

```
x1[1] <- 0
## tracemem[0x0000000013597028 -> 0x00000000170c7968]
```

The memory tracing says that the address of x1 has changed to a new one. More specifically, the piece of memory, that is, the original vector both x1 and x2 point to is copied to a new location. Now we have two copies of the same data in two different locations. Then, the first element of the copy is modified, and finally, x1 is made to point to the modified copy.

Now, x1 and x2 have different values: x1 points to the modified vector and x2 remains pointing to the original vector.

In other words, if multiple variables refer to the same object, modifying one variable will make a copy of the object. This mechanism is called **copy-on-modify**.

Another scenario where copy-on-modify happens is when we modify a function argument. Suppose we create the following function:

```
modify_first <- function(x) {
  x[1] <- 0
  x
}
```

When the function is executed, it attempts to modify the first element of argument x. Let's do some experiments with vectors and lists and see whether `modify_first()` can modify them.

For a number vector v1:

```
v1 <- c(1, 2, 3)
modify_first(v1)
```

```
## [1] 0 2 3
v1
## [1] 1 2 3
```

For a list `v2`:

```
v2 <- list(x = 1, y = 2)
modify_first(v2)
## $x
## [1] 0
##
## $y
## [1] 2
v2
## $x
## [1] 1
##
## $y
## [1] 2
```

In both experiments, the function only returned a modified version of the original object, but it did not modify the original object. However, directly modifying the vectors outside the function works:

```
v1[1] <- 0
v1
## [1] 0 2 3
v2[1] <- 0
v2
## $x
## [1] 0
##
## $y
## [1] 2
```

To use the modified version, we need to assign it to the original variable:

```
v3 <- 1:5
v3 <- modify_first(v3)
v3
## [1] 0 2 3 4 5
```

The preceding examples demonstrate that modifying a function argument also causes a copy to make sure that the modification does not affect things outside the function.

The copy-on-modify mechanism also happens when the attributes are modified. The following function removes the row names of a data frame and replaces its column names with capital letters:

```
change_names <- function(x) {
  if (is.data.frame(x)) {
    rownames(x) <- NULL
    if (ncol(x) <= length(LETTERS)) {
      colnames(x) <- LETTERS[1:ncol(x)]
    } else {
      stop("Too many columns to rename")
    }
  } else {
    stop("x must be a data frame")
  }
  x
}
```

To test the function, we will create a simple data frame with randomly generated data:

```
small_df <- data.frame(
  id = 1:3,
  width = runif(3, 5, 10),
  height = runif(3, 5, 10))
small_df
##   id    width   height
## 1  1 7.605076 9.991836
## 2  2 8.763025 7.360011
## 3  3 9.689882 8.550459
```

Now, we will call the function with the data frame and see the modified version:

```
change_names(small_df)
##   A     B        C
## 1 1 7.605076 9.991836
## 2 2 8.763025 7.360011
## 3 3 9.689882 8.550459
```

According to the copy-on-modify mechanism, small_df is copied the first time when its row names are removed, and then, all subsequent changes are made to the copied version instead of the original version. We can verify this by viewing small_df:

```
small_df
##   id    width   height
## 1  1 7.605076 9.991836
## 2  2 8.763025 7.360011
## 3  3 9.689882 8.550459
```

The original version has not changed at all.

Modifying objects outside a function

Despite the copy-on-modify mechanism, it is still possible to modify a vector outside a function. The <<- operator is designed to do the job. Suppose we have a variable x and create a function modify_x() that simply assigns a new value to x:

```
x <- 0
modify_x <- function(value) {
   x <<- value
}
```

When we call the function, the value of x will be replaced:

```
modify_x(3)
x
## [1] 3
```

This can be useful when you try to map a vector to a new list and do some counting at the same time. The following code creates a list of vectors with an increasing number of elements. In each iteration of lapply(), count is used to sum up the total number of elements in the vector generated:

```
count <- 0
lapply(1:3, function(x) {
   result <- 1:x
   count <<- count + length(result)
   result
})
## [[1]]
## [1] 1
##
## [[2]]
## [1] 1 2
##
## [[3]]
## [1] 1 2 3
count
## [1] 6
```

Another example in which <<- is useful is to flatten a nested list. Suppose we have a nested list like the one shown here:

```
nested_list <- list(
  a = c(1, 2, 3),
  b = list(
    x = c("a", "b", "c"),
    y = list(
      z = c(TRUE, FALSE),
      w = c(2, 3, 4))
  )
)
str(nested_list)
## List of 2
## $ a: num [1:3] 1 2 3
## $ b:List of 2
## ..$ x: chr [1:3] "a" "b" "c"
## ..$ y:List of 2
## .. ..$ z: logi [1:2] TRUE FALSE
##    .. ..$ w: num [1:3] 2 3 4
```

We want to flatten the list so that the nested levels are all brought to the first level. The following code solves the problem using rapply() and <<-.

First, we need to know that rapply() is a recursive version of lapply(). In each iteration, the supplied function is called with an atomic vector at a particular level in the list until all atomic vectors at all levels are exhausted. Calling rapply(nested_list, f) basically runs in the following manner:

```
f(c(1, 2, 3))
f(c("a", "b", "c"))
f(c(TRUE, FALSE))
f(c(2, 3, 4))
```

Keep in mind, that we should work out a solution to flatten nested_list. The solution that we will discuss is inspired by a Stackoverflow answer (http://stackoverflow.com/a/8139959/2969), which smartly uses rapply(). First, we will create an empty list to receive individual vectors in the nested list and a counter:

```
flat_list <- list()
i <- 1
```

Then, we will use `rapply()` to recursively apply a function to `nested_list`. In each iteration, the function receives an atomic vector in `nested_list` through x. The function sets the ith element of `flat_list` to x and increments the counter i:

```
res <- rapply(nested_list, function(x) {
flat_list[[i]] <<- x
i <<- i + 1
})
```

With the iterations done, all atomic vectors are stored in `flat_list` at the first level. The value returned by `rapply()` is as follows:

```
res
## a   b.x b.y.z b.y.w
## 2    3    4      5
```

As a result of `i <<- i + 1`, the values in `res` are of no much importance. However, the names of `res` are useful to indicate the original levels and names of each element in `flat_list`. So we let `flat_list` also have the names of `res` to indicate the origin of each element:

```
names(flat_list) <- names(res)
str(flat_list)
## List of 4
## $ a  : num [1:3] 1 2 3
## $ b.x : chr [1:3] "a" "b" "c"
## $ b.y.z: logi [1:2] TRUE FALSE
## $ b.y.w: num [1:3] 2 3 4
```

Finally, all elements in `nested_list` are stored in a flat way in `flat_list`.

Understanding lexical scoping

In the previous section, we introduced the copy-on-modify mechanism. The examples demonstrated two cases in which this mechanism happens. When an object has multiple names or is passed as an argument to a function, modifying it will cause the object to be copied, and it is the copied version that is actually modified.

To modify an object outside a function, we introduced the use of <<-, which finds the variable outside the function first and modifies that object instead of copying one locally. This leads to an important idea that a function has inside and outside. Inside a function, we can somehow refer to variables and functions outside.

For example, the following function uses two outside variables:

```
start_num <- 1
end_num <- 10
fun1 <- function(x) {
  c(start_num, x, end_num)
}
```

We first create two variables and define a function called `fun1`. The function simply puts together `start_num`, argument `x`, and `end_num` into a new vector. It is clear that `start_num` and `end_num` are not defined in the function but outside it while `x` is the argument of the function. Let's see if it works:

```
fun1(c(4, 5, 6))
## [1]  1  4  5  6 10
```

The function works by successfully getting the value of the two variables outside the function. You may guess that when we define the function, the values are captured so that `start_num` and `end_num` in `fun1` just take the values from outside. In fact, two experiments can be performed to prove it wrong.

The first experiment is simple. Let's remove the two variables:

```
rm(start_num, end_num)
fun1(c(4, 5, 6))
## Error in fun1(c(4, 5, 6)): object 'start_num' not found
```

Then, the function does not work anymore. If the values of the two variables are captured when the function is defined, the removal of them should not paralyze the function.

The second experiment is the other way around. Let's remove the function as well as the two variables. We will first define the function:

```
rm(fun1, start_num, end_num)
## Warning in rm(fun1, start_num, end_num): object 'start_num'
## not found
## Warning in rm(fun1, start_num, end_num): object 'end_num'
## not found
fun1 <- function(x) {
c(start_num, x, end_num)
}
```

If the creation of the function has to capture the two variables that are not present in it, the preceding code should result in an error saying `start_num` and `end_num` are missing. Clearly, there's no error, and the function is successfully created. Let's call it now:

```
fun1(c(4, 5, 6))
## Error in fun1(c(4, 5, 6)): object 'start_num' not found
```

The function does not work because the two variables are not found. We will then define the two variables and again call the function with the same argument:

```
start_num <- 1
end_num <- 10
fun1(c(4, 5, 6))
## [1]  1   4   5   6 10
```

The function works again. This leads to the conclusion that the function actually tries to look for the variables when it is called. Actually, during the execution of the function, when a symbol is encountered, it will first look for it inside the function. More specifically, if the symbol is passed in as an argument or created inside the function, the symbol will be resolved and its value is used.

Suppose we create a variable p first and then define a function `fun2` in which another p variable is created and used in the value to return:

```
p <- 0
fun2 <- function(x) {
  p <- 1
  x + p
}
```

When we call the function, which p will `fun2` use in x + p? Let's find out;

```
fun2(1)
## [1] 2
```

The output makes it clear that x + p uses p defined inside the function. The flow is simple. First, p <- 1 creates a new variable p with value 1 instead of changing p outside the function. Then, x + p is evaluated, with x being resolved as the passed-in argument and p as the local variable just defined. The rule is that only if a variable is not present inside the function will it be searched for outside.

However, what exactly does "outside" mean? The question is subtler than it appears to be. Suppose we create the following two functions:

```
f1 <- function(x) {
  x + p
}
g1 <- function(x) {
  p <- 1
  f1(x)
```

```
}
```

The first function f1 simply adds two variables: x is an argument and p is a variable yet to be found outside. The second function g1 defines a p variable inside and calls f1. The question is, "Will f1 find p inside g1 when g1 is called?"

```
g1(0)
## [1] 0
```

Unfortunately, f1 cannot find p inside g1 even though f1 is called in g1. If we define p and then call g1 again, the function works:

```
p <- 1
g1(0)
## [1] 1
```

What made g1 work is that when f1 is called and p cannot be found inside f1, it will search where f1 is defined instead of where it is called. This mechanism is called **lexical scoping**. In the preceding code, we defined p in the same scope where f1 is defined. Then, f1 can find p when it is called inside g1.

The same scoping rule also applies to how <<- finds variables. For example, the following code defines a variable m and two functions, f2 and g2, in the same scope. In f2, m is set to 2. However, in g2, a local m variable is defined and then f2 is called:

```
m <- 1
f2 <- function(x) {
  m <<- 2
  x
}
g2 <- function(x) {
  m <- 1
  f2(x)
  cat(sprintf("[g2] m: %d\n", m))
}
```

As soon as f2 is called, the value of m in g2 is printed. Let's call g2 and see what happens:

```
g2(1)
## [g2] m: 1
```

The printed text shows that the value of m in g2 remains unchanged, but the value of m outside f2 and g2 is changed as can be verified:

```
m
## [1] 2
```

The preceding experiment confirms that m <<- 2 follows the rule of lexical scoping.

The following two examples look even more complex. The functions are nested. In f, we not only create local variables such as p and q but also a local function f2, in which another local p variable is defined:

```
f <- function(x) {
  p <- 1
  q <- 2
  cat(sprintf("1. [f1] p: %d, q: %d\n", p, q))
  f2 <- function(x) {
    p <- 3
    cat(sprintf("2. [f2] p: %d, q: %d\n", p, q))
    c(x = x, p = p, q = q)
  }
  cat(sprintf("3. [f1] p: %d, q: %d\n", p, q))
  f2(x)
}
```

If you understand lexical scoping, you should be able to predict the result given an arbitrary input x. We add some cat() functions to make it easier to track the values of variables in each scope level. The cat() message includes an order, the function scope, and the values of p and q. Now, we will run f(0) and you may predict the result:

```
f(0)
## 1. [f1] p: 1, q: 2
## 3. [f1] p: 1, q: 2
## 2. [f2] p: 3, q: 2
## x p q
## 0 3 2
```

The executing order of the three cat() functions are 1, 3, and 2, and the values of p and q in each scope are consistent with lexical scoping rules. In the following example, we will also use <<-:

```
g <- function(x) {
  p <- 1
  q <- 2
  cat(sprintf("1. [f1] p: %d, q: %d\n", p, q))
  g2 <- function(x) {
    p <<- 3
    p <- 2
    cat(sprintf("2. [f2] p: %d, q: %d\n", p, q))
    c(x = x, p = p, q = q)
  }
  cat(sprintf("3. [f1] p: %d, q: %d\n", p, q))
  result <- g2(x)
```

```
    cat(sprintf("4. [f1] p: %d, q: %d\n", p, q))
    result
}
```

You may analyze the flow of the function by predicting the order of execution and the values of the printed variables:

```
g(0)
## 1. [f1] p: 1, q: 2
## 3. [f1] p: 1, q: 2
## 2. [f2] p: 2, q: 2
## 4. [f1] p: 3, q: 2
## x p q
## 0 2 2
```

If you do not succeed in predicting the behavior of the preceding function, go through the examples in this section more carefully.

Understanding how an environment works

In the previous sections, you learned about lazy evaluation, copy-on-modify, and lexical scoping. These mechanisms are highly related to a type of object called **environment**. In fact, lexical scoping is enabled exactly by the environment. Although environments look quite similar to lists, they are indeed fundamentally different in several aspects. In the following sections, we will get to know the behavior of environment objects by creating and manipulating them, and see the way its structure determines how R functions work.

Knowing the environment object

An environment is an object consisting of a set of names and has a parent environment. Each name (also known as a symbol or variable) points to an object. When we look up a symbol in an environment, it will search the set of symbols and return the object the symbol points to if it exists in the environment. Otherwise, it will continue to look up its parent environment. The following diagram illustrates the structure of an environment and the relationship between environments:

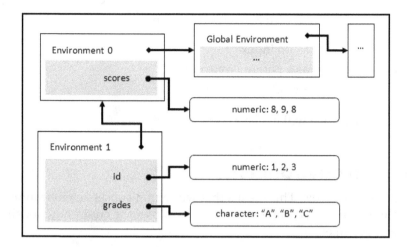

In the preceding diagram, **Environment 1** consists of two names (**id** and **grades**), and its parent environment is **Environment 0**, which consists of one name (**scores**). Each name in these environments points to an object stored somewhere in the memory. If we look up **id** in **Environment 1**, we'll get the numeric vector it points to directly. If we look up **scores** instead, **Environment 1** does not consist of **scores**, so it will look it up in its parent environment, **Environment 1**, and get its value successfully. For other names, it will look along the chain of parent environments until it is found or it will end up with an error of symbol not found.

In the following sections, we will go through these concepts in detail.

Creating and chaining environments

We can create a new environment using the `new.env()` function:

```
e1 <- new.env()
```

The environment is usually represented by hexadecimal digits, which is a memory address:

```
e1
## <environment: 0x0000000014a45748>
```

Extraction operators (`$` and `[[`) can be used to create variables in the environment, just like modifying a list:

```
e1$x <- 1
e1[["x"]]
## [1] 1
```

However, there are three major differences between an environment and a list:

- An environment has no index
- An environment has a parent environment
- Environments have reference semantics

In the following sections, we will explain them in detail.

Accessing an environment

An environment has no index. This means that we cannot subset an environment nor can we extract an element from it by index. If we try to subset the environment using a range of positions, we will get an error:

```
e1[1:3]
## Error in e1[1:3]: object of type 'environment' is not subsettable
```

We will get a different error when we try to extract a variable from an environment using index:

```
e1[[1]]
## Error in e1[[1]]: wrong arguments for subsetting an environment
```

The correct way to work with an environment is using names and environment-access functions. For example, we can detect whether a variable exists in an environment using exists():

```
exists("x", e1)
## [1] TRUE
```

For an existing variable, we can call get() to retrieve its value:

```
get("x", e1)
## [1] 1
```

We can call ls() to see all variable names in a given environment, as we mentioned in Chapter 3, *Managing Your Workspace*:

```
ls(e1)
## [1] "x"
```

If we use $ or [[to access variables that don't exist in the environment, we will get NULL, just like what we get when we extract an element from a list using a non-existing name:

```
e1$y
## NULL
e1[["y"]]
## NULL
```

However, if we use the get() function in a non-existing variable out of an environment, we will certainly receive an error, just like what happens when we refer to a non-existing variable without caution:

```
get("y", e1)
## Error in get("y", e1): object 'y' not found
```

To better handle the situation before an error occurs, we may use exists() to perform a detection before we use the get() function to the variable:

```
exists("y", e1)
## [1] FALSE
```

Chaining environments

An environment has a parent environment, which is the next place to look up a symbol if the symbol does not exist in the original environment. Suppose we are trying to use the get() function to a variable in an environment. If the variable is directly found in it, we get the value. Otherwise, get() will look for the variable in its parent environment.

In the following example, we will create a new environment e2, whose parent (or enclosing) environment is e1, just like we created in the previous section:

```
e2 <- new.env(parent = e1)
```

Different environments have different memory addresses:

```
e2
## <environment: 0x000000001772ef70>
e1
## <environment: 0x0000000014a45748>
```

However, the parent environment of e2 is, by definition, exactly the same environment e1 refers to, which can be verified by parent.env():

```
parent.env(e2)
## <environment: 0x0000000014a45748>
```

Now, we create a variable y in e2:

```
e2$y <- 2
```

We can use ls() to inspect all variable names in e2:

```
ls(e2)
## [1] "y"
```

We can also access the value of the variable using $, [[, exists() or get():

```
e2$y
## [1] 2
e2[["y"]]
## [1] 2
exists("y", e2)
## [1] TRUE
get("y", e2)
## [1] 2
```

However, the extraction operators ($ and [[) and the environment-access functions have a notable difference. The operators only work in the scope of a single environment, but the functions work along a chain of environments.

Note that we don't define any variable called x in e2. With no surprise, both operators extracting x result in NULL:

```
e2$x
## NULL
e2[["x"]]
## NULL
```

However, the parent environment plays a role when we use exists() and get(). Since x is not found in e2, the functions will continue the search in its parent environment e1:

```
exists("x", e2)
## [1] TRUE
get("x", e1)
## [1] 1
```

That's why we get positive results from both the preceding function calls. If we don't want the functions to search the parent environment, we can set inherits = FALSE. In this case, if the variable is not immediately available in the given environment, the search will not continue. Instead, exists() will return FALSE:

```
exists("x", e2, inherits = FALSE)
## [1] FALSE
```

Also, the `get()` function will result in an error:

```
get("x", e2, inherits = FALSE)
## Error in get("x", e2, inherits = FALSE): object 'x' not found
```

The chaining of environments work at many levels. For example, you may create an environment, e3, whose parent is e2. When you use the `get()` function to a variable from e3, the search will go along the chain of environments.

Using environments for reference semantics

Environments have reference semantics. This means that unlike data types such as atomic vectors and lists, an environment will not be copied when it is modified, whether it has multiple names or is passed as an argument to a function.

For example, we assign the value of e1 to another variable e3:

```
ls(e1)
## [1] "x"
e3 <- e1
```

If we have two variables pointing to the same list, modifying one would make a copy first and then modify the copied version, which does not influence the other list. Reference semantics behave otherwise. No copy is made when we modify the environment through either variable. So, we can see the changes through both e1 and e3 since they point to exactly the same environment.

The following code demonstrates how reference semantics work:

```
e3$y
## NULL
e1$y <- 2
e3$y
## [1] 2
```

First, there is no y defined in e3. Then, we created a new variable y in e1. Since e1 and e3 point to exactly the same environment, we can also access y through e3.

The same thing happens when we pass an environment as an argument to a function. Suppose we define the following function that tries to set z of e to 10:

```
modify <- function(e) {
  e$z <- 10
}
```

If we pass a list to this function, the modification will not work. Instead a local version is created and modified, but it is dropped after the function call ends:

```
list1 <- list(x = 1, y = 2)
list1$z
## NULL
modify(list1)
list1$z
## NULL
```

However, if we pass an environment to the function, modifying the environment does not produce a local copy but directly creates a new variable z in the environment:

```
e1$z
## NULL
modify(e1)
e1$z
## [1] 10
```

Knowing the built-in environments

Environment is quite a special type of object in R, but it is used everywhere from the implementation of a function call to the mechanism of lexical scoping. In fact, when you run a chunk of R code, you run it in a certain environment. To know which environment we are running the code in, we can call environment():

```
environment()
## <environment: R_GlobalEnv>
```

The output says that the current environment is the global environment. In fact, when a fresh R session gets ready for user input, the working environment is always the global environment. It is in this environment that we usually create variables and functions in data analysis.

As the previous examples demonstrated, an environment is also an object we can create and work with. For example, we can assign the current environment to a variable and create new symbols in this environment:

```
global <- environment()
global$some_obj <- 1
```

The preceding assignment is equivalent to directly calling some_obj <- 1, because this is already in the global environment. As long as you run the preceding code, the global environment is modified and some_obj gets a value:

```
some_obj
## [1] 1
```

There are other ways to access the global environment. For example, both `globalenv()` and `.GlobalEnv` refer to the global environment:

```
globalenv()
## <environment: R_GlobalEnv>
.GlobalEnv
## <environment: R_GlobalEnv>
```

The global environment (`globalenv()`) is the user workspace, while the base environment (`baseenv()`) provides basic functions and operators:

```
baseenv()
## <environment: base>
```

If you type `base::` in the RStudio editor, a long list of functions should appear. Most of the functions we introduced in the previous chapters are defined in the base environment, including, for example, functions to create basic data structures (for example, `list()` and `data.frame()`) and operators to work with them (for example, `[`, `:` and even `+`).

The global environment and the base environment are the most important built-in environments. Now, you may ask "What is the parent environment of the global environment? And what about the base environment? What about their grandparents?"

The following function can be used to find out the chain of a given environment:

```
parents <- function(env) {
  while (TRUE) {
    name <- environmentName(env)
    txt <- if (nzchar(name)) name else format(env)
    cat(txt, "\n")
    env <- parent.env(env)
  }
}
```

The preceding function recursively prints the names of the environment, the parent environment of each being the next one. Now, we can find out all levels of parent environments of the global environment:

```
parents(globalenv())
## R_GlobalEnv
## package:stats
## package:graphics
## package:grDevices
## package:utils
```

```
## package:datasets
## package:methods
## Autoloads
## base
## R_EmptyEnv
## Error in parent.env(env): the empty environment has no parent
```

Note that the chain terminates at an environment called the **empty environment**, which is the only environment that has nothing in it and has no parent environment. There is also a `emptyenv()` function that refers to the empty environment, but `parent.env(emptyenv())` will cause an error. This explains why `parents()` will always end up with an error.

The chain of environments is a combination of built-in environments and package environments. We can call `search()` to get the search path of symbol lookup in the perspective of the global environment:

```
search()
## [1] ".GlobalEnv" "package:stats"
## [3] "package:graphics" "package:grDevices"
## [5] "package:utils" "package:datasets"
## [7] "package:methods" "Autoloads"
## [9] "package:base"
```

Given the knowledge of symbol lookup along a chain of environments, we can figure out the process in detail of how the following code is evaluated in the global environment:

```
median(c(1, 2, 1 + 3))
```

The expression looks simple, but its evaluation process is more complex than it appears. First, look for `median` along the chain. It is found in the `stats` package environment. Then, look for `c`. It is found in the base environment. Finally, you may be surprised when you look for + (this is also a function!), as it is found in the base environment.

In fact, each time you attach a package, the package environment will be inserted before the global environment in the search path. If two packages export functions with conflict names, the functions defined in the package attached later will mask formerly defined ones since it becomes a closer parent to the global environment.

Understanding environments associated with a function

Environments govern the symbol lookup at not only the global level but also the function level. There are three important environments associated with function and its execution process: the executing environment, the enclosing environment, and the calling environment.

Each time a function is called, a new environment called is created to host the execution process. This is the executing environment of the function call. The arguments of the function and the variables we create in the function are actually the variables in the executing environment.

Like all other environments, the executing environment of a function is created with a parent environment. That parent environment, also called the enclosing environment of the function, is the environment where the function is defined. This means that during the execution of the function, any variable that is not defined in the executing environment will be looked for in the enclosing environment. This is exactly what makes lexical scoping possible.

Sometimes it is also useful to know the calling environment, that is, the environment in which the function is called. We can use `parent.frame()` to get the calling environment of the currently executing function.

To demonstrate these concepts, suppose we define the following function:

```r
simple_fun <- function() {
  cat("Executing environment: ")
  print(environment())
  cat("Enclosing environment: ")
  print(parent.env(environment()))
}
```

The function does nothing but prints the executing and enclosing environments when it is called:

```r
simple_fun()
## Executing environment: <environment: 0x0000000014955db0>
## Enclosing environment: <environment: R_GlobalEnv>
simple_fun()
## Executing environment: <environment: 0x000000001488f430>
## Enclosing environment: <environment: R_GlobalEnv>
simple_fun()
## Executing environment: <environment: 0x00000000146a23c8>
## Enclosing environment: <environment: R_GlobalEnv>
```

Note that each time the function is called, the executing environment is different, but the enclosing environment remains the same. In fact, when the function is defined, its enclosing environment is determined. We can call `environment()` over a function to get its enclosing environment:

```
environment(simple_fun)
## <environment: R_GlobalEnv>
```

The following example involves the three environments of three nested functions. In each function, the executing environment, enclosing environment, and calling environment are printed. If you firmly understand these concepts, I suggest that you make a prediction of which are the same and which are different:

```
f1 <- function() {
  cat("[f1] Executing in ")
  print(environment())
  cat("[f1] Enclosed by ")
  print(parent.env(environment()))
  cat("[f1] Calling from ")
  print(parent.frame())
  f2 <- function() {
    cat("[f2] Executing in ")
    print(environment())
    cat("[f2] Enclosed by ")
    print(parent.env(environment()))
    cat("[f2] Calling from ")
    print(parent.frame())
  }
  f3 <- function() {
    cat("[f3] Executing in ")
    print(environment())
    cat("[f3] Enclosed by ")
    print(parent.env(environment()))
    cat("[f3] Calling from ")
    print(parent.frame())
    f2()
  }
  f3()
}
```

Let's call `f1` and find out when each message is printed. The output requires some effort to read in its original form. We split the output into chunks for easier reading while preserving the order of output for consistency.

Note that temporarily created environments only have memory addresses (for example, 0x0000000016a39fe8) instead of a common name like the global environment (R_GlobalEnv). To make it easier to identify identical environments, we give the same memory addresses the same tags (for example, *A) at the end of each line of text output for the environments:

```
f1()
## [f1] Executing in <environment: 0x0000000016a39fe8> *A
## [f1] Enclosed by <environment: R_GlobalEnv>
## [f1] Calling from <environment: R_GlobalEnv>
```

When we call f1, its associated environments are printed as supposed, and then f2 and f3 are defined, and finally f3 is called, which continues producing the following text output:

```
## [f3] Executing in <environment: 0x0000000016a3def8> *B
## [f3] Enclosed by <environment: 0x0000000016a39fe8> *A
## [f3] Calling from <environment: 0x0000000016a39fe8> *A
```

Then, f2 is called in f3, which further produces the following text output:

```
## [f2] Executing in <environment: 0x0000000016a41f90> *C
## [f2] Enclosed by <environment: 0x0000000016a39fe8> *A
## [f2] Calling from <environment: 0x0000000016a3def8> *B
```

The printed messages show the following facts:

- Both the enclosing environment and calling environment of f1 are the global environment
- The enclosing environment and the calling environment of f3, as well as the enclosing environment of f2, are the executing environments of f1
- The calling environment of f2 is the executing environment of f3

The preceding facts are consistent with the following facts:

- f1 is both defined and called in the global environment
- f3 is both defined and called in f1
- f2 is defined in f1 but called in f3

If you managed to make the right predictions, you have a good understanding of how an environment and a function basically work. To go even deeper, I strongly recommend Hadley Wickham's Advanced R (http://amzn.com/1466586966?tag=devtools-2).

Summary

In this chapter, we went inside R and learned how R functions basically work. More specifically, you learned lazy evaluation, copy-on-modify, lexical scoping, and how environments work to allow these mechanisms. Having a concrete understanding of how R code is run not only helps you write the correct code but also makes it easier to find bugs from unexpected results.

In the next chapter, we will build on top of the foundation laid in this chapter. You will learn the basics of metaprogramming, which enables powerful features of interactive analysis.

9
Metaprogramming

In the previous chapter, you learned about the structure and features of an environment and also learned how to create and access an environment. Environment plays an important role in lazy evaluation, copy-on-modify, and lexical scoping, which are enabled by the environments associated with a function when it is created and called.

Now that we have a solid understanding of how functions work, we will go further in this chapter by learning to work with functions in more advanced forms. You will learn the metaprogramming facilities that make R flexible in interactive analysis. More specifically, we will cover the following topics in this chapter:

- Functional programming: closures and higher-order functions
- Computing on language with language objects
- Understanding non-standard evaluation

Understanding functional programming

In the previous chapter, you learned the behavior of a function in detail, including when an argument is evaluated (lazy evaluation), what happens when we try to modify an argument (copy-on-modify), and where to look for variables not defined within the function (lexical scoping). These technical terms that describe the behaviors may look more difficult than they actually are. In the following sections, you will learn about two types of functions: functions that are defined in functions and functions that work with other functions.

Creating and using closures

A function defined in a function is called a **closure_**. It is special because in the function body of the closure, not only the local arguments but also the variables created in the parent function are also available.

For example, suppose we have the following function:

```
add <- function(x, y) {
  x + y
}
```

This function has two arguments. Each time we call add(), we should supply two arguments. If we use closure, we can generate special versions of this function with a pre-specified argument. In the following section, we will create a simple closure to accomplish this.

Creating a simple closure

Here, we will create a function called addn, which has one argument y. This function does not do the actual plus calculation but creates a child function that adds y to whatever number x supplied:

```
addn <- function(y) {
  function(x) {
    x + y
  }
}
```

It may take extra efforts to realize that addn does not return a number like a typical function, but returns a closure: that is, a function defined in a function. The closure calculates x + y, where x refers to a local argument and y refers to an argument in its enclosing environment. In other words, addn() is no longer a calculator, but a calculator factory that manufactures calculators.

The factory function enables us to create specialized versions of calculators. For example, we can create two functions that add 1 and 2 to a numeric vector, respectively:

```
add1 <- addn(1)
add2 <- addn(2)
```

The two functions work as if the second argument of add(x, y) was fixed. The following code validates the calculators made by addn():

```
add1(10)
## [1] 11
add2(10)
## [1] 12
```

Take add1 as an example. The add1 <- addn(1) code evaluates addn(1), which results in a function assigned to add1:

```
add1
## function(x) {
## x + y
## }
## <environment: 0x00000000139b0e58>
```

When we print add1, it is a bit different because the environment of add1 is also attached. The environment of a function will be printed if it is not the current environment-in this case, the global environment. In the environment of add1, y is specified in addn(1), which can be verified by running the following code:

```
environment(add1)$y
## [1] 1
```

We can call environment() with add1 to access its enclosing environment, which captures y. That's exactly how closure works. We can do the same thing to add2 and see the value of y we specified with addn(2):

```
environment(add2)$y
## [1] 2
```

Making specialized functions

Closures are useful to make specialized functions. For example, due to the flexibility of the production of graphics, plot functions often provide a large number of arguments. If we frequently use only a particular subset of all arguments, we can make specialized versions that make the code easier to write and read.

The following `color_line` function is a version of `plot` specialized in color picking, but with plot type and line type being fixed. It is comparable to a factory that makes pens of all colors:

```
color_line<- function(col) {
  function(...) {
    plot(..., type = "l", lty = 1, col = col)
  }
}
```

If we want a red pen, we call `color_line` and get a specialized function that draws red lines. The resulted function is also open to other arguments such as title and font:

```
red_line<- color_line("red")
red_line(rnorm(30), main = "Red line plot")
```

This function produces the following line plot:

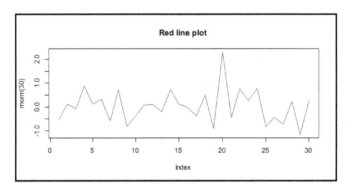

The preceding code looks more readable than the original version that does not employ such a specialized function:

```
plot(rnorm(30), type = "l", lty = 1, col = "red",
  main = "Red line plot")
```

Fitting normal distribution with maximal likelihood estimation

Closures are useful when we work with an algorithm with some given data. Optimization, for example, is a problem to find a set of parameters that maximizes or minimizes a pre-defined objective function subject to certain constraints and data. In statistics, many parameter estimation problems are, in essence, optimization problems. One good example that demonstrates the use of closures is **MLE (maximum likelihood estimation)**. When we estimate the parameters of a statistical model with data, we often use the method of maximal likelihood estimation (MLE, see https://en.wikipedia.org/wiki/Maximum_likelihood). The idea behind MLE is simple: the estimated values of parameters should make the observed data the most probable, given the model.

To perform MLE, we need a function that measures how probable it is to observe a given set of data under a specific model. Then, we apply optimization techniques to find out the values of parameters that maximizes the probability.

For example, we know that a set of observed data is generated by normal distribution, but the problem is, we don't know the parameters: mean and standard deviation. Then, we can use MLE to estimate them, given the observed data.

First, we know that the probability density function of a normal distribution with mean $\hat{A}\mu$ and standard deviation $\ddot{I}$ is:

$$f(x) = \frac{1}{\sqrt{2\pi}\sigma} \exp(-\frac{1}{2}\frac{(x - \mu_0)^2}{\sigma_0^2})$$

Therefore, the likelihood function given the observed data x is:

$$L(\mu, \sigma; x) = (2\pi\sigma^2)^{-n/2} \exp(-\frac{1}{2\sigma^2}\Sigma(x_i - \mu)^2)$$

To make the optimization easier, we will take a natural log and negate on both sides and get the negative log-likelihood function:

$$-l(\mu, \sigma; x) = \frac{n}{2}\ln(2\pi) + \frac{n}{2}\ln(\sigma^2) + \frac{1}{2\sigma^2}\Sigma(x_i - \mu)^2$$

The negative log-likelihood function has the same monotonicity as the original function. The optimization solution of this function is the same as the original function but can be much easier to solve. That's why we use this function in the estimation.

The following `nloglik` R function returns a closure of the two parameters of normal distribution given the observed data x:

```
nloglik<- function(x) {
  n <- length(x)
  function(mean, sd) {
    log(2 * pi) * n / 2 + log(sd ^ 2) * n / 2 + sum((x - mean) ^ 2) / (2 *
sd ^ 2)
  }
}
```

In this way, for any given set of observations, we call `nloglike` to get a negative log-likelihood function with respect to mean and standard deviation. It tells us how unlikely it is for us to observe the given data x assuming that the true model takes the values of `mean` and `sd` we specify.

For example, we use `rnorm()` to generate 10,000 random numbers that are normally distributed with mean 1 and standard deviation 2. Therefore, `mean` = 1 and `sd` = 2 are the true values of the distribution parameters:

```
data <- rnorm(10000, 1, 2)
```

Then, we turn to the `mle()` function in the `stats4` package. This function implements a number of numeric methods to find the minimum value of a given negative log-likelihood function with certain parameters. It takes a starting point of the numeric search, and a lower bound and a upper bound of the solution:

```
fit <- stats4::mle(nloglik(data),
  start = list(mean = 0, sd = 1), method = "L-BFGS-B",
  lower =c(-5, 0.01), upper = c(5, 10))
```

After some iterations, it finds an MLE solution and returns an S4 object, which includes the related data of the solution. To see how close the estimates are to the true value, we will extract the `coef` slot from the object:

```
fit@coef
## mean sd
## 1.007548 1.990121
```

It is obvious that the estimates are very close to the true values. Relatively speaking, both estimates have an error lower than 1 percent, as can be verified here:

```
(fit@coef - c(1, 2)) / c(1, 2)
## mean sd
##  0.007547752 -0.004939595
```

The following function is a composition of the histogram of `data` and the density functions of the normal distribution with both true parameters (red curve) and estimated parameters (blue curve):

```
hist(data, freq =FALSE, ylim =c(0, 0.25))
curve(dnorm(x, 1, 2), add =TRUE, col =rgb(1, 0, 0, 0.5), lwd =6)
curve(dnorm(x, fit@coef[["mean"]], fit@coef[["sd"]]),
    add =TRUE, col ="blue", lwd =2)
```

This produces the following histogram, plus a fitted normal density curve:

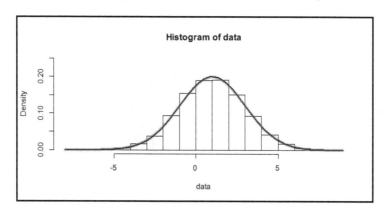

We can see that the density function produced by the estimated parameters is very close to the true model.

Using higher-order functions

In the previous section, we discussed closures, functions defined in parent functions. In this section, we will discuss higher-order functions, that is, functions that accept another function as an argument.

Before walking into this topic, we need more knowledge of how functions behave when they are passed around either as variables or as function arguments.

Creating aliases for functions

The first question is: if we assign an existing function to another variable, will it affect the enclosing environment of the function? If this is so, then the search paths of symbols that are not locally defined will be different.

The following code demonstrates why the enclosing environment of a function is not changed when it is assigned to another symbol. We define a simple function f1 that prints the executing environment, the enclosing environment, and the calling environment when it is called. Then, we define f2 that also prints the three environments, but in addition, it assigns the function of f1 to a local variable p and call p inside f2.

If p <- f1 defines the function locally, the enclosing environment of p will be the executing environment of f2. Otherwise, the enclosing environment will remain the global environment in which f1 is defined:

```
f1 <- function() {
  cat("[f1] executing in ")
  print(environment())
  cat("[f1] enclosed by ")
  print(parent.env(environment()))
  cat("[f1] calling from ")
  print(parent.frame())
}
f2 <- function() {
  cat("[f2] executing in ")
  print(environment())
  cat("[f2] enclosed by ")
  print(parent.env(environment()))
  cat("[f2] calling from ")
  print(parent.frame())
  p <- f1
  p()
}
f1()
## [f1] executing in <environment: 0x000000001435d700>
## [f1] enclosed by <environment: R_GlobalEnv>
## [f1] calling from <environment: R_GlobalEnv>
f2()
## [f2] executing in <environment: 0x0000000014eb2200>
## [f2] enclosed by <environment: R_GlobalEnv>
## [f2] calling from <environment: R_GlobalEnv>
## [f1] executing in <environment: 0x0000000014eaedf0>
## [f1] enclosed by <environment: R_GlobalEnv>
## [f1] calling from <environment: 0x0000000014eb2200>
```

We called the two functions in turn and found that p is called from the executing environment of f2, but the enclosing environment is unchanged. In other words, the search path of p and f1 are exactly the same. In fact, p <- f1 assigns exactly the same function f1 represents to p, and then, they both point to the same function.

Using functions as variables

Functions in R are not as special as they are in other programming languages. Everything is an object. Functions are objects too and can be referred to by variables.

Suppose we have a function like this:

```
f1 <- function(x, y) {
  if (x > y) {
    x + y
  } else {
    x - y
  }
}
```

In the preceding function, two conditional branches lead to different expressions that may result in different values. To achieve the same goal, we can also let the conditional branches result in different functions, store the result in a variable, and, finally, call the function the variable represents to get the result:

```
f2 <- function(x, y) {
  op <- if (x > y) `+` else `-`
  op(x, y)
}
```

Note that in R, everything we do is done by a function. The most basic operators + and – are functions too. They can be assigned to the variable op, and we can call op if it is indeed a function.

Passing functions as arguments

The previous examples demonstrate that we can easily pass functions around just like everything else, including passing functions in arguments.

In the following example, we will define two functions called add and product, respectively:

```
add <- function(x, y, z) {
  x + y + z
}
product <- function(x, y, z) {
  x * y * z
}
```

Then, we will define another function, `combine`, that tries to combine x, y, and z in some way specified by the argument `f`. Here, `f` is assumed to be a function that takes three arguments as we call it. In this way, `combine` is more flexible. It is not limited to a particular way of combining the inputs, but allows the user to specify:

```
combine <- function(f, x, y, z) {
    f(x, y, z)
}
```

We can pass `add` and `product`, we just defined in turn, to see if it works:

```
combine(add, 3, 4, 5)
## [1] 12
combine(product, 3, 4, 5)
## [1] 60
```

It is natural that when we call `combine(add, 3, 4, 5)`, the function body has `f = add` and `f(x, y, z)`, which result in `add(x, y, z)`. The same logic also applies to calling `combine` with `product`. Since `combine` accepts a function in its first argument, it is indeed a higher-order function.

Another reason we need higher-order functions is that the code is easier to read and write at a higher level of abstraction. In many cases, using higher-order functions make the code shorter yet more expressive. For example, for-loop is an ordinary flow-control device that iterates along a vector or list.

Suppose we need to apply a function named `f` to each element of vector x. If the function itself is vectorized, it is better to call `f(x)` directly. However, not every function supports vectorized operations, nor does every function need to be vectorized. If we want to do so, a for-loop, like the following one, solves the problem:

```
result<-list()
for (i in seq_along(x)) {
    result[[i]] <-f(x[[i]])
}
result
```

In the previous loop, `seq_along(x)` produces a sequence from 1 to the length of x, which is equivalent to `1:length(x)`. The code looks simple and easy to implement, but if we use it all the time, the drawback becomes significant.

Suppose the operation in each iteration gets more complicated: it would be hard to read. If you think about it, you will find that the code tells R *how* to finish the task instead of *what* the task is about. When you take a look at very long, sometimes nested loops, you would have a hard time to figure out what it is actually doing.

Instead, we can apply a function (f) to each element of a vector or list (x) by calling `lapply`, which we introduced in the previous chapters:

```
lapply(x, f)
```

In fact, `lapply` is essentially the same as the following code, although it is implemented in C:

```
lapply <- function(x, f, ...) {
  result <- list()
  for (i in seq_along(x)) {
      result[[i]] <-f(x[i], ...)
  }
}
```

This function is a higher-order function, because it works at a higher level of abstraction. Although it still uses a for-loop inside, it separates the work into two levels of abstraction so that each level looks simple.

In fact, `lapply` also supports extending f with additional arguments. For example, + has two arguments, as shown in the following code:

```
lapply(1:3, `+`, 3)
## [[1]]
## [1] 4
##
## [[2]]
## [1] 5
##
## [[3]]
## [1] 6
```

The preceding lines of code are equivalent to:

```
list(1 +3, 2 +3, 3 +3)
```

The preceding line of code is also equivalent to the case where we use a closure to produce the x+3 function:

```
lapply(1:3, addn(3))
## [[1]]
## [1] 4
##
## [[2]]
## [1] 5
##
## [[3]]
```

```
## [1] 6
```

As we mentioned in the previous chapters, `lapply` only returns a list. If we want a vector instead, we should use `sapply` in the interactive mode:

```
sapply(1:3, addn(3))
## [1] 4 5 6
```

Alternatively, we should use `vapply` in the programming code with type checking:

```
vapply(1:3, addn(3), numeric(1))
## [1] 4 5 6
```

In addition to these functions, R also offers several other apply-family functions, as we mentioned in the previous chapters, as well as `Filter`, `Map`, `Reduce`, `Find`, `Position`, and `Negate`. For more details, refer to `?Filter` in the documentation.

Moreover, the use of higher-order functions not only makes the code easier to read and more expressive, but these functions also separate the implementation of each level of abstraction so that they are independent from each other. It is much easier to improve simpler components than a whole bundle of logic coupled together.

For example, we can use apply-family functions to perform vector mapping, given a function. If each iteration is independent from the others, we can parallelize the mapping using multiple CPU cores so that more tasks can be done simultaneously. However, if we didn't use higher-order functions at the first place but a for-loop instead, it would take a while to convert it to parallel code.

For example, let's assume we use a for-loop to get the results. In each iteration, we perform a heavy computing task. Even if we find each iteration independently from the others, it is not always straightforward to convert it to parallel code:

```
result <- list()
for (i in seq_along(x)) {
  # heavy computing task
  result[[i]] <- f(x[[i]])
}
result
```

However, if we use the higher-order function `lapply()`, things will be much easier:

```
result <- lapply(x, f)
```

It would just take one small change to transform the code into a parallel version. Using `parallel::mclapply()`, we can apply `f` to each element of `x` with multiple cores:

```
result <- parallel::mclapply(x, f)
```

Unfortunately, `mclapply()` does not support Windows. More code is needed to perform parallel apply functions in Windows. We will cover this topic in the chapter on high-performance computing.

Computing on language

In the previous section, we introduced the functional programming facilities in R. You learned that functions are just another type of object we can pass around. When we create a new function, say `fun`, the environment we create will be associated with the function. This environment is called the enclosing environment of the function, which can be accessed via `environment(fun)`. Each time we call the function, a new executing environment that contains the unevaluated arguments (promises) will be created to host the execution of the function, which enables lazy evaluation. The parent of the executing environment is the enclosing environment of the function, which enables lexical scoping.

Functional programming allows us to write code in higher level of abstraction. Metaprogramming goes even further. It allows us to tweak the language itself and make certain language constructs easier to use in a certain scenario. Some popular R packages use metaprogramming in their functions to make things easier. In this section, I will show you the power of metaprogramming as well as its pros and cons, so that you can understand how related packages and functions work.

Before digging into the knowledge of how things work, we may look at a few built-in functions that use metaprogramming to make things easier.

Suppose we want to filter the built-in dataset `iris` for records with each numeric column being greater than 80 percent of all records.

The standard method is to subset the rows of the data frame by composing a logical vector:

```
iris[iris$Sepal.Length > quantile(iris$Sepal.Length, 0.8) &
    iris$Sepal.Width > quantile(iris$Sepal.Width, 0.8) &
    iris$Petal.Length > quantile(iris$Petal.Length, 0.8) &
    iris$Petal.Width > quantile(iris$Petal.Width, 0.8), ]
##     Sepal.Length  Sepal.Width  Petal.Length  Petal.Width
## 110     7.2          3.6           6.1           2.5
## 118     7.7          3.8           6.7           2.2
## 132     7.9          3.8           6.4           2.0
```

```
## Species
## 110 virginica
## 118 virginica
## 132 virginica
```

In the preceding code, each call of quantile() yields an 80 percent threshold for a column. Although the code works, it is quite redundant, because each time we use a column, we have to begin with iris$. In total, iris$ appears nine times.

The built-in function subset is useful to make things easier:

```
subset(iris,
    Sepal.Length > quantile(Sepal.Length, 0.8) &
    Sepal.Width > quantile(Sepal.Width, 0.8) &
    Petal.Length > quantile(Petal.Length, 0.8) &
    Petal.Width > quantile(Petal.Width, 0.8))
##      Sepal.Length Sepal.Width Petal.Length Petal.Width
## 110      7.2          3.6          6.1          2.5
## 118      7.7          3.8          6.7          2.2
## 132      7.9          3.8          6.4          2.0
## Species
## 110 virginica
## 118 virginica
## 132 virginica
```

The preceding code returns exactly the same results, but with cleaner code. But why does it work while omitting iris$ in the previous example does not work?

```
iris[Sepal.Length > quantile(Sepal.Length, 0.8) &
    Sepal.Width > quantile(Sepal.Width, 0.8) &
    Petal.Length > quantile(Petal.Length, 0.8) &
    Petal.Width > quantile(Petal.Width, 0.8), ]
## Error in `[.data.frame`(iris, Sepal.Length > quantile(Sepal.Length, 0.8)
## & : object 'Sepal.Length' not found
```

The preceding code does not work, because Sepal.Length and other columns are not defined in the scope (or environment) where we evaluate the subsetting expression. The magic function, subset, uses metaprogramming techniques to tweak the evaluation environment of its arguments so that Sepal.Length>quantile(Sepal.Length, 0.8) is evaluated in the environment with the columns of iris.

Moreover, subset not only works with rows, but is also useful in selecting columns. For example, we can also specify the select argument by directly using the column names as variables instead of using a character vector to select columns:

```
subset(iris,
```

```
    Sepal.Length > quantile(Sepal.Length, 0.8) &
    Sepal.Width > quantile(Sepal.Width, 0.8) &
    Petal.Length > quantile(Petal.Length, 0.8) &
    Petal.Width > quantile(Petal.Width, 0.8),
  select = c(Sepal.Length, Petal.Length, Species))
##      Sepal.Length Petal.Length  Species
## 110      7.2          6.1      virginica
## 118      7.7          6.7      virginica
## 132      7.9          6.4      virginica
```

See, `subset` tweaks how its second argument (`subset`) and third argument (`select`) are evaluated. The result is we can write simpler code with less redundancy.

In the next few sections, you will learn what happens behind the scene and how it is designed to work.

Capturing and modifying expressions

When we type an expression and hit the *Enter* (or return) key, R will evaluate the expression and show the output. Here is an example:

```
rnorm(5)
## [1]  0.54744813 1.15202065 0.74930997 -0.02514251
## [5]  0.99714852
```

It shows the five random numbers generated. The magic of `subset` is that it tweaks the environment where the argument is evaluated. This happens in two steps: first, capture the expression and then, interfere the evaluation of the expression.

Capturing expressions as language objects

Capturing an expression means preventing the expression from being evaluated, but storing the expression itself as a variable. The function that does this is `quote()`; we can call `quote()` to capture the expression between the parenthesis:

```
call1 <- quote(rnorm(5))
call1
## rnorm(5)
```

The preceding code does not result in five random numbers, but the function call itself. We can use `typeof()` and `class()` to see the type and class of the resulted object, `call1`:

```
typeof(call1)
## [1] "language"
```

```
class(call1)
## [1] "call"
```

We can see that `call1` is essentially a language object and it is a call. We can also write a function name in `quote()`:

```
name1 <- quote(rnorm)
name1
## rnorm
typeof(name1)
## [1] "symbol"
class(name1)
## [1] "name"
```

In this case, we don't get a call but a symbol (or name) instead.

In fact, `quote()` will return a call if a function call is captured and return a symbol if a variable name is captured. The only requirement is the validity of the code to capture; that is, as long as the code is syntactically correct, `quote()` will return the language object that represents the captured expression itself.

Even if the function does not exist or the variable as yet is undefined, the expression can be captured on its own:

```
quote(pvar)
## pvar
quote(xfun(a = 1:n))
## xfun(a = 1:n)
```

Of the preceding language objects, maybe `pvar`, `xfun`, and `n` are all as yet undefined, but we can `quote()` them anyway.

It is important to understand the difference between a variable and a symbol object, and between a function and a call object. A variable is a name of an object, and a symbol object is the name itself. A function is an object that is callable, and a call object is a language object that represents such a function call, which is as yet unevaluated. In this case, `rnorm` is a function and it is callable (for example, `rnorm(5)` returns five random numbers), but `quote(rnorm)` returns a symbol object and `quote(rnorm(5))` returns a call object, both of which are only the representations of the language itself.

We can convert the call object to a list so that we can see its internal structure:

```
as.list(call1)
## [[1]]
## rnorm
##
```

```
## [[2]]
## [1] 5
```

This shows that the call consists of two components: the symbol of the function and one argument. We can extract objects from a call object:

```
call1[[1]]
## rnorm
typeof(call1[[1]])
## [1] "symbol"
class(call1[[1]])
## [1] "name"
```

The first element of `call1` is a symbol:

```
call1[[2]]
## [1] 5
typeof(call1[[2]])
## [1] "double"
class(call1[[2]])
## [1] "numeric"
```

The second element of `call1` is a numeric value. From the previous examples, we know that `quote()` captures a variable name as a symbol object and a function call as a call object. Both of them are language objects. Like typical data structures, we can use `is.symbol()`/`is.name()` and `is.call()` to detect whether an object is a symbol or a call, respectively. More generally, we can also use `is.language()` to detect both the symbol and the call.

Another question is, "What if we call `quote()` on a literal value? What about a number or a string?" The following code creates a numeric value num1 and a quoted numeric value num2:

```
num1 <- 100
num2 <- quote(100)
```

They have exactly the same representation:

```
num1
## [1] 100
num2
## [1] 100
```

In fact, they have exactly the same value:

```
identical(num1, num2)
## [1] TRUE
```

Therefore, `quote()` does not transform a literal value (such as a number, logical value, string, and so on) to a language object, but it leaves it as it is. However, an expression that combines several literal values into a vector will still be transformed into a call object. Here is an example:

```
call2 <- quote(c("a", "b"))
call2
## c("a", "b")
```

It is consistent because `c()` is indeed a function that combines values and vectors. Moreover, if you look at the list representation of the call using `as.list()`, we can see the structure of the call:

```
as.list(call2)
## [[1]]
## c
##
## [[2]]
## [1] "a"
##
## [[3]]
## [1] "b"
```

The types of elements in the call can be revealed by `str()`:

```
str(as.list(call2))
## List of 3
##  $ : symbol c
##  $ : chr "a"
##  $ : chr "b"
```

Another noteworthy fact here is that simple arithmetic calculations are captured as calls too because they are surely function calls to arithmetic operators such as + and *, which are essentially built-in functions. For example, we can use the `quote()` function to the simplest arithmetic calculation, perform `1 + 1`:

```
call3 <- quote(1 + 1)
call3
## 1 + 1
```

The arithmetic representation is preserved, but it is a call and has exactly the same structure as of a call:

```
is.call(call3)
## [1] TRUE
str(as.list(call3))
## List of 3
```

```
##  $ : symbol +
##  $ : num 1
##  $ : num 1
```

Given all the preceding knowledge about capturing an expression, we can now capture a nested call; that is, a call that contains more calls:

```
call4 <- quote(sqrt(1 + x ^ 2))
call4
## sqrt(1 + x ^ 2)
```

We can use a function in the `pryr` package to view the recursive structure of the call. To install the package, run `install.package("pryr")`. Once the package is ready, we can call `pryr::call_tree` to do that:

```
pryr::call_tree(call4)
## \- ()
## \- `sqrt
## \- ()
## \- `+
## \-  1
## \- ()
## \- `^
## \- `x
## \-  2
```

For `call4`, the recursive structure is printed in a tree structure. The `\- ()` operator means a call, then `` `var `` represents a symbol object `var`, and others are literal values. In the preceding output, we can see that symbols and calls are captured and literal values are preserved.

If you are curious about the call tree of an expression, you can always use this function because it precisely reflects the way R processes the expression.

Modifying expressions

When we capture an expression as a call object, the call can be modified as if it were a list. For example, we can change the function to call by replacing the first element of the call with another symbol:

```
call1
## rnorm(5)
call1[[1]] <- quote(runif)
call1
## runif(5)
```

So, `rnorm(5)` is changed to `runif(5)`.

We can also add new argument to the call:

```
call1[[3]] <- -1
names(call1)[[3]] <- "min"
call1
## runif(5, min = -1)
```

Then, the call now has another parameter: `min = -1`.

Capturing expressions of function arguments

In the previous examples, you learned how to use `quote()` to capture a known expression, but `subset` works with arbitrary user-input expressions. Suppose we want to capture the expression of argument x.

The first implementation uses `quote()`:

```
fun1 <- function(x) {
  quote(x)
}
```

Let's see if `fun1` can capture the input expression when we call the function with `rnorm(5)`:

```
fun1(rnorm(5))
## x
```

Obviously, `quote(x)` only captures x and has nothing to do with the input expression `rnorm(5)`. To correctly capture it, we need to use `substitute()`. The function captures an expression and substitutes existing symbols with their expressions. The simplest usage of this function is to capture the expression of a function argument:

```
fun2 <- function(x) {
  substitute(x)
}
fun2(rnorm(5))
## rnorm(5)
```

With this implementation, `fun2` returns the input expression rather than x because x is replaced with the input expression, in this case, `rnorm(5)`.

The following examples demonstrate the behavior of `substitute` when we supply a list of language objects or literal values. In the first example, we substitute each symbol `x` in the given expression with `1`:

```
substitute(x + y + x ^ 2, list(x = 1))
## 1 + y + 1 ^ 2
```

In the second example, we substitute each symbol `f` that is supposed to be a function name with another quoted function name `sin`:

```
substitute(f(x + f(y)), list(f = quote(sin)))
## sin(x + sin(y))
```

Now, we are able to capture a certain expression with `quote()` and user-input expression with `substitute()`.

Constructing function calls

In addition to capturing expressions, we can directly build language objects with built-in functions. For example, `call1` is a captured call using `quote()`:

```
call1 <- quote(rnorm(5, mean = 3))
call1
## rnorm(5, mean = 3)
```

We can use `call()` to create a call of the same function with the same arguments:

```
call2 <- call("rnorm", 5,  mean = 3)
call2
## rnorm(5, mean = 3)
```

Alternatively, we can convert a list of call components to a call using `as.call()`:

```
call3 <- as.call(list(quote(rnorm), 5, mean = 3))
call3
## rnorm(5, mean = 3)
```

The three methods create identical calls; that is, they call a function of the same name and with the same arguments, which can be confirmed by calling `identical()` with the three resulted call objects:

```
identical(call1, call2)
## [1] TRUE
identical(call2, call3)
## [1] TRUE
```

Evaluating expressions

After capturing an expression, the next step is evaluating it. This can be done with `eval()`.

For example, if we type `sin(1)` and enter, the value will appear immediately:

```
sin(1)
## [1] 0.841471
```

To control the evaluation of `sin(1)`, We can use `quote()` to capture the expression and then `eval()` to evaluate the function call:

```
call1 <- quote(sin(1))
call1
## sin(1)
eval(call1)
## [1] 0.841471
```

We can capture any expression that is syntactically correct, which allows us to `quote()` an expression that uses undefined variables:

```
call2 <- quote(sin(x))
call2
## sin(x)
```

In `call2`, `sin(x)` uses an undefined variable x. If we directly evaluate it, an error occurs:

```
eval(call2)
## Error in eval(expr, envir, enclos): object 'x' not found
```

This error is similar to what happens when we directly run `sin(x)` without x being defined:

```
sin(x)
## Error in eval(expr, envir, enclos): object 'x' not found
```

The difference between directly running in console and using `eval()` is that `eval()` allows us to provide a list to evaluate the given expression. In this case, we don't have to create a variable x but supply a temporary list that contains x so that the expression will look up symbols in the list:

```
eval(call2, list(x = 1))
## [1] 0.841471
```

Alternatively, `eval()` also accepts an environment for symbol lookup. Here, we will create a new environment `e1` in which we create a variable x with value `1`, and then we use `eval()` in the call in `e1`:

```
e1 <- new.env()
e1$x <- 1
eval(call2, e1)
## [1] 0.841471
```

The same logic also applies when the captured expression has more undefined variables:

```
call3 <- quote(x ^ 2 + y ^ 2)
call3
## x ^ 2 + y ^ 2
```

Directly evaluating the expression without a complete specification of the undefined symbols will result in an error:

```
eval(call3)
## Error in eval(expr, envir, enclos): object 'x' not found
```

So does a partial specification, as follows:

```
eval(call3, list(x = 2))
## Error in eval(expr, envir, enclos): object 'y' not found
```

Only when we fully specify the values of the symbols in the expression can the evaluation result in a value:

```
eval(call3, list(x = 2, y = 3))
## [1] 13
```

The evaluation model of `eval(expr, envir, enclos)` is the same as calling a function. The function body is `expr`, and the executing environment is `envir`. If `envir` is given as a list, then the enclosing environment is `enclos`, or otherwise the enclosing environment is the parent environment of `envir`.

This model implies the exact behavior of symbol lookup. Suppose we use an environment instead to evaluate `call3`. Since `e1` only contains variable x, the evaluation does not proceed:

```
e1 <- new.env()
e1$x <- 2
eval(call3, e1)
## Error in eval(expr, envir, enclos): object 'y' not found
```

Then, we create a new environment whose parent is e1 and contains variable y. If we now evaluate call3 in e2, both x and y are found and the evaluation works:

```
e2 <- new.env(parent = e1)
e2$y <- 3
eval(call3, e2)
## [1] 13
```

In the preceding code, eval(call3, e2) tries to evaluate call3, with e2 being the executing environment. Now, we can go through the evaluating process to get a better understanding of how it works. The evaluation process is reflected by travelling recursively along the call tree produced by pryr::call_tree():

```
pryr::call_tree(call3)
## \- ()
## \- `+
## \- ()
## \- `^
## \- `x
## \- 2
## \- ()
## \- `^
## \- `y
## \- 2
```

First, it tries to find a function called +. It goes through e2 and e1, and does not find + until it reaches the base environment (baseenv()), where all the basic arithmetic operators are defined. Then, + needs to evaluate its arguments, so it looks for another function called ^ and finds it by going through the same flow. Then, again ^ needs to evaluate its arguments, so it looks for symbol x in e2. Environment e2 does not contain variable x, so it continues searching in e2 class's parent environment, e1, and finds x there. Finally, it looks for symbol y in e2 and finds it immediately. When the arguments a call needs are ready, the call can be evaluated to a result.

An alternative approach is to supply a list to envir and an enclosing environment:

```
e3 <- new.env()
e3$y <- 3
eval(call3, list(x = 2), e3)
## [1] 13
```

The evaluating process begins with an executing environment generated from the list whose parent environment is e3, as specified. Then, the process is exactly the same as the previous example.

Since everything we do is essentially calling functions, `quote()` and `substitute()` can capture everything, including assignment and other operations that do not look like calling functions. In fact, for example, `x <- 1` is essentially calling `<-` with `(x, 1)`, and `length(x) <- 10` is essentially calling `length<-` with `(x, 10)`.

To demonstrate the point, we may construct another example in which we create a new variable.

In the following example, we supply a list to generate the executing environment and `e3` as the enclosing environment:

```
eval(quote(z <- x + y + 1), list(x = 1), e3)
e3$z
## NULL
```

As a result, `z` is not created in `e3` but in a temporary executing environment created from the list. If we, instead, specify `e3` as the executing environment, the variable will be created in it:

```
eval(quote(z <- y + 1), e3)
e3$z
## [1] 4
```

In conclusion, `eval()` works in a way extremely close to the behavior of function calling, but `eval()` allows us to customize the evaluation of an expression by tweaking its executing and enclosing environment, which allows us to do good things such as `subset` as well as bad things such as follows:

```
eval(quote(1 + 1), list(`+` = `-`))
## [1] 0
```

Understanding non-standard evaluation

In the previous sections, you learned how to use `quote()` and `substitute()` to capture an expression as a language object, and you learned how to use `eval()` to evaluate it within a given list or environment. These functions constitute the facility of metaprogramming in R and allow us to tweak standard evaluation. The main application of metaprogramming is to perform non-standard evaluation to make certain usage easier. In the following sections, we will discuss a few examples to gain a better understanding of how it works.

Implementing quick subsetting using non-standard evaluation

Often, we need to take out a certain subset from a vector. The range of the subset may be the first few elements, last few elements, or some elements in the middle.

The first two cases can be easily handled by `head(x, n)` and `tail(x, n)`. The third case requires an input of the length of the vector.

For example, suppose we have an integer vector and want to take out elements from the third to the fifth last:

```
x <- 1:10
x[3:(length(x) -5)]
## [1] 3 4 5
```

The preceding subsetting expression uses x twice and looks a bit redundant. We can define a quick subsetting function that uses metaprogramming facilities to provide a special symbol to refer to the length of the input vector The following function, qs, is a simple implementation of this idea that allows us to use dot (.) to represent the length of the input vector x:

```
qs <- function(x, range) {
  range <- substitute(range)
   selector <- eval(range, list(. =length(x)))
   x[selector]
}
```

Using this function, we can use `3:(. - 5)` to represent the same range as the motivating example:

```
qs(x, 3:(. -5))
## [1] 3 4 5
```

We can also easily pick out a number by counting from the last element:

```
qs(x, . -1)
## [1] 9
```

Based on `qs()`, the following function is designed to trim both margins of n elements from the input vector x; that is, it returns a vector without the first n and last n elements of x:

```
trim_margin <- function(x, n) {
  qs(x, (n + 1):(. -n -1))
}
```

The function looks alright, but when we call it with an ordinary input, an error occurs:

```
trim_margin(x, 3)
## Error in eval(expr, envir, enclos): object 'n' not found
```

How come it couldn't find n? To understand why this happens, we need to analyze the path of symbol lookup when trim_margin is called. In the next section, we will go into this in detail and introduce the concept of dynamic scoping to resolve the problem.

Understanding dynamic scoping

Before trying to tackle the problem, let's use what you have learned to analyze what went wrong. When we call trim_margin(x, 3), we call qs(x, (n + 1):(. - n - 1)) in a fresh executing environment with x, and n. qs() is special because it uses non-standard evaluation. More specifically, it first captures range as a language object and then evaluates it with a list of additional symbols to provide, which, at the moment, only contains . = length(x).

The error just happens at eval(range, list(. = length(x))). The number of margin elements to trim, n, cannot be found here. There must be something wrong with the enclosing environment of evaluation. Now, we will take a closer look at the default value of the enclos argument of eval():

```
eval
## function (expr, envir = parent.frame(), enclos = if (is.list(envir) ||
## is.pairlist(envir)) parent.frame() else baseenv())
## .Internal(eval(expr, envir, enclos))
## <bytecode: 0x00000000106722c0>
## <environment: namespace:base>
```

The definition of eval() says that if we supply a list to envir, which is exactly what we have done, enclos will take parent.frame() by default, which is the calling environment of eval(); that is, the executing environment when we call qs(). Certainly, there is no n in any executing environment of qs.

Here, we exposed a shortcoming of using substitute() in trim_margin() because the expression is only fully meaningful in the correct context, that is, the executing environment of trim_margin(), which is also the calling environment of qs(). Unfortunately, substitute() only captures the expression; it does not capture the environment in which the expression is meaningful. Therefore, we have to do it ourselves.

Now, we know where the problem comes from. The solution is simple: always use the correct enclosing environment in which the captured expression is defined. In this case, we specify `enclos = parent.frame()` so that `eval()` looks for all symbols other than . in the calling environment of `qs()`, that is, the executing environment of `trim_margin()` where n is supplied.

The following lines of code are the fixed version of `qs()`:

```
qs <- function(x, range) {
  range <- substitute(range)
    selector <- eval(range, list(. =length(x)), parent.frame())
    x[selector]
}
```

We can test the function with the same code that went wrong previously:

```
trim_margin(x, 3)
## [1] 4 5 6
```

Now, the function works in the correct manner. In fact, this mechanism is the so-called **dynamic scoping**. Recall what you learned in the previous chapter. Each time a function is called, an executing environment is created. If a symbol cannot be found in the executing environment, it will search the enclosing environment.

With lexical scoping used in standard evaluation, the enclosing environment of a function is determined when the function is defined and so is the environment where it is defined.

However, with dynamic scoping used in non-standard evaluation, by contrast, the enclosing environment should be the calling environment in which the captured expression is defined so that symbols can be found either in the customized executing environment or in the enclosing environment, along with its parents.

In conclusion, when a function uses non-standard evaluation, it is important to ensure that dynamic scoping is correctly implemented.

Using formulas to capture expression and environment

To correctly implement dynamic scoping, we use `parent.frame()` to track the expression captured by `substitute()`. An easier way is to use a formula to capture the expression and environment at the same time.

In the chapter of working the data, we saw that a formula is often used to represent the relationship between variables. Most model functions (such as `lm()`) accept a formula to specify the relationship between a response variable and explanatory variables.

In fact, a formula object is much simpler than that. It automatically captures the expressions beside ~ and the environment where it is created. For example, we can directly create a formula and store it in a variable:

```
formula1 <- z ~ x ^ 2 + y ^ 2
```

We can see that the formula is essentially a language object with the `formula` class:

```
typeof(formula1)
## [1] "language"
class(formula1)
## [1] "formula"
```

If we convert the formula to a list, we can have a closer look at its structure:

```
str(as.list(formula1))
## List of 3
##  $ : symbol ~
##  $ : symbol z
##  $ : language x^2 + y^2
##  - attr(*, "class")= chr "formula"
##  - attr(*, ".Environment") =< environment: R_GlobalEnv>
```

We can see that `formula1` captured not only the expressions as language objects on both sides of ~, but also the environment where it was created. In fact, a formula is merely a call of function ~ with the arguments and calling environment captured. If both sides of ~ are specified, the length of the call is 3:

```
is.call(formula1)
## [1] TRUE
length(formula1)
## [1] 3
```

To access the language objects it captured, we can extract the second and the third elements:

```
formula1[[2]]
## z
formula1[[3]]
## x^2 + y^2
```

To access the environment where it was created, we can call `environment()`:

```
environment(formula1)
## <environment: R_GlobalEnv>
```

A formula can also be right-sided, that is, only the right side of ~ is specified. Here is an example:

```
formula2 <- ~x + y
str(as.list(formula2))
## List of 2
##  $ : symbol ~
##  $ : language x + y
##  - attr(*, "class")= chr "formula"
##  - attr(*, ".Environment")=<environment: R_GlobalEnv>
```

In this case, only one argument of ~ is supplied and captured so that we have a call of two language objects and we can access the expression it captured by extracting its second element:

```
length(formula2)
## [1] 2
formula2[[2]]
## x + y
```

With the knowledge of how the formula works, we can implement another version of qs() and trim_margin() using the formula.

The following function, qs2, behaves consistently with qs when range is a formula, or otherwise, it directly uses range to subset x:

```
qs2 <- function(x, range) {
  selector <- if (inherits(range, "formula")) {
eval(range[[2]], list(. = length(x)), environment(range))
  } else range
  x[selector]
}
```

Note that we use inherits(range, "formula") to check whether range is a formula and use environment(range) to implement dynamic scoping. Then, we can use a right-sided formula to activate non-standard evaluation:

```
qs2(1:10, ~3:(. -2))
## [1] 3 4 5 6 7 8
```

Otherwise, we can use standard evaluation:

```
qs2(1:10, 3)
## [1] 3
```

Now, we can re-implement `trim_margin` with qs2 using a formula:

```
trim_margin2 <- function(x, n) {
  qs2(x, ~ (n + 1):(. -n -1))
}
```

As can be verified, dynamic scoping works correctly because the formula used in `trim_margin2` automatically captures the executing environment, which is also the environment where the formula and n are defined:

```
trim_margin2(x, 3)
## [1] 4 5 6
```

Implementing subset with metaprogramming

With the knowledge of language objects, evaluation functions, and dynamic scoping, now we have the capability to implement a version of `subset`.

The underlying idea of the implementation is simple:

- Capture the row subsetting expression and evaluate it within the data frame which is, in essence, a list
- Capture the column-selecting expression and evaluate it in a named list of integer indices
- Use the resulting row selector (logical vector) and column selector (integer vector) to subset the data frame

Here is an implementation of the preceding logic:

```
subset2 <- function(x, subset = TRUE, select = TRUE) {
  enclos <- parent.frame()
  subset <- substitute(subset)
  select <- substitute(select)
  row_selector <- eval(subset, x, enclos)
  col_envir <- as.list(seq_along(x))
  names(col_envir) <- colnames(x)
  col_selector <- eval(select, col_envir, enclos)
  x[row_selector, col_selector]
}
```

The feature of row subsetting is easier to implement than the column selecting part. To perform row subsetting, we only need to capture `subset` and evaluate it within the data frame.

The column subsetting is trickier here. We will create a list of integer indices for the columns and give them the corresponding names. For example, a data frame with three columns (say, x, y, and z) needs a list of indices such as `list(a = 1, b = 2, c = 3)`, which allows us to select rows in the form of `select = c(x, y)` because `c(x, y)` is evaluated within the list.

Now, the behavior of `subset2` is very close to the built-in function `subset`:

```
subset2(mtcars, mpg >= quantile(mpg, 0.9), c(mpg, cyl, qsec))
##                  mpg  cyl  qsec
## Fiat 128        32.4   4   19.47
## Honda Civic     30.4   4   18.52
## Toyota Corolla  33.9   4   19.90
## Lotus Europa    30.4   4   16.90
```

Both implementations allow us to use `a:b` to select all columns between a and b, including both sides:

```
subset2(mtcars, mpg >= quantile(mpg, 0.9), mpg:drat)
##                  mpg  cyl disp  hp   drat
## Fiat 128        32.4   4  78.7  66   4.08
## Honda Civic     30.4   4  75.7  52   4.93
## Toyota Corolla  33.9   4  71.1  65   4.22
## Lotus Europa    30.4   4  95.1  113  3.77
```

Summary

In this chapter, you learned about the idea and usage of functional programming, including closures and higher order functions. We went further by digging into the metaprogramming facilities, including language objects, evaluation functions, formula, and the implementation of dynamic scoping to ensure user-input expressions are correctly handled when we customize the evaluation behavior. Since a number of popular packages use metaprogramming and non-standard evaluation to make interactive analysis easier, it is important to understand how it works so that we can be more confident to predict and debug the code.

In the next chapter, we will walk into another infrastructure of R: the object-oriented programming systems. You will learn the basic idea of object-oriented programming, how this idea is implemented in R, and how it can be useful. More specifically, we will begin with the looser S3 system, cover the stricter system S4 which offers a richer set of features, and introduce the reference class and newly implemented R5 system.

10
Object-Oriented Programming

In the previous chapter, you learned how functional programming and metaprogramming make it possible to customize the behavior of functions. We can create a function within a certain context, which is called a closure. We can also use higher order functions by passing functions around just like other objects.

In this chapter, you will learn how to customize the behavior of objects by walking into the world of object-oriented programming. R provides several different object-oriented systems to work with. At first glance, they look quite different from the object-oriented systems in other programming languages. However, the idea is mostly the same. I will briefly explain the concept of class and method of objects, and show you how they can be useful in unifying the way we work with data and models.

We will cover the following topics at the beginner level in the subsequent sections:

- The idea of object-oriented programming
- S3 system
- S4 system
- Reference class
- R6 package

Finally, we will compare these systems in several aspects.

Introducing object-oriented programming

If you are a developer from programming languages such as Java, Python, C++, C#, you should feel familiar with the object-oriented style of coding. However, if you are not familiar with any other object-oriented programming languages, you will probably be puzzled by this term, as it sounds a bit abstract. However, don't worry; this is much easier to understand than it looks if we think about the core of programming.

When we talk about programming, we are actually talking about using programming tools to solve problems. Before solving the problem, we need to model the problem first. Traditionally, we usually figured out an algorithm that takes several steps to solve a numeric computing problem. Then, we wrote some procedural code to implement the algorithm. For example, most statistical algorithms are implemented in a procedural style, that is, by transforming the input into the output according to the theory, step by step.

However, many problems are so closely bounded to the real world that it can be very intuitive to model the problem by defining some classes of objects as well as the interaction between them. In other words, by programming in an object-oriented style, we simply try to mimic the important features of the objects in concern at an appropriate level of abstraction.

There are many concepts involved in object-oriented programming. Here, we will only focus on the most important ones.

Understanding classes and methods

The most important concepts in this chapter are classes and methods. A class describes what the object is, and a method defines what it can do. There are countless real-world examples for these concepts. For example, `animal` can be a class. In this class, we can define methods such as make sound and move. The `vehicle` can be a class, too. In this class, we can define methods such as start, move, and stop. The `person` can be a class that has methods such as wake up, talk to another person, and go somewhere.

For a particular problem, we can define classes according to our need to model the objects we are dealing with and define methods for them to model the interaction between the objects. The objects need not be physical or tangible. One practical example is a bank account. It only exists in the data storage of banks, but it can be useful to model bank accounts with some data fields such as balance and owner, and some methods such as deposit, withdraw, and transfer between two accounts.

Understanding inheritance

Another important concept of object-oriented programming is inheritance, that is, we can define a class that inherits the behavior of a base (or super) class and has some new behavior. Usually, the base class is more abstract and general in concept, and the inheriting class is more concrete and specific. This is simply true for the concepts in our everyday life.

For example, dog and cat are two classes that inherit from the animal class. The animal class defines methods such as make sound and move. The dog and cat classes inherit these methods but implement them in different ways so that they make different sounds and move in different manners.

Also, car, bus, and airplane are classes that inherit from the vehicle class. The vehicle class defines methods such as start, move, and stop. The car, bus, and airplane classes inherit these functionalities but work in different ways. The car and bus can move in two dimensions on the surface, while airplane can move in three dimensions in the air.

There are some other concepts in the system of object-oriented programming, but we are not going to focus on them in this chapter. Let's keep in mind the concepts we mentioned and see how these concepts work in R programming.

Working with the S3 object system

The S3 object system in R is a simple, loose, object-oriented system. Every basic object type has an S3 class name. For example, integer, numeric, character, logical, list, data.frame, and so on are all S3 classes.

For example, the type of vec1 class is double, which means the internal type or storage mode of vec1 is double floating numbers. However, its S3 class is numeric:

```
vec1 <- c(1, 2, 3)
typeof(vec1)
## [1] "double"
class(vec1)
## [1] "numeric"
```

The type of data1 class is list, which means the internal type or storage mode of data1 is a list, but its S3 class is data.frame:

```
data1 <- data.frame(x = 1:3, y = rnorm(3))
typeof(data1)
## [1] "list"
class(data1)
```

```
## [1] "data.frame"
```

In the following sections, we'll explain the difference between the internal type of an object and its S3 class.

Understanding generic functions and method dispatch

As we mentioned earlier in this chapter, a class can possess a number of methods that define its behavior, mostly with other objects. In the S3 system, we can create generic functions and implement them for different classes as methods. This is how the S3 method dispatch works to make the class of an object important.

There are many simple examples of the S3 generic function in R. Each of them is defined for a general purpose and allows different classes of objects to have their own implementation for that purpose. Let's first take a look at the head() and tail() functions. Their functionality is simple: head() gets the first n records of a data object, while tail() gets the last n records of a data object. It is different from x[1:n] because it has different definitions of record for different classes of objects. For an atomic vector (numeric, character, and so on), the first n records just means the first n elements. However, for a data frame, the first n record means the first n rows rather than columns. Since a data frame is essentially a list, directly taking out the first n elements from a data frame is actually taking out the first n columns, which is not what head() is intended for.

First, let's type head and see what's inside the function:

```
head
## function (x, ...)
## UseMethod("head")
## <bytecode: 0x000000000f052e10>
## <environment: namespace:utils>
```

We find that there are no actual implementation details in this function. Instead, it calls UseMethod("head") to make head a so-called **generic function** to perform method dispatch, that is, it may behave in different ways for different classes.

Now, let's create two data objects of numeric class and data.frame class, respectively, and see how method dispatch works when we pass each object to the generic function head:

```
num_vec <- c(1, 2, 3, 4, 5)
data_frame <- data.frame(x = 1:5, y = rnorm(5))
```

For a numeric vector, `head` simply takes its first several elements.

```
head(num_vec, 3)
## [1] 1 2 3
```

However, for a data frame, `head` takes its first several rows rather than columns:

```
head(data_frame, 3)
##   x         y
## 1 1 0.8867848
## 2 2 0.1169713
## 3 3 0.3186301
```

Here, we can use a function to mimic the behavior of `head`. The following code is a simple implementation that takes the first n elements of any given object x:

```
simple_head <- function(x, n) {
  x[1:n]
}
```

For a numeric vector, it works in exactly the same way as `head`:

```
simple_head(num_vec, 3)
## [1] 1 2 3
```

However, for a data frame, it actually tries to take out the first n columns. Recall that the data frame is a list, and each column of the data frame is an element of the list. It may cause an error if n exceeds the number of columns of the data frame or, equivalently, the number of elements of the list:

```
simple_head(data_frame, 3)
## Error in `[.data.frame`(x, 1:n): undefined columns selected
```

To improve the implementation, we can check whether the input object x is a data frame before taking any measures:

```
simple_head2 <- function(x, n) {
  if (is.data.frame(x)) {
    x[1:n,]
  } else {
    x[1:n]
  }
}
```

Now, the behavior of `simple_head2` is almost the same with `head` for atomic vectors and data frames:

```
simple_head2(num_vec, 3)
## [1] 1 2 3
simple_head2(data_frame, 3)
##   x          y
## 1 1 0.8867848
## 2 2 0.1169713
## 3 3 0.3186301
```

However, `head` offers more than this. To see the methods implemented for `head`, we can call `methods()`, which returns a character vector:

```
methods("head")
## [1] head.data.frame*  head.default*    head.ftable*
## [4] head.function*    head.matrix      head.table*
## see '?methods' for accessing help and source code
```

It shows that there is already a bunch of built-in methods of `head` for a number of classes other than vectors and data frames. Note that the methods are all in the form of `method.class`. If we input a `data.frame` object, `head` will call `head.data.frame` internally. Similarly, if we input a `table` object, it will call `head.table` internally. What if we input a numeric vector? When no method is found that matches the class of the input object, it will turn to `method.default`, if defined. In this case, all atomic vectors are matched by `head.default`. The process through which a generic function finds the appropriate method for a certain input object is called **method dispatch**.

It looks like we can always check the class of the input object in a function to achieve the goal of method dispatch. However, it is easier to implement a method for another class to extend the functionality of a generic function because you don't have to modify the original generic function by adding specific class-checking conditions each time. We'll cover this later in this section.

Working with built-in classes and methods

S3 generic functions and methods are most useful in unifying the way we work with all kinds of models. For example, we can create a linear model and use generic functions to view the model from different perspectives:

```
lm1 <- lm(mpg ~ cyl + vs, data = mtcars)
```

In previous chapters, we mentioned that a linear model is essentially a list of data fields resulted from model fitting. That's why the type of lm1 is list, but its class is lm so that generic functions will choose methods for lm:

```
typeof(lm1)
## [1] "list"
class(lm1)
## [1] "lm"
```

The S3 method dispatch even happens without explicit calling of S3 generic functions. If we type lm1 and see what it is, the model object is printed:

```
lm1
##
## Call:
## lm(formula = mpg ~ cyl + vs, data = mtcars)
##
## Coefficients:
## (Intercept)          cyl           vs
##      39.6250      -3.0907      -0.9391
```

In fact, print is implicitly called:

```
print(lm1)
##
## Call:
## lm(formula = mpg ~ cyl + vs, data = mtcars)
##
## Coefficients:
## (Intercept)          cyl           vs
##      39.6250      -3.0907      -0.9391
```

We know that lm1 is essentially a list. Why does it not look like a list when it is printed? This is because print is a generic function, and it has a method for lm that prints the most important information of the linear model. We can get the actual method we call by getS3method("print", "lm"). In fact, print(lm1) goes to stats:::print.lm, which can be verified by checking whether they are identical:

```
identical(getS3method("print", "lm"), stats:::print.lm)
## [1] TRUE
```

Note that print.lm is defined in the stats package, but is not exported for public use, so we have to use ::: to access it. Generally, it is a bad idea to access internal objects in a package, because they may change in different releases and have no changes visible to the user. In most cases, we simply don't need to because generic functions such as print automatically choose the right method to call.

In R, `print` has methods implemented for many classes. The following code shows how many methods are implemented for different classes:

```
length(methods("print"))
## [1] 198
```

You can call `methods("print")` to view the whole list. In fact, if more packages are loaded, there will be more methods defined for classes in these packages.

While `print` shows a brief version of the model, `summary` shows detailed information. This function is also a generic function that has many methods for all kinds of model classes:

```
summary(lm1)
## 
## Call:
## lm(formula = mpg ~ cyl + vs, data = mtcars)
## 
## Residuals:
##     Min      1Q Median     3Q    Max
## -4.923 -1.953 -0.081  1.319  7.577
## 
## Coefficients:
##             Estimate Std. Error t value Pr(>|t|)
## (Intercept)  39.6250     4.2246   9.380 2.77e-10 ***
## cyl          -3.0907     0.5581  -5.538 5.70e-06 ***
## vs           -0.9391     1.9775  -0.475    0.638
## ---
## Signif. codes:
## 0 '***' 0.001 '**' 0.01 '*' 0.05 '.' 0.1 ' ' 1
## 
## Residual standard error: 3.248 on 29 degrees of freedom
## Multiple R-squared:  0.7283, Adjusted R-squared:  0.7096
## F-statistic: 38.87 on 2 and 29 DF,  p-value: 6.23e-09
```

The summary of a linear model provides not only what `print` shows but also some important statistics for the coefficients and the overall model. In fact, the output of `summary` is another object that can be accessed for the data it contains. In this case, it is a list of the `summary.lm` class, and it has its own method of `print`:

```
lm1summary <- summary(lm1)
typeof(lm1summary)
## [1] "list"
class(lm1summary)
## [1] "summary.lm"
```

To list what elements `lm1summary` contains, we can view the names on the list:

```
names(lm1summary)
## [1] "call"          "terms"        "residuals"
## [4] "coefficients"  "aliased"      "sigma"
## [7] "df"            "r.squared"    "adj.r.squared"
##[10] "fstatistic"    "cov.unscaled"
```

We can access each element in exactly the same way as we extract an element from a typical list. For example, to access the estimated coefficients of the linear model, we can use `lm1$coefficients`. Alternatively, we will use the following code to access the estimated coefficients:

```
coef(lm1)
## (Intercept)        cyl         vs
##   39.6250234  -3.0906748  -0.9390815
```

Here, `coef` is also a generic function that extracts the vector of coefficients from a model object. To access the detailed coefficient table in the model summary, we can use `lm1summary$coefficients` or, again, `coef`:

```
coef(lm1summary)
##                  Estimate  Std. Error    t value      Pr(>|t|)
## (Intercept) 39.6250234   4.2246061   9.3795782  2.765008e-10
## cyl         -3.0906748   0.5580883  -5.5379676  5.695238e-06
## vs          -0.9390815   1.9775199  -0.4748784  6.384306e-01
```

There are other useful model-related generic functions such as `plot`, `predict`, and so on. All these generic functions we mentioned are standard ways in R for users to interact with an estimated model. Different built-in models and those provided by third-party packages all try to implement these generic functions so that we don't need to remember different sets of functions to work with each model.

For example, we can use the `plot` function to the linear model with 2-by-2 partitions:

```
oldpar <- par(mfrow = c(2, 2))
plot(lm1)
par(oldpar)
```

This produces the following image with four parts:

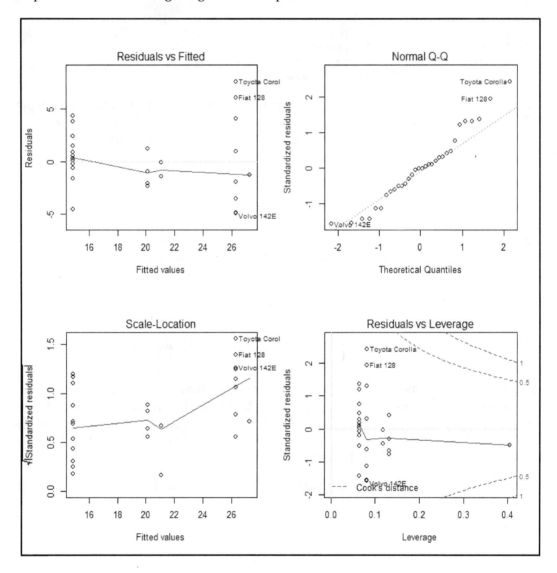

We can see that we used `plot` function to a linear model, which will result in four diagnostic plots that show the features of the residuals, which can be helpful in getting an impression on whether the model fit is good or bad. Note that if we directly call the `plot` function to a `lm` in a console, the four plots are interactively done in turn. To avoid this, we call `par()` to divide the plot area into 2-by-2 subareas.

Most statistical models are useful because they can be used to predict with new data. To do this, we use `predict`. In this case, we can supply the linear model and the new data to `predict`, and it will find the right method to make predictions with new data:

```
predict(lm1, data.frame(cyl = c(6, 8), vs = c(1, 1)))
##        1         2
## 20.14189 13.96054
```

This function can be used both in sample and out of sample. If we supply new data to the model, it is out-of-sample prediction. If the data we supply is already in the sample, it is in-sample prediction. Here, we can create a scatter plot between actual values (`mtcars$mpg`) and fitted values to see how well the fitted linear model predicts:

```
plot(mtcars$mpg, fitted(lm1))
```

The plot generated is shown as follows:

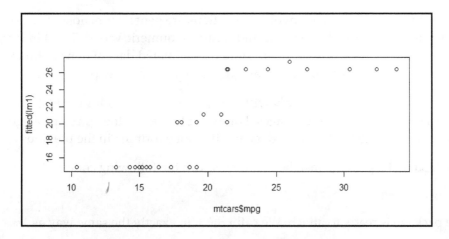

Here, `fitted` is also a generic function, which, in this case, is equivalent to `lm1$fitted.values`, fitted values are also equal to the predicted values with the original dataset using `predict(lm1, mtcars)`.

The difference between the actual values and fitted values of the response variable is called residuals. We can use another generic function `residuals` to access the numeric vector, or equivalently, use `lm1$residuals`. Here, we will make a density plot of the residuals:

```
plot(density(residuals(lm1)),
     main = "Density of lm1 residuals")
```

The plot generated is shown as follows:

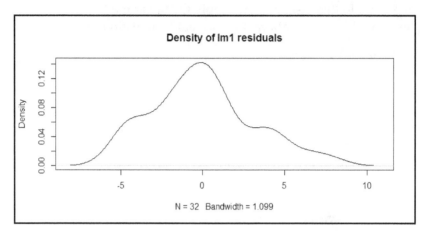

In the preceding function call, all involved functions are generic functions. The `residuals` function extracts the residuals from `lm1` and returns a numeric vector. The `density` function creates a list of class `density` to store the estimated data of density function of the residuals. Finally, `plot` turns to `plot.density` to create a density plot.

These generic functions work not only with `lm`, `glm`, and other built-in models, but also with models provided by other packages. For example, we use the `rpart` package to fit a regression tree model using the same data and the same formula in the previous example.

If you don't have the package installed, you need run the following code:

```
install.packages("rpart")
```

Now, the package is ready to attach. We call `rpart` in exactly the same way as `lm`:

```
library(rpart)
tree_model <- rpart(mpg ~ cyl + vs, data = mtcars)
```

We can do so because the package authors want the function call to be consistent with how we call built-in functions in R. The resulted object is a list of class `rpart`, which works in the same way with `lm` is a list of class `rpart`:

```
typeof(tree_model)
## [1] "list"
class(tree_model)
## [1] "rpart"
```

Like lm object, rpart also has a number of generic methods implemented. For example, we use the print function to print the model in its own way:

```
print(tree_model)
## n = 32
##
## node), split, n, deviance, yval
##        * denotes terminal node
##
## 1) root 32 1126.04700 20.09062
##    2) cyl >= 5 21   198.47240 16.64762
##      4) cyl >= 7 14    85.20000 15.10000 *
##      5) cyl < 7 7     12.67714 19.74286 *
##    3) cyl < 5 11   203.38550 26.66364 *
```

The output indicates that print has a method for rpart, which briefly shows what the regression tree looks like. In addition to print, summary gives more detailed information about the model fitting:

```
summary(tree_model)
## Call:
## rpart(formula = mpg ~ cyl + vs, data = mtcars)
##   n = 32
##
##            CP nsplit rel error    xerror       xstd
## 1 0.64312523      0 1.0000000 1.0844542 0.25608044
## 2 0.08933483      1 0.3568748 0.3858990 0.07230642
## 3 0.01000000      2 0.2675399 0.3875795 0.07204598
##
## Variable importance
## cyl   vs
##  65   35
##
## Node number 1: 32 observations,     complexity param=0.6431252
##    mean=20.09062, MSE=35.18897
##    left son=2 (21 obs) right son=3 (11 obs)
##    Primary splits:
##        cyl < 5    to the right, improve=0.6431252, (0 missing)
##        vs  < 0.5 to the left,  improve=0.4409477, (0 missing)
##    Surrogate splits:
##        vs < 0.5 to the left,   agree=0.844, adj=0.545, (0 split)
##
## Node number 2: 21 observations,     complexity param=0.08933483
##    mean=16.64762, MSE=9.451066
##    left son=4 (14 obs) right son=5 (7 obs)
##    Primary splits:
##        cyl < 7    to the right, improve=0.5068475, (0 missing)
```

```
##    Surrogate splits:
##        vs < 0.5 to the left,   agree=0.857, adj=0.571, (0 split)
##
## Node number 3: 11 observations
##    mean=26.66364, MSE=18.48959
##
## Node number 4: 14 observations
##    mean=15.1, MSE=6.085714
##
## Node number 5: 7 observations
##    mean=19.74286, MSE=1.81102
```

Likewise, `plot` and `text` also have methods for `rpart` to visualize it:

```
oldpar <- par(xpd = NA)
plot(tree_model)
text(tree_model, use.n = TRUE)
par(oldpar)
```

Then, we have the following tree graph:

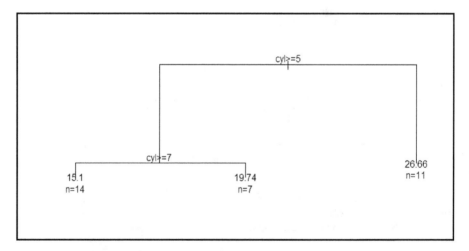

We can use `predict` to make predictions with new data, just like what we did with the linear model in the previous examples:

```
predict(tree_model, data.frame(cyl = c(6, 8), vs = c(1, 1)))
##        1        2
## 19.74286 15.10000
```

Note that not all models implement methods for all the generic functions. For example, since the regression tree is not a simple parametric model, it does not implement a method for `coef`:

```
coef(tree_model)
## NULL
```

Defining generic functions for existing classes

In the previous section, you learned how to use existing classes and methods to work with model objects. The S3 system, however, also allows us to create our own classes and generic functions.

Recall the example where we used conditional expressions to mimic the method dispatch of `head`. We mentioned that it works, but is often not the best practice. S3 generic functions are more flexible and easier to extend. To define a generic function, we usually create a function in which
`UseMethod` is called to trigger method dispatch. Then, we create method functions in the form of `method.class` for the classes we want the generic function to work with and usually a default method in the form of `method.default` to capture all other cases. Here is a simple rewriting of this example using generic function and methods. Here, we will create a new generic function, `generic_head`, with two arguments: the input object x and the number of records to take, n. The generic function only
calls `UseMethod("generic_head")` to ask R for method dispatch according to the class of x:

```
generic_head <- function(x, n)
  UseMethod("generic_head")
```

For atomic vectors (numeric, character, logical, and so on), the first n elements should be taken. We can define `generic_head.numeric`, `generic_head.character`, and so on respectively, but in this case, it looks better to define a default method to capture all cases that are not matched by other `generic_head.class` methods:

```
generic_head.default <- function(x, n) {
  x[1:n]
}
```

Now, `generic_head` has only one method, which is equivalent to not using generic function at all:

```
generic_head(num_vec, 3)
## [1] 1 2 3
```

Since we haven't defined the method for class `data.frame`, supplying a data frame will fall back to `generic_head.default`, which causes an error due to the invalid access of an out-of-bound column index:

```
generic_head(data_frame, 3)
## Error in `[.data.frame`(x, 1:n): undefined columns selected
```

However, let's assume we define a method for `data.frame`:

```
generic_head.data.frame <- function(x, n) {
  x[1:n,]
}
```

The generic function works as it is supposed to:

```
generic_head(data_frame, 3)
##   x         y
## 1 1 0.8867848
## 2 2 0.1169713
## 3 3 0.3186301
```

You may notice that the methods we implemented earlier are not robust because we don't have the argument checked. For example, if n is greater than the number of elements of the input object, the function will behave differently and usually in an undesirable way. I'll leave it as an exercise for you to make the methods more robust and behave appropriately for corner cases.

Creating objects of new classes

Now, it is time to have some examples of defining new classes. Note that `class(x)` gets the class of x, while `class(x) <- "some_class"` sets the class of x to `some_class`.

Using list as the underlying data structure

Just like `lm` and `rpart`, list is probably the most widely used underlying data structure to create a new class. This is because a class represents a type of object that can store different kinds of data with different lengths and has some methods to interact with other objects.

In the following example, we will define a function called `product` that creates a list of the class `product` with a name, price, and inventory. We'll define its own `print` method and add more behaviors as we go ahead:

```
product <- function(name, price, inventory) {
```

```
    obj <- list(name = name,
      price = price,
      inventory = inventory)
    class(obj) <- "product"
    obj
}
```

Note that we created a list first, replaced its class with `product`, and finally returned the object. In fact, the class of an object is a character vector. An alternative way is to use `structure()`:

```
product <- function(name, price, inventory) {
    structure(list(name = name,
      price = price,
      inventory = inventory),
      class = "product")
}
```

Now, we have a function that produced objects of the class `product`. In the following code, we will call `product()` and create an instance of this class:

```
laptop <- product("Laptop", 499, 300)
```

Like all previous objects, we can see its internal data structure and its S3 class for method dispatch:

```
typeof(laptop)
## [1] "list"
class(laptop)
## [1] "product"
```

Obviously, `laptop` is a list of class `product` as we created it. Since we haven't defined any methods for this class, its behavior is no different from an ordinary list object. If we type it, it will be printed as a list with its customized class attribute:

```
laptop
## $name
## [1] "Laptop"
##
## $price
## [1] 499
##
## $inventory
## [1] 300
##
## attr(,"class")
## [1] "product"
```

First, we can implement the `print` method for this class. Here, we want the class and the data fields in it to be printed in a compact style:

```
print.product <- function(x, ...) {
  cat("<product>\n")
  cat("name:", x$name, "\n")
  cat("price:", x$price, "\n")
  cat("inventory:", x$inventory, "\n")
  invisible(x)
}
```

It is a convention that the `print` method returns the input object itself for further use. If the printing is customized, then we often use `invisible` to suppress repeated printing of the same object that the function returns. You may try returning x directly and see what happens.

Then, we type the variable again. The `print` method will be dispatched to `print.product` since it is already defined:

```
laptop
## <product>
## name: Laptop
## price: 499
## inventory: 300
```

We can access the elements in `laptop` just like extracting elements from a list:

```
laptop$name
## [1] "Laptop"
laptop$price
## [1] 499
laptop$inventory
## [1] 300
```

If we create another instance and put the two instances into a list, `print.product` will still be called when the list is printed:

```
cellphone <- product("Phone", 249, 12000)
products <- list(laptop, cellphone)
products
## [[1]]
## <product>
## name: Laptop
## price: 499
## inventory: 300
##
## [[2]]
```

```
## <product>
## name: Phone
## price: 249
## inventory: 12000
```

This is because when `products` is printed as a list, it calls `print` on each of the elements, which also causes method dispatch.

Creating an S3 class is much simpler than most other programming languages that require formal definition of classes. It is important to have sufficient checking on the arguments to ensure that the created object is internally consistent with what the class represents.

For example, without proper checking, we can create a product with negative and non-integer inventory:

```
product("Basket", 150, -0.5)
## <product>
## name: Basket
## price: 150
## inventory: -0.5
```

To avoid this, we need to add some checking conditions in the object-generating function, `product`:

```
product <- function(name, price, inventory) {
  stopifnot(
    is.character(name), length(name) == 1,
    is.numeric(price), length(price) == 1,
    is.numeric(inventory), length(inventory) == 1,
  price > 0, inventory >= 0)
    structure(list(name = name,
      price = as.numeric(price),
      inventory = as.integer(inventory)),
      class = "product")
}
```

The function is enhanced, in that `name` must be a single string, `price` must be a single positive number, and `inventory` must be a single non-negative number. With this function, we cannot create ridiculous products by mistake, and such errors can be found in an early stage:

```
product("Basket", 150, -0.5)
## Error: inventory >= 0 is not TRUE
```

In addition to defining new classes, we can also define new generic functions. In the following code, we will define a new generic function called `value` and implement a method for `product` by measuring the value of the inventory of the product:

```
value <- function(x, ...)
  UseMethod("value")

value.default <- function(x, ...) {
  stop("value is undefined")
}

value.product <- function(x, ...) {
  x$price * x$inventory
}
```

For other classes, it calls `value.default` and stops. Now, `value` can be used with all instances of `product` we created:

```
value(laptop)
## [1] 149700
value(cellphone)
## [1] 2988000
```

The generic function also works with apply family functions by performing method dispatch for each element in the input vector or list:

```
sapply(products, value)
## [1]   149700 2988000
```

One more question is once we create the object of a certain class, does that mean that we can no longer change it? No, we still can change it. In this case, we can modify an existing element of `laptop`:

```
laptop$price <- laptop$price * 0.85
```

We can also create a new element in `laptop`:

```
laptop$value <- laptop$price * laptop$inventory
```

Now, we can take a look at it, and the changes are effective:

```
laptop
## <product>
## name: Laptop
## price: 424.15
## inventory: 300
```

What's worse is that we can even remove an element by setting it to NULL. This is why the S3 system is considered to be loose. You can't make sure that the object of a certain type has a fixed set of data fields and methods.

Using an atomic vector as the underlying data structure

In the previous section, we demonstrated an example of creating a new class from a list object. In fact, it is sometimes useful to create a new class of object from an atomic vector. In this section, I will show you a series of steps to create vectors with a percentage representation.

We first define a function, percent. This function simply checks whether the input is a numeric vector and alters its class to percent, which inherits from numeric:

```
percent <- function(x) {
  stopifnot(is.numeric(x))
  class(x) <- c("percent", "numeric")
  x
}
```

The inheritance here means that method dispatch first looks for methods of percent. If none is found, then it looks for methods of numeric. Therefore, the order of the class names matters. S3 inheritance will be covered in detail in the following section.

Now, we can create a percent vector from a numeric vector:

```
pct <- percent(c(0.1, 0.05, 0.25, 0.23))
pct
## [1] 0.10 0.05 0.25 0.23
## attr(,"class")
## [1] "percent" "numeric"
```

At the moment, there is no method implemented for percent. So, pct looks like an ordinary numeric vector with a customized class attribute. The purpose of this class is to show its values in percentage form, such as 25 percent instead of its original decimal representation.

To achieve this goal, we first implement as.character for the percent class by producing the correct string representation of the percentage form:

```
as.character.percent <- function(x, ...) {
  paste0(as.numeric(x) * 100, "%")
}
```

Now, we can get the desired string representation of a given percent vector:

```
as.character(pct)
## [1] "10%" "5%"  "25%" "23%"
```

Likewise, we need to implement format for percent by directly calling as.character:

```
format.percent <- function(x, ...) {
  as.character(x, ...)
}
```

Now, format has the same effect:

```
format(pct)
## [1] "10%" "5%"  "25%" "23%"
```

Now, we can implement print for percent by calling format.percent directly:

```
print.percent <- function(x, ...) {
  print(format.percent(x), quote = FALSE)
}
```

Note that we specify quote = FALSE when we print the formatted strings to make it look like numbers rather than strings. This is exactly the desired effect:

```
pct
## [1] 10% 5%  25% 23%
```

Note that arithmetic operators such as + and * automatically preserve the class of the output vector. As a result, the output vector is still printed in percentage form:

```
pct + 0.2
## [1] 30% 25% 45% 43%
pct * 0.5
## [1] 5%    2.5%  12.5% 11.5%
```

Unfortunately, other functions may not preserve the class of their input. For example, sum, mean, max, and min will drop the customized class and return a plain numeric vector instead:

```
sum(pct)
## [1] 0.63
mean(pct)
## [1] 0.1575
max(pct)
## [1] 0.25
min(pct)
## [1] 0.05
```

To make sure the percentage form is preserved when we perform these calculations, we need to implement these methods for the `percent` class:

```
sum.percent <- function(...) {
  percent(NextMethod("sum"))
}
mean.percent <- function(x, ...) {
  percent(NextMethod("mean"))
}
max.percent <- function(...) {
  percent(NextMethod("max"))
}
min.percent <- function(...) {
  percent(NextMethod("max"))
}
```

In the first method, `NextMethod("sum")` calls `sum` for numeric class, and the output numeric vector is wrapped with `percent` again. The same logic also applies to the implementation of the other three methods:

```
sum(pct)
## [1] 63%
mean(pct)
## [1] 15.75%
max(pct)
## [1] 25%
min(pct)
## [1] 5%
```

Now, these functions return values in percentage form, too. However, if we combine a percent vector with other numeric values, the percent class will be gone:

```
c(pct, 0.12)
## [1] 0.10 0.05 0.25 0.23 0.12
```

We can do the same thing to `c`:

```
c.percent <- function(x, ...) {
  percent(NextMethod("c"))
}
```

Now, combining percent vectors with numeric values result in percent vectors too:

```
c(pct, 0.12, -0.145)
## [1] 10%     5%     25%     23%     12%     -14.5%
```

However, from the other side, when we subset the percent vector or extract a value from it, the percent class will be dropped:

```
pct[1:3]
## [1] 0.10 0.05 0.25
pct[[2]]
## [1] 0.05
```

To fix this, we need to implement `[` and `[[` for percent in exactly the same way. You might be surprised to see a method called `[.percent`, but it will indeed match the percent class when we use these operators on a percent vector:

```
`[.percent` <- function(x, i) {
  percent(NextMethod("["))
}
`[[.percent` <- function(x, i) {
  percent(NextMethod("[["))
}
```

Now, both subsetting and extracting preserve the percent class:

```
pct[1:3]
## [1] 10% 5%   25%
pct[[2]]
## [1] 5%
```

With all these methods implemented, we can place a percent vector as a column of a data frame:

```
data.frame(id = 1:4, pct)
##    id pct
## 1   1 10%
## 2   2  5%
## 3   3 25%
## 4   4 23%
```

The percentage form is correctly preserved as a column in the data frame.

Understanding S3 inheritance

The S3 system is loose. You only need to create a function in the form of `method.class` to implement a method for a generic function. You only need to supply a character vector with multiple elements to indicate the inheritance relationship along the vector.

As we mentioned in the previous section, the class vector determines the order of matching classes in method dispatch. To demonstrate it, we will use a simple example in which we construct a number of classes with inheritance relationships.

Suppose we want to model some vehicles such as a car, bus, and airplane. These vehicles have something in common. They all have name, speed, and position, and they can move. To model them, we can define a base class called `vehicle`, which stores the common parts. We also define `car`, `bus`, and `airplane` that inherit from `vehicle` but have customized behaviors.

First, we will define a function to create the `vehicle` object, which is essentially an environment. We choose an environment over a list because we need its reference semantics, that is, we pass around the object, and modifying it will not cause a copy of the object. So, the object always refers to the same vehicle, no matter where it is passed around:

```
Vehicle <- function(class, name, speed) {
  obj <- new.env(parent = emptyenv())
  obj$name <- name
  obj$speed <- speed
  obj$position <- c(0, 0, 0)
  class(obj) <- c(class, "vehicle")
  obj
}
```

Note that `class(obj) <- c(class, "vehicle")` may look ambiguous because `class` is both a function argument and a basic function. In fact, `class(obj) <-` will look for the `class<-` function so that the usage does not cause ambiguity. The `Vehicle` function is a general creator of vehicle class objects with common data fields. The following function is specialized functions to create `car`, `bus` and `airplane` that inherit vehicle:

```
Car <- function(...) {
  Vehicle(class = "car", ...)
}
Bus <- function(...) {
  Vehicle(class = "bus", ...)
}
Airplane <- function(...) {
  Vehicle(class = "airplane", ...)
}
```

With the three preceding functions, we can create `car`, `bus`, and `airplane` objects. All inherit from the `vehicle` class. Now, we create an instance for each class:

```
car <- Car("Model-A", 80)
bus <- Bus("Medium-Bus", 45)
airplane <- Airplane("Big-Plane", 800)
```

Now, we will implement a common `print` method for `vehicle`:

```
print.vehicle <- function(x, ...) {
  cat(sprintf("<vehicle: %s>\n", class(x)[[1]]))
  cat("name:", x$name, "\n")
  cat("speed:", x$speed, "km/h\n")
  cat("position:", paste(x$position, collapse = ", "))
}
```

Since no `print.car`, `print.bus` or `print.airplane` is defined, typing those variables will print them with `print.vehicle`:

```
car
## <vehicle: car>
## name: Model-A
## speed: 80 km/h
## position: 0, 0, 0
bus
## <vehicle: bus>
## name: Medium-Bus
## speed: 45 km/h
## position: 0, 0, 0
airplane
## <vehicle: airplane>
## name: Big-Plane
## speed: 800 km/h
## position: 0, 0, 0
```

A vehicle is a carrier designed to be driven and to move. Naturally, we define a generic function called `move`, which modifies the position of a vehicle to reflect a user-supplied movement in a three-dimensional space. Since different vehicles move in different ways with distinct limitations, we can further implement several `move` methods for the various classes of vehicle we just defined:

```
move <- function(vehicle, x, y, z) {
  UseMethod("move")
}
move.vehicle <- function(vehicle, movement) {
  if (length(movement) != 3) {
    stop("All three dimensions must be specified to move a vehicle")
```

```
  }
  vehicle$position <- vehicle$position + movement
  vehicle
}
```

Here, we will limit the movement that can happen to a car and a bus to two dimensions.
Therefore, we will implement move.bus and move.car by checking the length of
the movement vector, which is only allowed to be 2. If the movement is valid, then, we
would force the third dimension of movement to be and then call NextMethod("move") to
call move.vehicle with vehicle and the latest value of movement:

```
move.bus <- move.car <- function(vehicle, movement) {
  if (length(movement) != 2) {
    stop("This vehicle only supports 2d movement")
  }
  movement <- c(movement, 0)
  NextMethod("move")
}
```

An airplane can move in either two or three dimensions. Therefore, move.airplane can be
flexible to accept both. If the movement vector is two dimensional, then the movement on
the third dimension is regarded as zero:

```
move.airplane <- function(vehicle, movement) {
  if (length(movement) == 2) {
    movement <- c(movement, 0)
  }
  NextMethod("move")
}
```

With move implemented for all three vehicles, we can test them with the three instances.
First, let's see if the following expression goes into an error if we want the car to move with
a three-dimensional vector:

```
move(car, c(1, 2, 3))
## Error in move.car(car, c(1, 2, 3)): This vehicle only supports 2d
movement
```

The method dispatch of the preceding function call finds move.car and stops for the
invalid movement. The following code is a two-dimensional movement, which is valid:

```
move(car, c(1, 2))
## <vehicle: car>
## name: Model-A
## speed: 80 km/h
## position: 1, 2, 0
```

Similarly, we can move the airplane in two dimensions:

```
move(airplane, c(1, 2))
## <vehicle: airplane>
## name: Big-Plane
## speed: 800 km/h
## position: 1, 2, 0
```

We can also move it in three dimensions:

```
move(airplane, c(20, 50, 80))
## <vehicle: airplane>
## name: Big-Plane
## speed: 800 km/h
## position: 21, 52, 80
```

Note that the position of `airplane` is accumulated because it is essentially an environment, so modifying `position` in `move.vehicle` does not cause a copy of it. Therefore, no matter where you pass it, there is only one instance of it. If you are not familiar with the reference semantics of environments, go through `Chapter 8`, *Inside R*.

Working with S4

In the previous section, we introduced the S3 system. Unlike the object-oriented systems in most other programming languages, the S3 system is much less strict than a system in which classes are defined with a fixed structure and certain method dispatch as the program compiles. When we define an S3 class, almost nothing can be sure. We can not only add or remove methods of the class at any time but also insert or delete data elements from the object as we wish. In addition, S3 only supports single dispatch, that is, methods are chosen according to the class of only one argument, mostly the first argument.

Then, R introduces a more formal and stricter object-oriented system, S4. This system allows us to define formal classes with pre-specified definition and inheritance structure. It also supports multiple dispatch, that is, methods are chosen according to the classes of multiple arguments.

In this section, you will learn how to define S4 classes and methods.

Defining S4 classes

Unlike S3 classes, which are simply represented by character vectors, S4 classes require formal definition of classes and methods. To define an S4 class, we need to call `setClass` and supply a representation of the class members, which are called **slots**. The representation is specified by the name and class of each slot. In this section, we'll redefine the product objects using an S4 class:

```
setClass("Product",
  representation(name = "character",
    price = "numeric",
    inventory = "integer"))
```

Once the class is defined, we can get the slots from its class definition by `getSlots()`:

```
getSlots("Product")
##        name       price   inventory
## "character"   "numeric"   "integer"
```

S4 is stricter than S3, not only because S4 requires class definition, but also because R will ensure that the classes of the members that create a new instance are consistent with the class representation. Now, we will use `new()` to create a new instance of an S4 class and specify the values of the slots:

```
laptop <- new("Product", name = "Laptop-A", price = 299, inventory = 100)
## Error in validObject(.Object): invalid class "Product" object: invalid
object for slot "inventory" in class "Product": got class "numeric", should
be or extend class "integer"
```

It might surprise you that the preceding code produces an error. If you take a closer look at the class representation, you will find that `inventory` must be an integer. In other words, `100` is a numeric value, which is not of class `integer`. It requires `100L` instead:

```
laptop <- new("Product", name = "Laptop-A", price = 299, inventory = 100L)
laptop
## An object of class "Product"
## Slot "name":
## [1] "Laptop-A"
##
## Slot "price":
## [1] 299
##
## Slot "inventory":
## [1] 100
```

Now, a new instance of `Product`, `laptop`, is created. It is printed as an object of class `Product`. The values of all slots are automatically printed.

For an S4 object, we can still use `typeof()` and `class()` to get some type information:

```
typeof(laptop)
## [1] "S4"
class(laptop)
## [1] "Product"
## attr(,"package")
## [1] ".GlobalEnv"
```

This time, the type is `S4` instead of `list` or other data types, and the class is the name of the S4 class. The S4 object is also a first-class citizen in R because it has a checking function:

```
isS4(laptop)
## [1] TRUE
```

Unlike accessing a list or environment with `$`, we need to use `@` to access a slot of an S4 object:

```
laptop@price * laptop@inventory
## [1] 29900
```

Alternatively, we can call `slot()` to access a slot with its name as a string. This is equivalent to accessing an element of a list or environment with double brackets (`[[]]`):

```
slot(laptop, "price")
## [1] 299
```

We can also modify an S4 object in the same way we modify a list:

```
laptop@price <- 289
```

However, we cannot supply to a slot something that is not consistent with the class representation:

```
laptop@inventory <- 200
## Error in (function (cl, name, valueClass) : assignment of an object of
## class "numeric" is not valid for @'inventory' in an object of class
## "Product"; is(value, "integer") is not TRUE
```

Neither can we create a new slot just like adding a new element to a list because the structure of an S4 object is fixed to its class representation:

```
laptop@value <- laptop@price * laptop@inventory
## Error in (function (cl, name, valueClass) : 'value' is not a slot in
## class "Product"
```

Now, we will create another instance with the values of slots partially supplied:

```
toy <- new("Product", name = "Toys", price = 10)
toy
## An object of class "Product"
## Slot "name":
## [1] "Toys"
##
## Slot "price":
## [1] 10
##
## Slot "inventory":
## integer(0)
```

The preceding code does not specify inventory, so the resulting object, toy, takes an empty integer vector as inventory. If you think it is not a good default value, we can specify a prototype of the class so that each instance will be created from it as a template:

```
setClass("Product",
  representation(name = "character",
    price = "numeric",
    inventory = "integer"),
  prototype(name = "Unnamed", price = NA_real_, inventory = 0L))
```

In the preceding prototype, we set the default value of price to be the numeric missing value and inventory to be integer zero. Note that NA is logical and cannot be used here because it is not consistent with the class representation.

Then, we will recreate toy with the same code:

```
toy <- new("Product", name = "Toys", price = 5)
toy
## An object of class "Product"
## Slot "name":
## [1] "Toys"
##
## Slot "price":
## [1] 5
##
## Slot "inventory":
## [1] 0
```

This time, `inventory` takes the default value `0L` from the prototype. However, what if we need more constraints on the input arguments? Although the classes of the arguments are checked, we can still supply values that are not meaningful as an instance of `Product`. For example, we can create a `bottle` class with negative inventory:

```
bottle <- new("Product", name = "Bottle", price = 1.5, inventory = -2L)
bottle
## An object of class "Product"
## Slot "name":
## [1] "Bottle"
##
## Slot "price":
## [1] 1.5
##
## Slot "inventory":
## [1] -2
```

The following code is a validation function that ensures that the slots of a `Product` object are meaningful. The validation function is somehow special because when there is no error about the input object, it should return `TRUE`. When there are errors, it should return a character vector that describe the errors. Therefore, it is best not to use `stop()` or `warning()` when a slot is not valid.

Here, we will validate the object by checking the length of each slot and whether they are missing values. Also, the price must be positive, and the inventory must be non-negative:

```
validate_product <- function(object) {
  errors <- c(
    if (length(object@name) != 1)
      "Length of name should be 1"
    else if (is.na(object@name))
      "name should not be missing value",
    if (length(object@price) != 1)
      "Length of price should be 1"
    else if (is.na(object@price))
      "price should not be missing value"
    else if (object@price <= 0)
      "price must be positive",
    if (length(object@inventory) != 1)
      "Length of inventory should be 1"
    else if (is.na(object@inventory))
      "inventory should not be missing value"
    else if (object@inventory < 0)
      "inventory must be non-negative")
  if (length(errors) == 0) TRUE else errors
}
```

We write a long combination of values to make up the error messages. This works because `if (FALSE) expr` returns `NULL` and `c(x, NULL)` returns x. At last, if no error message is produced, the function returns `TRUE`, otherwise it returns the error messages.

With this function defined, we can directly use it to validate `bottle`:

```
validate_product(bottle)
## [1] "inventory must be non-negative"
```

The validation results in an error message as supposed. Now, we need to make the class perform validation each time an instance is being created. We only need to specify the `validity` argument when we use `setClass` for `Product` class:

```
setClass("Product",
   representation(name = "character",
     price = "numeric",
     inventory = "integer"),
   prototype(name = "Unnamed",
     price = NA_real_, inventory = 0L),
   validity = validate_product)
```

Then, each time we try to create an instance of the `Product` class, the supplied values are automatically checked. Even the prototype is checked. Here are two cases that fail the validation:

```
bottle <- new("Product", name = "Bottle")
## Error in validObject(.Object): invalid class "Product" object: price
should not be missing value
```

The preceding code fails because the default value of `price` is `NA_real_` in the prototype. In the validation, however, the price cannot be a missing value:

```
bottle <- new("Product", name = "Bottle", price = 3, inventory = -2L)
## Error in validObject(.Object): invalid class "Product" object: inventory
must be non-negative
```

This fails because `inventory` must be a non-negative integer.

Note that the validation only occurs when we create a new instance of an S4 class. Once the object is created, however, the validation does not happen anymore. In other words, we can still set a slot to a bad value unless we explicitly validate it.

Understanding S4 inheritance

The S3 system is loose and flexible. Each S3 object of the same class may have different members. For S4, however, this cannot happen, that is, we cannot arbitrarily add a slot that is not in the class definition when we create a new instance of the class.

For example, we cannot put a `volume` slot when we create a new instance of `Product`:

```
bottle <- new("Product", name = "Bottle",
  price = 3, inventory = 100L, volume = 15)
## Error in initialize(value, ...): invalid name for slot of class
"Product": volume
```

Instead, we can only do this through proper inheritance. We need to create a new class that contains (or inherits from) the original class. In this case, we can define a `Container` class that inherits from `Product` and has a new numeric slot named `volume`:

```
setClass("Container",
  representation(volume = "numeric"),
  contains = "Product")
```

Since `Container` inherits from `Product`, any instance of `Container` has all the slots of `Product`. We can use `getSlots()` to view them:

```
getSlots("Container")
##       volume         name        price    inventory
##    "numeric"  "character"    "numeric"    "integer"
```

Now, we can create an instance of `Container` that has a `volume` slot:

```
bottle <- new("Container", name = "Bottle",
  price = 3, inventory = 100L, volume = 15)
```

Note that the validation of `Product` still functions when we create an instance of `Container`:

```
bottle <- new("Container", name = "Bottle",
  price = 3, inventory = -10L, volume = 15)
## Error in validObject(.Object): invalid class "Container" object:
inventory must be non-negative
```

Therefore, the checking ensures it is a valid `Product` class, but it still does not check anything about `Container`:

```
bottle <- new("Container", name = "Bottle",
  price = 3, inventory = 100L, volume = -2)
```

Just like we defined a validation function for Product, we can define another
for Container:

```
validate_container <- function(object) {
  errors <- c(
    if (length(object@volume) != 1)
      "Length of volume must be 1",
    if (object@volume <= 0)
      "volume must be positive"
  )
  if (length(errors) == 0) TRUE else errors
}
```

Then, we will redefine Container with this validation function:

```
setClass("Container",
  representation(volume = "numeric"),
  contains = "Product",
  validity = validate_container)
```

Note that we don't need to call validate_product in validate_container because both
validation functions will be called in turn to make sure all classes in the inheritance chain
are properly checked with their validation functions. You may add some text-printing code
to the validating functions to confirm that validate_product is always called
before validate_container when we create an instance of Container:

```
bottle <- new("Container", name = "Bottle",
  price = 3, inventory = 100L, volume = -2)
## Error in validObject(.Object): invalid class "Container" object: volume
must be positive
bottle <- new("Container", name = "Bottle",
  price = 3, inventory = -5L, volume = 10)
## Error in validObject(.Object): invalid class "Container" object:
inventory must be non-negative
```

Defining S4 generic functions

In the previous examples, we saw that S4 is much more formal than S3 because the S4 class
requires a class definition. Likewise, S4 generic functions are more formal too.

Here is an example where we define a series of S4 classes with a simple hierarchy of inheritance relationships. The example is about shapes. First, Shape is a root class. Both Polygon and Circle inherit from Shape, while Triangle and Rectangle inherit from Polygon. The inheritance structure of these shapes is illustrated here:

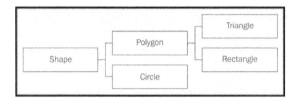

Each class except Shape has some necessary slots to describe itself:

```
setClass("Shape")
setClass("Polygon",
  representation(sides = "integer"),
  contains = "Shape")
setClass("Triangle",
  representation(a = "numeric", b = "numeric", c = "numeric"),
  prototype(a = 1, b = 1, c = 1, sides = 3L),
  contains = "Polygon")
setClass("Rectangle",
  representation(a = "numeric", b = "numeric"),
  prototype(a = 1, b = 1, sides = 4L),
  contains = "Polygon")
setClass("Circle",
  representation(r = "numeric"),
  prototype(r = 1, sides = Inf),
  contains = "Shape")
```

With these classes defined, we can set up a generic function to calculate the area of a Shape object. To do this, we need to call setGeneric() upon area and supply a function that calls standardGeneric("area") to make area a generic function and ready for S4 method dispatch. The valueClass is used to ensure that the return value of each method must be of class numeric:

```
setGeneric("area", function(object) {
  standardGeneric("area")
}, valueClass = "numeric")
## [1] "area"
```

Once the generic function is set up, we go on to implement different methods for different kinds of shapes. For `Triangle`, we use Heron's formula (`https://en.wikipedia.org/wiki/Heron's_formula`) to calculate its area, given the lengths of the three sides:

```
setMethod("area", signature("Triangle"), function(object) {
  a <- object@a
  b <- object@b
  c <- object@c
  s <- (a + b + c) / 2
  sqrt(s * (s - a) * (s - b) * (s - c))
})
## [1] "area"
```

For `Rectangle` and `Circle`, it is easy to write out the area formula for each of them:

```
setMethod("area", signature("Rectangle"), function(object) {
  object@a * object@b
})
## [1] "area"
setMethod("area", signature("Circle"), function(object) {
  pi * object@r ^ 2
})
## [1] "area"
```

Now, we can create an instance of `Triangle` and see whether `area()` dispatches to the correct method and returns the correct answer:

```
triangle <- new("Triangle", a = 3, b = 4, c = 5)
area(triangle)
## [1] 6
```

We also create an instance of `Circle` and see whether method dispatch works:

```
circle <- new("Circle", r = 3)
area(circle)
## [1] 28.27433
```

Both answers are correct. The `area()` function just works like an S3 generic function that performs method dispatch according to the class of the input object.

Understanding multiple dispatch

An S4 generic function is more flexible because it also supports multiple dispatch, that is, it can perform method dispatch according to the classes of multiple arguments.

Here, we will define another family of S4 classes: Object with a numeric height. Both Cylinder and Cone inherit from Object. Later, we will use multiple dispatch to calculate the volume of a certain type of geometric object with a certain shape of the bottom surface:

```
setClass("Object", representation(height = "numeric"))
setClass("Cylinder", contains = "Object")
setClass("Cone", contains = "Object")
```

Now, we will define a new generic function named volume. As its name suggests, this function is used to calculate the volume of an object that is described by the shape of the bottom surface and the form of the object:

```
setGeneric("volume",
  function(shape, object) standardGeneric("volume"))
## [1] "volume"
```

In the following code, we will implement two cases: one is for a rectangle-shaped cylinder and the other is for a rectangle-shaped cone:

```
setMethod("volume", signature("Rectangle", "Cylinder"),
  function(shape, object) {
    shape@a * shape@b * object@height
  })
## [1] "volume"
setMethod("volume", signature("Rectangle", "Cone"),
  function(shape, object) {
    shape@a * shape@b * object@height / 3
  })
## [1] "volume"
```

Note that all existing methods for volume require two arguments. Therefore, the method dispatch happens with both arguments, that is, it requires the classes of both input objects to match to choose the correct method. Now, we will test volume with an instance of Rectagle and an instance of Cylinder:

```
rectangle <- new("Rectangle", a = 2, b = 3)
cylinder <- new("Cylinder", height = 3)
volume(rectangle, cylinder)
## [1] 18
```

Since a relationship holds for a cylinder and a cone with the same height and the shape of bottom surface, the volume of the cylinder is three times that of the cone. To simplify the implementation of `volume` methods, we can directly put `Shape` in the method signature and call `area()` of the shape and directly use its area in the calculation:

```
setMethod("volume", signature("Shape", "Cylinder"),
   function(shape, object) {
      area(shape) * object@height
   })
## [1] "volume"
setMethod("volume", signature("Shape", "Cone"),
   function(shape, object) {
      area(shape) * object@height / 3
   })
## [1] "volume"
```

Now, `volume` is automatically applicable to `Circle`:

```
circle <- new("Circle", r = 2)
cone <- new("Cone", height = 3)
volume(circle, cone)
## [1] 12.56637
```

To make `volume` easier to use, we can also define a method that takes an instance of `Shape` and a numeric value as the height of the cylinder:

```
setMethod("volume", signature("Shape", "numeric"),
   function(shape, object) {
      area(shape) * object
   })
## [1] "volume"
```

Then, we can directly use numeric values in calculating the volume of the cylinder given its shape and height:

```
volume(rectangle, 3)
## [1] 18
```

Furthermore, we can simplify the notation by implementing a method of $*$:

```
setMethod("*", signature("Shape", "Object"),
   function(e1, e2) {
      volume(e1, e2)
   })
## [1] "*"
```

Now, we can calculate the volume by simply multiplying the shape and the object form:

```
rectangle * cone
## [1] 6
```

Note that an S4 object is not a list or environment, but it has copy-on-modify semantics. In this sense, when the value of a slot of an S4 object is modified by <- in a function, it behaves more like a list, that is, the S4 object is copied in the function and the original object is not modified.

For example, in the following code, we will define a function that tries to lengthen Object by multiplying its height with a numeric factor:

```
lengthen <- function(object, factor) {
  object@height <- object@height * factor
  object
}
```

When we apply this function on cylinder, which we previously created, its height is not changed at all. Instead, it is copied inside the function:

```
cylinder
## An object of class "Cylinder"
## Slot "height":
## [1] 3
lengthen(cylinder, 2)
## An object of class "Cylinder"
## Slot "height":
## [1] 6
cylinder
## An object of class "Cylinder"
## Slot "height":
## [1] 3
```

Working with the reference class

There is also a class system that has reference semantics. It is more like the class system in other object-oriented programming languages.

First, to define a reference class (**RC**), we supply a class definition to setRefClass(). Unlike the S4 class system where we use new() to create an instance, setRefClass() returns an instance generator. For example, we define a class named Vehicle, which has two fields: a numeric position and a numeric distance. We store the instance generator to a variable named Vehicle:

```
Vehicle <- setRefClass("Vehicle",
    fields = list(position = "numeric", distance = "numeric"))
```

To create an instance, we use `Vehicle$new` to create new instances of the `Vehicle` class:

```
car <- Vehicle$new(position = 0, distance = 0)
```

Unlike S4, the fields of RC are not slots, so we can use $ to access them:

```
car$position
## [1] 0
```

Each instance we create with `Vehicle$new` is an object of reference semantics. It behaves like a combination of S4 object and environment.

In the following code, we will create a function that modifies the fields in a `Vehicle` object. More specifically, we define `move` that modifies `position` in relative terms, and all movements are accumulated to `distance`:

```
move <- function(vehicle, movement) {
    vehicle$position <- vehicle$position + movement
    vehicle$distance <- vehicle$distance + abs(movement)
}
```

Now, we will call `move` with `car`, and the instance we created is modified rather than copied:

```
move(car, 10)
car
## Reference class object of class "Vehicle"
## Field "position":
## [1] 10
## Field "distance":
## [1] 10
```

Since RC itself is a class system more like ordinary object-oriented system, a better way to do this is to define its own methods of the class:

```
Vehicle <- setRefClass("Vehicle",
    fields = list(position = "numeric", distance = "numeric"),
    methods = list(move = function(x) {
        stopifnot(is.numeric(x))
        position <<- position + x
        distance <<- distance + abs(x)
    }))
```

Unlike S3 and S4 systems where methods are stored in the environment, RC directly include its methods. Therefore, we can directly call the method inside an instance. Note that to modify the value of a field in a method, we need to use <<- instead of <-. The following code is a simple test to check whether the method works and whether the reference object is modified:

```
bus <- Vehicle(position = 0, distance = 0)
bus$move(5)
bus
## Reference class object of class "Vehicle"
## Field "position":
## [1] 5
## Field "distance":
## [1] 5
```

From the preceding examples, we can see that RC looks more like the objects in C++ and Java. For more detailed introduction, read ?ReferenceClasses.

Working with R6

An enhanced version of RC is R6, a package that implements a more efficient reference class that supports public and private fields and methods, and some other powerful features.

Run the following code to install the package:

```
install.packages("R6")
```

The R6 class allows us to define classes that are even more like popular object-oriented programming languages. The following code is an example where we define the Vehicle class. It has some public fields and methods for users and some private fields and methods for internal use:

```
library(R6)
Vehicle <- R6Class("Vehicle",
  public = list(
    name = NA,
    model = NA,
    initialize = function(name, model) {
      if (!missing(name)) self$name <- name
      if (!missing(model)) self$model <- model
    },
    move = function(movement) {
      private$start()
      private$position <- private$position + movement
      private$stop()
```

```
    },
    get_position = function() {
      private$position
    }
  ),
  private = list(
    position = 0,
    speed = 0,
    start = function() {
      cat(self$name, "is starting\n")
      private$speed <- 50
    },
    stop = function() {
      cat(self$name, "is stopping\n")
      private$speed <- 0
    }
  ))
```

From the user side, we can only access the public fields and methods. Only the class methods have access to the private fields and methods. Although the vehicle has a position, we don't want the user to modify its value. Therefore, we put it in the private part and expose its value through get_position() so that it is hard for users to modify the position from outside:

```
car <- Vehicle$new(name = "Car", model = "A")
car
## <Vehicle>
##   Public:
##     clone: function (deep = FALSE)
##     get_position: function ()
##     initialize: function (name, model)
##     model: A
##     move: function (movement)
##     name: Car
##   Private:
##     position: 0
##     speed: 0
##     start: function ()
##     stop: function ()
```

When `car` is printed, all public and private fields and methods are displayed. Then, we will call the `move()` method, and we can find the position is changed with `get_position()`:

```
car$move(10)
## Car is starting
## Car is stopping
car$get_position()
## [1] 10
```

To demonstrate the inheritance of R6 class, we define a new class named `MeteredVehicle` that records the sum of distance it moves in history. To define the class, we need to add a private field `distance`, a public override of `move` that first calls `super$move()` to move the vehicle to get the right position and then accumulates the distance resulted from the movement in absolute terms:

```
MeteredVehicle <- R6Class("MeteredVehicle",
  inherit = Vehicle,
  public = list(
    move = function(movement) {
      super$move(movement)
      private$distance <<- private$distance + abs(movement)
    },
    get_distance = function() {
      private$distance
    }
  ),
  private = list(
    distance = 0
  ))
```

Now, we can do some experiments with `MeteredVehicle`. In the following code, we will create a `bus`:

```
bus <- MeteredVehicle$new(name = "Bus", model = "B")
bus
## <MeteredVehicle>
##   Inherits from: <Vehicle>
##   Public:
##     clone: function (deep = FALSE)
##     get_distance: function ()
##     get_position: function ()
##     initialize: function (name, model)
##     model: B
##     move: function (movement)
##     name: Bus
##   Private:
##     distance: 0
```

```
##      position: 0
##      speed: 0
##      start: function ()
##      stop: function ()
```

First, let bus move 10 units forward, and then, the position is changed and the distance is accumulated:

```
bus$move(10)
## Bus is starting
## Bus is stopping
bus$get_position()
## [1] 10
bus$get_distance()
## [1] 10
```

Then, let bus move 5 units backward. The position is closer to the origin, while the distance that sums up all movements becomes greater:

```
bus$move(-5)
## Bus is starting
## Bus is stopping
bus$get_position()
## [1] 5
bus$get_distance()
## [1] 15
```

 R6 also supports some other powerful features. For more details, read its vignettes at
https://cran.r-project.org/web/packages/R6/vignettes/Introductio
n.html.

Summary

In this chapter, you learned the basic concepts of object-oriented programming: class and methods and how they are connected by generic functions in R through method dispatch. You learned how to create S3, S4, RC, and R6 classes and methods. These systems share similar ideas but are distinct in implementation and usage. Hadley Wickham gives some nice suggestions in picking a system
(http://adv-r.had.co.nz/OO-essentials.html#picking-a-system).

After getting familiar with R's most important features, we will discuss more practical topics in the subsequent chapters. In the next chapter, you will learn about the packages and techniques used to access popular databases. You will gain necessary knowledge and techniques to connect R to relational databases such as SQLite and MySQL as well as the upcoming non-relational databases such as MongoDB and Redis.

11
Working with Databases

In the previous chapter, you learned the basic concepts of object-oriented programming. These include class and methods, and how they are connected by generic functions in R through method dispatch. You learned about the basic usage of S3, S4, RC, and R6, including defining classes and generic functions as well as implementing methods for certain classes.

Now that we have covered most of the important features of R, it is time we go ahead and discuss more practical topics. In this chapter, we will begin the discussion with how R can be used to work with databases, which is perhaps the first step of many data-analysis projects: extracting data from a database. More specifically, we will cover the following topics:

- Understanding relational databases
- Using SQL to query relational databases such as SQLite and MySQL
- Working with NoSQL databases such as MongoDB and Redis

Working with relational databases

In the previous chapters, we used a family of built-in functions such as `read.csv` and `read.table` to import data from separator-delimited files, such as those in the csv format. Using text formats to store data is handy and portable. When the data file is large, however, such a storage method may not be the best way.

There are three main reasons why text formats can no longer be easy to use. They are as follows:

1. Functions such as read.csv() are mostly used to load the whole file into memory, that is, a data frame in R. If the data is too large to fit into the computer memory, we simply cannot do it.
2. Even if the dataset is large, we usually don't have to load the whole dataset into memory when we work on a task. Instead, we often need to extract a subset of the dataset that meets a certain condition. The built-in data-importer functions simply do not support querying a csv file.
3. The dataset is still updating, that is, we need to insert records into the dataset periodically. If we use the csv format, inserting data can be painful, especially if we want to insert the records in the middle of the file and keep it in order.

Using a database is the best solution for these scenarios. It makes it much easier to store data that may exceed computer memory. Data in a database is queryable subject to user-supplied condition, which also makes it easier to update existing records and insert new records within a database.

A relational database is a collection of tables and relations between tables. A table in a relational database has the same representation with a data frame in R. Tables can have relations that make it easier to join the information of multiple tables.

In this section, we will start from the simplest database, SQLite (http://sqlite.org/), a portable, lightweight database engine.

To work with SQLite databases in R, we will use the RSQLite package. To install it from CRAN, run the following code:

```
install.packages("RSQLite")
```

Creating a SQLite database

First, let's see how to create a SQLite database. If we want to create an example database at data/example.sqlite, we need to ensure that the directory is available. If the directory does not exist, we have to create one:

```
if (!dir.exists("data")) dir.create("data")
```

Now, the `data/` directory is available. Next, we will load the `RSQLite` package and create a connection by supplying a database driver (`SQLite()`) and database file (`data/example.sqlite`). Although the file does not exist, the driver creates an empty file that is an empty SQLite database:

```
library(RSQLite)
## Loading required package: DBI
con <- dbConnect(SQLite(), "data/example.sqlite")
```

The database connection, `con`, is a layer between the user and the system. We can create a connection to a relational database and query, fetch, or update data through it. The connection will be used in all subsequent operations until we close the connection. In a typical relational database, we can create tables with a name and columns of certain names and data types, insert records as rows to a table, and update existing records. A table in a relational database looks very similar to a data frame in R.

Now, we will create a simple data frame that is to be inserted as a table to the database:

```
example1 <- data.frame(
id = 1:5,
type = c("A", "A", "B", "B", "C"),
score = c(8, 9, 8, 10, 9),
stringsAsFactors = FALSE)
example1
##   id type score
## 1  1    A     8
## 2  2    A     9
## 3  3    B     8
## 4  4    B    10
## 5  5    C     9
```

The data frame is ready and we will call `dbWriteTable()` to write this data frame as a table to the database:

```
dbWriteTable(con, "example1", example1)
## [1] TRUE
```

In the preceding code, we may well use other table names but still store the same data. Finally, we will disconnect the database using `dbDisconnect()` so that `con` is no longer available for data operations:

```
dbDisconnect(con)
## [1] TRUE
```

Writing multiple tables to a database

A SQLite database is a collection of tables. Therefore, we can store many tables in one database.

This time, we put the `diamonds` dataset in `ggplot2` and the `flights` dataset in `nycflights13` as two tables into one database. If you haven't installed these two packages, run the following code:

```
install.packages(c("ggplot2", "nycflights13"))
```

When the packages are available, we will call `data()` to load the two data frames:

```
data("diamonds", package ="ggplot2")
data("flights", package ="nycflights13")
```

We will repeat the same operation as we did earlier, but `dbWriteTable()` ends up with errors:

```
con <- dbConnect(SQLite(), "data/datasets.sqlite")
dbWriteTable(con, "diamonds", diamonds, row.names = FALSE)
## Error in (function (classes, fdef, mtable) : unable to find an inherited
method for function 'dbWriteTable' for signature '"SQLiteConnection",
"character", "tbl_df"'
dbWriteTable(con, "flights", flights, row.names = FALSE)
## Error in (function (classes, fdef, mtable) : unable to find an inherited
method for function 'dbWriteTable' for signature '"SQLiteConnection",
"character", "tbl_df"'
dbDisconnect(con)
## [1] TRUE
```

It can be useful to take a look at the class of these two variables:

```
class(diamonds)
## [1] "tbl_df"      "tbl"          "data.frame"
class(flights)
## [1] "tbl_df"      "tbl"          "data.frame"
```

Note that `diamonds` and `flights` are not simply of class `data.frame` but something more complex. To write them into the database, we need to convert them to plain `data.frame` objects using `as.data.frame()`:

```
con <- dbConnect(SQLite(), "data/datasets.sqlite")
dbWriteTable(con, "diamonds", as.data.frame(diamonds), row.names = FALSE)
## [1] TRUE
dbWriteTable(con, "flights", as.data.frame(flights), row.names = FALSE)
## [1] TRUE
```

```
dbDisconnect(con)
## [1] TRUE
```

Now, the database contains two tables.

Appending data to a table

As mentioned in the beginning of this section, appending records to a table in the database is fairly easy. Here is a simple example where we produce several chunks of data and append them to a database table in turn:

```
con <- dbConnect(SQLite(), "data/example2.sqlite")
chunk_size <- 10
id <- 0
for (i in 1:6) {
  chunk <- data.frame(id = ((i - 1L) * chunk_size):(i * chunk_size -1L),
    type = LETTERS[[i]],
    score =rbinom(chunk_size, 10, (10 - i) /10),
    stringsAsFactors =FALSE)
  dbWriteTable(con, "products", chunk,
    append = i > 1, row.names = FALSE)
}
dbDisconnect(con)
## [1] TRUE
```

Note that each chunk is a data frame with some determined data and some random numbers. Each time, we append these records to a table named `products`. The difference between this example and the previous ones is that when we call `dbWriteTable()`, we use `append = FALSE` for the first chunk to create that table in the database and use `append = TRUE` for each subsequent chunk to append to the existing table.

Accessing tables and table fields

Once we have a SQLite database, we can access not only the data we store in the tables, but also some metadata, such as the names of all tables and the columns of a table.

To demonstrate, we will connect to the SQLite database we created previously:

```
con <- dbConnect(SQLite(), "data/datasets.sqlite")
```

We can use `dbExistsTable()` to detect whether a table exists in the database:

```
dbExistsTable(con, "diamonds")
## [1] TRUE
dbExistsTable(con, "mtcars")
## [1] FALSE
```

Since we only wrote `diamonds` and `flights` in `datasets.sqlite` previously, `dbExistsTable()` returns the correct values. On the contrary to detecting table existence, we can use `dbListTables()` to list all the existing tables in the database:

```
dbListTables(con)
## [1] "diamonds" "flights"
```

For a certain table, we can also list the names of all columns (or fields) with `dbListFields()`:

```
dbListFields(con, "diamonds")
##   [1] "carat"   "cut"     "color"   "clarity" "depth"
##   [6] "table"   "price"   "x"       "y"       "z"
```

Contrary to `dbWriteTable()`, `dbReadTable()` reads the whole table into a data frame:

```
db_diamonds <- dbReadTable(con, "diamonds")
dbDisconnect(con)
## [1] TRUE
```

We can make a comparison between the data frame (`db_diamonds`) we read from the database and the original version (`diamonds`):

```
head(db_diamonds, 3)
##   carat     cut color clarity depth table price    x    y
## 1  0.23   Ideal     E     SI2  61.5    55   326 3.95 3.98
## 2  0.21 Premium     E     SI1  59.8    61   326 3.89 3.84
## 3  0.23    Good     E     VS1  56.9    65   327 4.05 4.07
##      z
## 1 2.43
## 2 2.31
## 3 2.31
head(diamonds, 3)
##   carat     cut color clarity depth table price    x    y
## 1  0.23   Ideal     E     SI2  61.5    55   326 3.95 3.98
## 2  0.21 Premium     E     SI1  59.8    61   326 3.89 3.84
## 3  0.23    Good     E     VS1  56.9    65   327 4.05 4.07
##      z
## 1 2.43
## 2 2.31
## 3 2.31
```

The data in both data frames looks exactly the same. However, if we use `identical()` to compare them, they are not really identical:

```
identical(diamonds, db_diamonds)
## [1] FALSE
```

To spot the difference, we can call `str()` to reveal the structure of both data frames. First, here is the structure of the data frame in the database:

```
str(db_diamonds)
## 'data.frame':    53940 obs. of  10 variables:
## $ carat  : num  0.23 0.21 0.23 0.29 0.31 0.24 0.24...
## $ cut    : chr  "Ideal" "Premium" "Good" "Premium" ...
## $ color  : chr  "E" "E" "E" "I" ...
## $ clarity: chr  "SI2" "SI1" "VS1" "VS2" ...
## $ depth  : num  61.5 59.8 56.9 62.4 63.3 62.8 62.3...
## $ table  : num  55 61 65 58 58 57 57 55 61 61 ...
## $ price  : int  326 326 327 334 335 336 336 337 337 ...
## $ x      : num  3.95 3.89 4.05 4.2 4.34 3.94 3.95...
## $ y      : num  3.98 3.84 4.07 4.23 4.35 3.96 3.98...
## $ z      : num  2.43 2.31 2.31 2.63 2.75 2.48 2.47...
```

Then, here is the structure of the original version:

```
str(diamonds)
## Classes 'tbl_df', 'tbl' and 'data.frame':    53940 obs. of   10
variables:
## $ carat  : num  0.23 0.21 0.23 0.29 0.31 0.24 0.24...
## $ cut    : Ord.factor w/ 5 levels "Fair"<"Good"<..: 5 4 2 4 2 3 3 3 1 3
...
## $ color  : Ord.factor w/ 7 levels "D"<"E"<"F"<"G"<..: 2 2 2 6 7 7 6 5 2
5 ...
## $ clarity: Ord.factor w/ 8 levels "I1"<"SI2"<"SI1"<..: 2 3 5 4 2 6 7 3
4 5 ...
## $ depth  : num  61.5 59.8 56.9 62.4 63.3 62.8 62.3 61.9 65.1 59.4 ...
## $ table  : num  55 61 65 58 58 57 57 55 61 61 ...
## $ price  : int  326 326 327 334 335 336 336 337 337...
## $ x      : num  3.95 3.89 4.05 4.2 4.34 3.94 3.95...
## $ y      : num  3.98 3.84 4.07 4.23 4.35 3.96 3.98...
## $ z      : num  2.43 2.31 2.31 2.63 2.75 2.48 2.47...
```

Now, the difference is obvious. In the original version, `cut`, `color`, and `clarity` are ordered factor variables that are essentially integers with some metadata (ordered levels). By contrast, in the database version, these columns are stored as text instead. This change is simply because SQLite does not have built-in support of ordered factors. Therefore, except for common data types (numbers, texts, logical, and so on), R-specific types will be converted to types supported by SQLite before the data frame is inserted.

Learning SQL to query relational databases

In the previous section, you learned how to write data into a SQLite database. In this section, you will learn how to query such a database so that we can get data from it according to our needs. We'll use data/datasets.sqlite (we created previously) in the following examples.

First, we need to establish a connection to the database:

```
con <- dbConnect(SQLite(), "data/datasets.sqlite")
dbListTables(con)
## [1] "diamonds" "flights"
```

There are two tables in the database. Then, we can select all data from diamonds using the select statement. Here, we want to select all columns (or fields). So, we will call dbGetQuery() with the database connection, con, and a query string:

```
db_diamonds <- dbGetQuery(con,
"select * from diamonds")
head(db_diamonds, 3)
##    carat       cut color clarity depth table price    x    y
## 1   0.23     Ideal     E     SI2  61.5    55   326 3.95 3.98
## 2   0.21   Premium     E     SI1  59.8    61   326 3.89 3.84
## 3   0.23      Good     E     VS1  56.9    65   327 4.05 4.07
##       z
## 1 2.43
## 2 2.31
## 3 2.31
```

Note that * means all fields (or, equivalently, columns). If we only need a subset of fields, we can name the fields in turn:

```
db_diamonds <-dbGetQuery(con,
"select carat, cut, color, clarity, depth, price
  from diamonds")
head(db_diamonds, 3)
##    carat       cut color clarity depth price
## 1   0.23     Ideal     E     SI2  61.5   326
## 2   0.21   Premium     E     SI1  59.8   326
## 3   0.23      Good     E     VS1  56.9   327
```

If we want to select all distinct cases that appear in the data, we can use select distinct. For example, the following code returns all distinct values of cut in diamonds:

```
dbGetQuery(con, "select distinct cut from diamonds")
##        cut
## 1    Ideal
```

```
## 2    Premium
## 3       Good
## 4 Very Good
## 5       Fair
```

Note that dbGetQuery() always returns data.frame, even though sometimes there is only one column. To retrieve the values as an atomic vector, just extract the first column from the data frame:

```
dbGetQuery(con, "select distinct clarity from diamonds")[[1]]
## [1] "SI2"  "SI1"  "VS1"  "VS2"  "VVS2" "VVS1" "I1"   "IF"
```

When we use select to select columns to query, sometimes, the column name is not exactly what we want. In this case, we can use A as B to get column B with the same data as A:

```
db_diamonds <- dbGetQuery(con,
"select carat, price, clarity as clarity_level from diamonds")
head(db_diamonds, 3)
##    carat price clarity_level
## 1   0.23   326           SI2
## 2   0.21   326           SI1
## 3   0.23   327           VS1
```

In some other cases, the value we want is not present in the database, but needs some calculation to figure out. Now, we will use A as B in which A can be an arithmetic calculation between existing columns:

```
db_diamonds <- dbGetQuery(con,
"select carat, price, x * y * z as size from diamonds")
head(db_diamonds, 3)
##    carat price     size
## 1   0.23   326 38.20203
## 2   0.21   326 34.50586
## 3   0.23   327 38.07688
```

What if we create a new column with existing columns and create another column with the new column, just like the following example?

```
db_diamonds <- dbGetQuery(con,
"select carat, price, x * y * z as size,
  price / size as value_density
  from diamonds")
## Error in sqliteSendQuery(con, statement, bind.data): error in statement:
no such column: size
```

We simply can't do this. In A as B, A must be composed of existing columns. However, if we insist on doing so, we can use nested query, that is, we select columns from a temporary table produced by a nested select:

```
db_diamonds <- dbGetQuery(con,
"select *, price / size as value_density from
  (select carat, price, x * y * z as size from diamonds)")
head(db_diamonds, 3)
##    carat price     size   value_density
## 1   0.23   326  38.20203      8.533578
## 2   0.21   326  34.50586      9.447672
## 3   0.23   327  38.07688      8.587887
```

In this case, size is defined in the temporary table when price/size is being computed.

The next important component of a database query is a condition. We can use where to specify the conditions that the results must satisfy. For example, we can select diamonds with Good cut:

```
good_diamonds <- dbGetQuery(con,
"select carat, cut, price from diamonds where cut = 'Good'")
head(good_diamonds, 3)
##    carat  cut price
## 1   0.23 Good   327
## 2   0.31 Good   335
## 3   0.30 Good   339
```

Note that records with good cut are only a small proportion of all records:

```
nrow(good_diamonds) /nrow(diamonds)
## [1] 0.09095291
```

If we have multiple conditions that must be met simultaneously, we can use and to combine these conditions. For example, we will select all records with Good cut and color E:

```
good_e_diamonds <- dbGetQuery(con,
"select carat, cut, color, price from diamonds
  where cut = 'Good' and color = 'E'")
head(good_e_diamonds, 3)
##    carat  cut color price
## 1   0.23 Good     E   327
## 2   0.23 Good     E   402
## 3   0.26 Good     E   554
nrow(good_e_diamonds) /nrow(diamonds)
## [1] 0.017297
```

Similar logical operations also include or and not.

In addition to the simple logical operations, we can also use in to filter records by examining whether the value of a field is contained in a given set. For example, we can select records with colors E and F:

```
color_ef_diamonds <- dbGetQuery(con,
 "select carat, cut, color, price from diamonds
   where color in ('E','F')")
nrow(color_ef_diamonds)
## [1] 19339
```

We can verify the result by the following table:

```
table(diamonds$color)
##
##     D     E     F     G     H     I     J
## 6775  9797  9542 11292  8304  5422  2808
```

To use in, we need to specify a set. Similar to in, we can also use between and which that allow us to specify a range:

```
some_price_diamonds <- dbGetQuery(con,
 "select carat, cut, color, price from diamonds
   where price between 5000 and 5500")
nrow(some_price_diamonds) /nrow(diamonds)
## [1] 0.03285132
```

In fact, the range does not have to be numeric. As long as the data type of the field is comparable, we can specify a range. For string column, we can write between 'string1' to 'string2' to filter records by lexical ordering.

Another useful operator for string column is like, which enables us to filter records with simple string patterns. For example, we can select all records with a cut variable that ends with Good. It can be either Good or Very Good. The notation is like '%Good' where % matches all strings:

```
good_cut_diamonds <- dbGetQuery(con,
 "select carat, cut, color, price from diamonds
   where cut like '%Good'")
nrow(good_cut_diamonds) /nrow(diamonds)
## [1] 0.3149425
```

Another major functionality of database query is sorting data with specified columns. We can do this with `order by`. For example, we can get the `carat` and `price` of all records but in an ascending order of `price`:

```
cheapest_diamonds <- dbGetQuery(con,
"select carat, price from diamonds
  order by price")
```

Therefore, we have a data frame of diamonds that is ordered from the cheapest to the most expensive ones:

```
head(cheapest_diamonds)
##    carat price
## 1   0.23   326
## 2   0.21   326
## 3   0.23   327
## 4   0.29   334
## 5   0.31   335
## 6   0.24   336
```

We can do the opposite by adding `desc` to the sorting column so that we get a data frame that is ordered in the opposite way:

```
most_expensive_diamonds <- dbGetQuery(con,
"select carat, price from diamonds
  order by price desc")
head(most_expensive_diamonds)
##    carat price
## 1   2.29 18823
## 2   2.00 18818
## 3   1.51 18806
## 4   2.07 18804
## 5   2.00 18803
## 6   2.29 18797
```

We can also sort the records with more than one column. For example, the following results are sorted by price in the ascending order first. If two records have equal price, the one with greater carat will be put ahead:

```
cheapest_diamonds <- dbGetQuery(con,
"select carat, price from diamonds
  order by price, carat desc")
head(cheapest_diamonds)
##    carat price
## 1   0.23   326
## 2   0.21   326
## 3   0.23   327
```

```
## 4    0.29    334
## 5    0.31    335
## 6    0.24    336
```

Like `select`, the column to sort can be computed from existing columns:

```
dense_diamonds <- dbGetQuery(con,
  "select carat, price, x * y * z as size from diamonds
    order by carat / size desc")
head(dense_diamonds)
##    carat  price      size
## 1   1.07   5909   47.24628
## 2   1.41   9752   74.41726
## 3   1.53   8971   85.25925
## 4   1.51   7188  133.10400
## 5   1.22   3156  108.24890
## 6   1.12   6115  100.97448
```

We can also query the sorted subset of all records using `where` and `order by` at the same time:

```
head(dbGetQuery(con,
  "select carat, price from diamonds
    where cut = 'Ideal' and clarity = 'IF' and color = 'J'
    order by price"))
##    carat price
## 1   0.30   489
## 2   0.30   489
## 3   0.32   521
## 4   0.32   533
## 5   0.32   533
## 6   0.35   569
```

If we only care about the first several results, we can use `limit` to constrain the number of records to retrieve:

```
dbGetQuery(con,
  "select carat, price from diamonds
    order by carat desc limit 3")
##    carat price
## 1   5.01 18018
## 2   4.50 18531
## 3   4.13 17329
```

In addition to column selection, conditional filtering, and sorting, we can also aggregate the records in database in groups. For example, we can count the number of records for each color:

```
dbGetQuery(con,
"select color, count(*) as number from diamonds
  group by color")
##    color number
## 1      D   6775
## 2      E   9797
## 3      F   9542
## 4      G  11292
## 5      H   8304
## 6      I   5422
## 7      J   2808
```

The results can be verified by calling `table()` with the original data:

```
table(diamonds$color)
##
##      D      E      F      G      H      I      J
##   6775   9797   9542  11292   8304   5422   2808
```

In addition to counting, we also have aggregating functions such as `avg()`, `max()`, `min()`, and `sum()`. For example, we can summarize the data by looking at the average price for each level of clarity:

```
dbGetQuery(con,
"select clarity, avg(price) as avg_price
    from diamonds
    group by clarity
    order by avg_price desc")
##    clarity avg_price
## 1      SI2  5063.029
## 2      SI1  3996.001
## 3      VS2  3924.989
## 4       I1  3924.169
## 5      VS1  3839.455
## 6     VVS2  3283.737
## 7       IF  2864.839
## 8     VVS1  2523.115
```

We can also examine the maximal carat at the five lowest prices:

```
dbGetQuery(con,
"select price, max(carat) as max_carat
    from diamonds
    group by price
```

```
    order by price
    limit 5")
##   price max_carat
## 1   326      0.23
## 2   327      0.23
## 3   334      0.29
## 4   335      0.31
## 5   336      0.24
```

We can also perform multiple calculations in a group. The following code calculates the range of prices and their average value for each clarity level:

```
dbGetQuery(con,
"select clarity,
    min(price) as min_price,
    max(price) as max_price,
    avg(price) as avg_price
  from diamonds
  group by clarity
  order by avg_price desc")
##   clarity min_price max_price avg_price
## 1     SI2       326     18804  5063.029
## 2     SI1       326     18818  3996.001
## 3     VS2       334     18823  3924.989
## 4      I1       345     18531  3924.169
## 5     VS1       327     18795  3839.455
## 6    VVS2       336     18768  3283.737
## 7      IF       369     18806  2864.839
## 8    VVS1       336     18777  2523.115
```

The following example calculates an average price for each clarity level weighted by carat, that is, a price with greater carat has more weight:

```
dbGetQuery(con,
"select clarity,
    sum(price * carat) / sum(carat) as wprice
  from diamonds
  group by clarity
  order by wprice desc")
##   clarity   wprice
## 1     SI2 7012.257
## 2     VS2 6173.858
## 3     VS1 6059.505
## 4     SI1 5919.187
## 5    VVS2 5470.156
## 6      I1 5233.937
## 7      IF 5124.584
## 8    VVS1 4389.112
```

Just like sorting with more than one column, we can also group the data by multiple columns. The following code computes the average price for each clarity and color pair, and shows the top five pairs with the highest average prices:

```
dbGetQuery(con,
"select clarity, color,
     avg(price) as avg_price
   from diamonds
   group by clarity, color
   order by avg_price desc
   limit 5")
##    clarity color avg_price
## 1       IF     D  8307.370
## 2      SI2     I  7002.649
## 3      SI2     J  6520.958
## 4      SI2     H  6099.895
## 5      VS2     I  5690.506
```

The most relational operation in a relational database should be table join, that is, joining a number of tables together by some columns. For example, we will create a data frame of cut, color, and clarity to select records with exactly the same field values of the three cases in diamond_selector:

```
diamond_selector <- data.frame(
cut = c("Ideal", "Good", "Fair"),
color = c("E", "I", "D"),
clarity = c("VS1", "I1", "IF"),
stringsAsFactors = FALSE
)
diamond_selector
##       cut color clarity
## 1 Ideal     E     VS1
## 2  Good     I      I1
## 3  Fair     D      IF
```

After creating the data frame, we write it to the database so that we can join diamonds and diamond_selector to filter the desirable records:

```
dbWriteTable(con, "diamond_selector", diamond_selector,
row.names = FALSE, overwrite = TRUE)
## [1] TRUE
```

We can specify the columns to match in the join-clause:

```
subset_diamonds <- dbGetQuery(con,
"select cut, color, clarity, carat, price
   from diamonds
```

```
   join diamond_selector using (cut, color, clarity)")
head(subset_diamonds)
##       cut color clarity carat price
## 1 Ideal     E     VS1  0.60  2774
## 2 Ideal     E     VS1  0.26   556
## 3 Ideal     E     VS1  0.70  2818
## 4 Ideal     E     VS1  0.70  2837
## 5  Good     I      I1  1.01  2844
## 6 Ideal     E     VS1  0.26   556
```

In total, we have only a tiny portion of all records that satisfy one of the three cases:

```
nrow(subset_diamonds) /nrow(diamonds)
## [1] 0.01121617
```

Finally, don't forget to disconnect the database to ensure that all resources are properly released:

```
dbDisconnect(con)
## [1] TRUE
```

In the previous examples, we only showed the basic use of SQL to query a relational database such as SQLite. In fact, SQL is richer and much more powerful than we have demonstrated. For more details, visit `http://www.w3schools.com/sql` and learn more.

Fetching query results chunk by chunk

In the beginning of the section, we mentioned that one of the advantages of using a relational database is that we can store a large amount of data. Usually, we only take out a subset of the database and do some research. However, sometimes, we need to go through an amount of data that exceeds the capacity of computer memory. Obviously, we cannot load all of the data into memory, but must process the data chunk by chunk.

Most reasonable relational databases support fetching a query result set chunk by chunk. In the following example, we will use `dbSendQuery()` instead of `dbGetQuery()` to get a result set. Then, we will repeat fetching chunks (a number of rows) from the result set until all results are fetched. In this way, we can process the data chunk by chunk without using a large amount of working memory:

```
con <- dbConnect(SQLite(), "data/datasets.sqlite")
res <- dbSendQuery(con,
"select carat, cut, color, price from diamonds
  where cut = 'Ideal' and color = 'E'")
while (!dbHasCompleted(res)) {
  chunk <- dbFetch(res, 800)
```

```
cat(nrow(chunk), "records fetched\n")
# do something with chunk
}
## 800 records fetched
## 800 records fetched
## 800 records fetched
## 800 records fetched
## 703 records fetched
dbClearResult(res)
## [1] TRUE
dbDisconnect(con)
## [1] TRUE
```

In practice, the database may have billions of records. The query may result in tens of millions of records. If you use dbGetQuery() to fetch the whole result set at once, your memory may not be sufficient. If the task can be finished by processing data chunks, it can be much cheaper to work chunk by chunk.

Using transactions for consistency

Popular relational databases have a strong ability to ensure consistency. When we insert or update data, we do it via transactions. If a transaction fails, we can undo the transaction and rollback the database to ensure that everything is consistent.

The following example is a simple simulation of the data accumulation process that may fail in the middle of the process. Suppose we need to accumulate the data of some products and store it in data/products.sqlite. Each time a chunk of data is produced, we need to append it to a table in the database. In each iteration, however, the process may fail with a probability of 20 percent:

```
set.seed(123)
con <- dbConnect(SQLite(), "data/products.sqlite")
chunk_size <- 10
for (i in 1:6) {
  cat("Processing chunk", i, "\n")
  if (runif(1) <= 0.2) stop("Data error")
  chunk <- data.frame(id = ((i - 1L) * chunk_size):(i * chunk_size - 1L),
    type = LETTERS[[i]],
    score = rbinom(chunk_size, 10, (10 - i) /10),
    stringsAsFactors = FALSE)
  dbWriteTable(con, "products", chunk,
    append = i > 1, row.names = FALSE)
}
## Processing chunk 1
## Processing chunk 2
```

```
## Processing chunk 3
## Processing chunk 4
## Processing chunk 5
## Error in eval(expr, envir, enclos): Data error
```

The accumulation fails when processing chunk 5. Then, we will count the records in the table:

```
dbGetQuery(con, "select COUNT(*) from products")
##    COUNT(*)
## 1       40
dbDisconnect(con)
## [1] TRUE
```

We can find that the table has stored a number of records. In some cases, we want either all records to be properly stored or we want nothing to be put into the database. In both cases, the database is consistent. However, if only half of the data is stored, some other problems may occur. To ensure that a series of database changes succeed or fail as a whole, we can call dbBegin() before we write any data, call dbCommit() after all changes are made, and call dbRollback() if anything goes wrong.

The following code is an enhanced version of the previous example. We use transactions to make sure either all chunks are written to the database or none. More specifically, we put the data-writing process in tryCatch. Before the writing begins, we begin a transaction by calling dbBegin(). Then, in tryCatch, we will write data chunk by chunk to the database. If everything goes well, we will call dbCommit() to commit the transaction so that all the changes are committed. If anything goes wrong, the error will be captured by the error function in which we produce a warning and rollback by dbRollback():

```
set.seed(123)
file.remove("data/products.sqlite")
## [1] TRUE
con <- dbConnect(SQLite(), "data/products.sqlite")
chunk_size <- 10
dbBegin(con)
## [1] TRUE
res <- tryCatch({
  for (i in 1:6) {
cat("Processing chunk", i, "\n")
    if (runif(1) <= 0.2) stop("Data error")
    chunk <- data.frame(id = ((i - 1L) * chunk_size):(i * chunk_size - 1L),
type = LETTERS[[i]],
score = rbinom(chunk_size, 10, (10 - i) /10),
stringsAsFactors = FALSE)
dbWriteTable(con, "products", chunk,
append = i > 1, row.names = FALSE)
```

```
    }
  dbCommit(con)
  }, error = function(e) {
  warning("An error occurs: ", e, "\nRolling back", immediate. = TRUE)
  dbRollback(con)
  })
## Processing chunk 1
## Processing chunk 2
## Processing chunk 3
## Processing chunk 4
## Processing chunk 5
## Warning in value[[3L]](cond): An error occurs: Error in
doTryCatch(return(expr), name, parentenv, handler): Data error
##
## Rolling back
```

We can see that the same error happens again. However, this time, the error is captured, the transaction cancelled, and the database rolled back. To verify, we can again count the number of records in the `products` table:

```
dbGetQuery(con, "select COUNT(*) from products")
## Error in sqliteSendQuery(con, statement, bind.data): error in statement:
no such table: products
dbDisconnect(con)
## [1] TRUE
```

It may be surprising that the counting query results in an error. Why does it not return 0? If we take a closer look at the example, we should understand that the first time we call `dbWriteTable()`, it creates a new table first and then inserts the data in the first chunk. In other words, the table creation is included in the transaction. So, when we roll back, the table creation is undone too. As a result, the preceding counting query produces an error because `products` does not exist at all. If the table exists before we begin a transaction, the count should be equal to the number of records before the transaction as if nothing happened.

Another example that requires strong consistency is account transfer. When we transfer an amount of money from one account to another, we need to ensure that the system withdraws the money from one account and deposits the same amount to the other account. The two changes must both happen or both fail to keep consistency. This can be easily done with transactions of relational databases.

Suppose we define a function that creates a SQLite database of a virtual bank. We will use `dbSendQuery()` to send commands to create a table of accounts and a table of transactions:

```
create_bank <- function(dbfile) {
  if (file.exists(dbfile)) file.remove(dbfile)
```

```
  con <- dbConnect(SQLite(), dbfile)
  dbSendQuery(con,
    "create table accounts
    (name text primary key, balance real)")
  dbSendQuery(con,
    "create table transactions
    (time text, account_from text, account_to text, value real)")
  con
}
```

The accounts table has two columns: `name` and `balance`. The transactions table has four columns: `time`, `account_from`, `account_to`, and `value`. The first table stores all the information of accounts, and the second one stores all historic transactions.

We will also define a function to create an account with a name and initial balance. The function uses `insert into` to write a new record to the accounts table:

```
create_account <- function(con, name, balance) {
  dbSendQuery(con,
    sprintf("insert into accounts (name, balance) values ('%s', %.2f)",
name, balance))
  TRUE
}
```

Note that we uses `sprintf` to produce the preceding SQL statement. It is acceptable for local and personal use, but it is generally not safe for web applications, because a hacker can easily write a partial expression to run any disastrous statements to manipulate the whole database.

Next, we will define a transfer function. The function checks whether the withdrawing account and receiving account both exist in the database. It ensures that the balance of the withdrawing account is sufficient for such an amount of transfer. If the transfer is valid, then it updates the balance of both accounts and adds a transaction record to the database:

```
transfer <- function(con, from, to, value) {
  get_account <- function(name) {
    account <- dbGetQuery(con,
      sprintf("select * from accounts
              where name = '%s'", name))
    if (nrow(account) == 0)
      stop(sprintf("Account '%s' does not exist", name))
    account
  }
  account_from <- get_account(from)
  account_to <- get_account(to)
  if (account_from$balance < value) {
    stop(sprintf("Insufficient money to transfer from '%s'",
```

```
                       from))
    } else {
      dbSendQuery(con,
        sprintf("update accounts set balance = %.2f
                where name = '%s'",
          account_from$balance - value, from))
    dbSendQuery(con,
    sprintf("update accounts set balance = %.2f
    where name = '%s'",
          account_to$balance + value, to))
        dbSendQuery(con,
          sprintf("insert into transactions (time, account_from,
                  account_to, value) values
          ('%s', '%s', '%s', %.2f)",
          format(Sys.time(), "%Y-%m-%d %H:%M:%S"),
          from, to, value))
    }
    TRUE
    }
```

Although we have some basic checking against possible insufficient funds of the withdrawing account, we still cannot ensure that the transfer is safe, because it can be interrupted by other causes. Therefore, we will implement a safe version of transfer in which we will use transaction to ensure that any changes made by transfer can be undone if anything goes wrong:

```
safe_transfer <- function(con, ...) {
  dbBegin(con)
  tryCatch({
    transfer(con, ...)
    dbCommit(con)
  }, error = function(e) {
    message("An error occurs in the transaction. Rollback...")
    dbRollback(con)
    stop(e)
  })
}
```

In fact, safe_transfer is a wrapper function of transfer. It just puts transfer in a sandbox of tryCatch. If an error occurs, we call dbRollback() to ensure that the database is consistent.

Before putting the functions into tests, we need functions to view the balance of a given account as well as all successful transactions that happened between accounts:

```
get_balance <- function(con, name) {
  res <- dbGetQuery(con,
```

```
    sprintf("select balance from accounts
          where name = '%s'", name))
  res$balance
}
get_transactions <- function(con, from, to) {
  dbGetQuery(con,
    sprintf("select * from transactions
      where account_from = '%s' and account_to = '%s'",
      from, to))
}
```

Now, we can do some tests. First, we will create a virtual bank using `create_bank()` that returns a SQLite connection to the database file. Then, we will create two accounts with some initial balance:

```
con <- create_bank("data/bank.sqlite")
create_account(con, "David", 5000)
## [1] TRUE
create_account(con, "Jenny", 6500)
## [1] TRUE
get_balance(con, "David")
## [1] 5000
get_balance(con, "Jenny")
## [1] 6500
```

Then, we will use `safe_transfer()` to transfer some money from David's account to Jenny's account:

```
safe_transfer(con, "David", "Jenny", 1500)
## [1] TRUE
get_balance(con, "David")
## [1] 3500
get_balance(con, "Jenny")
## [1] 8000
```

The transfer succeeds, and the balances of both accounts are changed in a consistent manner. Now, we will make another transfer. This time, the balance of David's account is not sufficient, so the transfer will end up with an error:

```
safe_transfer(con, "David", "Jenny", 6500)
## An error occurs in the transaction. Rollback...
## Error in transfer(con, ...): Insufficient money to transfer from 'David'
get_balance(con, "David")
## [1] 3500
get_balance(con, "Jenny")
## [1] 8000
```

The error is captured, and the function rolls back the database. The balances of both accounts do not change. Now, we will query all successful transactions:

```
get_transactions(con, "David", "Jenny")
##                      time    account_from  account_to value
## 1 2016-06-08 23:24:39         David         Jenny  1500
```

We can see the first transaction, but the failed transaction does not appear in the database. Finally, we should always remember to close the database connection:

```
dbDisconnect(con)
## [1] TRUE
```

Storing data in files to a database

When we deal with large data files, we may usually get stuck with issues of reading and writing data. There are two extremes in practice. One extreme is a really big text-format data source that is almost impossible to load into memory. The other is a large number of small pieces of data files that will require some effort to integrate them into one data frame.

For the first case, we can read the big source data chunk by chunk and append each chunk to a certain table in a database. The following function is designed for appending rows to a database table from a big source given an input file, an output database, a table name, and a chunk size. Consider that the input data may be too large to load into the memory, so the function will read one chunk each time to write to database and, thus, only require a small working memory:

```
chunk_rw <- function(input, output, table, chunk_size = 10000) {
  first_row <- read.csv(input, nrows = 1, header = TRUE)
  header <- colnames(first_row)
  n <- 0
  con <- dbConnect(SQLite(), output)
on.exit(dbDisconnect(con))
  while (TRUE) {
    df <- read.csv(input,
skip = 1 + n * chunk_size, nrows = chunk_size,
header = FALSE, col.names = header,
stringsAsFactors = FALSE)
    if (nrow(df) == 0) break;
dbWriteTable(con, table, df, row.names = FALSE, append = n > 0)
    n <- n + 1
cat(sprintf("%d records written\n", nrow(df)))
  }
}
```

The trick here is to correctly calculate the offset of each chunk in the input file.

To test the function, we will first write diamonds into a csv file and use chunk_rw() to write the csv file into a SQLite database chunk by chunk. With this method, the writing process only requires a much smaller working memory than is required for loading the whole data into memory:

```
write.csv(diamonds, "data/diamonds.csv", quote = FALSE, row.names = FALSE)
chunk_rw("data/diamonds.csv", "data/diamonds.sqlite", "diamonds")
## 10000 records written
## 10000 records written
## 10000 records written
## 10000 records written
## 10000 records written
## 3940 records written
```

Another extreme of loading data is that we need to read from many small data files. In this case, we can put all the data distributed in these files in a database so that we can easily query data from it. The following function is intended for putting the data of all csv files in a folder to one database:

```
batch_rw <- function(dir, output, table, overwrite = TRUE) {
  files <- list.files(dir, "\\.csv$", full.names = TRUE)
  con <- dbConnect(SQLite(), output)
on.exit(dbDisconnect(con))
  exist <- dbExistsTable(con, table)
  if (exist) {
    if (overwrite) dbRemoveTable(con, table)
    else stop(sprintf("Table '%s' already exists", table))
  }
  exist <- FALSE
  for (file in files) {
cat(file, "... ")
    df <- read.csv(file, header = TRUE,
stringsAsFactors = FALSE)
dbWriteTable(con, table, df, row.names = FALSE,
append = exist)
    exist <- TRUE
cat("done\n")
  }
}
```

To demonstrate, we have a number of small csv files in data/groups, and we use batch_rw() to put all the data into a database:

```
batch_rw("data/groups", "data/groups.sqlite", "groups")
## data/groups/group1.csv ... done
```

```
## data/groups/group2.csv ... done
## data/groups/group3.csv ... done
```

Now, all the data in the files is put into the database. We can query or read the whole table and see what is looks like:

```
con <- dbConnect(SQLite(), "data/groups.sqlite")
dbReadTable(con, "groups")
##      group   id   grade
## 1       1   I-1     A
## 2       1   I-2     B
## 3       1   I-3     A
## 4       2  II-1     C
## 5       2  II-2     C
## 6       3 III-1     B
## 7       3 III-2     B
## 8       3 III-3     A
## 9       3 III-4     C
dbDisconnect(con)
## [1] TRUE
```

In this section, you learned some basic knowledge and usage of SQLite database. However, many popular relational databases share many common features of functionality and the query language. With almost the same knowledge, you can work with MySQL via RMySQL, PostreSQL via RPostges, Microsoft SQL Server via RSQLServer, and ODBC-compatible databases (Microsoft Access and Excel) via RODBC. They share almost the same operating functions, so if you are familiar with one, you shouldn't have a problem working with others.

Working with NoSQL databases

In the previous section of this chapter, you learned the basics of relational databases and how to use SQL to query data. Relational data is mostly organized in a tabular form, that is, as a collection of tables with relations.

However, when the volume of data exceeds the capacity of a server, problems occur because the traditional model of relational databases does not easily support horizontal scalability, that is, storing data in a cluster of servers instead of a single one. This adds a new layer of complexibility of database management as the data is stored in a distributed form while still accessible as one logical database.

In recent years, NoSQL, or non-relational databases, have become much more popular than before due to the introduction of new database models and the remarkable performance they exhibit in big data analytics and real-time applications. Some non-relational databases are designed for high availability, scalability, and flexibility, and some for high performance.

The difference in storage model between relational databases and non-relational databases is notable. For example, for a shopping website, the goods and comments can be stored in a relational database with two tables: goods and comments. All the information of goods is stored in one table, and all comments on each good are stored in the other. The following code shows the basic structure of such tables:

```
products:
code,name,type,price,amount
A0000001,Product-A,Type-I,29.5,500
```

Each comment has a field that points to the product it is subject to:

```
comments:
code,user,score,text
A0000001,david,8,"This is a good product"
A0000001,jenny,5,"Just so so"
```

When a product has many related tables and the number of records is so large that the database must be distributed across a great number of servers, it would be hard to query such a database because executing a simple query can be extremely inefficient. If we use MongoDB to store such data, each good will stored as a document and all comments of this good are stored in an array as a field of the document. As a result, it would be easy to query the data, and the database can be easily distributed to a large number of servers.

Working with MongoDB

MongoDB is a popular non-relational database that provides a document-oriented way of storing data. Each product is a document in a collection. The product has some fields of descriptive information and has a field that is an array of comments. All comments are subdocuments so that each logical item can be stored in their own logical form.

Here is a JSON (https://en.wikipedia.org/wiki/JSON) representation of a good in the collection:

```
{
    "code":"A0000001",
    "name":"Product-A",
    "type":"Type-I",
    "price":29.5,
    "amount":500,
    "comments":[
```

```
{
    "user":"david",
    "score":8,
    "text":"This is a good product"
},
{
    "user":"jenny",
    "score":5,
    "text":"Just so so"
}
]
}
```

A relational database may contain many schemas. Each schema (or database) may consist of many tables. Each table may contain many records. Similarly, a MongoDB instance can host many databases. Each database can include many collections. Each collection may contain many documents. The main difference is that the records in a table of a relational database need to have the same structure, but a document in a collection of a MongoDB database is schema-less and is flexible enough to have nested structures.

In the preceding JSON code, for example, a good is represented by such a document in which `code`, `name`, `type`, `price`, and `amount` are data fields with simple data types while `comments` is an array of objects. Each comment is represented by an object in `comments` and has a structure of `user`, `score`, and `text`. All comments of a good are stored as an object in `comments`. Therefore, a good is highly self-contained in terms of product information and comments. If we need information of a product, we no longer need to join two tables but pick out several fields.

To install MongoDB, visit `https://docs.mongodb.com/manual/installation/` and follow the instructions. It supports nearly all major platforms.

Querying data from MongoDB

Suppose we have a working MongoDB instance running on a local machine. We can use the `mongolite` package to work with MongoDB. To install the package, run the following code:

```
install.packages("mongolite")
```

Once we have the package installed, we can create a Mongo connection by specifying the collection, database, and MongoDB address:

```
library(mongolite)
m <- mongo("students", "test", "mongodb://localhost")
```

First, we will create a connection to the local MongoDB instance. Initially, the `products` collection has no documents:

```
m$count()
## [1] 0
```

To insert the product with comments, we can directly supply the JSON document as a string to `m$insert()`:

```
m$insert('
{
  "code": "A0000001",
  "name": "Product-A",
  "type": "Type-I",
  "price": 29.5,
  "amount": 500,
  "comments": [
    {
      "user": "david",
      "score": 8,
      "text": "This is a good product"
    },
    {
      "user": "jenny",
      "score": 5,
      "text": "Just so so"
    }
  ]
}')
```

Now, the collection has one document:

```
m$count()
## [1] 1
```

Alternatively, we can use list object in R to represent the same structure. The following code inserts the second product with `list`:

```
m$insert(list(
  code = "A0000002",
  name = "Product-B",
  type = "Type-II",
  price = 59.9,
  amount = 200L,
  comments = list(
    list(user = "tom", score = 6L,
      text = "Just fine"),
    list(user = "mike", score = 9L,
```

```
        text = "great product!")
  )
), auto_unbox = TRUE)
```

Note that R does not provide a scalar type so that, by default, all vectors are interpreted as JSON arrays in MongoDB, unless `auto_unbox = TRUE`, which turns one-element vectors into scalars in JSON. Without `auto_unbox = TRUE`, one has to use either `jsonlite::unbox()` to ensure scalar output or `I()` to ensure array output.

Now, the collection has two documents:

```
m$count()
## [1] 2
```

Then, we can use `m$find()` to retrieve all documents in the collection, and the results are automatically simplified into a data frame for easier data manipulation:

```
products <- m$find()
##
 Found 2 records...
 Imported 2 records. Simplifying into dataframe...
str(products)
## 'data.frame':    2 obs. of  6 variables:
##  $ code    : chr  "A0000001" "A0000002"
##  $ name    : chr  "Product-A" "Product-B"
##  $ type    : chr  "Type-I" "Type-II"
##  $ price   : num  29.5 59.9
##  $ amount  : int  500 200
##  $ comments:List of 2
##   ..$ :'data.frame': 2 obs. of  3 variables:
##   .. ..$ user : chr  "david" "jenny"
##   .. ..$ score: int  8 5
##   .. ..$ text : chr  "This is a good product" "Just so so"
##   ..$ :'data.frame': 2 obs. of  3 variables:
##   .. ..$ user : chr  "tom" "mike"
##   .. ..$ score: int  6 9
##   .. ..$ text : chr  "Just fine" "great product!"
```

To avoid the automatic conversion, we can use `m$iterate()` to iterate over the collection and get list objects that represent the original form of storage:

```
iter <- m$iterate()
products <- iter$batch(2)
str(products)
## List of 2
##  $ :List of 6
##   ..$ code    : chr "A0000001"
```

```
##    ..$ name    : chr "Product-A"
##    ..$ type    : chr "Type-I"
##    ..$ price   : num 29.5
##    ..$ amount  : int 500
##    ..$ comments:List of 2
##    .. ..$ :List of 3
##    .. .. ..$ user : chr "david"
##    .. .. ..$ score: int 8
##    .. .. ..$ text : chr "This is a good product"
##    .. ..$ :List of 3
##    .. .. ..$ user : chr "jenny"
##    .. .. ..$ score: int 5
##    .. .. ..$ text : chr "Just so so"
##  $ :List of 6
##    ..$ code    : chr "A0000002"
##    ..$ name    : chr "Product-B"
##    ..$ type    : chr "Type-II"
##    ..$ price   : num 59.9
##    ..$ amount  : int 200
##    ..$ comments:List of 2
##    .. ..$ :List of 3
##    .. .. ..$ user : chr "tom"
##    .. .. ..$ score: int 6
##    .. .. ..$ text : chr "Just fine"
##    .. ..$ :List of 3
##    .. .. ..$ user : chr "mike"
##    .. .. ..$ score: int 9
##    .. .. ..$ text : chr "great product!"
```

To filter the collection, we can specify the conditional query and fields in m$find().

First, we will query documents with code of A0000001 and retrieve the name, price, and amount fields:

```
m$find('{ "code": "A0000001" }',
'{ "_id": 0, "name": 1, "price": 1, "amount": 1 }')
##
 Found 1 records...
 Imported 1 records. Simplifying into dataframe...
##       name price amount
## 1 Product-A  29.5    500
```

Then, we will query documents with price greater than or equal to 40, which is done by the $gte operator in the conditional query:

```
m$find('{ "price": { "$gte": 40 } }',
'{ "_id": 0, "name": 1, "price": 1, "amount": 1 }')
##
```

```
 Found 1 records...
 Imported 1 records. Simplifying into dataframe...
##         name price amount
## 1 Product-B 59.9    200
```

We can not only query the document fields, but also the object fields in an array field. The following code retrieves all documents with any comment that gives a 9-point score:

```
m$find('{ "comments.score": 9 }',
'{ "_id": 0, "code": 1, "name": 1}')
##
 Found 1 records...
 Imported 1 records. Simplifying into dataframe...
##          code      name
## 1 A0000002 Product-B
```

Similarly, the following code retrieves all documents with any comment that gives a score less than 6:

```
m$find('{ "comments.score": { "$lt": 6 }}',
'{ "_id": 0, "code": 1, "name": 1}')
##
 Found 1 records...
 Imported 1 records. Simplifying into dataframe...
##          code      name
## 1 A0000001 Product-A
```

Note that accessing the field of a subdocument is easily done by the . notation, which makes it pretty easy to work with nested structures:

```
## [1] TRUE
```

The m$insert() function also works with data frames in R. Now, we will create a new MongoDB connection to another collection:

```
m <- mongo("students", "test", "mongodb://localhost")
```

We will create a MongoDB connection, m, to work with the students collection in the test database in a local MongoDB instance:

```
m$count()
## [1] 0
```

Initially, the collection has no documents. To insert some data, we will create a simple data frame:

```
students <- data.frame(
   name = c("David", "Jenny", "Sara", "John"),
```

```
  age = c(25, 23, 26, 23),
  major = c("Statistics", "Physics", "Computer Science", "Statistics"),
  projects = c(2, 1, 3, 1),
  stringsAsFactors = FALSE
)
students
##      name age          major projects
## 1 David   25       Statistics        2
## 2 Jenny   23          Physics        1
## 3  Sara   26 Computer Science        3
## 4  John   23       Statistics        1
```

Then, we will insert the rows as documents into the collection:

```
m$insert(students)
##
Complete! Processed total of 4 rows.
```

Now, the collection has some documents:

```
m$count()
## [1] 4
```

We can retrieve all the documents from the collection using find():

```
m$find()
##
 Found 4 records...
 Imported 4 records. Simplifying into dataframe...
##      name age          major projects
## 1 David   25       Statistics        2
## 2 Jenny   23          Physics        1
## 3  Sara   26 Computer Science        3
## 4  John   23       Statistics        1
```

As we mentioned in the previous example, the way in which documents are stored in a MongoDB collection is different from the way columns are stored in a table of a relational database. A document in a MongoDB collection is more like a JSON document, but in fact, it is stored in binary form to achieve super performance and compactness. The m$find() function first retrieves the data in a JSON-like form and simplifies it into a data form for easy data manipulation.

To filter the data, we can specify the query condition by supplying documents to find(). For example, we want to find all documents whose name is Jenny:

```
m$find('{ "name": "Jenny" }')
##
```

```
   Found 1 records...
   Imported 1 records. Simplifying into dataframe...
## 	 name age   major projects
## 1 Jenny  23 Physics        1
```

The results are automatically coerced to a data frame to make it easier to use. Then, we will query all documents with a number of projects greater or equal to 2:

```
m$find('{ "projects": { "$gte": 2 }}')
##
 Found 2 records...
 Imported 2 records. Simplifying into dataframe...
##     name age            major projects
## 1 David  25        Statistics        2
## 2  Sara  26 Computer Science        3
```

To select fields, we will specify the `fields` argument of `find()`:

```
m$find('{ "projects": { "$gte": 2 }}',
'{ "_id": 0, "name": 1, "major": 1 }')
##
 Found 2 records...
 Imported 2 records. Simplifying into dataframe...
##     name            major
## 1 David        Statistics
## 2  Sara Computer Science
```

We can also sort the data by specifying the `sort` argument:

```
m$find('{ "projects": { "$gte": 2 }}',
fields ='{ "_id": 0, "name": 1, "age": 1 }',
sort ='{ "age": -1 }')
##
 Found 2 records...
 Imported 2 records. Simplifying into dataframe...
##     name age
## 1  Sara  26
## 2 David  25
```

To limit the documents returned, we will specify `limit`:

```
m$find('{ "projects": { "$gte": 2 }}',
fields ='{ "_id": 0, "name": 1, "age": 1 }',
sort ='{ "age": -1 }',
limit =1)
##
 Found 1 records...
 Imported 1 records. Simplifying into dataframe...
```

```
##     name age
## 1 Sara   26
```

Also, we can get all distinct values of a certain field of all documents:

```
m$distinct("major")
## [1] "Statistics"          "Physics"          "Computer Science"
```

We can get the distinct values with a condition:

```
m$distinct("major", '{ "projects": { "$gte": 2 } }')
## [1] "Statistics"        "Computer Science"
```

To update a document, we will call `update()`, find the documents in selection, and set the values of certain fields:

```
m$update('{ "name": "Jenny" }', '{ "$set": { "age": 24 } }')
## [1] TRUE
m$find()
##
 Found 4 records...
 Imported 4 records. Simplifying into dataframe...
##     name age              major projects
## 1 David   25        Statistics        2
## 2 Jenny   24           Physics        1
## 3  Sara   26 Computer Science        3
## 4  John   23        Statistics        1
```

Creating and removing indexes

Like relational databases, MongoDB also supports indexes. Each collection may have multiple indexes, and the fields of indexes are cached in memory for fast lookup. Properly created indexes can make document lookup extremely efficient.

Creating indexes in MongoDB with `mongolite` is easy. It can be done before or after we import data into the collection. However, if we already imported billions of documents, it can be time consuming to create an index. If we create many indexes before pouring any documents into the collection, the performance of inserting documents may be harmed.

Here, we will create an index for the `students` collection:

```
m$index('{ "name": 1 }')
##   v key._id key.name   name            ns
## 1 1       1       NA   _id_ test.students
## 2 1      NA        1 name_1 test.students
```

Now, if we find a document with the indexed field, the performance is super:

```
m$find('{ "name": "Sara" }')
##
 Found 1 records...
 Imported 1 records. Simplifying into dataframe...
##    name age               major projects
## 1 Sara   26 Computer Science        3
```

If no document satisfies the condition, an empty data frame will be returned:

```
m$find('{ "name": "Jane" }')
##
 Imported 0 records. Simplifying into dataframe...
## data frame with 0 columns and 0 rows
```

Finally, the collection can be abandoned with `drop()`:

```
m$drop()
## [1] TRUE
```

The performance boost of using an index is definitely not obvious if the amount of data is small. In the next example, we will create a data frame with many rows so that we can compare the performance of finding documents between using an index and not using one.

Here, we will use `expand.grid()` to create a data frame that exhausts all possible combinations of the provided vectors in the arguments:

```
set.seed(123)
m <- mongo("simulation", "test")
sim_data <- expand.grid(
type = c("A", "B", "C", "D", "E"),
category = c("P-1", "P-2", "P-3"),
group = 1:20000,
stringsAsFactors = FALSE)
head(sim_data)
##    type category group
## 1    A      P-1     1
## 2    B      P-1     1
## 3    C      P-1     1
## 4    D      P-1     1
## 5    E      P-1     1
## 6    A      P-2     1
```

The index columns are created. Next, we need to simulate some random numbers:

```
sim_data$score1 <- rnorm(nrow(sim_data), 10, 3)
sim_data$test1 <- rbinom(nrow(sim_data), 100, 0.8)
```

The data frame now looks like this:

```
head(sim_data)
##   type category group    score1 test1
## 1    A      P-1     1  8.318573    80
## 2    B      P-1     1  9.309468    75
## 3    C      P-1     1 14.676125    77
## 4    D      P-1     1 10.211525    79
## 5    E      P-1     1 10.387863    80
## 6    A      P-2     1 15.145195    76
```

Then, we will insert all the data into the `simulation` collection:

```
m$insert(sim_data)
Complete! Processed total of 300000 rows.
[1] TRUE
```

The first test is trying to answer how long it takes to query a document without any index:

```
system.time(rec <- m$find('{ "type": "C", "category": "P-3", "group": 87
}'))
##
 Found 1 records...
 Imported 1 records. Simplifying into dataframe...
##     user  system elapsed
##    0.000   0.000   0.104
rec
##   type category group   score1 test1
## 1    C      P-3    87 6.556688    72
```

The second test is about the performance of finding documents with joint conditions:

```
system.time({
  recs <- m$find('{ "type": { "$in": ["B", "D"]   },
    "category": { "$in": ["P-1", "P-2"] },
    "group": { "$gte": 25, "$lte": 75 } }')
})
##
Found 204 records...
 Imported 204 records. Simplifying into dataframe...
##     user  system elapsed
##    0.004   0.000   0.094
```

Then, the resulting data frame looks like this:

```
head(recs)
##   type category group    score1 test1
## 1    B      P-1    25 11.953580    80
## 2    D      P-1    25 13.074020    84
```

```
## 3      B          P-2      25 11.134503      76
## 4      D          P-2      25 12.570769      74
## 5      B          P-1      26  7.009658      77
## 6      D          P-1      26  9.957078      85
```

The third test is about the performance of finding documents using a non-index field:

```
system.time(recs2 <- m$find('{ "score1": { "$gte": 20 } }'))
##
Found 158 records...
 Imported 158 records. Simplifying into dataframe...
##     user  system elapsed
##    0.000   0.000   0.096
```

The resulting data frame looks like this:

```
head(recs2)
##    type category group   score1 test1
## 1     D       P-1    89 20.17111    76
## 2     B       P-3   199 20.26328    80
## 3     E       P-2   294 20.33798    75
## 4     E       P-2   400 21.14716    83
## 5     A       P-3   544 21.54330    73
## 6     A       P-1   545 20.19368    80
```

All three tests are done without creating an index for the collection. To make a contrast, we will now create an index:

```
m$index('{ "type": 1, "category": 1, "group": 1 }')
##   v key._id key.type key.category key.group
## 1 1       1       NA           NA        NA
## 2 1      NA        1            1         1
##                              name         ns
## 1                            _id_ test.simulation
## 2 type_1_category_1_group_1 test.simulation
```

Once the index is created, the query of the first test with index fields is quick:

```
system.time({
  rec <- m$find('{ "type": "C", "category": "P-3", "group": 87 }')
})
##
 Found 1 records...
 Imported 1 records. Simplifying into dataframe...
##     user  system elapsed
##    0.000   0.000   0.001
```

The second test also yields results quickly:

```
system.time({
   recs <- m$find('{ "type": { "$in": ["B", "D"]   },
      "category": { "$in": ["P-1", "P-2"] },
      "group": { "$gte": 25, "$lte": 75 } }')
})
##
 Found 204 records...
 Imported 204 records. Simplifying into dataframe...
##    user  system elapsed
##   0.000   0.000   0.002
```

However, the non-index fields do not contribute to the index search for documents:

```
system.time({
   recs2 <- m$find('{ "score1": { "$gte": 20 } }')
})
##
 Found 158 records...
 Imported 158 records. Simplifying into dataframe...
##    user  system elapsed
##   0.000   0.000   0.095
```

Another important feature of MongoDB is its aggregation pipeline. When we aggregate data, we supply an array of aggregate operations so that they are scheduled by the MongoDB instance. For example, the following code groups the data by `type`. Each group has a field count, average score, min test score, and max test score. Since the output can be long, we don't print it here. You may execute the code yourself and see the results:

```
m$aggregate('[
   { "$group": {
      "_id": "$type",
      "count": { "$sum": 1 },
      "avg_score": { "$avg": "$score1" },
      "min_test": { "$min": "$test1" },
      "max_test": { "$max": "$test1" }
   }
   }
]')
```

We can also use multiple fields as the key of a group, which is similar to `group by A, B` in SQL:

```
m$aggregate('[
   { "$group": {
      "_id": { "type": "$type", "category": "$category" },
      "count": { "$sum": 1 },
```

```
         "avg_score": { "$avg": "$score1" },
         "min_test": { "$min": "$test1" },
         "max_test": { "$max": "$test1" }
      }
   }
]')
```

The aggregation pipeline supports running aggregate operations in a streamline:

```
m$aggregate('[
   { "$group": {
         "_id": { "type": "$type", "category": "$category" },
         "count": { "$sum": 1 },
         "avg_score": { "$avg": "$score1" },
         "min_test": { "$min": "$test1" },
         "max_test": { "$max": "$test1" }
      }
   },
   {
      "$sort": { "_id.type": 1, "avg_score": -1 }
   }
]')
```

We can lengthen the pipeline by adding more operations. For example, the following code creates groups and aggregate data. Then, it sorts the documents with average score in the descending order, takes out the top three documents, and projects the fields into something useful:

```
m$aggregate('[
   { "$group": {
         "_id": { "type": "$type", "category": "$category" },
         "count": { "$sum": 1 },
         "avg_score": { "$avg": "$score1" },
         "min_test": { "$min": "$test1" },
         "max_test": { "$max": "$test1" }
      }
   },
   {
      "$sort": { "avg_score": -1 }
   },
   {
      "$limit": 3
   },
   {
      "$project": {
         "_id.type": 1,
         "_id.category": 1,
         "avg_score": 1,
```

```
        "test_range": { "$subtract": ["$max_test", "$min_test"] }
    }
  }
]')
```

In addition to the aggregate operators we used in the example, there are many other operators that are more powerful. For more details, visit https://docs.mongodb.com/manual/reference/operator/aggregation-pipeline/ and https://docs.mongodb.com/manual/reference/operator/aggregation-arithmetic/.

Another important feature of MongoDB is that it supports MapReduce (https://en.wikipedia.org/wiki/MapReduce) at an internal level. The MapReduce model is widely used in big data analytics in distributed clusters. In our environment, we can write an extremely simple MapReduce code that tries to produce a histogram of certain data:

```
bins <- m$mapreduce(
map = 'function() {
    emit(Math.floor(this.score1 / 2.5) * 2.5, 1);
  }',
reduce = 'function(id, counts) {
    return Array.sum(counts);
  }'
)
```

The first step of MapReduce is map. In this step, all values are mapped to a key-value pair. Then, the reduce step aggregates the key-value pair. In the preceding example, we simply calculated the number of records for each bin:

```
bins
##      _id  value
## 1   -5.0      6
## 2   -2.5    126
## 3    0.0   1747
## 4    2.5  12476
## 5    5.0  46248
## 6    7.5  89086
## 7   10.0  89489
## 8   12.5  46357
## 9   15.0  12603
## 10  17.5   1704
## 11  20.0    153
## 12  22.5      5
```

We can also create a bar plot from `bins`:

```
with(bins, barplot(value /sum(value), names.arg = `_id`,
main = "Histogram of scores",
```

```
xlab = "score1", ylab = "Percentage"))
```

The plot generated is shown as follows:

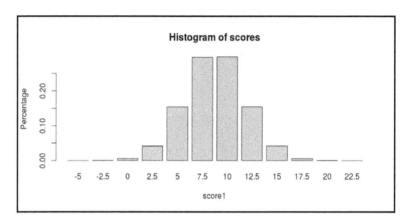

If the collection is no longer used, then we can use the `drop()` function to drop it:

```
m$drop()
## [1] TRUE
```

Since this section is at the introductory level, the more advanced use of MongoDB is beyond the scope of this book. If you are interested in MongoDB, go through the official tutorial at h ttps://docs.mongodb.com/manual/tutorial/.

Using Redis

Redis (http://redis.io/), unlike SQLite that stores data in tabular form or MongoDB that allows to store and query nested structures, is an in-memory data structure store. It stores key-values in memory and thus has very high performance of key lookup. However, it does not support query languages as used in SQL databases or MongoDB.

Redis is usually used as a high-performance data cache. We can store and manipulate a range of basic data structures in it. To install Redis, visit http://redis.io/download. Unfortunately, the Windows operating system is not officially supported, but the Microsoft Open Tech group develops and maintains a Win64 port of Redis at https://github.com/M SOpenTech/redis.

While SQL database stores tables and MongoDB stores documents, Redis stores key-value pairs as follows:

```
name: Something
type: 1
grade: A
```

The value can be more complex data structures (for example, hashmap, set, and sorted set) rather than simple values, and Redis provides a simple interface to work with these data structures in high performance and low latency.

Accessing Redis from R

To access a Redis instance from R, we can use the `rredis` package that provides simple functions to work with Redis. To install the package, run the following code:

```
install.packages("rredis")
```

Once the package is ready, we can connect to a Redis instance:

```
library(rredis)
redisConnect()
```

If we leave the arguments blank, it connects to the local Redis instance by default. It also lets us connect to a remote instance.

Setting and getting values from the Redis server

The most basic use of Redis is to store a value by calling `redisSet(key, value)`. In R, the value is, by default, serialized so that we can store any R objects in Redis:

```
redisSet("num1", 100)
## [1] "OK"
```

Now that the command has succeeded, we can retrieve the value with the same key:

```
redisGet("num1")
## [1] 100
```

We can store an integer vector:

```
redisSet("vec1", 1:5)
## [1] "OK"
redisGet("vec1")
## [1] 1 2 3 4 5
```

We can even store a data frame:

```
redisSet("mtcars_head", head(mtcars, 3))
## [1] "OK"
redisGet("mtcars_head")
##                   mpg cyl disp  hp drat    wt  qsec vs am gear
## Mazda RX4        21.0   6  160 110 3.90 2.620 16.46  0  1    4
## Mazda RX4 Wag    21.0   6  160 110 3.90 2.875 17.02  0  1    4
## Datsun 710       22.8   4  108  93 3.85 2.320 18.61  1  1    4
##                  carb
## Mazda RX4           4
## Mazda RX4 Wag       4
## Datsun 710          1
```

In fact, if other computers have access to your Redis instance, they will get the same data in R using `redisGet()`:

However, we can only get `NULL` if the key does not exist at all:

```
redisGet("something")
## NULL
```

Instead of getting `NULL`, we can use `redisExists()` to detect whether a key is defined:

```
redisExists("something")
## [1] FALSE
redisExists("num1")
## [1] TRUE
```

If we no longer need a key, we can delete it with `redisDelete()`:

```
redisDelete("num1")
## [1] "1"
## attr(,"redis string value")
## [1] TRUE
redisExists("num1")
## [1] FALSE
```

In addition to plain key-value pairs, Redis also supports more advanced data structures. For example, we can use `redisHSet()` to create a hash map of fruits in which different fruits have different numbers:

```
redisHSet("fruits", "apple", 5)
## [1] "1"
## attr(,"redis string value")
## [1] TRUE
redisHSet("fruits", "pear", 2)
## [1] "1"
```

```
## attr(,"redis string value")
## [1] TRUE
redisHSet("fruits", "banana", 9)
## [1] "1"
## attr(,"redis string value")
## [1] TRUE
```

We can call `redisHGet()` to get the value of a field of a hash map:

```
redisHGet("fruits", "banana")
## [1] 9
```

We can also get a list to represent the structure of the hash map:

```
redisHGetAll("fruits")
## $apple
## [1] 5
##
## $pear
## [1] 2
##
## $banana
## [1] 9
```

Alternatively, we can get the keys of the hash map:

```
redisHKeys("fruits")
## [[1]]
## [1] "apple"
## attr(,"redis string value")
## [1] TRUE
##
## [[2]]
## [1] "pear"
## attr(,"redis string value")
## [1] TRUE
##
## [[3]]
## [1] "banana"
## attr(,"redis string value")
## [1] TRUE
```

We can also get only the values of the hash map:

```
redisHVals("fruits")
## [[1]]
## [1] 5
##
## [[2]]
```

```
## [1] 2
##
## [[3]]
## [1] 9
```

Aditionally, we can simply get the number of fields in the hash map:

```
redisHLen("fruits")
## [1] "3"
## attr(,"redis string value")
## [1] TRUE
```

We can get the values of multiple fields at once:

```
redisHMGet("fruits", c("apple", "banana"))
## $apple
## [1] 5
##
## $banana
## [1] 9
```

We can also set the values of multiple fields by supplying a list:

```
redisHMSet("fruits", list(apple = 4, pear = 1))
## [1] "OK"
```

Now, the values of the fields are updated:

```
redisHGetAll("fruits")
## $apple
## [1] 4
##
## $pear
## [1] 1
##
## $banana
## [1] 9
```

In addition to the hash map, Redis also supports queue. We can push values from either left-hand side or the right-hand side of the queue. For example, we push integers from 1 to 3 from the right-hand side of a queue:

```
for (qi in 1:3) {
  redisRPush("queue", qi)
}
```

We can get the current length of the queue with `redisLLen()`:

```
redisLLen("queue")
## [1] "3"
## attr(,"redis string value")
## [1] TRUE
```

Now, the queue has three elements. Note that the value is a character vector rather than an integer. Therefore, we need to convert it if we need to use it as a number in other places.

Then, we can keep popping values from the left-hand side of the queue:

```
redisLPop("queue")
## [1] 1
redisLPop("queue")
## [1] 2
redisLPop("queue")
## [1] 3
redisLPop("queue")
## NULL
```

Note that the queue only has three elements to pop out. The fourth attempt returns NULL, which can be a criterion to check whether the queue is empty.

Finally, we should close the connection to Redis to release all resources:

```
redisClose()
```

Redis has more advanced features that are beyond the scope of this chapter. It supports not only data structure store, but also message broker, that is, we can use it to pass messages between different programs. For more advanced usage, read the official documentation at h ttp://redis.io/documentation.

Summary

In this chapter, you learned how to access different types of databases from R. We introduced the basic usage of relational databases such as SQLite and non-relational databases such as MongoDB and Redis. With the understanding of major differences in their functionality and feature sets, we need to choose an appropriate database to work with in our projects according to our purpose and needs.

In many data-related projects, data storage and data importing are the initial steps, but data cleaning and data manipulation cost most of the time. In the next chapter, we will move on to data-manipulation techniques. You will learn about a number of packages that are specially tailored for handy but powerful data manipulation. To better work with these packages, we'll need a better understanding of how they work, which requires the sound knowledge introduced in the previous chapters.

12
Data Manipulation

In the previous chapter, you learned the methods used to access different types of databases such as relational databases (SQLite and MySQL) and non-relational databases (MongoDB and Redis). Relational databases usually return data in a tabular form, while non-relational databases may support nested data structures and other features.

Even though the data is loaded into memory, it is usually far from ready for data analysis. Most data at this stage still needs cleaning and transforming, which, in fact, may take a large proportion of time before any statistical model and visualization can be applied. In this chapter, you'll learn about a set of built-in functions and several packages for data manipulation. The packages are extremely powerful. However, to better work with these packages, we need a concrete understanding of the knowledge introduced in the previous chapters.

In this chapter, we'll cover the following topics:

- Using basic functions to manipulate data frames
- Using SQL to query data frames via the `sqldf` package
- Using `data.table` to manipulate data
- Using `dplyr` pipelines to manipulate data frames
- Using `rlist` to work with nested data structures

Using built-in functions to manipulate data frames

Previously, you learned the basics of data frames. Here, we will review the built-in functions used to filter a data frame. Although a data frame is essentially a list of vectors, we can access it like a matrix since all column vectors are of the same length. To select rows that meet certain conditions, we will supply a logical vector as the first argument of [ ], while the second is left empty.

In R, these operations can be done with built-in functions. In this section, we will introduce some built-in functions that are most helpful to manipulate data into the form we need as model input or for presentation. Some of the functions or techniques are already presented in the previous chapters.

Most of the code in this section and subsequent sections are based on a group of fictitious data about some products. We will use the `readr` package to load the data for better handling of column types. If you don't have this package installed, run `install.packages("readr")`:

```
library(readr)
product_info <- read_csv("data/product-info.csv")
product_info
##     id       name  type    class released
## 1 T01     SupCar   toy  vehicle      yes
## 2 T02   SupPlane   toy  vehicle       no
## 3 M01      JeepX model  vehicle      yes
## 4 M02  AircraftX model  vehicle      yes
## 5 M03     Runner model   people      yes
## 6 M04     Dancer model   people       no
```

Once the data is loaded into memory as a data frame, we can take a look at its column types:

```
sapply(product_info, class)
##          id        name        type       class    released
## "character" "character" "character" "character" "character"
```

The `readr::read_csv` argument has different behavior from the built-in function `read.csv`. For example, it does not automatically convert string columns to factors (which can be problematic, but adds little value). Therefore, I recommend that you use functions provided by `readr` to read tabular data from file into R. If we were using the `read.csv` file, then all these columns would be factors with limited possible values.

Using built-in functions to manipulate data frames

Previously, you learned the basics of data frames. In this section, we will review the built-in functions to filter a data frame. Although a data frame is essentially a list of vectors, we can access it like a matrix since all column vectors are of the same length. To select rows that meet certain conditions, we will supply a logical vector as the first argument of [], while the second is left empty. In the following examples, we will use a series of product information points and statistics we introduced earlier to demonstrate basic data-filtering methods and summary techniques.

For example, we will take out all rows of `toy` type:

```
product_info[product_info$type == "toy", ]
##     id     name type    class released
## 1 T01   SupCar  toy  vehicle      yes
## 2 T02 SupPlane  toy  vehicle       no
```

Alternatively, we could take out all rows that are not released:

```
product_info[product_info$released == "no", ]
##     id     name  type    class released
## 2 T02 SupPlane   toy  vehicle       no
## 6 M04   Dancer model   people       no
```

To filter columns, we will supply a character vector as the second argument while the first is left empty, which is exactly what we did when we subset a matrix:

```
product_info[, c("id", "name", "type")]
##     id      name  type
## 1 T01    SupCar   toy
## 2 T02  SupPlane   toy
## 3 M01     JeepX model
## 4 M02 AircraftX model
## 5 M03    Runner model
## 6 M04    Dancer model
```

Alternatively, we can filter the data frame by regarding it as a list. We will supply only one character vector of column names in [] and omit the comma:

```
product_info[c("id", "name", "class")]
##     id      name   class
## 1 T01    SupCar vehicle
## 2 T02  SupPlane vehicle
## 3 M01     JeepX vehicle
## 4 M02 AircraftX vehicle
```

```
## 5 M03    Runner  people
## 6 M04    Dancer  people
```

To filter a data frame by both row and column, we will supply a vector as the first argument to select rows and a vector as the second to select columns:

```
product_info[product_info$type == "toy", c("name", "class", "released")]
##         name   class released
## 1    SupCar vehicle      yes
## 2 SupPlane vehicle       no
```

If the row-filtering condition is based on values of certain columns, the preceding code can be very redundant, especially when the condition gets more complicated. Another built-in function that simplifies code is `subset`, as we introduced previously:

```
subset(product_info,
  subset = type == "model" & released == "yes",
  select = name:class)
##         name  type   class
## 3      JeepX model vehicle
## 4  AircraftX model vehicle
## 5     Runner model  people
```

The `subset` function uses non-standard evaluation so that we can directly use the columns of the data frame without typing `product_info` many times, because the expressions are meant to be evaluated in the context of the data frame.

Similarly, we can use `with` to evaluate an expression in the context of the data frame, that is, the columns of the data frame can be used as symbols in the expression without repeatedly specifying the data frame:

```
with(product_info, name[released == "no"])
## [1] "SupPlane" "Dancer"
```

The expression can be more than a simple subsetting. We can summarize the data by counting the occurrences of each possible value of a vector. For example, we can create a table of the occurrences of types of records that are released:

```
with(product_info, table(type[released == "yes"]))
##
## model   toy
##     3     1
```

In addition to the table of product information, we also have a table of product statistics that describe some properties of each product:

```
product_stats <- read_csv("data/product-stats.csv")
product_stats
##      id material size weight
## 1 T01    Metal  120   10.0
## 2 T02    Metal  350   45.0
## 3 M01 Plastics   50     NA
## 4 M02 Plastics   85    3.0
## 5 M03     Wood   15     NA
## 6 M04     Wood   16    0.6
```

Now, think how we can get the names of products with the top three largest sizes. One way is to sort the records in product_stats by size in descending order, select id values of the top three records, and use these values to filter rows of product_info by id:

```
top_3_id <- product_stats[order(product_stats$size, decreasing = TRUE),
"id"][1:3]
product_info[product_info$id %in% top_3_id, ]
##     id     name type   class released
## 1 T01   SupCar  toy vehicle      yes
## 2 T02 SupPlane  toy vehicle       no
## 4 M02 AircraftX model vehicle     yes
```

Although it works as supposed, this approach looks quite redundant. Note that product_info and product_stats actually describe the same set of products from different perspectives. The connection between these two tables is the id column. Each id is unique and refers to the same product. To access both sets of information, we can put the two tables together into one data frame. The simplest way to do this is use merge:

```
product_table <- merge(product_info, product_stats, by = "id")
product_table
##     id     name  type   class released material size weight
## 1 M01    JeepX model vehicle      yes Plastics   50     NA
## 2 M02 AircraftX model vehicle     yes Plastics   85    3.0
## 3 M03   Runner model  people      yes     Wood   15     NA
## 4 M04   Dancer model  people       no     Wood   16    0.6
## 5 T01   SupCar   toy vehicle      yes    Metal  120   10.0
## 6 T02 SupPlane   toy vehicle       no    Metal  350   45.0
```

Now, we create a new data frame that is a combined version of product_table and product_info, with a shared id column. In fact, if you reorder the records in the second table, the two tables still can be correctly merged.

With the combined version, we can do things more easily. For example, with the merged version, we can sort the data frame with any column in one table that we loaded without having to manually work with the other:

```
product_table[order(product_table$size), ]
##     id      name  type   class released material size weight
## 3 M03    Runner model  people      yes     Wood   15     NA
## 4 M04    Dancer model  people       no     Wood   16    0.6
## 1 M01     JeepX model vehicle      yes Plastics   50     NA
## 2 M02 AircraftX model vehicle      yes Plastics   85    3.0
## 5 T01    SupCar   toy vehicle      yes    Metal  120   10.0
## 6 T02  SupPlane   toy vehicle       no    Metal  350   45.0
```

To solve the problem, we can directly use the merged table and get the same answer:

```
product_table[order(product_table$size, decreasing = TRUE), "name"][1:3]
## [1] "SupPlane"  "SupCar"     "AircraftX"
```

The merged data frame allows us to sort the records by a column in one data frame and filter the records by a column in the other. For example, we will first sort the product records by weight in descending order and select all records of the model type:

```
product_table[order(product_table$weight, decreasing = TRUE), ][
    product_table$type == "model",]
##     id      name  type   class released material size weight
## 6 T02  SupPlane   toy vehicle       no    Metal  350   45.0
## 5 T01    SupCar   toy vehicle      yes    Metal  120   10.0
## 2 M02 AircraftX model vehicle      yes Plastics   85    3.0
## 4 M04    Dancer model  people       no     Wood   16    0.6
```

Sometimes, the column values are literal but can be converted to standard R data structures to better represent the data. For example, the released column in product_info only takes yes and no, which can be better represented with a logical vector. We can use <- to modify the column values, as you learned previously. However, it is usually better to create a new data frame with the existing columns properly adjusted and new columns added without polluting the original data. To do this, we can use transform:

```
transform(product_table,
    released = ifelse(released == "yes", TRUE, FALSE),
    density = weight / size)
##     id      name  type   class released material size weight
## 1 M01     JeepX model vehicle     TRUE Plastics   50     NA
## 2 M02 AircraftX model vehicle     TRUE Plastics   85    3.0
## 3 M03    Runner model  people     TRUE     Wood   15     NA
## 4 M04    Dancer model  people    FALSE     Wood   16    0.6
## 5 T01    SupCar   toy vehicle     TRUE    Metal  120   10.0
## 6 T02  SupPlane   toy vehicle    FALSE    Metal  350   45.0
```

```
##        density
## 1            NA
## 2 0.03529412
## 3            NA
## 4 0.03750000
## 5 0.08333333
## 6 0.12857143
```

The result is a new data frame with `released` converted to a logical vector and a new column, `density`, added. You can easily verify that `product_table` is not modified at all.

Also, note that `transform` works in a way similar to `subset` because both functions use non-standard evaluation to allow direct use of data frame columns as symbols in the arguments so that we don't have to type `product_table$` before columns all the time.

In the preceding data, a number of columns contain missing values represented by NA. Under many circumstances, we don't want any missing values to be present in our data. Therefore, we need to somehow deal with them. To demonstrate the various techniques, we will load another table that contains missing values. The table is the test results of the quality, durability, and waterproofing of each product in the previous dataset we used. It is the test results of the quality, durability, and waterproofing of each product. We will store the data in `product_tests`:

```
product_tests <- read_csv("data/product-tests.csv")
product_tests
##      id quality durability waterproof
## 1 T01      NA          10         no
## 2 T02      10           9         no
## 3 M01       6           4        yes
## 4 M02       6           5        yes
## 5 M03       5          NA        yes
## 6 M04       6           6        yes
```

Note that the values in both `quality` and `durability` contain missing values (NA). To exclude all rows with missing values, we can use `na.omit()`:

```
na.omit(product_tests)
##      id quality durability waterproof
## 2 T02      10           9         no
## 3 M01       6           4        yes
## 4 M02       6           5        yes
## 6 M04       6           6        yes
```

Another way is to use `complete.cases()` to get a logical vector, indicating all complete rows (without any missing value):

```
complete.cases(product_tests)
## [1] FALSE  TRUE   TRUE   TRUE FALSE   TRUE
```

Then, we can use this logical vector to filter the data frame. For example, we can get the `id` of all complete rows:

```
product_tests[complete.cases(product_tests), "id"]
## [1] "T02" "M01" "M02" "M04"
```

Alternatively, we can get the id of all incomplete rows:

```
product_tests[!complete.cases(product_tests), "id"]
## [1] "T01" "M03"
```

Note that `product_info`, `product_stats`, and `product_tests` all share an `id` column; we can merge them all together. Unfortunately, there's no built-in function to merge an arbitrary number of data frames. We can only merge two existing data frames at a time, or we'll have to merge them recursively:

```
product_full <- merge(product_table, product_tests, by = "id")
product_full
##     id      name  type    class released material size weight
## 1 M01     JeepX model  vehicle      yes Plastics   50     NA
## 2 M02 AircraftX model  vehicle      yes Plastics   85    3.0
## 3 M03    Runner model   people      yes     Wood   15     NA
## 4 M04    Dancer model   people       no     Wood   16    0.6
## 5 T01    SupCar   toy  vehicle      yes    Metal  120   10.0
## 6 T02  SupPlane   toy  vehicle       no    Metal  350   45.0
##   quality durability waterproof
## 1       6          4        yes
## 2       6          5        yes
## 3       5         NA        yes
## 4       6          6        yes
## 5      NA         10         no
## 6      10          9         no
```

With the fully merged table, we can use `tapply`, another apply-family function specialized to work with tabular data, to summarize the data using certain methods over given columns. For example, we can calculate the mean value of `quality` of each `type`:

```
mean_quality1 <- tapply(product_full$quality,
  list(product_full$type),
  mean, na.rm = TRUE)
mean_quality1
```

```
## model    toy
##  5.75 10.00
```

Note that we not only supply `mean` but also specify `na.rm = TRUE` to ignore the missing values in `quality`. The result looks like a numeric vector. We will use `str()`, so let's take a look at its structure:

```
str(mean_quality1)
##  num [1:2(1d)] 5.75 10
##  - attr(*, "dimnames")=List of 1
##   ..$ : chr [1:2] "model" "toy"
```

In fact, it is a one-dimensional array:

```
is.array(mean_quality1)
## [1] TRUE
```

The `tapply` function produces an array instead of a simple numeric vector, because it can be easily generalized to work with multiple grouping. For example, we can compute the mean value of `quality` for each `type` and `class` pair:

```
mean_quality2 <- tapply(product_full$quality,
  list(product_full$type, product_full$class),
  mean, na.rm = TRUE)
mean_quality2
##        people vehicle
## model     5.5       6
## toy        NA      10
```

Now, we have a two-dimensional array, whose values can be extracted by two arguments:

```
mean_quality2["model", "vehicle"]
## [1] 6
```

Moreover, we can supply more columns for grouping. In the following code, we will use the `with()` function to reduce redundant typing of `product_full`:

```
mean_quality3 <- with(product_full,
  tapply(quality, list(type, material, released),
    mean, na.rm = TRUE))
mean_quality3
## , , no
##
##        Metal Plastics Wood
## model     NA       NA    6
## toy       10       NA   NA
##
## , , yes
```

```
##
##          Metal Plastics Wood
## model      NA        6    5
## toy       NaN       NA   NA
```

Now, a three-dimensional array is produced. Even though na.rm = TRUE is specified, many cells are still missing values. This is because no value is present for the grouping:

```
str(mean_quality3)
##   num [1:2, 1:3, 1:2] NA 10 NA NA 6 NA NA NaN 6 NA ...
##   - attr(*, "dimnames")=List of 3
##     ..$ : chr [1:2] "model" "toy"
##     ..$ : chr [1:3] "Metal" "Plastics" "Wood"
##     ..$ : chr [1:2] "no" "yes"
```

We can access the cell value by supplying three arguments:

```
mean_quality3["model", "Wood", "yes"]
## [1] 5
```

In summary, tapply groups the input data frame with n specified variables and produces an array with n dimensions. This approach to summarizing data can be hard to work with, especially when there are more columns for grouping. This is mostly because array is usually high-dimensional, hard to represent, and not flexible for further manipulation. Later in this chapter, you will learn several different methods that make group summary much easier.

Reshaping data frames using reshape2

Previously, you learned how to filter, sort, merge, and summarize data frames. These operations only work on rows and columns separately. Sometimes, however, we need to do something more complex.

For example, the following code loads a dataset of tests on quality and durability on different dates of two products:

```
toy_tests <- read_csv("data/product-toy-tests.csv")
toy_tests
##    id      date sample quality durability
## 1 T01 20160201    100       9          9
## 2 T01 20160302    150      10          9
## 3 T01 20160405    180       9         10
## 4 T01 20160502    140       9          9
## 5 T02 20160201     70       7          9
## 6 T02 20160303     75       8          8
```

```
## 7 T02 20160403        90          9            8
## 8 T02 20160502        85         10            9
```

Each row of the preceding data frame represents a record of tests of a particular product (id) on a certain date. If we need to compare the quality or durability of the two products at the same time, it can be hard to work with such format of data. Instead, we need the data to be transformed like the following code so that we can compare the values of the two products more easily:

```
date           T01    T02
20160201         9      9
20160301        10      9
```

The reshape2 package is designed for such a transform. If you don't have it installed, run the following command:

```
install.packages("reshape2")
```

Once the package is installed, we can use reshape2::dcast to transform the data so that we can easily compare the quality of different products on the same date. More specifically, it reshapes toy_tests so that the date column is shared, the values in id are spread as columns, and the values for each date and id are quality data:

```
library(reshape2)
toy_quality <- dcast(toy_tests, date ~ id, value.var = "quality")
toy_quality
##         date T01 T02
## 1 20160201    9   7
## 2 20160302   10  NA
## 3 20160303   NA   8
## 4 20160403   NA   9
## 5 20160405    9  NA
## 6 20160502    9  10
```

As you can see, toy_tests is immediately transformed. The quality values of both products are aligned with date. Although each month the two products conduct a test, the date may not exactly match with each other. This results in missing values if one product has a value on a day, but the other has no corresponding value on exactly the same day.

One way to fill the missing value is to use the approach called **Last Observation Carried Forward (LOCF)**, which means that if a non-missing value is followed by a missing value, then the non-missing value is carried forward to replace the missing value, until all subsequent missing values are replaced. One implementation of LOCF is provided by the zoo package. Run the following command to install the package if you don't have it:

```
install.packages("zoo")
```

To demonstrate how it works, we will use `zoo::na.locf()` to perform this technique over a very simple numeric vector with missing values:

```
zoo::na.locf(c(1, 2, NA, NA, 3, 1, NA, 2, NA))
## [1] 1 2 2 2 3 1 1 2 2
```

It is straightforward that all missing values are replaced with previous non-missing values. To do the same thing with `T01` and `T02` columns of `toy_quality`, we can sub-assign the processed vector to the columns:

```
toy_quality$T01 <- zoo::na.locf(toy_quality$T01)
toy_quality$T02 <- zoo::na.locf(toy_quality$T02)
```

However, if `toy_tests` contains thousands of products, it is ridiculous to write thousands of lines of code to do similar things like this. A better practice would be using exclusive sub-assignment as follows:

```
toy_quality[-1] <- lapply(toy_quality[-1], zoo::na.locf)
toy_quality
##         date T01 T02
## 1 20160201   9   7
## 2 20160302  10   7
## 3 20160303  10   8
## 4 20160403  10   9
## 5 20160405   9   9
## 6 20160502   9  10
```

We will use `lapply()` to perform LOCF over all columns of `toy_quality`, except `date`, and assign the resulting list to the subset of `toy_quality` without the `date` column. This works because sub-assignment of a data frame accepts a list and still preserves the class of data frame.

However, although the data does not contain any missing values, the meaning of each row is changed. Originally, product `T01` does not take a test on `20160303`. The value should be interpreted as the last test value of quality on or before the day. Another drawback is that in the original data, both products take tests every month, but the preceding reshaped data frame is not aligned to `date` of regular frequency.

One way to fix the drawbacks is to use year-month data instead of an exact date. In the following code, we will create a new column `ym`, that is, the first 6 characters of `toy_tests`. For example, `substr(20160101, 1, 6)` will result in `201601`:

```
toy_tests$ym <- substr(toy_tests$date, 1, 6)
toy_tests
##    id     date sample quality durability     ym
## 1 T01 20160201    100       9          9 201602
```

```
## 2 T01 20160302   150    10      9 201603
## 3 T01 20160405   180     9     10 201604
## 4 T01 20160502   140     9      9 201605
## 5 T02 20160201    70     7      9 201602
## 6 T02 20160303    75     8      8 201603
## 7 T02 20160403    90     9      8 201604
## 8 T02 20160502    85    10      9 201605
```

This time, we will use the `ym` column for alignment instead of `date`:

```
toy_quality <- dcast(toy_tests, ym ~ id,
    value.var = "quality")
toy_quality
##        ym T01 T02
## 1 201602   9   7
## 2 201603  10   8
## 3 201604   9   9
## 4 201605   9  10
```

Now, the missing values are gone, and the quality scores of both products in each month are naturally presented.

Sometimes, we need to combine a number of columns into one that indicates the measure and another that stores the value. For example, the following code uses `reshape2::melt` to combine the two measures (`quality` and `durability`) of the original data into a column named `measure` and a column of the measured value:

```
toy_tests2 <- melt(toy_tests, id.vars = c("id", "ym"),
   measure.vars = c("quality", "durability"),
   variable.name = "measure")
toy_tests2
##       id      ym    measure value
## 1    T01 201602    quality     9
## 2    T01 201603    quality    10
## 3    T01 201604    quality     9
## 4    T01 201605    quality     9
## 5    T02 201602    quality     7
## 6    T02 201603    quality     8
## 7    T02 201604    quality     9
## 8    T02 201605    quality    10
## 9    T01 201602 durability     9
## 10   T01 201603 durability     9
## 11   T01 201604 durability    10
## 12   T01 201605 durability     9
## 13   T02 201602 durability     9
## 14   T02 201603 durability     8
## 15   T02 201604 durability     8
```

```
## 16 T02 201605 durability     9
```

The variable names are now contained in the data, which can be directly used by some packages. For example, we can use `ggplot2` to plot data in such a format. The following code is an example of a scatter plot with facet grid of different combination of factors:

```
library(ggplot2)
ggplot(toy_tests2, aes(x = ym, y = value)) +
    geom_point() +
    facet_grid(id ~ measure)
```

Then, we can see a scatter plot grouped by product `id` and `measure` with `ym` as *x* values and `value` as *y* values:

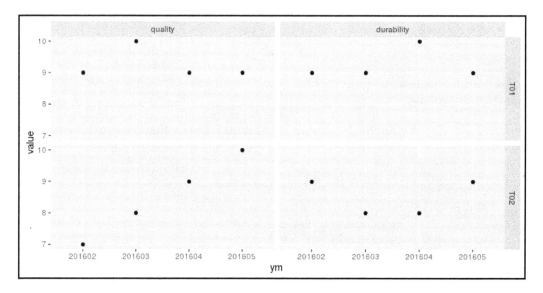

The plot can be easily manipulated because the grouping factor (`measure`) is contained as data rather than columns, which is easier to represent from the perspective of the `ggplot2` package:

```
ggplot(toy_tests2, aes(x = ym, y = value, color = id)) +
    geom_point() +
    facet_grid(. ~ measure)
```

This time, we will present the points of the two products in different colors:

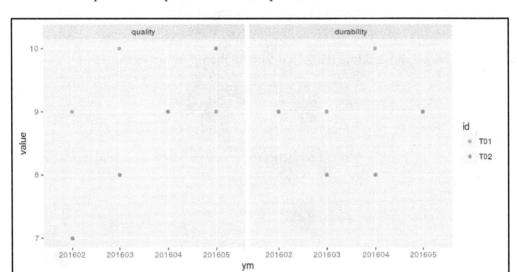

Using SQL to query data frames via the sqldf package

In the previous chapter, you learned how to compose SQL statements to query data from relational databases such as SQLite and MySQL. Is there a way to directly use SQL to query data frames in R as if these data frames are tables in relational databases? The `sqldf` package says yes.

This package takes advantage of SQLite, thanks to its lightweight structure and easiness to embed into an R session. Run the following command to install this package if you don't have it:

```
install.packages("sqldf")
```

First, let's attach the package, as shown in the following code:

```
library(sqldf)
## Loading required package: gsubfn
## Loading required package: proto
## Loading required package: RSQLite
## Loading required package: DBI
```

Note that when we attach `sqldf`, a number of other packages are automatically loaded. The `sqldf` package depends on these packages, because what it does is basically transferring data and converting data types between R and SQLite.

Then, we will reload the product tables we used in the previous sections:

```
product_info <- read_csv("data/product-info.csv")
product_stats <- read_csv("data/product-stats.csv")
product_tests <- read_csv("data/product-tests.csv")
toy_tests <- read_csv("data/product-toy-tests.csv")
```

The magic of this package is that we can directly query the data frames in our working environment with SQL. For example, we can select all records of `product_info`:

```
sqldf("select * from product_info")
## Loading required package: tcltk
##     id      name  type   class released
## 1 T01    SupCar   toy vehicle      yes
## 2 T02  SupPlane   toy vehicle       no
## 3 M01     JeepX model vehicle      yes
## 4 M02 AircraftX model vehicle      yes
## 5 M03    Runner model  people      yes
## 6 M04    Dancer model  people       no
```

The `sqldf` package supports simple select queries that are supported by SQLite. For example, we can select a certain set of columns:

```
sqldf("select id, name, class from product_info")
##     id      name   class
## 1 T01    SupCar vehicle
## 2 T02  SupPlane vehicle
## 3 M01     JeepX vehicle
## 4 M02 AircraftX vehicle
## 5 M03    Runner  people
## 6 M04    Dancer  people
```

We can filter records by a certain condition:

```
sqldf("select id, name from product_info where released = 'yes'")
##     id      name
## 1 T01    SupCar
## 2 M01     JeepX
## 3 M02 AircraftX
## 4 M03    Runner
```

We can compute a new column and give it a name:

```
sqldf("select id, material, size / weight as density from product_stats")
##    id material    density
## 1 T01    Metal 12.000000
## 2 T02    Metal  7.777778
## 3 M01 Plastics         NA
## 4 M02 Plastics 28.333333
## 5 M03     Wood         NA
## 6 M04     Wood 26.666667
```

We can sort records by certain columns in given orders:

```
sqldf("select * from product_stats order by size desc")
##    id material size weight
## 1 T02    Metal  350   45.0
## 2 T01    Metal  120   10.0
## 3 M02 Plastics   85    3.0
## 4 M01 Plastics   50     NA
## 5 M04     Wood   16    0.6
## 6 M03     Wood   15     NA
```

The package also supports querying multiple data frames such as `join`. In the following code, we will merge `product_info` and `product_stats` by `id`, just like what we did with `merge()` previously:

```
sqldf("select * from product_info join product_stats using (id)")
##    id     name  type   class released material size weight
## 1 T01   SupCar   toy vehicle      yes    Metal  120   10.0
## 2 T02 SupPlane   toy vehicle       no    Metal  350   45.0
## 3 M01    JeepX model vehicle      yes Plastics   50     NA
## 4 M02 AircraftX model vehicle      yes Plastics   85    3.0
## 5 M03   Runner model  people      yes     Wood   15     NA
## 6 M04   Dancer model  people       no     Wood   16    0.6
```

Moreover, it also supports nested query. In the following code, we will select all records in `product_info` that are made of wood:

```
sqldf("select * from product_info where id in
  (select id from product_stats where material = 'Wood')")
##    id   name  type  class released
## 1 M03 Runner model people      yes
## 2 M04 Dancer model people       no
```

Alternatively, we can use `join` with the same `where` condition to achieve the same goal. For many relational databases, `join` usually works faster than `in` when the data is large:

```
sqldf("select * from product_info join product_stats using (id)
  where material = 'Wood'")
##   id   name  type  class released material size weight
## 1 M03 Runner model people      yes     Wood   15     NA
## 2 M04 Dancer model people       no     Wood   16    0.6
```

In addition to `join`, we can easily summarize data by group. For example, we group `product_tests` by `waterproof` into two groups: `yes` and `no`. For each group, we compute the average values of `quality` and `durability`, respectively:

```
sqldf("select waterproof, avg(quality), avg(durability) from product_tests
  group by waterproof")
##   waterproof avg(quality) avg(durability)
## 1         no        10.00             9.5
## 2        yes         5.75             5.0
```

For the `toy_tests` data, it is easy to aggregate data for each product. Here is an example of averaging `quality` and `durability` values across time for each product:

```
sqldf("select id, avg(quality), avg(durability) from toy_tests
  group by id")
##    id avg(quality) avg(durability)
## 1 T01         9.25            9.25
## 2 T02         8.50            8.50
```

To make the results more informative, we can join `product_info` with the grouped summary table so that the product information and average measures are presented together:

```
sqldf("select * from product_info join
  (select id, avg(quality), avg(durability) from toy_tests
    group by id) using (id)")
##    id     name type   class released avg(quality)
## 1 T01   SupCar  toy vehicle      yes         9.25
## 2 T02 SupPlane  toy vehicle       no         8.50
##    avg(durability)
## 1            9.25
## 2            8.50
```

Using `sqldf` and SQL to query data frames looks very handy, but the limitations are obvious too.

First, since `sqldf` is, by default, based on SQLite, the limitation of the package is also the limitation of SQLite database, that is, the built-in group aggregate functions are limited. The official webpage (`https://sqlite.org/lang_aggfunc.html`) provides a list of functions: `avg()`, `count()`, `group_concat()`, `max()`, `min()`, `sum()`, and `total()`. If we need more than that, for example, `quantile()`, it won't be easy. In R, we can use much more advanced algorithms to aggregate columns.

Second, since we need to supply a string of select statements to query data, it is not very convenient to generate SQL dynamically when part of it is determined by R variables. Therefore, we need to use `sprintf()` to allow the values of R variables to appear in the SQL statement.

Third, the limitation of `sqldf` is also the limitation of SQL. It is hard to compute new columns with more complex algorithms. For example, if we need to compute a ranking column based on an existing numeric column, it would not be very easy to implement. However, in R, we just need `order()`. Another thing is that it is hard or verbose to implement more complex filter operations such as ranking-based data filtering. For example, how do you select the first one or two products ordered by `size` in descending order grouped by `material`? Such a query requires a lot more thinking and tricks.

However, if we use the `plyr` package, such a task is a piece of cake. If you have the package installed, run the following code:

```
install.packages("plyr")
```

To demonstrate how simple it is, we will use `plyr::ddply` to do this. We will supply `material` as the data splitter, that is, `product_stats` is divided into several parts for each value taken by `material`. We also supply a function to transform the input data frame (each part) to a new data frame. Then, the `ddply` function combines these data frames together:

```
plyr::ddply(product_stats, "material",
  function(x) {
    head(x[order(x$size, decreasing = TRUE),], 1L)
  })
##     id material size weight
## 1 T02    Metal  350   45.0
## 2 M02 Plastics   85    3.0
## 3 M04     Wood   16    0.6
```

The anonymous function we supplied is called with three parts of `product_stats` with distinct `material`, each part having identical `material`.

Another example is to select top two test results with the most samples:

```
plyr::ddply(toy_tests, "id",
  function(x) {
    head(x[order(x$sample, decreasing = TRUE), ], 2)
  })
##    id      date sample quality durability
## 1 T01 20160405    180       9         10
## 2 T01 20160302    150      10          9
## 3 T02 20160403     90       9          8
## 4 T02 20160502     85      10          9
```

The anonymous function we supplied is called with two parts of `toy_tests`: one part is a data frame with `id` being `T01` and the other `T02`. For each part, we order the sub-dataframe by `sample` in the descending order and take the top two records. The task is easily finished.

In addition, `ddply`, `plyr` provides a variety of functions of many possible pairs of input-output data types. To learn more, visit `http://had.co.nz/plyr/` and `https://github.com/hadley/plyr`.

Using data.table to manipulate data

In the first section, we reviewed some built-in functions used to manipulate data frames. Then, we introduced `sqldf`, which makes simple data query and summary easier. However, both approaches have their limitations. Using built-in functions can be verbose and slow, and it is not easy to summarize data because SQL is not as powerful as the full spectrum of R functions.

The `data.table` package provides a powerful enhanced version of `data.frame`. It is blazing fast and has the ability to handle large data that fits into memory. It invents a natural syntax of data manipulation using `[]`. Run the following command to install the package from CRAN if you don't have it yet:

```
install.packages("data.table")
```

Once the package is successfully installed, we will load the package and see what it offers:

```
library(data.table)
##
## Attaching package: 'data.table'
## The following objects are masked from 'package:reshape2':
##
##     dcast, melt
```

Note that we previously loaded the `reshape2` package in which `dcast` and `melt` are defined. The `data.table` package also provides enhanced version of `dcast` and `melt` with more powerful functionality, better performance, and higher memory efficiency. We'll take a look at them later in this section.

Creating `data.table` is very much like creating `data.frame`:

```
dt <- data.table(x = 1:3, y = rnorm(3), z = letters[1:3])
dt
##    x          y z
## 1: 1 -0.50219235 a
## 2: 2  0.13153117 b
## 3: 3 -0.07891709 c
```

We can see its structure with `str()`:

```
str(dt)
## Classes 'data.table' and 'data.frame':   3 obs. of   3 variables:
##  $ x: int  1 2 3
##  $ y: num  -0.5022 0.1315 -0.0789
##  $ z: chr  "a" "b" "c"
##  - attr(*, ".internal.selfref")=<externalptr>
```

It is clear that `dt` is of class `data.table` and `data.frame`, which means that `data.table` inherits from `data.frame`. In other words, it inherits some behaviors of `data.frame`, but override others as enhancements.

First, we still load the product data. However, this time, we will use `fread()` provided by `data.table` package. The `fread()` function is super-fast, has great memory efficiency, and directly returns `data.table`:

```
product_info <- fread("data/product-info.csv")
product_stats <- fread("data/product-stats.csv")
product_tests <- fread("data/product-tests.csv")
toy_tests <- fread("data/product-toy-tests.csv")
```

If we take a look at `product_info`, its appearance is only slightly different from that of a data frame:

```
product_info
##      id     name  type   class released
## 1: T01   SupCar   toy vehicle      yes
## 2: T02 SupPlane   toy vehicle       no
## 3: M01    JeepX model vehicle      yes
## 4: M02 AircraftX model vehicle      yes
## 5: M03   Runner model  people      yes
## 6: M04   Dancer model  people       no
```

Again, we will look at its structure:

```
str(product_info)
## Classes 'data.table' and 'data.frame':   6 obs. of   5 variables:
##  $ id      : chr  "T01" "T02" "M01" "M02" ...
##  $ name    : chr  "SupCar" "SupPlane" "JeepX" "AircraftX" ...
##  $ type    : chr  "toy" "toy" "model" "model" ...
##  $ class   : chr  "vehicle" "vehicle" "vehicle" "vehicle" ...
##  $ released: chr  "yes" "no" "yes" "yes" ...
##  - attr(*, ".internal.selfref") =< externalptr>
```

As compared to `data.frame`, if we supply only one argument to subset `data.table`, it means selecting rows rather than columns:

```
product_info[1]
##       id   name type    class released
## 1: T01 SupCar  toy vehicle      yes
product_info[1:3]
##       id     name  type    class released
## 1: T01    SupCar   toy vehicle      yes
## 2: T02  SupPlane   toy vehicle       no
## 3: M01     JeepX model vehicle      yes
```

If the number we supply in `[]` is negative, it means excluding the record, which is fully consistent with subsetting a vector:

```
product_info[-1]
##       id      name  type    class released
## 1: T02  SupPlane   toy vehicle       no
## 2: M01     JeepX model vehicle      yes
## 3: M02 AircraftX model vehicle      yes
## 4: M03    Runner model  people      yes
## 5: M04    Dancer model  people       no
```

In addition, `data.table` also provides a number of symbols that represent important components of `data.table`. One of the most useful symbols is `.N`, which means the number of rows. If we want to select the last row, we no longer need `nrow(product_info)`:

```
product_info[.N]
##       id   name  type  class released
## 1: M04 Dancer model people       no
```

We can easily select the first and last rows:

```
product_info[c(1, .N)]
##       id   name  type   class released
## 1: T01 SupCar   toy vehicle      yes
```

```
## 2: M04 Dancer model  people      no
```

The syntax of `data.table` subsetting automatically evaluates the expressions in the context of the data, that is, we can directly use column names as symbols, just like how we use `subset`, `transform`, and `with`. For example, we can directly use `released` in the first argument to select rows of products that are released:

```
product_info[released == "yes"]
##      id      name  type    class released
## 1: T01    SupCar   toy  vehicle      yes
## 2: M01     JeepX model  vehicle      yes
## 3: M02 AircraftX model  vehicle      yes
## 4: M03    Runner model   people      yes
```

The first argument in the square brackets is a row filter, while the second is evaluated within the context of the filtered data. For example, we can directly use `id` to represent `product_info$id` because `id` is evaluated within the context of `product_info`:

```
product_info[released == "yes", id]
## [1] "T01" "M01" "M02" "M03"
```

The way to select columns of a data frame does not work here. If we put a character vector in the second argument, then we'll get the character vector itself because a string is indeed a string:

```
product_info[released == "yes", "id"]
## [1] "id"
```

To disable this behavior, we can specify `with = FALSE` so that the second argument accepts a character vector to select columns, and it always returns a `data.table`, no matter how many columns are specified:

```
product_info[released == "yes", "id", with = FALSE]
##      id
## 1: T01
## 2: M01
## 3: M02
## 4: M03
product_info[released == "yes", c("id", "name"), with = FALSE]
##      id      name
## 1: T01    SupCar
## 2: M01     JeepX
## 3: M02 AircraftX
## 4: M03    Runner
```

We can also write some other expressions as the second argument. For example, we can generate a table of the number of released products for each combination of `type` and `class`:

```
product_info[released == "yes", table(type, class)]
##         class
## type     people vehicle
##    model      1       2
##    toy        0       1
```

However, if a list is produced, it will be transformed to `data.table` instead:

```
product_info[released == "yes", list(id, name)]
##       id      name
## 1: T01    SupCar
## 2: M01     JeepX
## 3: M02 AircraftX
## 4: M03    Runner
```

In this way, we can easily create a new `data.table` package with existing columns replaced:

```
product_info[, list(id, name, released = released == "yes")]
##       id      name released
## 1: T01    SupCar     TRUE
## 2: T02 SupPlane    FALSE
## 3: M01     JeepX     TRUE
## 4: M02 AircraftX     TRUE
## 5: M03    Runner     TRUE
## 6: M04    Dancer    FALSE
```

We can also easily create a new `data.table` package with new columns based on existing columns:

```
product_stats[, list(id, material, size, weight,
  density = size / weight)]
##       id material size weight   density
## 1: T01    Metal  120   10.0 12.000000
## 2: T02    Metal  350   45.0  7.777778
## 3: M01 Plastics   50     NA        NA
## 4: M02 Plastics   85    3.0 28.333333
## 5: M03     Wood   15     NA        NA
## 6: M04     Wood   16    0.6 26.666667
```

For simplicity, data.table provides .() to be short for list():

```
product_info[, .(id, name, type, class)]
##      id      name   type    class
## 1: T01    SupCar    toy  vehicle
## 2: T02  SupPlane    toy  vehicle
## 3: M01     JeepX  model  vehicle
## 4: M02  AircraftX model  vehicle
## 5: M03    Runner  model   people
## 6: M04    Dancer  model   people
product_info[released == "yes", .(id, name)]
##      id      name
## 1: T01    SupCar
## 2: M01     JeepX
## 3: M02 AircraftX
## 4: M03    Runner
```

By supplying the ordered indices, we can easily sort the records by the given criterion:

```
product_stats[order(size, decreasing = TRUE)]
##      id material size weight
## 1: T02    Metal  350   45.0
## 2: T01    Metal  120   10.0
## 3: M02 Plastics   85    3.0
## 4: M01 Plastics   50     NA
## 5: M04     Wood   16    0.6
## 6: M03     Wood   15     NA
```

Previously, we always created a new data.table package after subsetting.
The data.table package also provides := for in-place assignment of columns. For example, the original data of product_stats is shown as follows:

```
product_stats
##      id material size weight
## 1: T01    Metal  120   10.0
## 2: T02    Metal  350   45.0
## 3: M01 Plastics   50     NA
## 4: M02 Plastics   85    3.0
## 5: M03     Wood   15     NA
## 6: M04     Wood   16    0.6
```

We will use := to create a new column directly in product_stats:

```
product_stats[, density := size / weight]
```

Nothing shows here, but the original `data.table` package is modified:

```
product_stats
##       id material size weight   density
## 1: T01    Metal  120   10.0 12.000000
## 2: T02    Metal  350   45.0  7.777778
## 3: M01 Plastics   50     NA        NA
## 4: M02 Plastics   85    3.0 28.333333
## 5: M03     Wood   15     NA        NA
## 6: M04     Wood   16    0.6 26.666667
```

We can use `:=` to replace an existing column:

```
product_info[, released := released == "yes"]
product_info
##       id      name  type   class released
## 1: T01    SupCar   toy vehicle     TRUE
## 2: T02  SupPlane   toy vehicle    FALSE
## 3: M01     JeepX model vehicle     TRUE
## 4: M02 AircraftX model vehicle     TRUE
## 5: M03    Runner model  people     TRUE
## 6: M04    Dancer model  people    FALSE
```

The `data.table` package provides `:=` mainly because in-place modification has a much higher performance since it avoids unnecessary copies of data.

Using key to access rows

Another distinct feature of `data.table` is the support of indexing, that is, we can create a key on `data.table`, so accessing records by key can be extremely efficient. For example, we will use `setkey()` to make `id` the key of `product_info`:

```
setkey(product_info, id)
```

Note that the function behaves in a very different way from most R functions. It does not return a new copy of the data table but directly installs a key to the original input. The data frame, however, looks unchanged:

```
product_info
##       id      name  type   class released
## 1: M01     JeepX model vehicle     TRUE
## 2: M02 AircraftX model vehicle     TRUE
## 3: M03    Runner model  people     TRUE
## 4: M04    Dancer model  people    FALSE
## 5: T01    SupCar   toy vehicle     TRUE
## 6: T02  SupPlane   toy vehicle    FALSE
```

Also, its key is created:

```
key(product_info)
## [1] "id"
```

Now, we can use a key to access the records in `product_info`. For example, we can directly write a value of `id` to get the records with that `id`:

```
product_info["M01"]
##      id  name  type   class released
## 1: M01 JeepX model vehicle     TRUE
```

If we use this with a `data.table` package without a key, an error occurs and reminds you to set a key:

```
product_stats["M01"]
## Error in `[.data.table`(product_stats, "M01"): When i is a data.table
(or character vector), x must be keyed (i.e. sorted, and, marked as sorted)
so data.table knows which columns to join to and take advantage of x being
sorted. Call setkey(x, ...) first, see ?setkey.
```

We can also use `setkeyv()` to set key, but it only accepts a character vector:

```
setkeyv(product_stats, "id")
```

This function is much easier to use if we have a dynamically determined vector to be the key. Now, we can use key to access `product_stats` too:

```
product_stats["M02"]
##      id material size weight  density
## 1: M02 Plastics   85      3 28.33333
```

If two tables have the same key, we can easily join them together:

```
product_info[product_stats]
##       id      name  type   class released material size
## 1: M01     JeepX model vehicle     TRUE Plastics   50
## 2: M02 AircraftX model vehicle     TRUE Plastics   85
## 3: M03    Runner model  people     TRUE     Wood   15
## 4: M04    Dancer model  people    FALSE     Wood   16
## 5: T01    SupCar   toy vehicle     TRUE    Metal  120
## 6: T02  SupPlane   toy vehicle    FALSE    Metal  350
##     weight    density
## 1:     NA         NA
## 2:    3.0 28.333333
## 3:     NA         NA
## 4:    0.6 26.666667
## 5:   10.0 12.000000
```

```
## 6:    45.0  7.777778
```

The key of a `data.table` package can be more than one element. For example, to locate a record of `toy_tests`, we need to specify both `id` and `date`. In the following code, we will set a key of the two columns on `toy_tests`:

```
setkey(toy_tests, id, date)
```

Now, we can get a row by supplying both elements in the key:

```
toy_tests[.("T01", 20160201)]
##       id      date sample quality durability
## 1: T01 20160201    100       9          9
```

If we only supply the first element, we would get a subset of the data with all records that match the first element:

```
toy_tests["T01"]
##       id      date sample quality durability
## 1: T01 20160201    100       9          9
## 2: T01 20160302    150      10          9
## 3: T01 20160405    180       9         10
## 4: T01 20160502    140       9          9
```

However, if we only supply the second element, we can't get anything but an error. It is because the algorithm it behind requires the key to be ordered:

```
toy_tests[.(20160201)]
## Error in bmerge(i, x, leftcols, rightcols, io, xo, roll, rollends,
nomatch, : x.'id' is a character column being joined to i.'V1' which is
type 'double'. Character columns must join to factor or character columns.
```

Also, we cannot get any data if we supply a key in a wrong order:

```
toy_tests[.(20160201, "T01")]
## Error in bmerge(i, x, leftcols, rightcols, io, xo, roll, rollends,
nomatch, : x.'id' is a character column being joined to i.'V1' which is
type 'double'. Character columns must join to factor or character columns.
```

Summarizing data by groups

Another important argument of subsetting a data.table is by, which is used to split the data into multiple parts, and for each part, evaluate the second argument. In this section, we'll demonstrate how the by syntax makes it much easier to summarize data by groups. For example, the simplest usage of by is counting the records in each group. In the following code, we will count the number of both released and unreleased products:

```
product_info[, .N, by = released]
##    released N
## 1:    TRUE 4
## 2:   FALSE 2
```

The group can be defined by more than one variable. For example, a tuple of type and class can be a group, and for each group, we will count the number of records:

```
product_info[, .N, by = .(type, class)]
##     type  class N
## 1: model vehicle 2
## 2: model  people 2
## 3:   toy vehicle 2
```

We can also perform statistical calculations for each group. Here, we will compute the mean value of quality for both waterproof products and non-waterproof ones:

```
product_tests[, mean(quality, na.rm = TRUE),
  by = .(waterproof)]
##    waterproof    V1
## 1:         no 10.00
## 2:        yes  5.75
```

Note that the mean values are stored in V1 because we didn't supply a name for the column, so the package uses its default column names. To avoid that, we will use expression in form of .(y = f(x)) instead:

```
product_tests[, .(mean_quality = mean(quality, na.rm = TRUE)),
  by = .(waterproof)]
##    waterproof mean_quality
## 1:         no        10.00
## 2:        yes         5.75
```

We can chain multiple `[]` in turn. In the following example, we will first join `product_info` and `product_tests` by shared key `id` and then calculate the mean values of `quality` and `durability` for each group of `type` and `class` of released products:

```
product_info[product_tests][released == TRUE,
  .(mean_quality = mean(quality, na.rm = TRUE),
    mean_durability = mean(durability, na.rm = TRUE)),
  by = .(type, class)]
##      type   class mean_quality mean_durability
## 1:    toy vehicle          NaN            10.0
## 2: model vehicle            6             4.5
## 3: model  people            5             NaN
```

Note that the values of `by` columns will be unique in the resulting `data.table`. We can use `keyby` instead of `by` to ensure it is automatically used as key by the resulted `data.table`:

```
type_class_tests <- product_info[product_tests][released == TRUE,
  .(mean_quality = mean(quality, na.rm = TRUE),
    mean_durability = mean(durability, na.rm = TRUE)),
  keyby = .(type, class)]
type_class_tests
##      type   class mean_quality mean_durability
## 1: model  people            5             NaN
## 2: model vehicle            6             4.5
## 3:    toy vehicle          NaN            10.0
key(type_class_tests)
## [1] "type"  "class"
```

Then, we can directly use a tuple of key values to access the records:

```
type_class_tests[.("model", "vehicle"), mean_quality]
## [1] 6
```

You can clearly see that using keys can be much more convenient than using logical comparisons when we try to find certain records in a table. However, its true advantage is not demonstrated yet because the data is not large enough. Using key to search records can be much faster than iterative logical comparison for large data, because searching by key takes advantage of binary search while iteration wastes a lot of time doing unnecessary computation.

Here is an example to make a contrast. First, we will create a data of 10 million rows with an index column `id` and two numeric columns filled with random numbers:

```
n <- 10000000
test1 <- data.frame(id = 1:n, x = rnorm(n), y = rnorm(n))
```

Now, we want to see find a row of `id` being `8765432`. Let's see how long it takes:

```
system.time(row <- test1[test1$id == 876543, ])
##    user  system elapsed
##   0.156   0.036   0.192
row
##               id          x         y
## 876543 876543 0.02300419 1.291588
```

It seems no big deal, but suppose you need to frequently do this, say, hundreds of times per second, then your machine simply can't return a result in time.

Then, we will use `data.table` to do this. First, we will call `setDT()` to transform `data.frame` to `data.table`. This function performs some magic to transform the object in place, no copy made. When we use the `setDT()` function, we also provide a key `id` so that the resulted `data.table` has `id` as its keyed column:

```
setDT(test1, key = "id")
class(test1)
## [1] "data.table" "data.frame"
```

Now, `test1` is transformed to `data.table`. Then, we will search the same element:

```
system.time(row <- test1[.(8765432)])
##    user  system elapsed
##   0.000   0.000   0.001
row
##            id          x          y
## 1: 8765432 0.2532357 -2.121696
```

The results are the same, but the time `data.table` takes is much shorter than `data.frame`.

Reshaping data.table

Previously, you learned how to reshape a data frame with the `reshape2` package. The `data.table` package provides faster and more powerful implementations of `dcast` and `melt` for the `data.table` object.

For example, we will reshape `toy_tests` by aligning the quality scores of each product to year-month tuples:

```
toy_tests[, ym := substr(date, 1, 6)]
toy_quality <- dcast(toy_tests, ym ~ id, value.var = "quality")
toy_quality
##        ym T01 T02
## 1: 201602   9   7
## 2: 201603  10   8
## 3: 201604   9   9
## 4: 201605   9  10
```

First, we used `:=` to create a new column ym directly in `toy_tests` and use dcast to transform it in the same way with the previous example of reshape2. The result looks the same with the output of `reshape2::dcast` for `data.frame`.

While `reshape2::dcast` does not support multi-value `value.var`, `data.table::dcast` works with multiple value variables, as shown here:

```
toy_tests2 <- dcast(toy_tests, ym ~ id, value.var = c("quality",
"durability"))
toy_tests2
##        ym quality_T01 quality_T02 durability_T01
## 1: 201602           9           7              9
## 2: 201603          10           8              9
## 3: 201604           9           9             10
## 4: 201605           9          10              9
##    durability_T02
## 1:              9
## 2:              8
## 3:              8
## 4:              9
```

The column names, except the first, are no longer values of id but are value variables with values of id concatenated by the underscore symbol. In addition, the key of the output `data.table` is automatically set to the variables that appear on the left-hand side of the reshaping formula
ym ~ id:

```
key(toy_tests2)
## [1] "ym"
```

The key implies that we can access the records directly by supplying a value of ym. However, the following code ends up with an error:

```
toy_tests2[.(201602)]
## Error in bmerge(i, x, leftcols, rightcols, io, xo, roll, rollends,
nomatch, : x.'ym' is a character column being joined to i.'V1' which is
type 'double'. Character columns must join to factor or character columns.
```

There's something wrong with the data types. We can run the following code to see the class of each column:

```
sapply(toy_tests2, class)
##                  ym    quality_T01    quality_T02 durability_T01
##      "character"      "integer"      "integer"      "integer"
## durability_T02
##      "integer"
```

The problem lies in the class of ym:. It is a character vector, but we supplied a key of numeric values. Therefore, the search fails with unmatched data types. If we supply a string, we can get the corresponding record:

```
toy_tests2["201602"]
##          ym quality_T01 quality_T02 durability_T01
## 1: 201602           9           7              9
##      durability_T02
## 1:              9
```

But how did ym become a character vector in the first place? Recall ym := substr(date, 1, 6) where date is an integer vector, but substr() will coerce date to a character vector and then take out the first six characters. Therefore, it is natural that the result is a character vector. This is simply demonstrated as follows:

```
class(20160101)
## [1] "numeric"
class(substr(20160101, 1, 6))
## [1] "character"
```

The point here is that we need to be careful about the data types of the key columns.

Using in-place set functions

If we use data.frame, to change the names or the column order will cause copies of the data structure. In recent R versions, the copy is made fewer when we rename columns, but it is still hard to reorder the columns of a data frame without making a new copy. This should not be a problem when the data is small, but if the data is very large, the performance and memory pressure it imposes can really be an issue.

An enhanced version of data.frame, data.table provides a family of set functions with reference semantics, that is, they modify data.table in place and avoid unnecessary copying, thus exhibiting astonishing performance.

Take product_stats as an example. We can call setDF() to change data.table to data.frame in place without making copies:

```
product_stats
##        id material size weight   density
## 1: M01 Plastics   50    NA        NA
## 2: M02 Plastics   85   3.0 28.333333
## 3: M03    Wood   15    NA        NA
## 4: M04    Wood   16   0.6 26.666667
## 5: T01   Metal  120  10.0 12.000000
## 6: T02   Metal  350  45.0  7.777778
setDF(product_stats)
class(product_stats)
## [1] "data.frame"
```

We can call setDT() to make any data.frame to data.table and set up a key if specified:

```
setDT(product_stats, key = "id")
class(product_stats)
## [1] "data.table" "data.frame"
```

We can call setnames to change the name of the given columns to their new names:

```
setnames(product_stats, "size", "volume")
product_stats
##        id material volume weight   density
## 1: M01 Plastics     50    NA        NA
## 2: M02 Plastics     85   3.0 28.333333
## 3: M03    Wood     15    NA        NA
## 4: M04    Wood     16   0.6 26.666667
## 5: T01   Metal    120  10.0 12.000000
## 6: T02   Metal    350  45.0  7.777778
```

If we add a new column, the column should appear as the last one. For example, we will add an index column for all rows using .I representing 1:.N:

```
product_stats[, i := .I]
product_stats
##       id material volume weight   density i
## 1: M01 Plastics      50     NA        NA 1
## 2: M02 Plastics      85    3.0 28.333333 2
## 3: M03     Wood      15     NA        NA 3
## 4: M04     Wood      16    0.6 26.666667 4
## 5: T01    Metal     120   10.0 12.000000 5
## 6: T02    Metal     350   45.0  7.777778 6
```

By convention, the index column should, in most cases, appear as the first column. We can supply a new order of column names to setcolorder() so that the columns are directly reordered without making copies:

```
setcolorder(product_stats,
  c("i", "id", "material", "weight", "volume", "density"))
product_stats
##    i  id material weight volume   density
## 1: 1 M01 Plastics     NA     50        NA
## 2: 2 M02 Plastics    3.0     85 28.333333
## 3: 3 M03     Wood     NA     15        NA
## 4: 4 M04     Wood    0.6     16 26.666667
## 5: 5 T01    Metal   10.0    120 12.000000
## 6: 6 T02    Metal   45.0    350  7.777778
```

Understanding dynamic scoping of data.table

The most commonly used syntax of data.table is data[i, j, by], where i, j, and by are all evaluated with dynamic scoping. In other words, we can use not only the columns directly, but also the predefined symbols such as .N, .I, and .SD to refer to important components of the data, as well as symbols and functions that can be accessed in the calling environment.

Before demonstrating this, we will create a new data.table named market_data with a consecutive column of date:

```
market_data <- data.table(date = as.Date("2015-05-01") + 0:299)
head(market_data)
##          date
## 1: 2015-05-01
## 2: 2015-05-02
## 3: 2015-05-03
```

```
## 4: 2015-05-04
## 5: 2015-05-05
## 6: 2015-05-06
```

Then, we will add two new columns to `market_data` by calling `:=` as a function:

```
set.seed(123)
market_data[, `:=`(
  price = round(30 * cumprod(1 + rnorm(300, 0.001, 0.05)), 2),
  volume = rbinom(300, 5000, 0.8)
)]
```

Note that `price` is a simple random walk, and `volume` is randomly drawn from a binomial distribution:

```
head(market_data)
##           date price volume
## 1: 2015-05-01 29.19   4021
## 2: 2015-05-02 28.88   4000
## 3: 2015-05-03 31.16   4033
## 4: 2015-05-04 31.30   4036
## 5: 2015-05-05 31.54   3995
## 6: 2015-05-06 34.27   3955
```

Then, we will plot the data:

```
plot(price ~ date, data = market_data,
  type = "l",
  main = "Market data")
```

The plot generated is shown as follows:

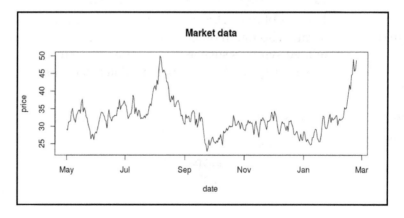

Once the data is ready, we can aggregate the data and see how dynamic scoping can be used to make things easier.

First, we will look at the range of the `date` column:

```
market_data[, range(date)]
## [1] "2015-05-01" "2016-02-24"
```

The data can be reduced to monthly **open-high-low-close (OHLC)** data easily by group aggregate:

```
monthly <- market_data[,
  .(open = price[[1]], high = max(price),
    low = min(price), close = price[[.N]]),
  keyby = .(year = year(date), month = month(date))]
head(monthly)
##      year month  open  high   low close
## 1: 2015     5 29.19 37.71 26.15 28.44
## 2: 2015     6 28.05 37.63 28.05 37.21
## 3: 2015     7 36.32 40.99 32.13 40.99
## 4: 2015     8 41.52 50.00 30.90 30.90
## 5: 2015     9 30.54 34.46 22.89 27.02
## 6: 2015    10 25.68 33.18 24.65 29.32
```

In the `j` expression, we can generate an OHLC record with each `data.table` grouped by `year` and `month`. If the output of `j` is a `list`, or `data.frame`, or `data.table`, then the output will be stacked together to result in one `data.table`.

In fact, the `j` expression can be anything, even with `by` specified. More specifically, `j` is evaluated within the context of each `data.table` as a subset of the original data split by the value of the `by` expression. For example, the following code does not aggregate data by group, but plot a price chart for each year:

```
oldpar <- par(mfrow = c(1, 2))
market_data[, {
  plot(price ~ date, type = "l",
    main = sprintf("Market data (%d)", year))
}, by = .(year = year(date))]
par(oldpar)
```

The plot generated is shown as follows:

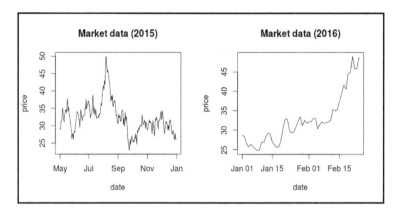

Note that we don't specify the `data` argument of `plot` because it is evaluated in the context of `market_data` grouped by `year` where `price` and `date` are already defined.

Moreover, the `j` expression can be model-fitting code. Here is an example of batch fitting of linear models. First, we will load `diamonds` data from the `ggplot2` package:

```
data("diamonds", package = "ggplot2")
setDT(diamonds)
head(diamonds)
##      carat       cut color clarity depth table price    x
## 1:   0.23     Ideal     E     SI2  61.5    55   326 3.95
## 2:   0.21   Premium     E     SI1  59.8    61   326 3.89
## 3:   0.23      Good     E     VS1  56.9    65   327 4.05
## 4:   0.29   Premium     I     VS2  62.4    58   334 4.20
## 5:   0.31      Good     J     SI2  63.3    58   335 4.34
## 6:   0.24 Very Good     J    VVS2  62.8    57   336 3.94
##       y    z
## 1: 3.98 2.43
## 2: 3.84 2.31
## 3: 4.07 2.31
## 4: 4.23 2.63
## 5: 4.35 2.75
## 6: 3.96 2.48
```

The data contains 53940 records of diamonds with 10 properties. Here, we will fit linear regression models on each group of `cut` to see how `carat` and `depth` may provide some information of `log(price)` in each group.

In the following code, the j expression involves fitting a linear model and coercing its coefficients into a list. Note that the j expression is evaluated for each value of the keyby expression. Since a list is returned, the estimated linear coefficients for each group will be stacked as one data.table is shown as follows:

```
diamonds[, {
  m <- lm(log(price) ~ carat + depth)
  as.list(coef(m))
}, keyby = .(cut)]
##            cut (Intercept)    carat        depth
## 1:       Fair    7.730010 1.264588 -0.014982439
## 2:       Good    7.077469 1.973600 -0.014601101
## 3: Very Good    6.293642 2.087957 -0.002890208
## 4:    Premium    5.934310 1.852778  0.005939651
## 5:      Ideal    8.495409 2.125605 -0.038080022
```

Dynamic scoping also allows us to combine the use of symbols that are predefined, inside or outside data.table. For example, we can define a function to calculate the annual average values of a user-defined column of market_data:

```
average <- function(column) {
  market_data[, .(average = mean(.SD[[column]])),
    by = .(year = year(date))]
}
```

In the preceding j expression, .SD means the grouped data.table for each value of year. We can use .SD[[x]] to extract the values of column x, just like extracting an element by name from a list.

Then, we can run the following code to calculate the average prices for each year:

```
average("price")
##    year  average
## 1: 2015 32.32531
## 2: 2016 32.38364
```

We will just change the argument to volume to calculate the average volumes for each year:

```
average("volume")
##    year  average
## 1: 2015 3999.931
## 2: 2016 4003.382
```

Also, we can use a specially invented syntax to create a dynamic number of columns with dynamically determined names.

Suppose we add three new alternative price columns, each adds some random noise to the original `price` values. Instead of repeat calling `market_data[, price1 := ...]` and `market_data[, price2 := ...]`, we can use `market_data[, (columns) := list(...)]` to set columns dynamically, where `columns` is a character vector of column names and `list(...)` is the values for each corresponding column in `columns`:

```
price_cols <- paste0("price", 1:3)
market_data[, (price_cols) := lapply(1:3,
  function(i) round(price + rnorm(.N, 0, 5), 2))]
head(market_data)
##          date price volume price1 price2 price3
## 1: 2015-05-01 29.19   4021  30.55  27.39  33.22
## 2: 2015-05-02 28.88   4000  29.67  20.45  36.00
## 3: 2015-05-03 31.16   4033  34.31  26.94  27.24
## 4: 2015-05-04 31.30   4036  29.32  29.01  28.04
## 5: 2015-05-05 31.54   3995  36.04  32.06  34.79
## 6: 2015-05-06 34.27   3955  30.12  30.96  35.19
```

On the other hand, if we get a table with many columns and we need to perform some computation on a subset of them, we can also use similar syntax to solve the problem. Imagine that the price-related columns may have missing values. We need to perform `zoo::na.locf()` on each price column. First, we will use regular expression to get all the price columns:

```
cols <- colnames(market_data)
price_cols <- cols[grep("^price", cols)]
price_cols
## [1] "price"  "price1" "price2" "price3"
```

Then, we will use similar syntax but add an additional argument, `.SDcols = price_cols`, in order to limit the columns of `.SD` to be only the price columns we get. The following code calls `zoo::na.locf()` on each price column, and the old values of each column are replaced:

```
market_data[, (price_cols) := lapply(.SD, zoo::na.locf),
  .SDcols = price_cols]
```

In this section, we have demonstrated the usage of `data.table` and how it makes data manipulation much easier. To see the full feature list of `data.table`, visit `https://github.com/Rdatatable/data.table/wiki`. To quickly review the usage, go through the data table cheat sheet (`https://www.datacamp.com/community/tutorials/data-table-cheat-sheet`).

Using dplyr pipelines to manipulate data frames

Another popular package is `dplyr`, which invents a grammar of data manipulation. Instead of using the subset function (`[]`), `dplyr` defines a set of basic `erb` functions as the building blocks of data operations and imports a pipeline operator to chain these functions to perform complex multistep tasks.

Run the following code to install `dplyr` from CRAN if you don't have it yet:

```
install.packages("dplyr")
```

First, we will reload the product tables again to reset all data to their original forms:

```
library(readr)
product_info <- read_csv("data/product-info.csv")
product_stats <- read_csv("data/product-stats.csv")
product_tests <- read_csv("data/product-tests.csv")
toy_tests <- read_csv("data/product-toy-tests.csv")
```

Then, we will load the `dplyr` package:

```
library(dplyr)
##
## Attaching package: 'dplyr'
## The following objects are masked from 'package:data.table':
##
##     between, last
## The following objects are masked from 'package:stats':
##
##     filter, lag
## The following objects are masked from 'package:base':
##
##     intersect, setdiff, setequal, union
```

The following output indicates that `dplyr` generalizes a number of built-in functions, so they are masked after the package is attached.

Now, we can start to play with the verb functions it provides. First, we will use `select` to select columns from the provided data frame by creating a new table with the given columns:

```
select(product_info, id, name, type, class)
## Source: local data frame [6 x 4]
##
```

```
##      id      name  type    class
##   (chr)     (chr) (chr)    (chr)
## 1   T01    SupCar   toy  vehicle
## 2   T02  SupPlane   toy  vehicle
## 3   M01     JeepX model  vehicle
## 4   M02  AircraftX model vehicle
## 5   M03    Runner model   people
## 6   M04    Dancer model   people
```

The printing of the preceding table is a bit different from the way both `data.frame` and `data.table` are printed. It not only shows the table itself, but also includes a header indicating the size of the data frame and the data types of each column.

It is clear that `select()` uses non-standard evaluation that allows us to directly use column names of the given data frame as arguments. It works in a way similar to how `subset()`, `transform()`, and `with()` work.

We can use `filter` to filter the data frame by logical condition, which is also evaluated in the context of the data frame:

```
filter(product_info, released == "yes")
## Source: local data frame [4 x 5]
##
##      id      name  type    class released
##   (chr)     (chr) (chr)    (chr)    (chr)
## 1   T01    SupCar   toy  vehicle      yes
## 2   M01     JeepX model  vehicle      yes
## 3   M02  AircraftX model vehicle      yes
## 4   M03    Runner model   people      yes
```

If we want to filter records with multiple conditions, we only need to write each condition as an argument of `filter()`:

```
filter(product_info,
   released == "yes", type == "model")
## Source: local data frame [3 x 5]
##
##      id      name  type    class released
##   (chr)     (chr) (chr)    (chr)    (chr)
## 1   M01     JeepX model  vehicle      yes
## 2   M02  AircraftX model vehicle      yes
## 3   M03    Runner model   people      yes
```

The `mutate` function is used to create a new data frame with new columns added or existing columns replaced, like `transform`, but also supports in-place assignment, `:=`, if the provided data is a `data.table`:

```
mutate(product_stats, density = size / weight)
## Source: local data frame [6 x 5]
##
##        id material  size weight    density
##     (chr)    (chr) (int)  (dbl)      (dbl)
## 1    T01    Metal   120   10.0  12.000000
## 2    T02    Metal   350   45.0   7.777778
## 3    M01  Plastics    50     NA         NA
## 4    M02  Plastics    85    3.0  28.333333
## 5    M03     Wood    15     NA         NA
## 6    M04     Wood    16    0.6  26.666667
```

The `arrange` function is used to create a new data frame sorted by one or more columns. The `desc()` function indicates the descending order:

```
arrange(product_stats, material, desc(size), desc(weight))
## Source: local data frame [6 x 4]
##
##        id material  size weight
##     (chr)    (chr) (int)  (dbl)
## 1    T02    Metal   350   45.0
## 2    T01    Metal   120   10.0
## 3    M02  Plastics    85    3.0
## 4    M01  Plastics    50     NA
## 5    M04     Wood    16    0.6
## 6    M03     Wood    15     NA
```

The `dplyr` function provides a rich set of join operations, including `inner_join`, `left_join`, `right_join`, `full_join`, `semi_join`, and `anti_join`. If two tables to join have records that do not match, these join operations may behave very differently. For `product_info` and `product_tests`, the records match exactly, so `left_join` should return the same results as `merge`:

```
product_info_tests <- left_join(product_info, product_tests, by = "id")
product_info_tests
## Source: local data frame [6 x 8]
##
##        id      name   type     class released quality durability
##     (chr)     (chr)  (chr)     (chr)    (chr)   (int)      (int)
## 1    T01    SupCar    toy   vehicle      yes      NA         10
## 2    T02  SupPlane    toy   vehicle       no      10          9
## 3    M01     JeepX  model   vehicle      yes       6          4
## 4    M02  AircraftX model   vehicle      yes       6          5
## 5    M03    Runner  model    people      yes       5         NA
## 6    M04    Dancer  model    people       no       6          6
## Variables not shown: waterproof (chr)
```

To know more about the difference between those join operations, run `?dplyr::join`.

To summarize the data by groups, we need to first create a grouped table by `group_by()`. Then, we will use `summarize()` to aggregate the data. For example, we will divide `product_info_tests` with `type` and `class`, and then for each type class group, we will calculate the average values of `quality` and `durability`:

```
summarize(group_by(product_info_tests, type, class),
    mean_quality = mean(quality, na.rm = TRUE),
    mean_durability = mean(durability, na.rm = TRUE))
## Source: local data frame [3 x 4]
## Groups: type [?]
##
##     type    class mean_quality mean_durability
##    (chr)    (chr)        (dbl)           (dbl)
## 1 model   people          5.5             6.0
## 2 model  vehicle          6.0             4.5
## 3   toy  vehicle         10.0             9.5
```

From the preceding code examples, you learned the verb functions `select()`, `filter()`, `mutate()`, `arrange()`, `group_by()`, and `summarize()`. Each of them is designed to do a small thing, but together they can perform comprehensive data operations when properly composed. Apart from these functions, `dplyr` imports the pipeline operator `%>%` from the `magrittr` package to compose functions into pipelines.

Suppose we have `product_info` and `product_tests`. We need to analyze the released product by computing the average values of quality and durability for each type class group, and present the summary data in descending order of the average quality. This can be done nicely with the `dplyr` verb functions composed by the pipeline operator:

```
product_info %>%
    filter(released == "yes") %>%
    inner_join(product_tests, by = "id") %>%
    group_by(type, class) %>%
    summarize(
        mean_quality = mean(quality, na.rm = TRUE),
        mean_durability = mean(durability, na.rm = TRUE)) %>%
    arrange(desc(mean_quality))
## Source: local data frame [3 x 4]
## Groups: type [2]
##
##     type    class mean_quality mean_durability
##    (chr)    (chr)        (dbl)           (dbl)
## 1 model  vehicle            6             4.5
## 2 model   people            5             NaN
## 3   toy  vehicle          NaN            10.0
```

But how does `%>%` work? The pipeline operator basically does only one thing: put the result on the left-hand side of the first argument of the function call on the right-hand side, that is, `x %>% f(...)` will be basically evaluated as `f(x, ...)`. Since `%>%` is a package-defined binary operator, it allows us to chain function calls to either avoid redundant intermediate values or decompose nested calls.

Suppose we need to transform `d0` to `d3` through three steps. In each step, we need to call a function with the previous result and an argument. If we manipulate data like this, there will be many intermediate results, and sometimes, it consumes a lot of memory when the data is large:

```
d1 <- f1(d0, arg1)
d2 <- f2(d1, arg2)
d3 <- f3(d2, arg3)
```

If we want to avoid intermediate results, we'll have to write nested calls. This task does not look straightforward at all, especially when there are numerous arguments in each function call:

```
f3(f2(f1(d0, arg1), arg2), arg3)
```

Using the pipeline operator, the workflow can be rearranged as follows:

```
d0 %>%
  f1(arg1) %>%
  f2(arg2) %>%
  f3(arg3)
```

The code looks much cleaner and straightforward. The whole expression not only looks like a pipeline but also works like a pipeline. The `d0 %>% f1(arg1)` equation is evaluated as `f1(d0, arg1)`, which is sent to `f2(., arg2)`, which is sent to `f3(., arg3)`. The output of each step becomes the input of the next step.

Therefore, the pipeline operator not only works with `dplyr` functions, but also works with all other functions. Suppose we want to make a density plot of the diamond prices:

```
data(diamonds, package = "ggplot2")
plot(density(diamonds$price, from = 0),
  main = "Density plot of diamond prices")
```

The plot generated is shown as follows:

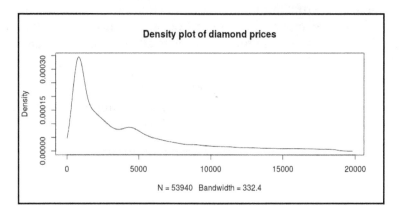

Using the pipeline operator, we can rewrite code as follows:

```
diamonds$price %>%
  density(from = 0) %>%
  plot(main = "Density plot of diamonds prices")
```

Like `data.table`, `dplyr` also supplies `do()` to perform arbitrary operation on each group of data. For example, we can group `diamonds` by `cut`, and for each group, we can fit a linear model of `log(price) ~ carat`. Different from `data.table`, we need to specify the names of such operations so that the results can be stored as columns. Also, the expression in `do()` is not directly evaluated in the context of the grouped data. Instead, we need to use `.` to represent the data:

```
models <- diamonds %>%
  group_by(cut) %>%
  do(lmod = lm(log(price) ~ carat, data = .))
models
## Source: local data frame [5 x 2]
## Groups: <by row>
##
##         cut    lmod
##      (fctr)   (chr)
## 1      Fair <S3:lm>
## 2      Good <S3:lm>
## 3 Very Good <S3:lm>
## 4   Premium <S3:lm>
## 5     Ideal <S3:lm>
```

Note that a new column lmod is created. It is not a typical data column of atomic vectors. Rather, it is a list of linear model objects, that is, the model for each value of cut is stored in the list-typed column lmod. We can access each model using an index:

```
models$lmod[[1]]
##
## Call:
## lm(formula = log(price) ~ carat, data = .)
##
## Coefficients:
## (Intercept)         carat
##       6.785         1.251
```

The do() function can be very helpful to perform highly customized operations. For example, suppose we need to analyze toy_tests data by summarizing the quality and durability for each product. Consider what we should do if, we only need the top three test records with most samples, and the quality and durability of each product should be a weighted average of the measure and the sample.

Using dplyr functions and pipeline, the preceding task can be easily done with the following code:

```
toy_tests %>%
  group_by(id) %>%
  arrange(desc(sample)) %>%
  do(head(., 3)) %>%
  summarize(
    quality = sum(quality * sample) / sum(sample),
    durability = sum(durability * sample) / sum(sample))
## Source: local data frame [2 x 3]
##
##      id   quality durability
##    (chr)    (dbl)      (dbl)
## 1   T01 9.319149   9.382979
## 2   T02 9.040000   8.340000
```

Note that when the data is grouped, all subsequent operations are performed by group. To see the intermediate result, we will run the code before do(head(., 3)):

```
toy_tests %>%
  group_by(id) %>%
  arrange(desc(sample))
## Source: local data frame [8 x 5]
## Groups: id [2]
##
##      id     date sample quality durability
##    (chr)   (int)  (int)   (int)      (int)
```

```
## 1    T01 20160405    180         9         10
## 2    T01 20160302    150        10          9
## 3    T01 20160502    140         9          9
## 4    T01 20160201    100         9          9
## 5    T02 20160403     90         9          8
## 6    T02 20160502     85        10          9
## 7    T02 20160303     75         8          8
## 8    T02 20160201     70         7          9
```

We get all records sorted by `sample` in descending order. Then, `do(head(., 3))` will evaluate `head(., 3)` for each group where `.` represents the data in the group:

```
toy_tests %>%
  group_by(id) %>%
  arrange(desc(sample)) %>%
  do(head(., 3))
## Source: local data frame [6 x 5]
## Groups: id [2]
##
##         id    date sample quality durability
##      (chr)   (int)  (int)   (int)      (int)
## 1    T01 20160405    180       9         10
## 2    T01 20160302    150      10          9
## 3    T01 20160502    140       9          9
## 4    T02 20160403     90       9          8
## 5    T02 20160502     85      10          9
## 6    T02 20160303     75       8          8
```

Now, we will get the top three records with most samples. It is handy to summarize the data as supposed.

The `dplyr` function defines a very intuitive grammar of data manipulation and provides high-performance verb functions that are designed for use in pipeline. To learn more, I recommend that you read the package vignettes (`https://cran.rstudio.com/web/packages/dplyr/vignettes/introduction.html`) and visit the interactive tutorial (`https://www.datacamp.com/courses/dplyr-data-manipulation-r-tutorial`) at DataCamp.

Using rlist to work with nested data structures

In the previous chapter, you learned about both relational databases that store data in tables and non-relational databases that support nested data structures. In R, the most commonly used nested data structure is a list object. All previous sections focus on manipulating tabular data. In this section, let's play with the `rlist` package I developed, which is designed for manipulating non-tabular data.

The design of `rlist` is very similar to `dplyr`. It provides mapping, filtering, selecting, sorting, grouping, and aggregating functionality for list objects. Run the following code to install the `rlist` package from CRAN:

```
install.packages("rlist")
```

We have the non-tabular version of the product data stored in `data/products.json`. In this file, each product has a JSON representation as follows:

```
{
    "id": "T01",
    "name": "SupCar",
    "type": "toy",
    "class": "vehicle",
    "released": true,
    "stats": {
      "material": "Metal",
      "size": 120,
      "weight": 10
    },
    "tests": {
      "quality": null,
      "durability": 10,
      "waterproof": false
    },
    "scores": [8, 9, 10, 10, 6, 5]
}
```

All products are stored in an JSON array like `[ {...}, {...} ]`. Instead of storing data in different tables, we put everything relating to a product in one object. To work with data in this format, we can use `rlist` functions. First, let's load the `rlist` package:

```
library(rlist)
```

To load the data into R as a list, we can use `jsonlite::fromJSON()` or simply `list.load()` provided by `rlist`:

```
products <- list.load("data/products.json")
str(products[[1]])
## List of 8
##  $ id      : chr "T01"
##  $ name    : chr "SupCar"
##  $ type    : chr "toy"
##  $ class   : chr "vehicle"
##  $ released: logi TRUE
##  $ stats   :List of 3
##   ..$ material: chr "Metal"
##   ..$ size    : int 120
##   ..$ weight  : int 10
##  $ tests   :List of 3
##   ..$ quality   : NULL
##   ..$ durability: int 10
##   ..$ waterproof: logi FALSE
##  $ scores  : int [1:6] 8 9 10 10 6 5
```

Now, `products` contains the information of all products. Each element of `products` represents a product with all related information.

To evaluate an expression within the context of each element, we can call `list.map()`:

```
str(list.map(products, id))
## List of 6
##  $ : chr "T01"
##  $ : chr "T02"
##  $ : chr "M01"
##  $ : chr "M02"
##  $ : chr "M03"
##  $ : chr "M04"
```

It iteratively evaluates `id` on each element of `products` and returns a new list containing all the corresponding results. The `list.mapv()` function simplifies the list and only returns a vector:

```
list.mapv(products, name)
## [1] "SupCar"   "SupPlane"  "JeepX"     "AircraftX"
## [5] "Runner"   "Dancer"
```

To filter `products`, we can call `list.filter()` with logical conditions. All elements of `products` for which the conditions yield TRUE will be picked out:

```
released_products <- list.filter(products, released)
list.mapv(released_products, name)
## [1] "SupCar"    "JeepX"      "AircraftX" "Runner"
```

Note that `rlist` functions have design similar to `dplyr` functions, that is, the input data is always the first argument. We can, thus, use a pipeline operator to pipe the results forward:

```
products %>%
  list.filter(released) %>%
  list.mapv(name)
## [1] "SupCar"    "JeepX"      "AircraftX" "Runner"
```

We can use `list.select()` to select the given fields of each element of the input list:

```
products %>%
  list.filter(released, tests$waterproof) %>%
  list.select(id, name, scores) %>%
  str()
## List of 3
##  $ :List of 3
##   ..$ id    : chr "M01"
##   ..$ name  : chr "JeepX"
##   ..$ scores: int [1:6] 6 8 7 9 8 6
##  $ :List of 3
##   ..$ id    : chr "M02"
##   ..$ name  : chr "AircraftX"
##   ..$ scores: int [1:7] 9 9 10 8 10 7 9
##  $ :List of 3
##   ..$ id    : chr "M03"
##   ..$ name  : chr "Runner"
##   ..$ scores: int [1:10] 6 7 5 6 5 8 10 9 8 9
```

Alternatively, we can make new fields in `list.select()` based on the existing fields:

```
products %>%
  list.filter(mean(scores) >= 8) %>%
  list.select(name, scores, mean_score = mean(scores)) %>%
  str()
## List of 3
##  $ :List of 3
##   ..$ name      : chr "SupCar"
##   ..$ scores    : int [1:6] 8 9 10 10 6 5
##   ..$ mean_score: num 8
##  $ :List of 3
##   ..$ name      : chr "SupPlane"
```

```
##    ..$ scores     : int [1:5] 9 9 10 10 10
##    ..$ mean_score: num 9.6
##  $ :List of 3
##    ..$ name       : chr "AircraftX"
##    ..$ scores     : int [1:7] 9 9 10 8 10 7 9
##    ..$ mean_score: num 8.86
```

We can also sort the list elements by certain fields or values using `list.sort()` and stack all elements into a data frame using `list.stack()`:

```
products %>%
  list.select(name, mean_score = mean(scores)) %>%
  list.sort(-mean_score) %>%
  list.stack()
##         name mean_score
## 1   SupPlane   9.600000
## 2  AircraftX   8.857143
## 3     SupCar   8.000000
## 4     Dancer   7.833333
## 5      JeepX   7.333333
## 6     Runner   7.300000
```

To group a list, we will call `list.group()` to make a nested list in which all elements are divided by the values of the field:

```
products %>%
  list.select(name, type, released) %>%
  list.group(type) %>%
  str()
## List of 2
##  $ model:List of 4
##    ..$ :List of 3
##    .. ..$ name    : chr "JeepX"
##    .. ..$ type    : chr "model"
##    .. ..$ released: logi TRUE
##    ..$ :List of 3
##    .. ..$ name    : chr "AircraftX"
##    .. ..$ type    : chr "model"
##    .. ..$ released: logi TRUE
##    ..$ :List of 3
##    .. ..$ name    : chr "Runner"
##    .. ..$ type    : chr "model"
##    .. ..$ released: logi TRUE
##    ..$ :List of 3
##    .. ..$ name    : chr "Dancer"
##    .. ..$ type    : chr "model"
##    .. ..$ released: logi FALSE
##  $ toy  :List of 2
```

```
##    ..$ :List of 3
##    .. ..$ name    : chr "SupCar"
##    .. ..$ type    : chr "toy"
##    .. ..$ released: logi TRUE
##    ..$ :List of 3
##    .. ..$ name    : chr "SupPlane"
##    .. ..$ type    : chr "toy"
##    .. ..$ released: logi FALSE
```

The `rlist` function also provides many other functions that try to make non-tabular data manipulation easier. For example, `list.table()` enhances `table()` to directly work with a list of elements:

```
products %>%
    list.table(type, class)
##           class
## type    people vehicle
##    model     2       2
##    toy       0       2
```

It also supports multi-dimensional tables by evaluating each argument in the context of the input list:

```
products %>%
    list.filter(released) %>%
    list.table(type, waterproof = tests$waterproof)
##           waterproof
## type    FALSE TRUE
##    model     0    3
##    toy       1    0
```

Although the storage of data is non-tabular, we can easily perform comprehensive data manipulation and get the results presented in the tabular form. For example, suppose we need to compute the mean score and number of scores of the top two products with the highest mean scores but also with at least five scores.

We can decompose such a task into smaller data manipulation subtasks, which can be easily done by `rlist` functions. Due to the number of steps involved in the data operations, we will use pipeline to organize the workflow:

```
products %>%
    list.filter(length(scores) >= 5) %>%
    list.sort(-mean(scores)) %>%
    list.take(2) %>%
    list.select(name,
        mean_score = mean(scores),
        n_score = length(scores)) %>%
```

```
    list.stack()
##           name mean_score n_score
## 1  SupPlane   9.600000       5
## 2 AircraftX   8.857143       7
```

The code looks straightforward, and it is easy to predict or analyze what happens in each step. If the final result can be represented in the tabular form, we can call `list.stack()` to bind all list elements together into a data frame.

To learn more about `rlist` functions, read the `rlist` tutorial (`https://renkun.me/rlist-tutorial/`). There are other packages that deal with nested data structures but may have different philosophy, such as purrr (`https://github.com/hadley/purrr`). If you are interested, visit and learn more on their websites.

Summary

In this chapter, you learned a number of basic functions and various packages for data manipulation. Using built-in functions to manipulate data can be redundant. Several packages are tailored for filtering and aggregating data based on different techniques and philosophies. The `sqldf` packages use embedded SQLite databases so that we can directly write SQL statements to query data frame in our working environment. On the other hand, `data.table` provides an enhanced version of `data.frame` and a powerful syntax, and `dplyr` defines a grammar of data manipulation by providing a set of pipeline friendly verb functions. The `rlist` class provides a set of pipeline friendly functions for non-tabular data manipulation. No single package is best for all situations. Each of them represents a way of thinking, and which best fits a certain problem depends on how you understand the problem and your experience of working with data.

Processing data and doing simulation require considerable computing power. However, from the beginning to today, performance is not the top priority for R. Although R is very powerful in interactive analysis, visualization, and reporting, its implementation is considered slow compared to some other popular scripting languages when it is used to process a large amount of data. In the next chapter, we'll introduce several techniques from performance measure and profiling to vectorization, MKL-powered R kernel, parallel computing, and Rcpp. These techniques will help you achieve high performance when you really need it.

13
High-Performance Computing

In the previous chapter, you learned about a number of built-in functions and various packages tailored for data manipulation. Although these packages rely on different techniques and may be built under a different philosophy, they all make data filtering and aggregating much easier.

However, data processing is more than simple filtering and aggregating. Sometimes, it involves simulation and other computationintensive tasks. Compared to high-performance programming languages such as C and C++, R is much slower due to its dynamic design and the current implementation that prioritizes stability, ease, and power in statistical analysis and visualization over performance and language features. However, well-written R code can still be fast enough for most purposes.

In this chapter, I'll demonstrate the following techniques to help you write R code with high performance:

- Measuring code performance
- Profiling code to find bottleneck
- Using built-in functions and vectorization
- Using multiple cores by parallel computing
- Writing C++ with Rcpp and related packages

Understanding code performance issues

From the very beginning, R is designed for statistical computing and data visualization and is widely used by academia and industry. For most data analysis purposes, correctness is more important than performance. In other words, getting a correct result in 1 minute should be better than getting an incorrect one in 20 seconds. A result that is three times faster is not automatically three times more valid than a slow but correct result. Therefore, performance should not be a concern before you are sure about the correctness of your code.

Let's assume that you are 100 percent sure that your code is correct but it runs a bit slowly. Now, is it necessary for you to optimize the code so that it can run faster. Well, it depends. Before making a decision, it is helpful to divide the time of problem solving into three parts: time of development, execution, and future maintenance.

Suppose we have been working on a problem for an hour. Since we didn't take performance into account at the beginning, the code does not run very fast. It takes us 50 minutes to think about the problem and implement the solution. Then, it takes 1 minute to run and produce an answer. Since the code aligns well with the problem and looks straightforward, future improvements can be easily integrated into the solution, so it takes us less time to maintain.

Then, suppose another developer has been working on the same problem but attempts to write an extremely high-performance code at the beginning. It takes time to work out a solution to the problem, but takes much more time to optimize the structure of the code so that it can run faster. It may take two hours to think of and implement a high-performance solution. Then, it takes 0.1 second to run and produce an answer. Since the code is particularly optimized to squeeze the hardware, it is probably not flexible for future refinement, especially when the problem is updated, which would cost more time to maintain.

The second developer can happily claim that her code has 600 times the performance of our code, but it may not be worth doing so because it may cost much more human time. In many cases, human time is more expensive than computer time.

However, if the code is frequently used, say, if billions of iterations are required, a small improvement of performance of each iteration can help save a large amount of time. In this case, code performance really matters.

Let's take an example of a simple algorithm that produces a numeric vector of cumulative sum, that is, each element of the output vector is the sum of all previous elements of the input vector. The code will be examined in different contexts in the discussion that follows.

Although R provides a built-in function, `cumsum`, to do this, we will implement an R version at the moment to help understand performance issues. The algorithm is easy to implement as follows:

```
x <- c(1, 2, 3, 4, 5)
y <- numeric()
sum_x <- 0
for (xi in x) {
  sum_x <- sum_x + xi
  y <- c(y, sum_x)
}
y
## [1]  1  3  6 10 15
```

The algorithm only uses a `for` loop to accumulate each element of the input vector x into `sum_x`. In each iteration, it appends `sum_x` to the output vector y. We can rewrite the algorithm as the following function:

```
my_cumsum1 <- function(x) {
  y <- numeric()
  sum_x <- 0
  for (xi in x) {
    sum_x <- sum_x + xi
    y <- c(y, sum_x)
  }
  y
}
```

An alternative implementation is to use index to access the input vector x and access/modify the output vector y:

```
my_cumsum2 <- function(x) {
  y <- numeric(length(x))
  if (length(y)) {
    y[[1]] <- x[[1]]
    for (i in 2:length(x)) {
      y[[i]] <- y[[I - 1]] + x[[i]]
    }
  }
  y
}
```

We know that R provides a built-in function `cumsum()` to do exactly the same thing. The two preceding implementations should yield exactly the same results as `cumsum()`. Here, we will generate some random numbers and check whether they are consistent:

```
x <- rnorm(100)
all.equal(cumsum(x), my_cumsum1(x))
## [1] TRUE
all.equal(cumsum(x), my_cumsum2(x))
## [1] TRUE
```

In the preceding code, `all.equal()` checks whether all corresponding elements of two vectors are equal. From the results, we are sure that `my_cumsum1()`, `my_cumsum2()` and `cumsum()` are consistent. In the next section, we'll measure the time required for each version of `cumsum`.

Measuring code performance

Although the three functions will output the same results given the same input, their performance difference can be quite obvious. To reveal the difference in performance, we need tools to measure the execution time of code. The simplest one is `system.time()`.

To measure the execution time of any expression, we just wrap the code with the function. Here, we will measure how much time it takes by `my_cumsum1()` to compute over a numeric vector of 100 elements:

```
x <- rnorm(100)
system.time(my_cumsum1(x))
##    user  system elapsed
##       0       0       0
```

The timer results in three columns: `user`, `system`, and `elapsed`. It is the user time that we should pay more attention to. It measures the CPU time charged for executing the code. For more details, run `?proc.time` and see the difference between these measures.

The results suggest that the code simply runs too fast to measure. We can try timing `my_cumsum2()`, and the results are mostly the same:

```
system.time(my_cumsum2(x))
##    user  system elapsed
##   0.000   0.000   0.001
```

The same thing happens with the built-in function `cumsum()` too:

```
system.time(cumsum(x))
##    user  system elapsed
##       0       0       0
```

The timing does not really work because the input is too small. Now, we will generate a vector of `1000` numbers and do it again:

```
x <- rnorm(1000)
system.time(my_cumsum1(x))
##    user  system elapsed
##   0.000   0.000   0.003
system.time(my_cumsum2(x))
##    user  system elapsed
##   0.004   0.000   0.001
system.time(cumsum(x))
##    user  system elapsed
##       0       0       0
```

Now, we are sure that `my_cumsum1()` and `my_cumsum2()` indeed take some time to compute the results but show no remarkable contrast. However, `cumsum()` is still too fast to measure.

We will again use a larger input for all three functions and see whether their performance difference can be revealed:

```
x <- rnorm(10000)
system.time(my_cumsum1(x))
##    user  system elapsed
##   0.208   0.000   0.211
system.time(my_cumsum2(x))
##    user  system elapsed
##   0.012   0.004   0.013
system.time(cumsum(x))
##    user  system elapsed
##       0       0       0
```

The result is quite clear: `my_cumsum1()` looks more than 10 times slower than `my_cumsum2()`, and `cumsum()` is still way too fast than both our implementations.

Note that the performance difference may not be constant, especially when we provide even larger inputs as follows:

```
x <- rnorm(100000)
system.time(my_cumsum1(x))
##    user  system elapsed
```

```
## 25.732    0.964   26.699
system.time(my_cumsum2(x))
##     user   system elapsed
##    0.124    0.000    0.123
system.time(cumsum(x))
##     user   system elapsed
##        0        0        0
```

The preceding results make quite an astonishing contrast: my_cumsum1() can be 200 times slower than my_cumsum2() when the length of input vector is at 100,000 level. The cumsum() function is consistently super fast in all previous results.

The system.time() function can help measure the execution time of a code chunk, but it is not very accurate. On the one hand, each time, the measure can result in different values so that we should repeat the timing for enough times to make a valid comparison. On the other hand, the resolution of the timer may not be high enough to address the real difference in performance of the code of interest.

A package named microbenchmark serves as a more accurate solution to comparing the performance of different expressions. To install the package, run the following code:

```
install.packages("microbenchmark")
```

When the package is ready, we will load the package and call microbenchmark() to directly compare the performance of the three functions:

```
library(microbenchmark)
x <- rnorm(100)
microbenchmark(my_cumsum1(x), my_cumsum2(x), cumsum(x))
## Unit: nanoseconds
##             expr    min       lq      mean   median       uq
##    my_cumsum1(x)  58250  64732.5  68353.51  66396.0  71840.0
##    my_cumsum2(x) 120150 127634.5 131042.40 130739.5 133287.5
##        cumsum(x)    295    376.5    593.47    440.5    537.5
##     max neval cld
##   88228   100  b
##  152845   100   c
##    7182   100 a
```

Note that microbenchmark(), by default, runs each expression 100 times so that it can provide more quantiles of the execution time. Maybe to your surprise, my_cumsum1() is a bit faster than my_cumsum2() when the input vector has 100 elements. Also, note that the unit of the time numbers is nanoseconds (1 second is 1,000,000,000 nanoseconds).

Then, we will try an input of 1000 numbers:

```
x <- rnorm(1000)
microbenchmark(my_cumsum1(x), my_cumsum2(x), cumsum(x))
## Unit: microseconds
##            expr      min        lq       mean    median
##   my_cumsum1(x) 1600.186 1620.5190 2238.67494 1667.5605
##   my_cumsum2(x) 1034.973 1068.4600 1145.00544 1088.4090
##       cumsum(x)    1.806    2.1505    3.43945    3.4405
##         uq       max neval cld
## 3142.4610 3750.516   100   c
## 1116.2280 2596.908   100   b
##    4.0415   11.007   100  a
```

Now, my_cumsum2() gets a bit faster than my_cumsum1(), but both are way slower than the built-in cumsum(). Note that the unit becomes microseconds now.

For input of 5000 numbers, the performance difference between my_cumsum1() and my_cumsum2() gets even greater:

```
x <- rnorm(5000)
microbenchmark(my_cumsum1(x), my_cumsum2(x), cumsum(x))
## Unit: microseconds
##            expr       min        lq        mean     median
##   my_cumsum1(x) 42646.201 44043.050 51715.59988 44808.9745
##   my_cumsum2(x)  5291.242  5364.568  5718.19744  5422.8950
##       cumsum(x)    10.183    11.565    14.52506    14.6765
##          uq         max neval cld
## 46153.351 135805.947   100   c
##  5794.821  10619.352   100   b
##    15.536     37.202   100  a
```

The same thing happens with an input of 10000 elements:

```
x <- rnorm(10000)
microbenchmark(my_cumsum1(x), my_cumsum2(x), cumsum(x), times = 10)
## Unit: microseconds
##            expr        min         lq        mean     median
##   my_cumsum1(x) 169609.730 170687.964 198782.7958 173248.004
##   my_cumsum2(x)  10682.121  10724.513  11278.0974  10813.395
##       cumsum(x)     20.744     25.627     26.0943     26.544
##        uq        max neval cld
## 253662.89 264469.677    10   b
##  11588.99  13487.812    10   a
##     27.64     29.163    10   a
```

In all previous benchmarks, the performance of `cumsum()` looks very stable and does not increase significantly as the length of input increases.

To better understand the performance dynamics of the three functions, we will create the following function to visualize how they perform, provided an input of different lengths:

```
library(data.table)
benchmark <- function(ns, times = 30) {
  results <- lapply(ns, function(n) {
    x <- rnorm(n)
    result <- microbenchmark(my_cumsum1(x), my_cumsum2(x), cumsum(x),
times = times, unit = "ms")
    data <- setDT(summary(result))
    data[, n := n]
    data
  })
  rbindlist(results)
}
```

The logic of the function is straightforward: ns is a vector of all lengths of input vectors we want to test with these functions. Note that `microbenchmark()` returns in a data frame of all tests results, and `summary(microbenchmark())` returns the summary table we saw previously. We tag each summary with n, stack all benchmark results, and use the `ggplot2` package to visualize the results.

First, we will do the benchmarking from 100 to 3000 elements of step 100:

```
benchmarks <- benchmark(seq(100, 3000, 100))
```

Then, we will create a plot to show contrast between the performance of the three functions:

```
library(ggplot2)
ggplot(benchmarks, aes(x = n, color = expr)) +
  ggtitle("Microbenchmark on cumsum functions") +
  geom_point(aes(y = median)) +
  geom_errorbar(aes(ymin = lq, ymax = uq))
```

This produces the following benchmarks of the three versions of `cumsum` we intend to compare:

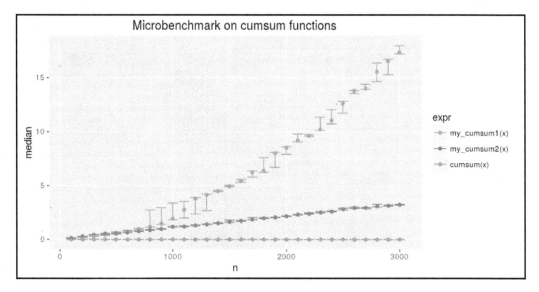

In the preceding chart, we put together the results of all three functions. The dots indicate the median, and the error bar shows the 75th and 25th quantile.

It is very clear that the performance of `my_cumsum1()` decreases faster for longer input, the performance of `my_cumsum2()` almost decreases linearly as the input gets longer, while `cumsum(x)` is extremely fast and its performance does not seem to decay significantly as the input gets longer.

For small input, `my_cumsum1()` can be faster than `my_cumsum2()`, as we demonstrated earlier. We can do a benchmarking that focuses more on small input:

```
benchmarks2 <- benchmark(seq(2, 600, 10), times = 50)
```

This time, we will limit the length of input vector from 2 to 500 of stop 10. Since the functions will be executed almost twice the number of times than the previous benchmarking, to keep the total execution time down, we will reduce `times` from the default 100 to 50:

```
ggplot(benchmarks2, aes(x = n, color = expr)) +
    ggtitle("Microbenchmark on cumsum functions over small input") +
    geom_point(aes(y = median)) +
    geom_errorbar(aes(ymin = lq, ymax = uq))
```

The following graphics illustrates the performance difference at smaller inputs:

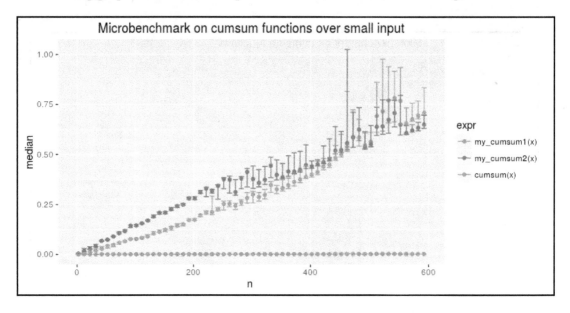

From the chart, we can see that for small input of less than around 400 numbers, `my_cumsum1()` is faster than `my_cumsum2()`. The performance of `my_cumsum1()` decays much faster than `my_cumsum2()` as the input gets more elements.

The dynamics of performance ranking can be better illustrated by a benchmarking of input from 10 to 800 elements:

```
benchmarks3 <- benchmark(seq(10, 800, 10), times = 50)
ggplot(benchmarks3, aes(x = n, color = expr)) +
  ggtitle("Microbenchmark on cumsum functions with break even") +
  geom_point(aes(y = median)) +
  geom_errorbar(aes(ymin = lq, ymax = uq))
```

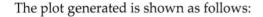
The plot generated is shown as follows:

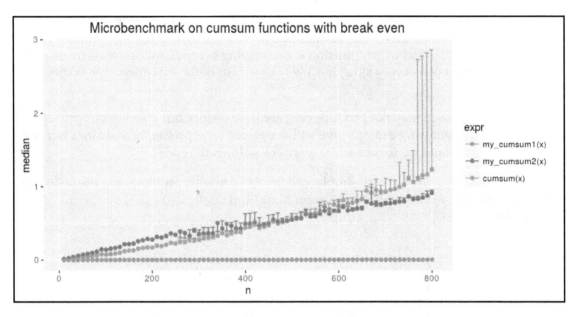

In conclusion, a small difference in implementation may result in big performance gaps. For a small input, the gap is usually not obvious, but when the input gets larger, the performance difference can be very significant and thus should not be ignored. To compare the performance of multiple expressions, we can use `microbenchmark` instead of `system.time()` to get more accurate and more useful results.

Profiling code

In the previous section, you learned how to use `microbenchmark()` to benchmark expressions. This can be useful when we have several alternative solutions to a problem and want to see which has better performance and when we optimize an expression and want to see whether the performance actually gets better than the original code.

However, it is usually the case that, when we feel the code is slow, it is not easy to locate the expression that contributes most to slowing down the entire program. Such an expression is called a "performance bottleneck." To improve code performance, it is best to resolve the bottleneck first.

Fortunately, R provides profiling tools to help us find the bottleneck, that is, the code that runs most slowly, which should be the top focus for improving code performance.

Profiling code with Rprof

R provides a built-in function, Rprof(), for code profiling. When profiling starts, a sampling procedure is running with all subsequent code until the profiling is ended. The sampling basically looks at which function R is executing every 20 milliseconds by default. In this way, if a function is very slow, it is likely that most of the execution time is spent on that function call.

The sampling approach may not produce very accurate results, but it serves our purpose in most cases. In the following example, we will use Rprof() to profile the code in which we call my_cumsum1() and try to find which part slows down the code.

The way of using Rprof() is very simple: call Rprof() to start profiling, run the code you want to profile, call Rprof(NULL) to stop profiling, and finally call summaryRprof() to see the profiling summary:

```
x <- rnorm(1000)
tmp <- tempfile(fileext = ".out")
Rprof(tmp)
for (i in 1:1000) {
  my_cumsum1(x)
}
Rprof(NULL)
summaryRprof(tmp)
## $by.self
##              self.time self.pct total.time total.pct
## "c"              2.42    82.88       2.42     82.88
## "my_cumsum1"     0.46    15.75       2.92    100.00
## "+"              0.04     1.37       0.04      1.37
## $by.total
##              total.time total.pct self.time self.pct
## "my_cumsum1"       2.92    100.00      0.46    15.75
## "c"                2.42     82.88      2.42    82.88
## "+"                0.04      1.37      0.04     1.37
##
## $sample.interval
## [1] 0.02
##
## $sampling.time
## [1] 2.92
```

Note that we used tempfile() to create a temporary file to store profiling data. If we don't supply such a file to Rprof(), it will automatically create Rprof.out in the current working directory. The default also applies to summaryRprof().

The profiling results summarize the profiling data into a readable format: $by.self sorts the timing by self.time, while $by.total sorts by total.time. More specifically, the self.time of a function is the time spent executing code in the function only, and the total.time of a function is the total execution time of the function.

To figure out which part slows down the function, we should pay more attention to self.time because it addresses the independent time of execution of each function.

The preceding profiling results show that c takes up a major part of the execution time, that is,

y <- c(y, sum_x) contributes most to slowing down the function.

We can do the same thing to my_cumsum2(). The profiling results suggest that most time is spent on my_cumsum2(), but that is normal because that's the only thing we do in the code. No particular function in my_cumsum2() takes up major part of time to execute:

```
tmp <- tempfile(fileext = ".out")
Rprof(tmp)
for (i in 1:1000) {
    my_cumsum2(x)
}
Rprof(NULL)
summaryRprof(tmp)
## $by.self
##              self.time self.pct total.time total.pct
## "my_cumsum2"      1.42    97.26       1.46    100.00
## "-"               0.04     2.74       0.04      2.74
##
## $by.total
##              total.time total.pct self.time self.pct
## "my_cumsum2"       1.46    100.00      1.42    97.26
## "-"                0.04      2.74      0.04     2.74
##
## $sample.interval
## [1] 0.02
##
## $sampling.time
## [1] 1.46
```

In a practical situation, the code we want to profile is usually complicated enough. It may involve many different functions. Such a profiling summary can be less helpful if we only see the timing of each function it tracks. Fortunately, Rprof() supports line profiling, that is, it can tell us the timing of each line of code when we specify line.profiling = TRUE and use source(..., keep.source = TRUE).

We will create a script file at code/my_cumsum1.R with the following code:

```
my_cumsum1 <- function(x) {
   y <- numeric()
   sum_x <- 0
   for (xi in x) {
     sum_x <- sum_x + xi
     y <- c(y, sum_x)
   }
   y
}

x <- rnorm(1000)

for (i in 1:1000) {
   my_cumsum1(x)
}
```

Then, we will profile this script file with Rprof() and source():

```
tmp <- tempfile(fileext = ".out")
Rprof(tmp, line.profiling = TRUE)
source("code/my_cumsum1.R", keep.source = TRUE)
Rprof(NULL)
summaryRprof(tmp, lines = "show")
## $by.self
##                    self.time self.pct total.time total.pct
## my_cumsum1.R#6          2.38    88.15       2.38     88.15
## my_cumsum1.R#5          0.26     9.63       0.26      9.63
## my_cumsum1.R#4          0.06     2.22       0.06      2.22
##
## $by.total
##                    total.time total.pct self.time self.pct
## my_cumsum1.R#14         2.70    100.00       0.00     0.00
## my_cumsum1.R#6          2.38     88.15       2.38    88.15
## my_cumsum1.R#5          0.26      9.63       0.26     9.63
## my_cumsum1.R#4          0.06      2.22       0.06     2.22
##
## $by.line
##                    self.time self.pct total.time total.pct
## my_cumsum1.R#4          0.06     2.22       0.06      2.22
## my_cumsum1.R#5          0.26     9.63       0.26      9.63
## my_cumsum1.R#6          2.38    88.15       2.38     88.15
## my_cumsum1.R#14         0.00     0.00       2.70    100.00
##
## $sample.interval
## [1] 0.02
##
```

```
## $sampling.time
## [1] 2.7
```

This time, it no longer shows function names but line numbers in the script file. We can easily locate the lines that cost most time by looking at the top rows in `$by.self`. The `my_cumsum1.R#6` file refers to `y <- c(y, sum_x)`, which is consistent with the previous profiling results.

Profiling code with profvis

The `Rprof()` function provides useful information to help us find which part of the code is too slow so that we can improve the implementation. RStudio also released an enhanced profiling tool, `profvis` (`https://rstudio.github.io/profvis/`), which provides interactive visualization for profiling R code.

It is an R package and has been integrated into RStudio. To install the package, run the following code:

```
install.packages("profvis")
```

As soon as the package is installed, we can use `profvis` to profile an expression and visualize the results:

```
library(profvis)
profvis({
  my_cumsum1 <- function(x) {
    y <- numeric()
    sum_x <- 0
    for (xi in x) {
      sum_x <- sum_x + xi
      y <- c(y, sum_x)
    }
    y
  }

  x <- rnorm(1000)

  for (i in 1:1000) {
    my_cumsum1(x)
  }
})
```

When the profiling is finished, a new tab will appear with an interactive user interface:

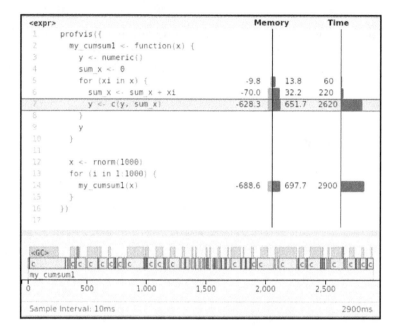

The upper pane shows the code, memory usage, and timing, whereas the lower pane shows the timeline of function calling as well as when garbage collection occurs. We can click and select a certain line of code and see the timeline of function execution. Compared with the results produced by summaryRprof(), this interactive visualization provides much richer information that enables us to know more about how the code is executed over a long time. In this way, we can easily identify the slow code and some patterns that may induce problems.

We can do exactly the same thing with my_cumsum2():

```
profvis({
  my_cumsum2 <- function(x) {
    y <- numeric(length(x))
    y[[1]] <- x[[1]]
    for (i in 2:length(x)) {
      y[[i]] <- y[[i-1]] + x[[i]]
    }
    y
  }

  x <- rnorm(1000)
```

```
    for (i in 1:1000) {
        my_cumsum2(x)
    }
})
```

This time, the profiling results in the following statistics:

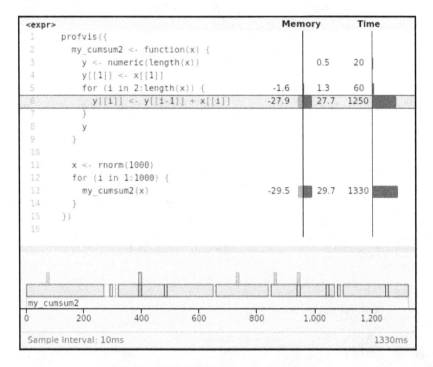

We can easily identify which part takes the most time and decide whether it is acceptable. In all code, there is always a part that takes most time, but this does not indicate that it is too slow. If the code serves our purpose and the performance is acceptable, then there may not be a need to optimize the performance at the risk of modifying the code into an incorrect version.

Understanding why code can be slow

In the previous sections, you learned about the tools for timing and profiling code. To solve the same problem, one function can be blazing fast, and the other can be ridiculously slow. It is helpful to understand what can make code slow.

First, R is a dynamic programming language. By design, it provides highly flexible data structures and code-execution mechanisms. Therefore, it is hard for the code interpreter to know in advance how to deal with the next function call until it is actually called. This is not the case for strong-typed static programming languages such as C and C++. Many things are determined at compile time rather than runtime, so the program knows a lot ahead of time, and optimization can be intensively performed. By contrast, R trades flexibility for performance, but well-written R code can exhibit acceptable, if not good, performance.

The top reason why R code can be slow is that our code may intensively create, allocate, or copy data structures. This is exactly why `my_cumsum1()` and `my_cumsum2()` show great difference in performance when the input gets longer. The `my_cumsum1()` function always grows the vector, which means that in each iteration the vector is copied to a new address and a new element is appended. As a result, the more iterations we have, the more elements it has to copy, and then the code gets slower.

This can be made explicit by the following benchmarking: `grow_by_index` means we initialize an empty list. The `preallocated` function means we initialize a list with pre-allocated positions, that is, a list of n `NULL` values with all positions allocated. In both cases, we modify the ith element of the list, but the difference is that we'll grow the first list in each iteration, and this does not happen with the second list because it is already fully allocated:

```
n <- 10000
microbenchmark(grow_by_index = {
  x <- list()
  for (i in 1:n) x[[i]] <- i
}, preallocated = {
  x <- vector("list", n)
  for (i in 1:n) x[[i]] <- i
}, times = 20)
## Unit: milliseconds
##          expr        min         lq       mean     median
##  grow_by_index 258.584783 261.639465 299.781601 263.896162
##   preallocated   7.151352   7.222043   7.372342   7.257661
##            uq        max neval cld
##  351.887538 375.447134    20   b
##    7.382103   8.612665    20   a
```

The results are clear: intensively growing a list can significantly slow down the code, while modifying a pre-allocated list within range is fast. The same logic also applies to atomic vectors and matrices. Growing a data structure in R is generally slow because it triggers reallocation, that is, copying the original data structure to a new memory address. This is very expensive in R, especially when the data is large.

However, accurate pre-allocation is not always feasible because it requires that we know the total number prior to the iteration. Sometimes, we can only ask for a result to store repeatedly without knowing the exact total number. In this case, maybe it is still a good idea to pre-allocate a list or vector with a reasonable length. When the iteration is over, if the number of iterations does not reach the pre-allocated length, we can take a subset of the list or vector. In this way, we can avoid intensive reallocation of data structures.

Boosting code performance

In the previous section, we demonstrated how to use profiling tools to identify a performance bottleneck in the code. In this section, you will learn about a number of approaches to boosting code performance.

Using built-in functions

Previously, we demonstrated the performance difference between my_cumsum1(), my_cumsum2() and the built-in function cumsum(). Although my_cumsum2() is faster than my_cumsum1(), when the input vector contains many numbers, cumsum() is much faster than them. Also, its performance does not decay significantly even as the input gets longer. If we evaluate cumsum, we can see that it is a primitive function:

```
cumsum
## function (x)  .Primitive("cumsum")
```

A primitive function in R is implemented in C/C++/Fortran, compiled to native instructions, and thus, is extremely efficient. Another example is diff(). Here, we will implement computing vector difference sequence in R:

```
diff_for <- function(x) {
  n <- length(x) - 1
  res <- numeric(n)
  for (i in seq_len(n)) {
    res[[i]] <- x[[i + 1]] - x[[i]]
  }
  res
}
```

We can verify that the implementation is correct:

```
diff_for(c(2, 3, 1, 5))
## [1]  1 -2  4
```

Therefore, both `diff_for()` and built-in `diff()` must return the same result for the same input:

```
x <- rnorm(1000)
all.equal(diff_for(x), diff(x))
## [1] TRUE
```

However, there's a big gap in performance between the two functions.

```
microbenchmark(diff_for(x), diff(x))
## Unit: microseconds
##          expr       min        lq       mean    median
##   diff_for(x) 1034.028 1078.9075 1256.01075 1139.1270
##       diff(x)   12.057   14.2535   21.72772   17.5705
##            uq       max neval cld
##   1372.1145 2634.128   100   b
##     25.4525   75.850   100   a
```

Built-in functions are, in most cases, way faster than equivalent R implementations. This is true not only for vector functions, but also for matrices. For example, here is a simple 3 by 4 integer matrix:

```
mat <- matrix(1:12, nrow = 3)
mat
##      [,1] [,2] [,3] [,4]
## [1,]    1    4    7   10
## [2,]    2    5    8   11
## [3,]    3    6    9   12
```

We can write a function to transpose the matrix:

```
my_transpose <- function(x) {
    stopifnot(is.matrix(x))
    res <- matrix(vector(mode(x), length(x)),
      nrow = ncol(x), ncol = nrow(x),
      dimnames = dimnames(x)[c(2, 1)])
    for (i in seq_len(ncol(x))) {
      for (j in seq_len(nrow(x))) {
        res[i, j] <- x[j, i]
      }
    }
    res
  }
```

In the function, we will first create a matrix of the same type as the input, but with the number and names of rows and columns exchanged, respectively. Then, we will iterate over columns and rows to transpose the matrix:

```
my_transpose(mat)
##      [,1] [,2] [,3]
## [1,]    1    2    3
## [2,]    4    5    6
## [3,]    7    8    9
## [4,]   10   11   12
```

The built-in function of matrix transpose is t(). We can easily verify that both functions return the same results:

```
all.equal(my_transpose(mat), t(mat))
## [1] TRUE
```

However, they may exhibit great difference in performance:

```
microbenchmark(my_transpose(mat), t(mat))
## Unit: microseconds
##                expr    min     lq     mean  median      uq
##   my_transpose(mat) 22.795 24.633 29.47941 26.0865 35.5055
##              t(mat)  1.576  1.978  2.87349  2.3375  2.7695
##      max neval cld
## 71.509   100   b
## 16.171   100   a
```

The performance difference gets even more significant when the input matrix is larger. Here, we will create a new matrix with 1000 rows and 25 columns. While the results are the same, the performance can be very different:

```
mat <- matrix(rnorm(25000), nrow = 1000)
all.equal(my_transpose(mat), t(mat))
## [1] TRUE
microbenchmark(my_transpose(mat), t(mat))
## Unit: microseconds
##                expr       min        lq      mean
##   my_transpose(mat) 21786.241 22456.3990 24466.055
##              t(mat)    36.611    46.2045    61.047
##      median        uq        max neval cld
## 23821.5905 24225.142 113395.811   100   b
##    57.7505    68.694    142.126   100   a
```

Note that `t()` is a generic function that works with both matrix and data frame. S3 dispatching to find the right method for the input, also has some overhead. Therefore, directly calling `t.default()` on a matrix is slightly faster:

```
microbenchmark(my_transpose(mat), t(mat), t.default(mat))
## Unit: microseconds
##                 expr        min         lq        mean
##    my_transpose(mat) 21773.751 22498.6420 23673.26089
##               t(mat)    37.853    48.8475    63.57713
##       t.default(mat)    35.518    41.0305    52.97680
##       median         uq        max neval cld
##    23848.6625 24139.7675 29034.267   100   b
##       61.3565    69.6655   140.061   100   a
##       46.3095    54.0655   146.755   100   a
```

All previous examples show that, in most cases, it is much better to use built-in functions if provided than reinventing the wheel in R. These functions get rid of the overhead of R code and, thus, can be extremely efficient even if the input is huge.

Using vectorization

A special subset of built-in functions are arithmetic operators such as +, −, *, /, ^, and %%. These operators are not only extremely efficient but also vectorized.

Suppose we implement + in R:

```
add <- function(x, y) {
   stopifnot(length(x) == length(y),
      is.numeric(x), is.numeric(y))
   z <- numeric(length(x))
   for (i in seq_along(x)) {
     z[[i]] <- x[[i]] + y[[i]]
   }
   z
}
```

Then, we would randomly generate x and y. The `add(x, y)`, and x + y arguments should return exactly the same results:

```
x <- rnorm(10000)
y <- rnorm(10000)
all.equal(add(x, y), x + y)
## [1] TRUE
```

The following benchmarking shows that the performance difference is huge:

```
microbenchmark(add(x, y), x + y)
## Unit: microseconds
##        expr       min           lq       mean      median
##   add(x, y) 9815.495   10055.7045 11478.95003 10712.7710
##       x + y   10.260      12.0345    17.31862    13.3995
##         uq         max neval cld
## 12598.366  18754.504   100   b
##    22.208     56.969   100   a
```

Now, suppose we need to calculate the sum of the reciprocal of first n positive integers squared. We can easily implement the algorithm using a for loop as the following function algo1_for:

```
algo1_for <- function(n) {
  res <- 0
  for (i in seq_len(n)) {
    res <- res + 1 /i ^ 2
  }
  res
}
```

The function takes an input n, iterates n times to accumulate as supposed, and returns the result.

A better approach is to use vectorized calculation directly without any necessity of a for loop, just like how algo1_vec() is implemented:

```
algo1_vec <- function(n) {
  sum(1 / seq_len(n) ^ 2)
}
```

The two functions yield the same results, given an ordinary input:

```
algo1_for(10)
## [1] 1.549768
algo1_vec(10)
## [1] 1.549768
```

However, their performance is very different:

```
microbenchmark(algo1_for(200), algo1_vec(200))
## Unit: microseconds
##             expr     min        lq       mean     median        uq
##   algo1_for(200) 91.727  101.2285  104.26857   103.6445   105.632
##   algo1_vec(200)  2.465    2.8015    3.51926     3.0355     3.211
##        max neval cld
```

```
##   206.295    100   b
##    19.426    100   a
microbenchmark(algo1_for(1000), algo1_vec(1000))
## Unit: microseconds
##               expr     min       lq      mean   median
##   algo1_for(1000) 376.335 498.9320 516.63954 506.859
##   algo1_vec(1000)   8.718   9.1175   9.82515   9.426
##         uq      max neval cld
##   519.2420 1823.502   100   b
##     9.8955   20.564   100   a
```

Vectorization is a highly recommended way of writing R code. It is not only of high performance but, also makes the code easier to understand.

Using byte-code compiler

In the previous section, we saw the power of vectorization. Sometimes, however, the problem dictates a for loop, and it is hard to vectorize the code. In this case, we may consider using R byte-code compiler to compile the function so that the function no longer needs parsing and may run faster.

First, we will load the compiler package, which is distributed along with R. We will use cmpfun() to compile a given R function. For example, we will compile diff_for() and store the compiled function as diff_cmp():

```
library(compiler)
diff_cmp <- cmpfun(diff_for)
diff_cmp
## function(x) {
##    n <- length(x) - 1
##    res <- numeric(n)
##    for (i in seq_len(n)) {
##      res[[i]] <- x[[i + 1]] - x[[i]]
##    }
##    res
## }
## <bytecode: 0x93aec08>
```

When we look at diff_cmp(), it does not look very different from diff_for(), but it has an additional tag of the bytecode address.

Then, we will run the benchmarking again with diff_cmp() this time:

```
x <- rnorm(10000)
microbenchmark(diff_for(x), diff_cmp(x), diff(x))
```

```
## Unit: microseconds
##          expr        min            lq        mean       median
##   diff_for(x)  10664.387  10940.0840  11684.3285  11357.9330
##   diff_cmp(x)    732.110    740.7610    760.1985    751.0295
##       diff(x)     80.824     91.2775    107.8473    103.8535
##         uq        max neval cld
## 12179.98  16606.291   100   c
##   763.66   1015.234   100   b
##   115.11    219.396   100   a
```

It looks amazing that the compiled version, `diff_cmp()`, is much faster than `diff_for()` even though we didn't modify anything but compiled it into bytecode.

Now, we will do the same thing with `algo1_for()`:

```
algo1_cmp <- cmpfun(algo1_for)
algo1_cmp
## function(n) {
##   res <- 0
##   for (i in seq_len(n)) {
##     res <- res + 1 / i ^ 2
##   }
##   res
## }
## <bytecode: 0xa87e2a8>
```

Then, we will conduct the benchmarking with the compiled version included:

```
n <- 1000
microbenchmark(algo1_for(n), algo1_cmp(n), algo1_vec(n))
## Unit: microseconds
##            expr      min         lq       mean     median        uq
##   algo1_for(n)  490.791  499.5295  509.46589  505.7560  517.5770
##   algo1_cmp(n)   55.588   56.8355   58.10490   57.8270   58.7140
##   algo1_vec(n)    8.688    9.2150    9.79685    9.4955    9.8895
##        max neval cld
## 567.680   100   c
##  69.734   100   b
##  19.765   100   a
```

Again, the compiled version becomes more than six times faster than the original version, even if we didn't change a bit of code.

However, compiling is no magic if it is used to compile a fully vectorized function. Here, we will compile `algo1_vec()` and compare its performance with the original version:

```
algo1_vec_cmp <- cmpfun(algo1_vec)
microbenchmark(algo1_vec(n), algo1_vec_cmp(n), times = 10000)
```

```
## Unit: microseconds
##             expr   min     lq      mean median    uq
##      algo1_vec(n)  8.47  8.678  20.454858  8.812  9.008
##  algo1_vec_cmp(n)  8.35  8.560   9.701012  8.687  8.864
##        max neval cld
##  96376.483 10000   a
##   1751.431 10000   a
```

Note that the compiled function shows no significant performance improvement. To know more about how the compiler works, type `?compile` and read the documentation.

Using Intel MKL-powered R distribution

The R distribution we normally use is single threaded, that is, only one CPU thread is used to execute all R code. The good thing is that the execution model is simple and safe, but it does not take advantage of multicore computing.

Microsoft R Open (MRO, see `https://mran.microsoft.com/open/`) is an enhanced distribution of R. Powered by Intel Math Kernel Library (MKL, see `https://software.intel.com/en-us/intel-mkl`), MRO enhances the matrix algorithms by automatically taking advantage of multithreading computation. On a multicore computer, MRO can be 10-80 times faster than the official R implementation at matrix multiplication, Cholesky factorization, QR decomposition, singular value decomposition, principal component analysis, and linear discriminant analysis. For more details, visit `https://mran.microsoft.com/documents/rro/multithread/` and see the benchmarking.

Using parallel computing

As we mentioned in the previous section, R is single threaded in design but still allows multiprocessing parallel computing, that is, running multiple R sessions to compute. This technique is supported by a parallel library, which is also distributed along with R.

Suppose we need to do a simulation: we need to generate a random path that follows a certain random process and see whether at any point, the value goes beyond a fixed margin around the starting point.

The following code generates one realization:

```
set.seed(1)
sim_data <- 100 * cumprod(1 + rnorm(500, 0, 0.006))
plot(sim_data, type = "s", ylim = c(85, 115),
```

```
    main = "A simulated random path")
  abline(h = 100, lty = 2, col = "blue")
  abline(h = 100 * (1 + 0.1 * c(1, -1)), lty = 3, col = "red")
```

The plot generated is shown as follows:

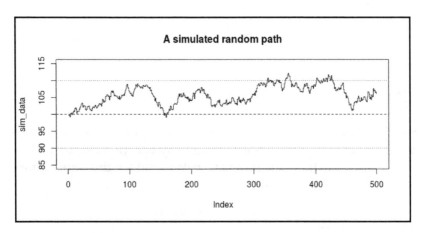

The preceding graph shows the path and 10 percent margin. It is clear that between index 300 and 500, the value goes beyond the upper margin multiple times.

This is just one path. A valid simulation requires that the generator run as many times as necessary to produce statistically meaningful results. The following function parameterizes the random path generator and returns a list of summary indicators of interest. Note that `signal` indicates whether any point on the path goes beyond the margin:

```
simulate <- function(i, p = 100, n = 10000,
    r = 0, sigma = 0.0005, margin = 0.1) {
  ps <- p * cumprod(1 + rnorm(n, r, sigma))
  list(id = i,
    first = ps[[1]],
    high = max(ps),
    low = min(ps),
    last = ps[[n]],
    signal = any(ps > p * (1 + margin) | ps < p * (1 - margin)))
}
```

Then, we can run the generator for one time and see its summarized result:

```
simulate(1)
## $id
## [1] 1
##
## $first
```

```
## [1] 100.0039
##
## $high
## [1] 101.4578
##
## $low
## [1] 94.15108
##
## $last
## [1] 96.13973
##
## $signal
## [1] FALSE
```

To perform the simulation, we need to run the function many times. In practice, we may need to run at least millions of realizations, which may take us a considerable amount of time. Here, we will measure how much time it costs to run ten thousand iterations of this simulation:

```
system.time(res <- lapply(1:10000, simulate))
##    user  system elapsed
##   8.768   0.000   8.768
```

When the simulation is finished, we can convert all results into one data table:

```
library(data.table)
res_table <- rbindlist(res)
head(res_table)
##    id     first     high      low     last signal
## 1:  1 100.03526 100.7157 93.80330 100.55324  FALSE
## 2:  2 100.03014 104.7150 98.85049 101.97831  FALSE
## 3:  3  99.99356 104.9834 95.28500  95.59243  FALSE
## 4:  4  99.93058 103.4315 96.10691  97.22223  FALSE
## 5:  5  99.99785 100.6041 94.12958  95.97975  FALSE
## 6:  6 100.03235 102.1770 94.65729  96.49873  FALSE
```

We can calculate the realized probability of `signal == TRUE`:

```
res_table[, sum(signal) /.N]
## [1] 0.0881
```

What if the problem gets more practical and requires us to run millions of times? In this case, some researchers may turn to programming languages implemented with much higher performance such as C and C++, which are extremely efficient and flexible. They are great tools in implementing algorithms but require more effort to deal with the compiler, linker, and data input/output.

Note that each iteration in the preceding simulation is completely independent of each other, so it is better accomplished by parallel computing.

Since different operating systems have different implementations of process and threading model, some features that are available for Linux and MacOS are not available for Windows. Thus, performing parallel computing on Windows can be a bit more verbose.

Using parallel computing on Windows

On Windows, we need to create a local cluster of multiple R sessions to run parallel computing:

```
library(parallel)
cl <- makeCluster(detectCores())
```

The detectCores() function returns the number of cores your computer is equipped with. Creating a cluster of more than that number of nodes is allowed but usually does no good because your computer cannot perform more tasks than that simultaneously.

Then, we can call parLapply(), the parallel version of lapply():

```
system.time(res <- parLapply(cl, 1:10000, simulate))
##     user   system  elapsed
##    0.024   0.008    3.772
```

Note that the time consumed is reduced to more than half of the original time. Now, we no longer need the cluster. We can call stopCluster() to kill the R sessions just created:

```
stopCluster(cl)
```

When we call parLapply(), it automatically schedules the task for each cluster node. More specifically, all cluster nodes run simulate() with one of 1:10000 exclusively at the same time so that the computation is done in parallel. Finally, all results are collected so that we get a list just like the results from lapply():

```
length(res)
## [1] 10000
res_table <- rbindlist(res)
res_table[, sum(signal) /.N]
## [1] 0.0889
```

The parallel code looks simple because `simulate()` is self-contained and does not rely on user-defined external variables or datasets. If we run a function in parallel that refers to a variable in the master session (the current session that creates the cluster), it will not find the variable:

```
cl <- makeCluster(detectCores())
n <- 1
parLapply(cl, 1:3, function(x) x + n)
## Error in checkForRemoteErrors(val): 3 nodes produced errors; first
error: object 'n' not found
stopCluster(cl)
```

All nodes fail because each of them starts as a fresh R session with no user variables defined. To let the cluster nodes get the value of the variable they need, we have to export them to all nodes.

The following example demonstrates how this works. Suppose we have a data frame of numbers. We want to take random samples from the data frame:

```
n <- 100
data <- data.frame(id = 1:n,  x = rnorm(n), y = rnorm(n))

take_sample <- function(n) {
  data[sample(seq_len(nrow(data)),
    size = n, replace = FALSE), ]
}
```

If we perform the sampling in parallel, all nodes must share the data frame and the function. To do this, we can use `clusterEvalQ()` to evaluate an expression on each cluster node. First, we will make a cluster just as we did earlier:

```
cl <- makeCluster(detectCores())
```

The `Sys.getpid()` function returns the process ID of the current R session. Since there are four nodes in the cluster, each is an R session with a unique process ID. We can call `clusterEvalQ()` with `Sys.getpid()` and see the process ID of each node:

```
clusterEvalQ(cl, Sys.getpid())
## [[1]]
## [1] 20714
##
## [[2]]
## [1] 20723
##
## [[3]]
## [1] 20732
##
```

```
## [[4]]
## [1] 20741
```

To see the variables in the global environment of each node, we can call `ls()`, just like we call in our own working environment:

```
clusterEvalQ(cl, ls())
## [[1]]
## character(0)
##
## [[2]]
## character(0)
##
## [[3]]
## character(0)
##
## [[4]]
## character(0)
```

As we mentioned, all cluster nodes are, by default, initialized with an empty global environment. To export `data` and `take_sample` to each node, we can call `clusterExport()`:

```
clusterExport(cl, c("data", "take_sample"))
clusterEvalQ(cl, ls())
## [[1]]
## [1] "data"        "take_sample"
##
## [[2]]
## [1] "data"        "take_sample"
##
## [[3]]
## [1] "data"        "take_sample"
##
## [[4]]
## [1] "data"        "take_sample"
```

Now, we can see that all nodes have `data` and `take_sample`. Now, we can let each node call `take_sample()`:

```
clusterEvalQ(cl, take_sample(2))
## [[1]]
##    id         x           y
## 88 88 0.6519981  1.43142886
## 80 80 0.7985715 -0.04409101
##
## [[2]]
##    id         x           y
```

```
## 65 65 -0.4705287 -1.0859630
## 35 35  0.6240227 -0.3634574
##
## [[3]]
##    id        x          y
## 75 75 0.3994768 -0.1489621
## 8   8 1.4234844  1.8903637
##
## [[4]]
##    id        x          y
## 77 77 0.4458477  1.420187
## 9   9 0.3943990 -0.196291
```

Alternatively, we can use clusterCall() and <<- to create global variables in each node, while <- only creates local variables in the function:

```
invisible(clusterCall(cl, function() {
  local_var <- 10
  global_var <<- 100
}))
clusterEvalQ(cl, ls())
## [[1]]
## [1] "data"      "global_var"  "take_sample"
##
## [[2]]
## [1] "data"      "global_var"  "take_sample"
##
## [[3]]
## [1] "data"      "global_var"  "take_sample"
##
## [[4]]
## [1] "data"      "global_var"  "take_sample"
```

Note that clusterCall() returns the returned value from each node. In the preceding code, we will use invisible() to suppress the values they return.

Since each cluster node is started in a fresh state, they only load basic packages. To let each node load the given packages, we can also use clusterEvalQ(). The following code lets each node attach the data.table package so that parLapply() can run a function in which data.table functions are used on each node:

```
clusterExport(cl, "simulate")
invisible(clusterEvalQ(cl, {
  library(data.table)
}))
res <- parLapply(cl, 1:3, function(i) {
  res_table <- rbindlist(lapply(1:1000, simulate))
```

```
    res_table[, id := NULL]
    summary(res_table)
})
```

A list of data summary is returned:

```
res
## [[1]]
##      first              high                low
##  Min.   : 99.86   Min.   : 99.95   Min.   : 84.39
##  1st Qu.: 99.97   1st Qu.:101.44   1st Qu.: 94.20
##  Median :100.00   Median :103.32   Median : 96.60
##  Mean   :100.00   Mean   :103.95   Mean   : 96.04
##  3rd Qu.:100.03   3rd Qu.:105.63   3rd Qu.: 98.40
##  Max.   :100.17   Max.   :121.00   Max.   :100.06
##      last             signal
##  Min.   : 84.99   Mode :logical
##  1st Qu.: 96.53   FALSE:911
##  Median : 99.99   TRUE :89
##  Mean   : 99.92   NA's :0
##  3rd Qu.:103.11
##  Max.   :119.66
##
## [[2]]
##      first              high                low
##  Min.   : 99.81   Min.   : 99.86   Min.   : 83.67
##  1st Qu.: 99.96   1st Qu.:101.48   1st Qu.: 94.32
##  Median :100.00   Median :103.14   Median : 96.42
##  Mean   :100.00   Mean   :103.91   Mean   : 96.05
##  3rd Qu.:100.04   3rd Qu.:105.76   3rd Qu.: 98.48
##  Max.   :100.16   Max.   :119.80   Max.   :100.12
##      last             signal
##  Min.   : 85.81   Mode :logical
##  1st Qu.: 96.34   FALSE:914
##  Median : 99.69   TRUE :86
##  Mean   : 99.87   NA's :0
##  3rd Qu.:103.31
##  Max.   :119.39
##
## [[3]]
##      first              high                low
##  Min.   : 99.84   Min.   : 99.88   Min.   : 85.88
##  1st Qu.: 99.97   1st Qu.:101.61   1st Qu.: 94.26
##  Median :100.00   Median :103.42   Median : 96.72
##  Mean   :100.00   Mean   :104.05   Mean   : 96.12
##  3rd Qu.:100.03   3rd Qu.:105.89   3rd Qu.: 98.35
##  Max.   :100.15   Max.   :117.60   Max.   :100.03
##      last             signal
```

```
##   Min.   : 86.05    Mode :logical
##   1st Qu.: 96.70    FALSE:920
##   Median :100.16    TRUE :80
##   Mean   :100.04    NA's :0
##   3rd Qu.:103.24
##   Max.   :114.80
```

When we don't need the cluster any more, we will run the following code to release it:

```
stopCluster(cl)
```

Using parallel computing on Linux and MacOS

Using parallel computing on Linux and MacOS can be much easier than on Windows. Without having to manually create a socket-based cluster, `mclapply()` directly forks the current R session into multiple R sessions, with everything preserved to continue running in parallel and schedule tasks for each child R session:

```
system.time(res <- mclapply(1:10000, simulate,
  mc.cores = detectCores()))
##    user  system elapsed
##   9.732   0.060   3.415
```

Therefore, we don't have to export the variables because they are immediately available in each fork process:

```
mclapply(1:3, take_sample, mc.cores = detectCores())
## [[1]]
##     id          x           y
## 62 62 0.1679572  -0.5948647
##
## [[2]]
##     id          x           y
## 56 56 1.5678983   0.08655707
## 39 39 0.1015022  -1.98006684
##
## [[3]]
##     id           x            y
## 98 98  0.13892696  -0.1672610
## 4   4  0.07533799  -0.6346651
## 76 76 -0.57345242  -0.5234832
```

Also, we can create jobs to be done in parallel with much flexibility. For example, we will create a job that generates 10 random numbers:

```
job1 <- mcparallel(rnorm(10), "job1")
```

As long as the job is created, we can choose to collect the results from the job with `mccollect()`. Then, the function will not return until the job is finished:

```
mccollect(job1)
## $`20772`
##  [1]  1.1295953 -0.6173255  1.2859549 -0.9442054  0.1482608
##  [6]  0.4242623  0.9463755  0.6662561  0.4313663  0.6231939
```

We can also programmatically create a number of jobs to run in parallel. For example, we create 8 jobs, and each sleeps for a random time. Then, `mccollect()` won't return until all jobs are finished sleeping. Since the jobs are run in parallel, the time `mccollect()` takes won't be too long:

```
jobs <- lapply(1:8, function(i) {
  mcparallel({
    t <- rbinom(1, 5, 0.6)
    Sys.sleep(t)
    t
  }, paste0("job", i))
})
system.time(res <- mccollect(jobs))
##    user  system elapsed
##   0.012   0.040   4.852
```

This allows us to customize the task-scheduling mechanism.

Using Rcpp

As we mentioned, parallel computing works when each iteration is independent so that the final results do not rely on the order of execution. However, not all tasks are so ideal like this. Therefore, the use of parallel computing may be undermined. What if we really want the algorithm to run fast and easily interact with R? The answer is by writing the algorithm in C++ via Rcpp (http://www.rcpp.org/).

C++ code usually runs very fast, because it is compiled to native instructions and is thus much closer to hardware level than a scripting language like R. Rcpp is a package that enables us to write C++ code with seamless R and C++ integration. With Rcpp, we can write C++ code in which we can call R functions and take advantage of R data structures. It allows us to write high-performance code and preserve the power of data manipulation in R at the same time.

To use Rcpp, we first need to ensure that the system is prepared for computing native code with the right toolchain. Under Windows, Rtools is needed and can be found at `https://cran.r-project.org/bin/windows/Rtools/`. Under Linux and MacOS, a properly installed C/C++ toolchain is required.

Once the toolchain is properly installed, run the following code to install the package:

```
install.packages("Rcpp")
```

Then, we will create a C++ source file at `code/rcpp-demo.cpp` with the following code:

```cpp
#include <Rcpp.h>
usingnamespace Rcpp;

// [[Rcpp::export]]
NumericVector timesTwo(NumericVector x) {
  return x * 2;
}
```

The preceding code is written in C++. If you are not familiar with C++ syntax, you can quickly pick up the simplest part by going through `http://www.learncpp.com/`. The language design and supported features are much richer and more complex than R. Don't expect to be an expert in a short period of time, but getting started with the basics usually allows you to write simple algorithms.

If you read the preceding code, it looks very different from typical R code. Since C++ is a strong-typed language, we need to specify the types of function arguments and the return type of functions. A function that is commented with `[[Rcpp::export]]` will be captured by Rcpp, and when we source the code in RStudio or use `Rcpp::sourceCpp` directly, these C++ functions will be automatically compiled and ported to our working environment in R.

The preceding C++ function simply takes a numeric vector and returns a new numeric vector with all x elements doubled. Note that the `NumericVector` class is provided by `Rcpp.h` included at the beginning of the source file. In fact, `Rcpp.h` provides the C++ proxy of all commonly used R data structures. Now, we will call `Rcpp::sourceCpp()` to compile and load the source file:

```
Rcpp::sourceCpp("code/rcpp-demo.cpp")
```

The function compiles the source code, links it to necessary shared libraries, and exposes an R function to the environment. The beauty is that all of these are done automatically, which makes it much easier to write algorithms for non-professional C++ developers. Now, we have an R function to call it:

```
timesTwo
## function (x)
## .Primitive(".Call")(<pointer: 0x7f81735528c0>, x)
```

We can see that timeTwo in R does not look like an ordinary function, but performs a native call to the C++ function. The function works with single numeric input:

```
timesTwo(10)
## [1] 20
```

It also works with a multi-element numeric vector:

```
timesTwo(c(1, 2, 3))
## [1] 2 4 6
```

Now, we can use very simple C++ language constructs to reimplement the algo1_for algorithm in C++. Now, we will create a C++ source file at code/rcpp-algo1.cpp with the following code:

```
#include <Rcpp.h>
 using namespace Rcpp;

 // [[Rcpp::export]]
 double algo1_cpp(int n) {
   double res = 0;
   for (double i = 1; i < n; i++) {
     res += 1 / (i * i);
   }
   return res;
 }
```

Note that we don't use any R but C++ data structures in algo1_cpp. When we source the code, Rcpp will handle all the porting for us:

```
Rcpp::sourceCpp("code/rcpp-algo1.cpp")
```

The function works with a single numeric input:

```
algo1_cpp(10)
## [1] 1.539768
```

If we supply a numeric vector, an error will occur:

```
algo1_cpp(c(10, 15))
## Error in eval(expr, envir, enclos): expecting a single value
```

Now, we can do the benchmarking again. This time, we will add `algo1_cpp` to the list of alternative implementations. Here, we will compare the version using a `for` loop in R, the byte-code compiled version using for loop in R, the vectorized version, and the C++ version:

```
n <- 1000
microbenchmark(
  algo1_for(n),
  algo1_cmp(n),
  algo1_vec(n),
  algo1_cpp(n))
## Unit: microseconds
##           expr      min       lq      mean    median        uq
##   algo1_for(n) 493.312 507.7220 533.41701 513.8250 531.5470
##   algo1_cmp(n)  57.262  59.1375  61.44986  60.0160  61.1190
##   algo1_vec(n)  10.091  10.8340  11.60346  11.3045  11.7735
##   algo1_cpp(n)   5.493   6.0765   7.13512   6.6210   7.2775
##       max neval cld
##   789.799   100   c
##   105.260   100   b
##    23.007   100  a
##    22.131   100  a
```

It is amazing that the C++ version is even faster than the vectorized version. Although the functions used by the vectorized version are primitive functions and are already very fast, they still have some overhead due to method dispatching and argument checking. Our C++ version is specialized to the task, so it can be slightly faster than the vectorized version.

Another example is the C++ implementation of `diff_for()` as the following code shows:

```
#include <Rcpp.h>
usingnamespace Rcpp;

// [[Rcpp::export]]
NumericVector diff_cpp(NumericVector x) {
  NumericVector res(x.size() - 1);
  for (int i = 0; i < x.size() - 1; i++) {
    res[i] = x[i + 1] - x[i];
  }
  return res;
}
```

In the preceding C++ code, `diff_cpp()` takes a numeric vector and returns a numeric vector. The function simply creates a new vector, and calculates and stores the differences between the consecutive two elements in x iteratively. Then, we will source the code file:

```
Rcpp::sourceCpp("code/rcpp-diff.cpp")
```

It is easy to verify whether the function works as supposed:

```
diff_cpp(c(1, 2, 3, 5))
## [1] 1 1 2
```

Then, we will do the benchmarking again with five different calls: the version using a for loop in R (`diff_for`), the byte-code compiled version (`diff_cmp`), the vectorized version (`diff`), the vectorized version without method dispatch (`diff.default`), and our C++ version (`diff_cpp`):

```
x <- rnorm(1000)
microbenchmark(
    diff_for(x),
    diff_cmp(x),
    diff(x),
    diff.default(x),
    diff_cpp(x))
## Unit: microseconds
##              expr      min         lq       mean     median
##       diff_for(x) 1055.177 1113.8875 1297.82994 1282.9675
##       diff_cmp(x)   75.511   78.4210   88.46485   88.2135
##           diff(x)   12.899   14.9340   20.64854   18.3975
##   diff.default(x)   10.750   11.6865   13.90939   12.6400
##       diff_cpp(x)    5.314    6.4260    8.62119    7.5330
##          uq        max neval cld
##    1400.8250 2930.690    100   c
##      90.3485  179.620    100  b
##      24.2335   65.172    100 a
##      15.3810   25.455    100 a
##       8.9570   54.455    100 a
```

It appears that the C++ version is the fastest.

In recent years, a rapidly growing number of R packages have used Rcpp to either boost performance or directly link to popular libraries that provide high-performance algorithms. For example, RcppArmadillo and RcppEigen provide high-performance linear algebra algorithms, RcppDE provides fast implementations for global optimization by differential evolution in C++, and so on.

To know more about Rcpp and related packages, visit its official website (http://www.rcpp.org/). I also recommend the book*Seamless R and C++ Integration with Rcpp* by Rcpp's author Dirk Eddelbuettel at http://www.rcpp.org/book/.

OpenMP

As we mentioned in the section on parallel computing, an R session runs in a single thread. However, in Rcpp code, we can use multithreading to boost the performance. One multithreading technique is OpenMP (http://openmp.org), which is supported by most modern C++ compilers (see http://openmp.org/wp/openmp-compilers/).

Several articles discuss and demonstrate the use of OpenMP with Rcpp at http://gallery.rcpp.org/tags/openmp/. Here, we will provide a simple example. We will create a C++ source file with the following code at code/rcpp-diff-openmp.cpp:

```cpp
// [[Rcpp::plugins(openmp)]]
#include <omp.h>
#include <Rcpp.h>
usingnamespace Rcpp;

// [[Rcpp::export]]
NumericVector diff_cpp_omp(NumericVector x) {
  omp_set_num_threads(3);
  NumericVector res(x.size() - 1);
#pragma omp parallel for
  for (int i = 0; i < x.size() - 1; i++) {
    res[i] = x[i + 1] - x[i];
  }
  return res;
}
```

Note that Rcpp will recognize the comment in the first line and add necessary options to the compiler so that OpenMP is enabled. To use OpenMP, we need to include omp.h. Then, we can set the number of threads by calling omp_set_num_threads(n) and use #pragma omp parallel for to indicate that the following for loop should be parallelized. If the number of threads is set to 1, then the code also runs normally.

We will source the C++ code file:

```
Rcpp::sourceCpp("code/rcpp-diff-openmp.cpp")
```

First, let's see whether the function works properly:

```
diff_cpp_omp(c(1, 2, 4, 8))
## [1] 1 2 4
```

Then, we will start benchmarking with a 1000-number input vector:

```
x <- rnorm(1000)
microbenchmark(
    diff_for(x),
    diff_cmp(x),
    diff(x),
    diff.default(x),
    diff_cpp(x),
    diff_cpp_omp(x))
## Unit: microseconds
##               expr       min        lq       mean     median
##        diff_for(x) 1010.367 1097.9015 1275.67358 1236.7620
##        diff_cmp(x)   75.729   78.6645   88.20651   88.9505
##            diff(x)   12.615   16.4200   21.13281   20.5400
##   diff.default(x)   10.555   12.1690   16.07964   14.8210
##        diff_cpp(x)    5.640    6.4825    8.24118    7.5400
##   diff_cpp_omp(x)    3.505    4.4390   26.76233    5.6625
##          uq       max neval cld
## 1393.5430 2839.485    100   c
##   94.3970  186.660    100  b
##   24.4260   43.893    100 a
##   18.4635   72.940    100 a
##    8.6365   50.533    100 a
##   13.9585 1430.605    100 a
```

Unfortunately, even with multi-threading, `diff_cpp_omp()` is slower than its single-threaded C++ implementation. This is because using multithreading has some overhead. If the input is small, the time to initialize multiple threads may take a significant part of the whole computing time. However, if the input is large enough, the advantage of multi-threading will exceed its cost. Here, we will use `100000` numbers as the input vector:

```
x <- rnorm(100000)
microbenchmark(
    diff_for(x),
    diff_cmp(x),
    diff(x),
    diff.default(x),
    diff_cpp(x),
    diff_cpp_omp(x))
## Unit: microseconds
##               expr        min          lq        mean
##        diff_for(x) 112216.936 114617.4975 121631.8135
```

```
##      diff_cmp(x)    7355.241    7440.7105    8800.0184
##          diff(x)     863.672     897.2060    1595.9434
##   diff.default(x)    844.186     877.4030    3451.6377
##      diff_cpp(x)     418.207     429.3125     560.3064
##   diff_cpp_omp(x)    125.572     149.9855     237.5871
##       median           uq            max neval cld
## 115284.377 116165.3140 214787.857    100    c
##   7537.405   8439.9260 102712.582    100   b
##   1029.642   2195.5620   8020.990    100  a
##    931.306   2365.6920  99832.513    100  a
##    436.638    552.5110   2165.091    100  a
##    166.834    190.7765   1983.299    100  a
```

The cost of creating multiple threads is small relative to the performance boost of using them. As a result, the version powered by OpenMP is even faster than the simple C++ version.

In fact, the feature set of OpenMP is much richer than we have demonstrated. For more details, read the official documentation. For more examples, I recommend *Guide into OpenMP: Easy multithreading programming for C++* by Joel Yliluoma at http://bisqwit.iki.fi/story/howto/openmp/.

RcppParallel

Another approach to taking advantage of multi-threading with Rcpp is RcppParallel (http://rcppcore.github.io/RcppParallel/). This package includes Intel TBB (https://www.threadingbuildingblocks.org/) and TinyThread (http://tinythreadpp.bitsnbites.eu/). It provides thread-safe vector and matrix wrapper data structures as well as high-level parallel functions.

To perform multi-threading parallel computing with RcppParallel, we need to implement a Worker to handle how a slice of input is transformed to the output. Then, RcppParallel will take care of the rest of the work such as multithreading task scheduling.

Here's a short demo. We will create a C++ source file with the following code at code/rcpp-parallel.cpp. Note that we need to declare to Rcpp that it depends on RcppParallel and uses C++ 11 for using lambda function.

Here, we will implement a `Worker` called `Transformer` that transforms each element x of a matrix to `1 / (1 + x ^ 2)`. Then, in `par_transform`, we will create an instance of `Transformer` and call `parallelFor` with it so that it automatically takes advantage of multithreading:

```
// [[Rcpp::plugins(cpp11)]]
// [[Rcpp::depends(RcppParallel)]]
#include <Rcpp.h>
#include <RcppParallel.h>

using namespace Rcpp;
using namespace RcppParallel;

struct Transformer : public Worker {
  const RMatrix<double> input;
  RMatrix<double> output;
  Transformer(const NumericMatrix input, NumericMatrix output)
    : input(input), output(output) {}
  void operator()(std::size_t begin, std::size_t end) {
    std::transform(input.begin() + begin, input.begin() + end,
      output.begin() + begin, [](double x) {
        return 1 / (1 + x * x);
      });
  }
};

// [[Rcpp::export]]
NumericMatrix par_transform (NumericMatrix x) {
  NumericMatrix output(x.nrow(), x.ncol());
  Transformer transformer(x, output);
  parallelFor(0, x.length(), transformer);
  return output;
}
```

We can easily verify that the function works with a small matrix:

```
mat <- matrix(1:12, nrow = 3)
mat
##      [,1] [,2] [,3] [,4]
## [1,]    1    4    7   10
## [2,]    2    5    8   11
## [3,]    3    6    9   12
par_transform(mat)
##      [,1]       [,2]       [,3]        [,4]
## [1,]  0.5 0.05882353 0.02000000 0.009900990
## [2,]  0.2 0.03846154 0.01538462 0.008196721
## [3,]  0.1 0.02702703 0.01219512 0.006896552
all.equal(par_transform(mat), 1 / (1 + mat ^ 2))
```

```
## [1] TRUE
```

It produces exactly the same results as the vectorized R expression. Now, we can take a look at its performance when the input matrix is very large:

```
mat <- matrix(rnorm(1000 * 2000), nrow = 1000)
microbenchmark(1 /(1 + mat ^ 2), par_transform(mat))
## Unit: milliseconds
##                   expr      min        lq      mean    median
##        1/(1 + mat ^ 2) 14.50142 15.588700 19.78580 15.768088
##     par_transform(mat)  7.73545  8.654449 13.88619  9.277798
##          uq       max neval cld
##   18.79235 127.1912    100    b
##   11.65137 110.6236    100    a
```

It appears that the multi-threading version is almost 1x faster than the vectorized version.

RcppParallel is more powerful than we have demonstrated. For more detailed introduction and examples, visit http://rcppcore.github.io/RcppParallel.

Summary

In this chapter, you learned when performance may or may not matter, how to measure the performance of R code, how to use profiling tools to identify the slowest part of code, and why such code can be slow. Then, we introduced the most important ways to boost the code performance: using built-in functions if possible, taking advantage of vectorization, using the byte-code compiler, using parallel computing, writing code in C++ via Rcpp, and using multi-threading techniques in C++. High-performance computing is quite an advanced topic, and there's still a lot more to learn if you want to apply it in practice. This chapter demonstrates that using R does not always mean slow code. Instead, we can achieve high performance if we want.

In the next chapter, we will introduce another useful topic: web scraping. To scrape data from webpages, we need to understand how web pages are structured and how to extract data from their source code. You will learn the basic idea and representation of HTML, XML, and CSS, and how to analyze a target webpage so that we can correctly extract the information we want from webpages.

14
Web Scraping

R provides a platform with easy access to statistical computing and data analysis. Given a data set, it is handy to perform data transformation and apply analytic models and numeric methods with either flexible data structures or high performance, as discussed in previous chapters.

However, the input data set is not always as immediately available as tables provided by well-organized commercial databases. Sometimes, we have to collect data by ourselves. Web content is an important source of data for a wide range of research fields. To collect (scrape or harvest) data from the Internet, we need appropriate techniques and tools. In this chapter, we'll introduce the basic knowledge and tools of web scraping, including:

- Looking inside web pages
- Learning CSS and XPath selector
- Analyzing HTML code and extracting data

Looking inside web pages

Web pages are made to present information. The following screenshot shows a simple web page located at `data/simple-page.html` that has a heading and a paragraph:

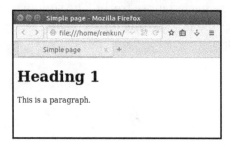

All modern web browsers support such web pages. If you open `data/simple-page.html` with any text editor, it will show the code behind the web page as follows:

```
<!DOCTYPE html>
<html>
<head>
  <title>Simple page</title>
</head>
<body>
  <h1>Heading 1</h1>
  <p>This is a paragraph.</p>
</body>
</html>
```

The preceding code is an example of HTML (Hyper Text Markup Language). It is the most widely used language on the Internet. Different from any programming language to be finally translated into computer instructions, HTML describes the layout and content of a web page, and web browsers are designed to render the code into a web page according to web standards.

Modern web browsers use the first line of HTML to determine which standard is used to render the web page. In this case, the latest standard, HTML 5, is used.

If you read through the code, you'll probably notice that HTML is nothing but a nested structure of tags such as `<html>`, `<title>`, `<body>`, `<h1>`, and `<p>`. Each tag begins with `<tag>` and is closed with `</tag>`.

In fact, these tags are not arbitrarily named, nor are they allowed to contain other arbitrary tags. Each has a specific meaning to the web browser and is only allowed to contain a subset of tags, or even none.

The `<html>` tag is the root element of all HTML. It most commonly contains `<head>` and `<body>`. The `<head>` tag usually contains `<title>` to show on the title bar and browser tabs and other metadata of the web page, while `<body>` plays the main role in determining the layout and contents of the web page.

In the `<body>` tag, tags can be nested more freely. The simple page only contains a level-1 heading (`<h1>`) and a paragraph (`<p>`) while the following web page contains a table with two rows and two columns:

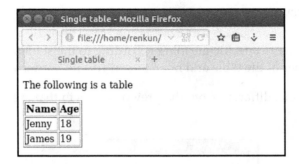

The HTML code behind the web page is stored in `data/single-table.html`:

```
<!DOCTYPE html>
<html>
<head>
  <title>Single table</title>
</head>
<body>
  <p>The following is a table</p>
  <table id="table1" border="1">
    <thead>
      <tr>
        <th>Name</th>
        <th>Age</th>
      </tr>
    </thead>
    <tbody>
      <tr>
        <td>Jenny</td>
        <td>18</td>
      </tr>
      <tr>
        <td>James</td>
        <td>19</td>
      </tr>
    </tbody>
  </table>
</body>
</html>
```

Note that a `<table>` tag is structured row by row: `<tr>` represents a table row, `<th>` a table header cell, and `<td>` a table cell.

Also notice that an HTML element such as `<table>` may have additional attributes in the form of `<table attr1="value1" attr2="value2">`. The attributes are not arbitrarily defined. Instead, each has a specific meaning according to the standard. In the preceding code, `id` is the identifier of the table and `border` controls its border width.

The following page looks different from the previous ones in that it shows some styling of contents:

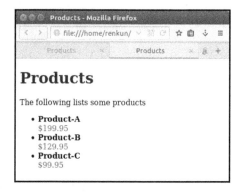

If you take a look at its source code at `data/simple-products.html`, you'll find some new tags such as `<div>` (a section), `<ul>` (unrecorded list), `<li>` (list item), and `<span>` (also a section used for applying styles); additionally, many HTML elements have an attribute called `style` to define their appearance:

```
<!DOCTYPE html>
<html>
<head>
  <title>Products</title>
</head>
<body>
  <h1 style="color: blue;">Products</h1>
  <p>The following lists some products</p>
  <div id="table1" style="width: 50px;">
    <ul>
      <li>
        <span style="font-weight: bold;">Product-A</span>
        <span style="color: green;">$199.95</span>
      </li>
      <li>
        <span style="font-weight: bold;">Product-B</span>
        <span style="color: green;">$129.95</span>
      </li>
      <li>
        <span style="font-weight: bold;">Product-C</span>
```

```
      <span style="color: green;">$99.95</span>
    </li>
  </ul>
  </div>
</body>
</html>
```

Values in style is written in the form of `property1: value1; property2: value2;`.
However, the styles of the list items are a bit redundant because all product names share the same style and this is also true for all product prices. The following HTML at `data/products.html` uses CSS (**Cascading Style Sheets**) instead to avoid redundant styling definitions:

```
<!DOCTYPE html>
<html>
<head>
  <title>Products</title>
  <style>
    h1 {
      color: darkblue;
    }
    .product-list {
      width: 50px;
    }
    .product-list li.selected .name {
      color: 1px blue solid;
    }
    .product-list .name {
      font-weight: bold;
    }
    .product-list .price {
      color: green;
    }
  </style>
</head>
<body>
  <h1>Products</h1>
  <p>The following lists some products</p>
  <div id="table1" class="product-list">
    <ul>
      <li>
        <span class="name">Product-A</span>
        <span class="price">$199.95</span>
      </li>
      <li class="selected">
        <span class="name">Product-B</span>
        <span class="price">$129.95</span>
```

```
      </li>
      <li>
        <span class="name">Product-C</span>
        <span class="price">$99.95</span>
      </li>
    </ul>
  </div>
</body>
</html>
```

Note that we add `<style>` in `<head>` to declare a global stylesheet in the web page. We also switch `style` to `class` for content elements (`div`, `li`, and `span`) to use those pre-defined styles. The syntax of CSS is briefly introduced in the following code.

Match all `<h1>` elements:

```
h1 {
  color: darkblue;
}
```

Match all elements with the `product-list` class:

```
.product-list {
  width: 50px;
}
```

Match all elements with the `product-list` class, and then match all nested elements with the `name` class:

```
.product-list .name {
  font-weight: bold;
}
```

Match all elements with the `product-list` class, then match all nested `<li>` elements with the `selected` class, and finally match all nested elements with the `name` class:

```
.product-list li.selected .name {
  color: 1px blue solid;
}
```

Note that simply using `style` cannot achieve this. The following screenshot shows the rendered web page:

Each CSS entry consists of a CSS selector (for example, `.product-list`) to match HTML elements and the styles (for example, `color: red;`) to apply. CSS selectors are not only used to apply styling, but are also commonly used to extract contents from web pages so the HTML elements of interest are properly matched. This is an underlying technique behind web scraping.

CSS is much richer than demonstrated in the preceding code. For web scraping, we use the following examples to show the most commonly used CSS selectors:

Syntax	Match
`*`	All elements
`h1, h2, h3`	`<h1>`,`<h2>`,`<h3>`
`#table1`	`<* id="table1">`
`.product-list`	`<* class="product-list">`
`div#container`	`<div id="container">`
`div a`	`<div><a>` and `<div><p><a>`
`div > a`	`<div><a>` but not`<div><p><a>`
`div > a.new`	`<div><a class="new">`
`ul > li:first-child`	First `<li>` in`<ul>`
`ul > li:last-child`	Last `<li>` in`<ul>`
`ul > li:nth-child(3)`	3rd `<li>` in`<ul>`

`p + *`	Next element of \<p\>
`img[title]`	\<img\> with title attribute
`table[border=1]`	\<table border="1"\>

In each level, `tag#id.class[]` can be used with `tag`, `#id.class`, and `[]` optionally. For more information on CSS selectors, visit `https://developer.mozilla.org/en-US/docs/Web/CSS/CSS_Selectors`. To learn more about HTML tags, visit `http://www.w3schools.com/tags/`.

Extracting data from web pages using CSS selectors

In R, the easiest-to-use package for web scraping is `rvest`. Run the following code to install the package from CRAN:

```
install.packages("rvest")
```

First, we load the package and use `read_html()` to read `data/single-table.html` and try to extract the table from the web page:

```
library(rvest)
## Loading required package: xml2
single_table_page <- read_html("data/single-table.html")
single_table_page
## {xml_document}
## <html>
## [1] <head>\n  <title>Single table</title>\n</head>
## [2] <body>\n  <p>The following is a table</p>\n  <table i ...
```

Note that `single_table_page` is a parsed HTML document, which is a nested data structure of HTML nodes.

A typical process for scraping information from such a web page using `rvest` functions is: First, locate the HTML nodes from which we need to extract data. Then, use either the CSS selector or XPath expression to filter the HTML nodes so that the nodes we need are selected and those we don't need are omitted. Finally, use proper selectors with `html_nodes()` to take a subset of nodes, `html_attrs()` to extract attributes, and `html_text()` to extract text from the parsed web page.

The package also provides simple functions that directly extract data from a web page and return a data frame. For example, to extract all <table> elements from it, we directly call html_table():

```
html_table(single_table_page)
## [[1]]
##     Name Age
## 1  Jenny  18
## 2  James  19
```

To extract the first <table> element, we use html_node() to select the first node with the CSS selector table and then use html_table() with the node to get a data frame:

```
html_table(html_node(single_table_page, "table"))
##     Name Age
## 1  Jenny  18
## 2  James  19
```

A more natural way to do this is to use pipelines, just like using %>% with dplyr functions introduced in Chapter 12, *Data Manipulation*. Recall that %>% basically evaluates x %>% f(...) as f(x, ...) so that a nested call can be unnested and become much more readable. The preceding code can be rewritten as the following using %>%:

```
single_table_page %>%
  html_node("table") %>%
  html_table()
##     Name Age
## 1  Jenny  18
## 2  James  19
```

Now we read data/products.html and use html_nodes() to match the <span class="name"> nodes:

```
products_page <- read_html("data/products.html")
products_page %>%
  html_nodes(".product-list li .name")
## {xml_nodeset (3)}
## [1] <span class="name">Product-A</span>
## [2] <span class="name">Product-B</span>
## [3] <span class="name">Product-C</span>
```

Note that the nodes we want to select are of the name class in <li> nodes of a node of the product-list class, therefore we can use .product-list li.name to select all such nodes. Go through the CSS table if you feel you are not familiar with the notation.

To extract the contents from the selected nodes, we use `html_text()`, which returns a character vector:

```
products_page %>%
    html_nodes(".product-list li .name") %>%
    html_text()
## [1] "Product-A" "Product-B" "Product-C"
```

Similarly, the following code extracts the product prices:

```
products_page %>%
    html_nodes(".product-list li .price") %>%
    html_text()
## [1] "$199.95" "$129.95" "$99.95"
```

In the preceding code, `html_nodes()` returns a collection of HTML nodes while `html_text()` is smart enough to extract the inner text from each HTML node and returns a character vector.

Note that these prices are still in their raw format represented by a string rather than number. The following code extracts the same data and transforms it into a more useful form:

```
product_items <- products_page %>%
    html_nodes(".product-list li")
products <- data.frame(
    name = product_items %>%
        html_nodes(".name") %>%
        html_text(),
    price = product_items %>%
        html_nodes(".price") %>%
        html_text() %>%
        gsub("$", "", ., fixed = TRUE) %>%
        as.numeric(),
    stringsAsFactors = FALSE
)
products
##         name   price
## 1 Product-A 199.95
## 2 Product-B 129.95
## 3 Product-C  99.95
```

Note that the intermediate results of selected nodes can be stored as a variable and used repeatedly. Then the subsequent `html_nodes()` and `html_node()` calls only match the inner nodes.

Since product prices should be numeric values, we use `gsub()` to remove `$` from the raw prices and convert the results to a numeric vector. The call of `gsub()` in the pipeline is somehow special because the previous result (represented by `.`) should be put to the third argument instead of the first one.

In this case, `.product-list li .name` can be reduced to `.name` and the same also applies to `.product-list li .price`. In practice, however, a CSS class may be used extensively and such a general selector may match too many elements that are not desired. Therefore, it is better to use a more descriptive and sufficiently strict selector to match the interested nodes.

Learning XPath selectors

In the previous section, we learned about CSS selectors and how to use them as well as functions provided by the `rvest` package to extract contents from web pages.

CSS selectors are powerful enough to serve most needs of HTML node matching. However, sometimes an even more powerful technique is required to select nodes that meet more special conditions.

Take a look at the following web page a bit more complex than `data/products.html`:

This web page is stored as a standalone HTML file at `data/new-products.html`. The full source code is long we will only show the `<body>`. here. Please go through the source code to get an impression of its structure:

```html
<body>
  <h1>New Products</h1>
  <p>The following is a list of products</p>
  <div id="list" class="product-list">
    <ul>
      <li>
        <span class="name">Product-A</span>
        <span class="price">$199.95</span>
        <div class="info bordered">
          <p>Description for Product-A</p>
          <ul>
            <li><span class="info-key">Quality</span> <span class="info-value">Good</span></li>
            <li><span class="info-key">Duration</span> <span class="info-value">5</span><span class="unit">years</span></li>
          </ul>
        </div>
      </li>
      <li class="selected">
        <span class="name">Product-B</span>
        <span class="price">$129.95</span>
        <div class="info">
          <p>Description for Product-B</p>
          <ul>
            <li><span class="info-key">Quality</span> <span class="info-value">Medium</span></li>
            <li><span class="info-key">Duration</span> <span class="info-value">2</span><span class="unit">years</span></li>
          </ul>
        </div>
      </li>
      <li>
        <span class="name">Product-C</span>
        <span class="price">$99.95</span>
        <div class="info">
          <p>Description for Product-C</p>
          <ul>
            <li><span class="info-key">Quality</span> <span class="info-value">Good</span></li>
            <li><span class="info-key">Duration</span> <span class="info-value">4</span><span class="unit">years</span></li>
          </ul>
        </div>
      </li>
```

```
      </ul>
    </div>
    <p>All products are available for sale!</p>
  </body>
```

The source code of the web page contains a stylesheet and a product list of detailed information. Each product has a description and more properties to show. In the following code, we load the web page as we did in the previous examples:

```
page <- read_html("data/new-products.html")
```

The structure of the HTML code is simple and clear. Before digging into XPath, we need to know a little about XML. Well-written and well-organized HTML documents can be basically regarded as a specialization of **XML (eXtensive Markup Language)** documents. Different from HTML, XML allows arbitrary tags and attributes. The following is a simple XML document:

```
<?xml version="1.0"?>
<root>
  <product id="1">
    <name>Product-A<name>
    <price>$199.95</price>
  </product>
  <product id="2">
    <name>Product-B</name>
    <price>$129.95</price>
  </product>
</root>
```

XPath is a technique designed for extracting data from XML documents. In this section, we compare XPath expressions with CSS selectors and see how they can be useful to extract data from web pages.

The html_node() and html_nodes() support XPath expressions via the xpath= argument. The following table shows some important comparisons between CSS selectors and equivalent XPath expressions:

CSS	XPath	Match
li > *	//li/*	All children of <li>
li[attr]	//li[@attr]	All <li> with attr attribute
li[attr=value]	//li[@attr='value']	<li attr="value">
li#item	//li[@id='item']	<li id="item">

li.info	//li[contains(@class,'info')]	<li class="info">
li:first-child	//li[1]	First <li>
li:last-child	//li[last()]	Last <li>
li:nth-child(n)	//li[n]	n th<li>
(N/A)	//p[a]	All <p> with a child <a>
(N/A)	//p[position() <= 5]	The first five <p> nodes
(N/A)	//p[last()-2]	The last third last <p>
(N/A)	//li[value>0.5]	All <li> with child <value> whose value > 0.5

Note that CSS selectors usually match nodes at all sub-levels. In XPath, // tag and / tag are defined to match nodes differently. More specifically, // tag refers to <tag> nodes at all sub-levels while / tag only refers to <tag> nodes at the first sub-level.

To demonstrate the usage, the following are some examples:

Select all <p> nodes:

```
page %>% html_nodes(xpath = "//p")
## {xml_nodeset (5)}
## [1] <p>The following is a list of products</p>
## [2] <p>Description for Product-A</p>
## [3] <p>Description for Product-B</p>
## [4] <p>Description for Product-C</p>
## [5] <p>All products are available for sale!</p>
```

Select all <li> with the class attribute:

```
page %>% html_nodes(xpath = "//li[@class]")
## {xml_nodeset (1)}
## [1] <li class="selected">\n          <span class="name">Pro ...
```

Select all <li> as children of <div id="list"><ul>:

```
page %>% html_nodes(xpath = "//div[@id='list']/ul/li")
## {xml_nodeset (3)}
## [1] <li>\n          <span class="name">Product-A</span>\n   ...
## [2] <li class="selected">\n          <span class="name">Pro ...
## [3] <li>\n          <span class="name">Product-C</span>\n   ...
```

Select all `<span class="name">` as children of `<li>` inside `<div id="list">`:

```
page %>% html_nodes(xpath = "//div[@id='list']//li/span[@class='name']")
## {xml_nodeset (3)}
## [1] <span class="name">Product-A</span>
## [2] <span class="name">Product-B</span>
## [3] <span class="name">Product-C</span>
```

Select all `<span class="name">` as children in `<li class="selected">`:

```
page %>%
  html_nodes(xpath = "//li[@class='selected']/span[@class='name']")
## {xml_nodeset (1)}
## [1] <span class="name">Product-B</span>
```

All the preceding examples can be achieved with equivalent CSS selectors. The following examples, however, are not possible with CSS selectors.

Select all `<div>` with a child `<p>`:

```
page %>% html_nodes(xpath = "//div[p]")
## {xml_nodeset (3)}
## [1] <div class="info bordered">\n          <p>Description ...
## [2] <div class="info">\n          <p>Description for Prod ...
## [3] <div class="info">\n          <p>Description for Prod ...
```

Select all `<span class="info-value">Good</span>`:

```
page %>%
  html_nodes(xpath = "//span[@class='info-value' and text()='Good']")
## {xml_nodeset (2)}
## [1] <span class="info-value">Good</span>
## [2] <span class="info-value">Good</span>
```

Select all product names with good quality:

```
page %>%
  html_nodes(xpath = "//li[div/ul/li[1]/span[@class='info-value' and
text()='Good']]/span[@class='name']")
## {xml_nodeset (2)}
## [1] <span class="name">Product-A</span>
## [2] <span class="name">Product-C</span>
```

Select all product names with a duration greater than three years:

```
page %>%
  html_nodes(xpath = "//li[div/ul/li[2]/span[@class='info-value' and
text()>3]]/span[@class='name']")
## {xml_nodeset (2)}
## [1] <span class="name">Product-A</span>
## [2] <span class="name">Product-C</span>
```

XPath is very flexible and can be a powerful tool to match nodes in web pages. To learn more, visit
http://www.w3schools.com/xsl/xpath_syntax.aspac.

Analysing HTML code and extracting data

In the previous sections, we learned the basics of HTML, CSS, and XPath. To scrape real-world web pages, the problem now becomesa question of writing the proper CSS or XPath selectors. In this section, we introduce some simple ways to figure out working selectors.

Suppose we want to scrape all available R packages at
https://cran.rstudio.com/web/packages/available_packages_by_name.html. The web page looks simple. To figure out the selector expression, right-click on the table and select **Inspect Element** in the context menu, which should be available in most modern web browsers:

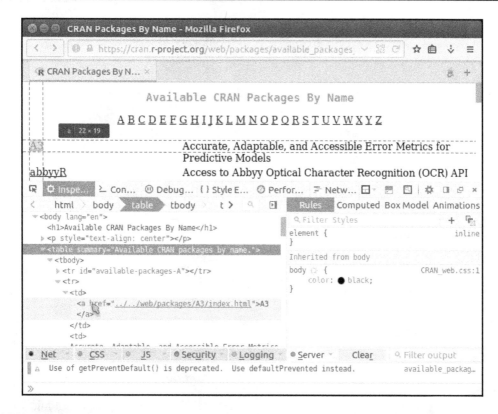

Then the inspector panel shows up and we can see the underlying HTML of the web page. In Firefox and Chrome, the selected node is highlighted so it can be located more easily:

The HTML contains a unique `<table>` so we can directly use `table` to select it and use `html_table()` to extract it out as a data frame:

```
page <-
read_html("https://cran.rstudio.com/web/packages/available_packages_by_name
.html")
pkg_table <- page %>%
  html_node("table") %>%
  html_table(fill = TRUE)
head(pkg_table, 5)
##              X1
## 1
## 2             A3
## 3        abbyyR
## 4           abc
## 5 ABCanalysis
##
X2
## 1
<NA>
## 2 Accurate, Adaptable, and Accessible Error Metrics for
Predictive\nModels
## 3                  Access to Abbyy Optical Character Recognition (OCR)
API
## 4                        Tools for Approximate Bayesian Computation
(ABC)
## 5                                              Computed ABC
Analysis
```

Note that the original table has no headers. The resulted data frame uses default headers instead and the first row is empty. The following code is written to fix these problems:

```
pkg_table <- pkg_table[complete.cases(pkg_table), ]
colnames(pkg_table) <- c("name", "title")
head(pkg_table, 3)
##      name
## 2      A3
## 3 abbyyR
## 4     abc
##
title
## 2 Accurate, Adaptable, and Accessible Error Metrics for
Predictive\nModels
## 3                  Access to Abbyy Optical Character Recognition (OCR)
API
## 4                        Tools for Approximate Bayesian Computation
(ABC)
```

The next example is to extract the latest stock price of MSFT at `http://finance.yahoo.com` `/quote/MSFT`. Using the element inspector, we find that the price is contained by a `<span>` with very long classes that are generated by the program:

Looking several levels up, we can find a path, `div#quote-header-info > section > span`, to navigate to this very node. Therefore, we can use this CSS selector to find and extract the stock price:

```
page <- read_html("https://finance.yahoo.com/quote/MSFT")
page %>%
  html_node("div#quote-header-info > section > span") %>%
  html_text() %>%
  as.numeric()
## [1] 56.68
```

On the right side of the web page, there is a table of corporate key statistics:

Key Statistics >	
Market Cap	440.22B
P/E Ratio (ttm)	26.85
Diluted EPS	N/A
Beta	1.05
Earnings Date	N/A
Dividend & Yield	1.44 (2.54%)
Ex-Dividend Date	N/A
1y Target Est	N/A

Before extracting it out, we again inspect the table and its enclosing nodes, and try to find a selector that navigates to this table:

It is obvious that the `<table>` of interest is enclosed by a `<div id="key-statistics"`. Thus we can directly use `#key-statistics table` to match the table node and turn it into a data frame:

```
page %>%
  html_node("#key-statistics table") %>%
  html_table()
##                  X1        X2
## 1         Market Cap   442.56B
## 2      P/E Ratio (ttm)    26.99
## 3        Diluted EPS      N/A
```

```
## 4              Beta           1.05
## 5      Earnings Date           N/A
## 6 Dividend & Yield 1.44 (2.56%)
## 7 Ex-Dividend Date            N/A
## 8      1y Target Est          N/A
```

With similar techniques, we can create a function that returns the company name and price given a stock ticker symbol (for example, MSFT):

```
get_price <- function(symbol) {
  page <- read_html(sprintf("https://finance.yahoo.com/quote/%s", symbol))
  list(symbol = symbol,
    company = page %>%
      html_node("div#quote-header-info > div:nth-child(1) > h6") %>%
      html_text(),
    price = page %>%
      html_node("div#quote-header-info > section > span:nth-child(1)") %>%
      html_text() %>%
      as.numeric())
}
```

The CSS selectors are restrictive enough to navigate to the right HTML nodes. To test this function, we run the following code:

```
get_price("AAPL")
## $symbol
## [1] "AAPL"
##
## $company
## [1] "Apple Inc."
##
## $price
## [1] 104.19
```

Another example is scraping top R questions at
`http://stackoverflow.com/questions/tagged/r?sort=votes`, shown as follows:

With a similar method, it is easy to find out that the question list is contained by a container whose `id` is `questions`. Therefore, we can load the page and select and store the question container with `#questions`:

```
page <-
read_html("https://stackoverflow.com/questions/tagged/r?sort=votes&pageSize
=5")
questions <- page %>%
  html_node("#questions")
```

To extract the question titles, we take a closer look at the HTML structure behind the first question:

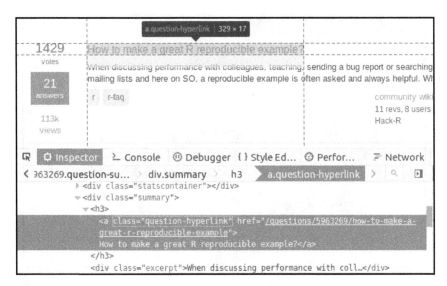

It is easy to find out that each question title is contained in `<div class="summary"><h3>`:

```
questions %>%
  html_nodes(".summary h3") %>%
  html_text()
## [1] "How to make a great R reproducible example?"
## [2] "How to sort a dataframe by column(s)?"
## [3] "R Grouping functions: sapply vs. lapply vs. apply. vs. tapply vs.
by vs. aggregate"
## [4] "How to join (merge) data frames (inner, outer, left, right)?"
## [5] "How can we make xkcd style graphs?"
```

Note that `<a class="question-hyperlink">` also provides an even easier CSS selector that returns the same results:

```
questions %>%
  html_nodes(".question-hyperlink") %>%
  html_text()
```

If we are also interested in the votes of each question, we can again inspect the votes and see how they can be described with a CSS selector:

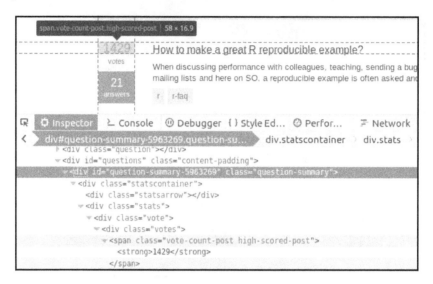

Fortunately, all vote panels share the same structure and it is quite straightforward to find out their pattern. Each question is contained in a `<div>` with the `question-summary` class in which the vote is in a `<span>` with the `.vote-count-post` class:

```
questions %>%
  html_nodes(".question-summary .vote-count-post") %>%
  html_text() %>%
  as.integer()
## [1] 1429  746  622  533  471
```

Similarly, the following code extracts the number of answers:

```
questions %>%
  html_nodes(".question-summary .status strong") %>%
  html_text() %>%
  as.integer()
## [1] 21 15  8 11  7
```

If we go ahead with extracting the tags of each question, it becomes a bit tricky because different questions may have different numbers of tags. In the following code, we first select the tag containers of all questions and extract the tags in each container by iteration.

```
questions %>%
  html_nodes(".question-summary .tags") %>%
  lapply(function(node) {
```

```
    node %>%
      html_nodes(".post-tag") %>%
      html_text()
  }) %>%
  str
## List of 5
##  $ : chr [1:2] "r" "r-faq"
##  $ : chr [1:4] "r" "sorting" "dataframe" "r-faq"
##  $ : chr [1:4] "r" "sapply" "tapply" "r-faq"
##  $ : chr [1:5] "r" "join" "merge" "dataframe" ...
##  $ : chr [1:2] "r" "ggplot2"
```

All the preceding scraping happens in one web page. What if we need to collect data across multiple web pages? Suppose we visit the page of each question (for example, `http://stackoverflow.com/q/5963269/2906900`). Notice that there is an info box on the up-right. We need to extract such info boxes of each question in list:

asked	5 years ago
viewed	113403 times
active	5 days ago

Inspecting tells us `#qinfo` is the key of the info box on each question page. Then we can select all question hyperlinks, extract the URLs of all questions, iterate over them, read each question page, and extract the info box using that key:

```
questions %>%
  html_nodes(".question-hyperlink") %>%
  html_attr("href") %>%
  lapply(function(link) {
    paste0("https://stackoverflow.com", link) %>%
      read_html() %>%
      html_node("#qinfo") %>%
      html_table() %>%
      setNames(c("item", "value"))
  })
## [[1]]
##      item           value
## 1   asked   5 years ago
## 2 viewed 113698 times
## 3 active    7 days ago
##
## [[2]]
##      item           value
## 1   asked   6 years ago
## 2 viewed 640899 times
```

```
## 3 active  2 months ago
##
## [[3]]
##      item        value
## 1  asked   5 years ago
## 2 viewed 221964 times
## 3 active  1 month ago
##
## [[4]]
##      item        value
## 1  asked   6 years ago
## 2 viewed 311376 times
## 3 active   15 days ago
##
## [[5]]
##      item        value
## 1  asked  3 years ago
## 2 viewed  53232 times
## 3 active 4 months ago
```

Besides all these, `rvest` also supports creating an HTTP session to simulate page navigation. To learn more, read the `rvest` documentation. For many scraping tasks, you can also simplify the finding of selectors by using the tools provided by `http://selectorgadget.com/`.

There are more advanced techniques of web scraping such as dealing with AJAX and dynamic web pages using JavaScript, but they are beyond the scope of this chapter. For more usage, read the documentation for the `rvest` package.

Note that `rvest` is largely inspired by Python packages Robobrowser and BeautifulSoup. These packages are more powerful and thus popular in web scraping in some aspects than `rvest`. If the source is complex and large in scale, you might do well to learn to use these Python packages. Go to `https://www.crummy.com/software/BeautifulSoup/` for more information.

Summary

In this chapter, we learned how web pages are written in HTML and stylized by CSS. CSS selectors can be used to match HTML nodes so that their contents can be extracted. Well-written HTML documents can also be queried by XPath Expression, which has more features and is more flexible. Then we learned how to use the element inspector in modern web browsers to figure out a restrictive selector to match the HTML nodes of interest so that the needed data can be extracted from web pages.

In this next chapter, we will learn a series of techniques that boost your productivity, from R Markdown documents, diagrams, to interactive shiny apps. These tools make it much easier to create quality, reproducible, and interactive documents, which are very nice ways to present data, ideas, and prototypes.

15
Boosting Productivity

In the previous chapter, we learned to use R to extract information from web pages. To understand how this works, we learned several languages such as HTML, CSS, and XPath. In fact, R has much more to offer than just a statistical computing environment. The R community provides tools for everything from data collection, to data manipulation, statistical modeling, visualization, and all the way to reporting and presentation.

In this chapter, we will learn about a number of packages that boost our productivity. We'll review several languages we learned throughout this book and get to know another one: markdown. We'll see how R and markdown can be combined to produce powerful dynamic documents. More specifically, we'll:

- Get to know markdown and R Markdown
- Embed tables, charts, diagrams and interactive plots
- Create interactive apps

Writing R Markdown documents

The work of data analysts is more than putting data into models and drawing some conclusions. We usually need to go through a complete workflow from data collecting, to data cleaning, visualization, modeling, and finally writing a report or making a presentation.

In the previous chapters, we improved our productivity by learning the R programming language from different aspects. In this chapter, we will further boost our productivity by focusing on the final step: reporting and presentation. In the following sections, we'll learn a very simple language to write documents: markdown.

Getting to know markdown

Throughout this book, we have already learned a bunch of languages. These languages are very different and may confuse beginners. But if you keep in mind their purposes, it won't be hard to use them together. Before learning markdown, we'll take a quick review of the languages we learned in the previous chapters.

The first is, of course, the R programming language. A programming language is designed for solving problems. R is specially designed and tailored for statistical computing and is empowered by the community to be capable of doing many other things; the example is shown as follows:

```
n <- 100
x <- rnorm(n)
y <- 2 * x + rnorm(n)
m <- lm(y ~ x)
coef(m)
```

In Chapter 12, *Data Manipulation*, we learned SQL to query relational databases. It is designed to be a programming language but is used to express relational database operations such as inserting or updating records and querying data:

```
SELECT name, price
FROM products
WHERE category = 'Food'
ORDER BY price desc
```

The R programming language is executed by the R interpreter and SQL is executed by a database engine. However, we also learned languages that are not designed for execution but to represent data. Perhaps the most commonly used data representation languages in programming world are JSON and XML:

```
[
  {
    "id": 1,
    "name": "Product-A",
    "price": 199.95
  },
  {
    "id": 2,
    "name": "Product-B",
    "price": 129.95
  }
]
```

The specification of JSON defines elements such as value (1, "text"), array ([]), and object ({}), and so on, while XML does not provide type support but allows the usage of attributes and nodes:

```
<?xml version="1.0"?>
<root>
  <product id="1">
    <name>Product-A<name>
    <price>$199.95</price>
  </product>
  <product id="2">
    <name>Product-B</name>
    <price>$129.95</price>
  </product>
</root>
```

In the previous chapter on web scraping, we learned the basics of HTML which is quite similar to XML. Most web pages are written in HTML due to its flexible representation of contents and layouts:

```
<!DOCTYPE html>
<html>
<head>
  <title>Simple page</title>
</head>
<body>
  <h1>Heading 1</h1>
  <p>This is a paragraph.</p>
</body>
</html>
```

In this chapter, we'll learn markdown, a lightweight markup language with a syntax designed for plain text formatting and which can be converted to many other document formats. After getting familiar with markdown, we'll go further with R Markdown, which is designed for dynamic documents and is actively supported by RStudio and the rest of the R community. The format is so simple that we can use any plain text editor to write markdown documents.

The following code block shows its syntax:

```
# Heading 1

This is a top level section. This paragraph contains both __bold__ text and
_italic_ text. There are more than one syntax to represent **bold** text
and *italic* text.

## Heading 2

This is a second level section. The following are some bullets.

* Point 1
* Point 2
* Point 3

### Heading 3

This is a third level section. Here are some numbered bullets.

1. hello
2. world

Link: [click here](https://r-project.org)
Image: ![image-title](https://www.r-project.org/Rlogo.png)
Image link: [![image-
title](https://www.r-project.org/Rlogo.png)](https://r-project.org)
```

The syntax is extremely simple: Some characters are devoted to representing different formats. In a plain text editor, we cannot preview the formats as it indicates. But when converted to a HTML document, the texts will be formatted according to the syntax.

The following screenshot shows the preview of a markdown document in Abricotine (`http://abricotine.brrd.fr/`), an open-source markdown editor with live preview:

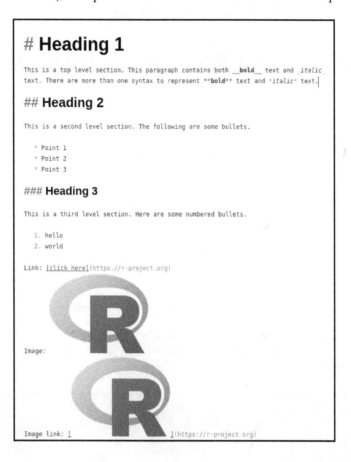

There are also online markdown editors with fantastic features. One of my favorites is StackEdit (`https://stackedit.io/`). You can create a new blank document and copy the above markdown texts into the editor, and then the you can see the instant preview as an HTML page:

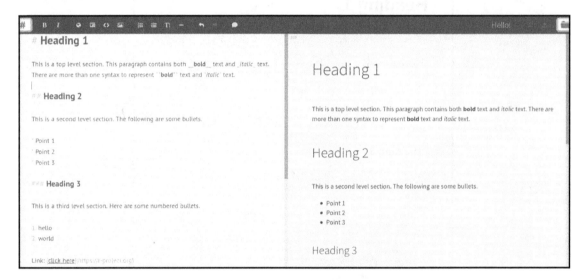

Markdown is widely used in online discussion. The largest open-source repository host, GitHub (`https://github.com`), supports markdown in writing issues as shown in the following screenshot:

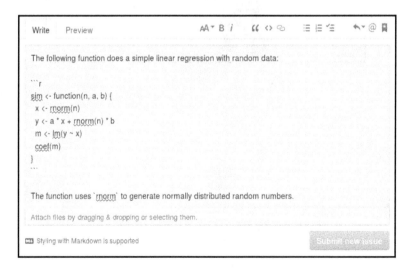

Note that backticks (`` ` ``) are used to create source code symbols and three-backticks (`` ``` ``X) are used to contain a code block written in language X. Code blocks are shown in fixed-width font which is better for presenting program code. Also, we can preview what we have written so far:

Write   Preview

The following function does a simple linear regression with random data:

```
sim <- function(n, a, b) {
  x <- rnorm(n)
  y <- a * x + rnorm(n) * b
  m <- lm(y ~ x)
  coef(m)
}
```

The function uses `rnorm` to generate normally distributed random numbers.

Another special symbol, $, is used to quote math formulas. Single dollar ($) indicates inline math whereas double dollars ($$) displays math (in a new line). The math formula should be written in LaTeX math syntax (https://en.wikibooks.org/wiki/LaTeX/Mathematics).

The following math equation is not that simple: `$$x^2+y^2=z^2$$`, where x,y, and z are integers.

Not all markdown editors support the preview of math formulas. In StackEdit, the preceding markdown is previewed as follows:

The following math equation is not that simple:

$$x^2 + y^2 = z^2$$

where x, y, and z are integers.

In addition, many markdown renderers support the table syntax shown as follows:

```
| Sepal.Length| Sepal.Width| Petal.Length| Petal.Width|Species |
|------------:|-----------:|------------:|-----------:|:-------|
|          5.1|         3.5|          1.4|         0.2|setosa  |
|          4.9|         3.0|          1.4|         0.2|setosa  |
|          4.7|         3.2|          1.3|         0.2|setosa  |
|          4.6|         3.1|          1.5|         0.2|setosa  |
|          5.0|         3.6|          1.4|         0.2|setosa  |
|          5.4|         3.9|          1.7|         0.4|setosa  |
```

In StackEdit, the preceding text table is rendered as follows:

Sepal.Length	Sepal.Width	Petal.Length	Petal.Width	Species
5.1	3.5	1.4	0.2	setosa
4.9	3.0	1.4	0.2	setosa
4.7	3.2	1.3	0.2	setosa
4.6	3.1	1.5	0.2	setosa
5.0	3.6	1.4	0.2	setosa
5.4	3.9	1.7	0.4	setosa

Integrating R into Markdown

Markdown is easy to write and read, and has most necessary features for writing reports such as simple text formatting, embedding images, links, tables, quotes, math formula, and code blocks.

Although writing plain texts in markdown is easy, creating reports with many images and tables is not, especially when the images and tables are produced dynamically by code. R Markdown is the killer app that integrates R into markdown.

More specifically, the markdowns we showed earlier in this chapter are all static documents; that is, they were determined when we wrote them. However, R Markdown is a combination of R code and markdown texts. The output of R code can be text, table, images, and interactive widgets. It can be rendered as an HTML web page, a PDF document, and even a Word document. Visit `http://rmarkdown.rstudio.com/formats.html` to learn more about supported formats.

To create an R Markdown document, click the menu item, as shown in the following screenshot:

If you don't have `rmarkdown` and `knitr` installed, RStudio will install these necessary packages automatically. Then you can write a title and author and choose a default output format, as shown in the following screenshot:

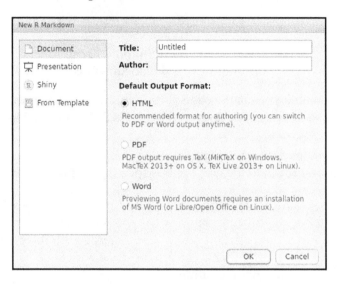

Then a new R Markdown document will be created. The new document is not empty but a demo document that shows the basics of writing texts and embedding R code which produces images. In the template document, we can see some code chunks like:

```
17
18 ``` {r cars}
19 summary(cars)
20 ```
21
```

The preceding chunk evaluates `summary(cars)` and will produce some text output:

```
25
26 ``` {r pressure, echo=FALSE}
27 plot(pressure)
28 ```
```

The preceding chunk evaluates `plot(pressure)` and will produce an image. Note that we can specify options for each chunk in the form of `{r [chunk_name], [options]}` where `[chunk_name]` is optional and is used to name the produced image and `[options]` is optional and may specify whether the code should appear in the output document, the width and height of the produced graphics, and so on. To find more options, visit `http://yihui.name/knitr/options/`.

To render the document, just click on the **Knit** button:

When the document is properly saved to disk, RStudio will call functions to render the document into a web page. More specifically, the document is rendered in two steps:

1. The `knitr` module runs the code of each chunk and places the code and output according to the chunk options so that Rmd is fully rendered as a static markdown document.
2. The `pandoc` module renders the resulted markdown document as HTML, PDF, or DOCX according to the Rmd options specified in file header.

As we are editing an R Markdown document in RStudio, we can choose which format to produce anytime and then it will automatically call the `knitr` module to render the document into markdown and then run the `pandoc` module with the proper arguments to produce a document in that format. This can also be done with code using functions provided by `knitr` and `rmarkdown` modules.

In the new document dialog, we can also choose presentation and create slides using R Markdown. Since writing documents and writing slides are similar, we won't go into detail on this topic.

Embedding tables and charts

Without R code chunks, R Markdown is no different from a plain markdown document. With code chunks, the output of code is embedded into the document so that the final content is dynamic. If a code chunk uses a random number generator without fixing the random seed, each time we knit the document we will get different results.

By default, the output of a code chunk is put directly beneath the code in fixed-width font starting with ## as if the code is run in the console. This form of output works but is not always satisfactory, especially when we want to present the data in more straightforward forms.

Embedding tables

When writing a report, we often need to put tables within the contents. In an R Markdown document, we can directly evaluate a `data.frame` variable. Suppose we have the following `data.frame`:

```
toys <- data.frame(
    id = 1:3,
    name = c("Car", "Plane", "Motocycle"),
    price = c(15, 25, 14),
    share = c(0.3, 0.1, 0.2),
    stringsAsFactors = FALSE
)
```

To output the variable in plain text, we only need to type the variable name in a code chunk:

```
toys
##     id       name price share
## 1   1        Car     15   0.3
## 2   2      Plane     25   0.1
## 3   3  Motocycle     14   0.2
```

Note that HTML, PDF, and Word documents all support native tables. To produce a native table for the chosen format, we can use `knitr::kable()` to produce the markdown representation of the table just like the following:

```
| id|name      | price| share|
|--:|:----------|-----:|-----:|
|  1|Car        |    15|   0.3|
|  2|Plane      |    25|   0.1|
|  3|Motocycle  |    14|   0.2|
```

When `pandoc` renders the resulted markdown document to other formats, it will produce a native table from the markdown representation:

```
knitr::kable(toys)
```

The table generated native table is shown as follows:

id	name	price	share
1	Car	15	0.3
2	Plane	25	0.1
3	Motocycle	14	0.2

There are other packages that produce native tables but with enhanced features. For example, the `xtable` package not only supports converting `data.frame` to LaTeX, it also provides pre-defined templates to present the results of a number of statistical models.

```
xtable::xtable(lm(mpg ~ cyl + vs, data = mtcars))
```

When the preceding code is knitted with the `results='asis'` option, the linear model will be shown as the following table in the output PDF document:

	Estimate	Std. Error	t value	Pr(>|t|)
(Intercept)	39.6250	4.2246	9.38	0.0000
cyl	-3.0907	0.5581	-5.54	0.0000
vs	-0.9391	1.9775	-0.47	0.6384

The most well-known data software is perhaps Microsoft Excel. A very interesting feature of Excel is conditional formatting. To implement such features in R, I developed `formattable` package. To install, run `install.packages("formattable")`. It enables cell formatting in a data frame to exhibit more comparative information:

```
library(formattable)
formattable(toys,
  list(price = color_bar("lightpink"), share = percent))
```

The generated table is shown as follows:

id	name	price	share
1	Car	15	30.00%
2	Plane	25	10.00%
3	Motocycle	14	20.00%

Sometimes, the data has many rows, which makes embedding such a table into the document not a good idea. But JavaScript libraries such as DataTables (`https://datatables.net/`) make it easier to embed large data sets in a web page because it automatically performs paging and also supports search and filtering. Since an R Markdown document can be rendered into an HTML web page, it is natural to leverage the JavaScript package. An R package called DT (`http://rstudio.github.io/DT/`) ports DataTables to R data frames and we can easily put a large data set into a document to let the reader explore and inspect the data in detail:

```
library(DT)
datatable(mtcars)
```

The generated table is shown as follows:

Show 10 ÷ entries   Search: [   ]

	mpg	cyl	disp	hp	drat	wt	qsec	vs	am	gear	carb
Mazda RX4	21	6	160	110	3.9	2.62	16.46	0	1	4	4
Mazda RX4 Wag	21	6	160	110	3.9	2.875	17.02	0	1	4	4
Datsun 710	22.8	4	108	93	3.85	2.32	18.61	1	1	4	1
Hornet 4 Drive	21.4	6	258	110	3.08	3.215	19.44	1	0	3	1
Hornet Sportabout	18.7	8	360	175	3.15	3.44	17.02	0	0	3	2
Valiant	18.1	6	225	105	2.76	3.46	20.22	1	0	3	1
Duster 360	14.3	8	360	245	3.21	3.57	15.84	0	0	3	4
Merc 240D	24.4	4	146.7	62	3.69	3.19	20	1	0	4	2
Merc 230	22.8	4	140.8	95	3.92	3.15	22.9	1	0	4	2
Merc 280	19.2	6	167.6	123	3.92	3.44	18.3	1	0	4	4

Showing 1 to 10 of 32 entries   Previous [1] 2 3 4 Next

The preceding packages, `formattable` and `DT` are two examples of a wide range of HTML widgets (`http://www.htmlwidgets.org/`). Many of them are adapted from popular JavaScript libraries since there are already a good number of high quality JavaScript libraries in the community.

Embedding charts and diagrams

Embedding charts is as easy as embedding tables as we demonstrated. If a code chunk produces a plot, `knitr` will save the image to a file with the name of the code chunk and write `[name](image-file.png)` below the code so that when `pandoc` renders the document the image will be found and inserted to the right place:

```
set.seed(123)
x <- rnorm(1000)
y <- 2 * x + rnorm(1000)
m <- lm(y ~ x)
plot(x, y, main = "Linear regression", col = "darkgray")
abline(coef(m))
```

The plot generated is shown as follows:

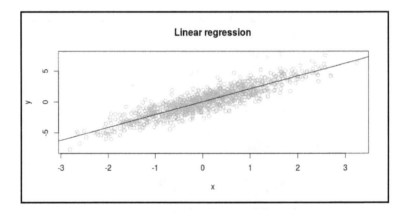

The default image size may not apply to all scenarios. We can specify chunk options `fig.height` and `fig.width` to alter the size of the image.

In addition to creating charts with basic graphics and packages like `ggplot2`, we can also create diagrams and graphs using `DiagrammeR` package. To install the package from CRAN, run `install.packages("DiagrammeR")`.

This package uses Graphviz (`https://en.wikipedia.org/wiki/Graphviz`) to describe the relations and styling of a diagram. The following code produces a very simple directed graph:

```
library(DiagrammeR)
grViz("
digraph rmarkdown {
  A -> B;
  B -> C;
```

```
  C -> A;
}")
```

The generated graph is shown as follows:

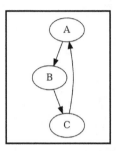

DiagrammeR also provides a more programmable way to construct diagrams. It exports a set of functions to perform operations on a graph. Each function takes a graph and outputs a modified graph. Therefore it is easy to use pipeline to connect all operations to produce a graph in a streamline. For more details, visit the package website at `http://rich-iannone.github.io/DiagrammeR`.

Embedding interactive plots

Previously, we demonstrated both static tables (`knitr::kable`, `xtable`, and `formattable`) and interactive tables (`DT`). Similar things happen to plots too. We can not only place static images in the document as we did in the previous section, but also create dynamic and interactive plots in either the viewer or the output document.

In fact, there are more packages designed to produce interactive graphics than tables. Most of them take advantage of existing JavaScript libraries and make R data structures easier to work with them. In the following code, we introduce some of the most popular packages used to create interactive graphics.

The ggvis (`http://ggvis.rstudio.com/`) developed by RStudio uses Vega (`https://vega.github.io/vega/`) as its graphics backend:

```
library(ggvis)
mtcars %>%
  ggvis(~mpg, ~disp, opacity := 0.6) %>%
  layer_points(size := input_slider(1, 100, value = 50, label = "size"))
%>%
  layer_smooths(span = input_slider(0.5, 1, value = 1, label = "span"))
```

The plot generated is shown as follows:

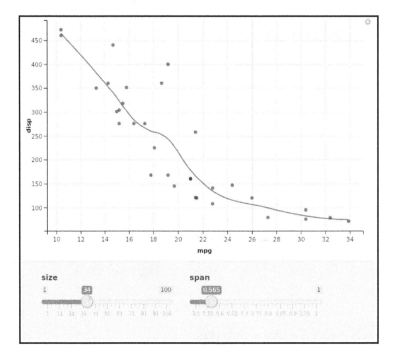

Note that its grammar is a bit like ggplot2. It best works with a pipeline operator.

Another package is called dygraphs (https://rstudio.github.io/dygraphs/) which uses the JavaScript library (http://dygraphs.com/) of the same name. This package specializes in plotting time series data with interactive capabilities.

In the following example, we use the temperature data of airports provided in the nycflights13 package. To plot the daily temperature time series of each airport present in the data, we need to summarize the data by computing the mean temperature on each day, reshape the long-format data to wide-format, and convert the results to an xts time series object with a date index and temperature columns corresponding to each airport:

```
library(dygraphs)
library(xts)
library(dplyr)
library(reshape2)
data(weather, package = "nycflights13")
temp <- weather %>%
  group_by(origin, year, month, day) %>%
  summarize(temp = mean(temp)) %>%
```

```
  ungroup() %>%
  mutate(date = as.Date(sprintf("%d-%02d-%02d",
    year, month, day))) %>%
  select(origin, date, temp) %>%
  dcast(date ~ origin, value.var = "temp")

temp_xts <- as.xts(temp[-1], order.by = temp[[1]])
head(temp_xts)
##                EWR      JFK       LGA
## 2013-01-01 38.4800 38.8713 39.23913
## 2013-01-02 28.8350 28.5425 28.72250
## 2013-01-03 29.4575 29.7725 29.70500
## 2013-01-04 33.4775 34.0325 35.26250
## 2013-01-05 36.7325 36.8975 37.73750
## 2013-01-06 37.9700 37.4525 39.70250
```

Then we supply `temp_xts` to `dygraph()` to create an interactive time series plot with a range selector and dynamic highlighting:

```
dygraph(temp_xts, main = "Airport Temperature") %>%
  dyRangeSelector() %>%
  dyHighlight(highlightCircleSize = 3,
    highlightSeriesBackgroundAlpha = 0.3,
    hideOnMouseOut = FALSE)
```

The plot generated is shown as follows:

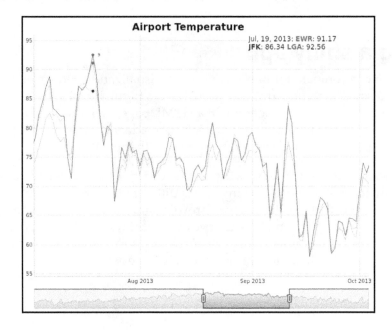

If the code is run in R terminal, the web browser will launch and show a web page containing the plot. If the code is run in RStudio, the plot will show up in the **Viewer** pane. If the code is a chunk in R Markdown document, the plot will be embedded into the rendered document.

The main advantage of interactive graphics over static plots is that interactivity allows users to further examine and explore the data rather than forcing users to view it from a fixed perspective.

There are other remarkable packages of interactive graphics. For example, `plotly` (`https://plot.ly/r/`) and `highcharter` (`http://jkunst.com/highcharter/`) are nice packages to produce a wide range of interactive plots based on JavaScript backends.

In addition to the features we demonstrated in the previous sections, R Markdown can also be used to create presentation slides, journal articles, books and websites. Visit the official website at `http://rmarkdown.rstudio.com` to learn more.

Creating interactive apps

In the previous section, we demonstrated the use of R Markdown that is designed for creating dynamic documents. In this section, we will take a quick tour of creating interactive apps where we use a graphical user interface to interact with the data.

Creating a shiny app

R itself is a great environment for data analysis and visualization. However, it is not usual to deliver R and some analytic scripts to the customers to run by themselves. The outcome of data analysis can be presented not only in a HTML page, PDF document, or a Word document, but also in an interactive app that allows readers to interact with the data by modifying some parameters and see what happens with the outcome.

A powerful package, `shiny` (`http://shiny.rstudio.com/`), developed by RStudio, is designed exactly for this purpose. A shiny app is different from the interactive graphics we demonstrated previously. It works in a web browser and the developer has all the say about what appears in the web page and how users can interact with it. To achieve this, a shiny app basically consists of two important parts: An HTTP server that interacts with the web browser, and an R session that interacts with the HTTP server.

The following is a minimal shiny app. We write an R script to define its user interface (`ui`) and `server` logic. The user interface is a `bootstrapPage` which contains a `numericInput` to take an integer of sample size and a `textOutput` to show the mean of the randomly generated sample. The logic behind `server` is to simply generate random numbers according to the sample size (n) in the `input` and put the mean of the random sample to the `output`:

```
library(shiny)

ui <- bootstrapPage(
  numericInput("n", label = "Sample size", value = 10, min = 10, max =
100),
  textOutput("mean")
)

server <- function(input, output) {
  output$mean <- renderText(mean(rnorm(input$n)))
}

app <- shinyApp(ui, server)
runApp(app)
```

The definition is now complete and we can source the code in RStudio to play with this minimal shiny app, as shown in the following screenshot:

Each time we change the number of the sample size, the HTTP server will ask the R backend to rerun the server logic and refresh the output mean.

Although the preceding example is not useful, it at least demonstrates the basic components of a shiny app. Now we look at a more complicated but useful example.

The following example is a visualizer of many paths generated by geometric Brownian motion which is often used to model stock prices. As we know, a geometric Brownian motion is characterized by starting value, expected growth rate (`r`), volatility (`sigma`), duration (`T`) and the number of `periods`. Expect for `T` = 1, we allow users to modify all other parameters.

Now we can define the user interface of the shiny app according to the parameters we want to expose to users. The `shiny` package provides a rich set of input controls listed as follows:

```
shiny_vars <- ls(getNamespace("shiny"))
shiny_vars[grep("Input$", shiny_vars)]
##  [1] "checkboxGroupInput"      "checkboxInput"
##  [3] "dateInput"               "dateRangeInput"
##  [5] "fileInput"               "numericInput"
##  [7] "passwordInput"           "selectInput"
##  [9] "selectizeInput"          "sliderInput"
## [11] "textInput"               "updateCheckboxGroupInput"
## [13] "updateCheckboxInput"     "updateDateInput"
## [15] "updateDateRangeInput"    "updateNumericInput"
## [17] "updateSelectInput"       "updateSelectizeInput"
## [19] "updateSliderInput"       "updateTextInput"
```

To control the randomness of the generated paths, we allow users to specify the random seed (`seed`) so that the same seed produces the same paths. In the following code where `ui` is defined, we use `numericInput` for `seed` and `sliderInput` for other parameters. The `sliderInput` control has a certain range and step so that we can force a parameter to take reasonable values.

The user interface not only defines the input part but also the output part, that is, where to show what. The following is all output types shiny provides:

```
shiny_vars[grep("Output$", shiny_vars)]
## [1] "dataTableOutput"   "htmlOutput"
## [3] "imageOutput"       "plotOutput"
## [5] "tableOutput"       "textOutput"
## [7] "uiOutput"          "verbatimTextOutput"
```

In this example, the shiny app only shows a plot of all paths put together to indicate different possibilities with the same set of parameters:

```
library(shiny)
ui <- fluidPage(
  titlePanel("Random walk"),
  sidebarLayout(
    sidebarPanel(
      numericInput("seed", "Random seed", 123),
      sliderInput("paths", "Paths", 1, 100, 1),
      sliderInput("start", "Starting value", 1, 10, 1, 1),
      sliderInput("r", "Expected return", -0.1, 0.1, 0, 0.001),
      sliderInput("sigma", "Sigma", 0.001, 1, 0.01, 0.001),
      sliderInput("periods", "Periods", 10, 1000, 200, 10)),
    mainPanel(
      plotOutput("plot", width = "100%", height = "600px")
```

```
  ))
 )
```

Once the user interface is defined, we need to implement the server logic which is basically about generating random paths according to user-specified parameters and put them together in the same plot.

The following code is a simple implementation of the server logic. First we set the random seed. Then we iteratively call `sde::GBM` to generate random paths from geometric Brownian motion. To install the package, run `install.packages("sde")` before calling GBM:

The GBM package is responsible for generating one path while `sapply` is used to combine all generated paths into a matrix (`mat`) where each column represents a path. Finally, we use `matplot` to plot each path in different colors together in one chart.

The calculation is done in `render*` functions no matter whether it is a text, image, or a table. The following lists all the render functions shiny provides:

```
shiny_vars[grep("^render", shiny_vars)]
## [1] "renderDataTable" "renderImage"     "renderPage"
## [4] "renderPlot"      "renderPrint"     "renderReactLog"
## [7] "renderTable"     "renderText"      "renderUI"
```

In this example, we only need `renderPlot()` and to put the plotting code in it. The `output$plot` function will go to `plotOutput("plot")` in the user interface when the input is modified:

```
server <- function(input, output) {
  output$plot <- renderPlot({
    set.seed(input$seed)
    mat <- sapply(seq_len(input$paths), function(i) {
      sde::GBM(input$start,
        input$r, input$sigma, 1, input$periods)
    })
    matplot(mat, type = "l", lty = 1,
      main = "Geometric Brownian motions")
  })
}
```

Now both user interface and server logic are ready. We can combine them together to create a shiny app and run it in the web browser.

```
app <- shinyApp(ui, server)
runApp(app)
```

When the parameters are modified, the plot will be refreshed automatically:

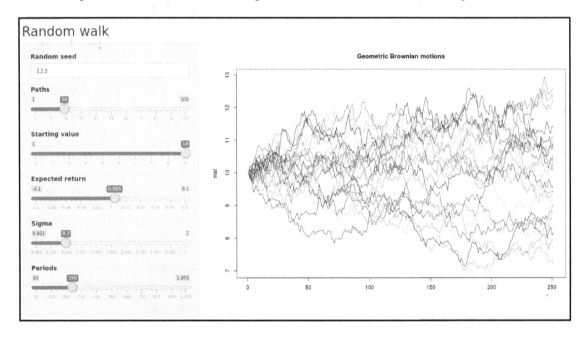

If we set a significantly positive annualized expected return, the generated paths will tend to grow more than decline:

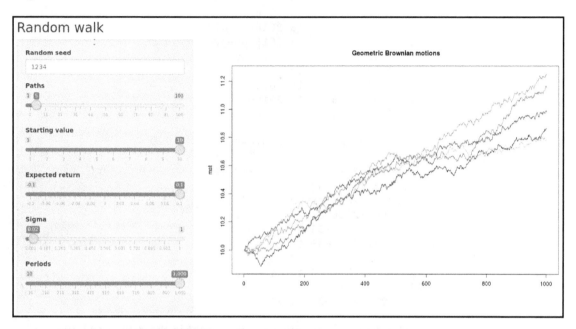

Using shinydashboard

In addition to the functions `shiny` provides, RStudio also develops `shinydashboard` (http://rstudio.github.io/shinydashboard/) which is specialized in presenting data for overview or monitoring purposes.

The following example demonstrates how easy it is to create a simple dashboard to show the most popular R packages on CRAN with the most downloads in weekly and monthly time scale.

The data source is provided by `cranlogs` (http://cranlogs.r-pkg.org). First run the following code to install the packages we need:

```
install_packages(c("shinydashboard", "cranlogs"))
```

Then we take a quick view of the data source of CRAN downloads:

```
library(cranlogs)
cran_top_downloads()
## No encoding supplied: defaulting to UTF-8.
```

```
##    rank  package count       from          to
## 1     1     Rcpp  9682 2016-08-18 2016-08-18
## 2     2   digest  8937 2016-08-18 2016-08-18
## 3     3  ggplot2  8269 2016-08-18 2016-08-18
## 4     4     plyr  7816 2016-08-18 2016-08-18
## 5     5  stringi  7471 2016-08-18 2016-08-18
## 6     6  stringr  7242 2016-08-18 2016-08-18
## 7     7 jsonlite  7100 2016-08-18 2016-08-18
## 8     8 magrittr  6824 2016-08-18 2016-08-18
## 9     9   scales  6397 2016-08-18 2016-08-18
## 10   10     curl  6383 2016-08-18 2016-08-18
cran_top_downloads("last-week")
## No encoding supplied: defaulting to UTF-8.
##    rank  package count       from          to
## 1     1     Rcpp 50505 2016-08-12 2016-08-18
## 2     2   digest 46086 2016-08-12 2016-08-18
## 3     3  ggplot2 39808 2016-08-12 2016-08-18
## 4     4     plyr 38593 2016-08-12 2016-08-18
## 5     5 jsonlite 36984 2016-08-12 2016-08-18
## 6     6  stringi 36271 2016-08-12 2016-08-18
## 7     7  stringr 34800 2016-08-12 2016-08-18
## 8     8     curl 33739 2016-08-12 2016-08-18
## 9     9      DBI 33595 2016-08-12 2016-08-18
## 10   10 magrittr 32880 2016-08-12 2016-08-18
```

After getting familiar with the form of data we want to present in the dashboard, we can now think about constructing the dashboard in exactly the same way as constructing a typical shiny app. To make the most of `shinydashboard`, it is better to go through `http://rstudio.github.io/shinydashboard/structure.html` to get a general idea of the nice components it provides.

Similarly to shiny app, we start by creating the user interface. This time, we use `dashboardPage`, `dashboardSidebar` and `dashboardBody`. In the dashboard, we want to present the package download dynamics and tables of the most popular packages with top downloads in both monthly and weekly scales.

We put the menu of monthly and weekly in the side bar so users can choose which to see. In each tab page, we can put plots and tables together. In this example, we use `formattable` to add color bars on the download column to make the numbers more comparable and straightforward.

```
library(shiny)
library(shinydashboard)
library(formattable)
library(cranlogs)
```

```
ui <- dashboardPage(
  dashboardHeader(title = "CRAN Downloads"),
  dashboardSidebar(sidebarMenu(
    menuItem("Last week",
      tabName = "last_week", icon = icon("list")),
    menuItem("Last month",
      tabName = "last_month", icon = icon("list"))
  )),
  dashboardBody(tabItems(
    tabItem(tabName = "last_week",
      fluidRow(tabBox(title = "Total downloads",
        tabPanel("Total", formattableOutput("last_week_table"))),
        tabBox(title = "Top downloads",
          tabPanel("Top", formattableOutput("last_week_top_table"))))),
    tabItem(tabName = "last_month",
      fluidRow(tabBox(title = "Total downloads",
        tabPanel("Total", plotOutput("last_month_barplot"))),
        tabBox(title = "Top downloads",
          tabPanel("Top", formattableOutput("last_month_top_table")))))))
  ))
)
```

Note that `plotOutput` is provided by `shiny` while `formattableOutput` is provided by `formattable` package. In fact, developers can create all kinds of HTML widgets that can be embedded into a shiny app as long as the package properly defines the `render*` function and `*Output` function to produce the correct HTML code.

Then we define the server logic. Since the output relies purely on the data source, we download the data before calling `formattable` and `plot`.

```
server <- function(input, output) {
  output$last_week_table <- renderFormattable({
    data <- cran_downloads(when = "last-week")
    formattable(data, list(count = color_bar("lightblue")))
  })
  output$last_week_top_table <- renderFormattable({
    data <- cran_top_downloads("last-week")
    formattable(data, list(count = color_bar("lightblue"),
      package = formatter("span",
        style = "font-family: monospace;")))
  })
  output$last_month_barplot <- renderPlot({
    data <- subset(cran_downloads(when = "last-month"),
      count > 0)
    with(data, barplot(count, names.arg = date),
      main = "Last month downloads")
  })
```

```
output$last_month_top_table <- renderFormattable({
  data <- cran_top_downloads("last-month")
  formattable(data, list(count = color_bar("lightblue"),
    package = formatter("span",
      style = "font-family: monospace;")))
})
}
```

In fact, if the data is updating, we can create a dynamic dashboard where the tables and charts periodically refresh. Using `?reactiveTimer` and `?reactive` will be the key to achieve this. Read the documentation for more information.

Both the user interface and the server logic are ready, so we can run the app now:

```
runApp(shinyApp(ui, server))
```

By default, the shiny app shows the first page at the first visit. The following is a screenshot of the **Last week** tab page which consists of two tab panels of `formattable` data frames:

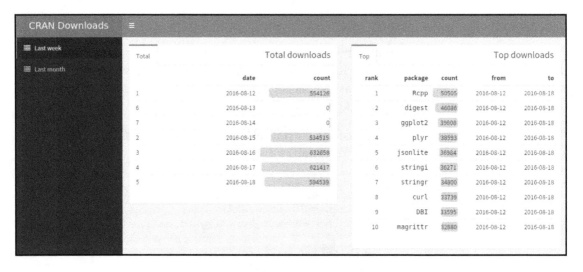

The following screenshot shows the **Last month** tab page which consists of a histogram and a `formattable` data frame:

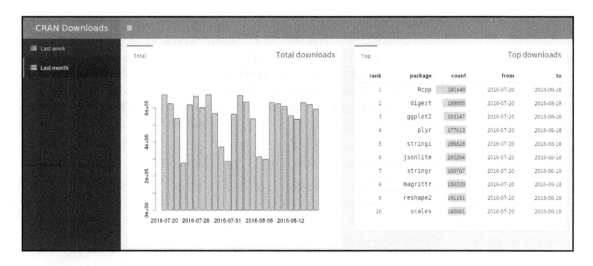

To see more examples and the code behind them, visit
`http://rstudio.github.io/shinydashboard/examples.html`.

Summary

In this chapter, we demonstrated the use of R Markdown to produce dynamic documents where tables, graphics, and interactive plots can be easily embedded. Then we saw a few simple examples of shiny apps which are basically web-based interactive apps with an R backend. With these powerful productivity tools, data analysis can be made more interesting and full of fun because the outcome can be demonstrated in a nice, interactive way, which is usually better for conveying more information, drawing more insights and making better decisions.

Now we have finished this book. We started learning R by getting familiar with the fundamental concepts, data structures and language constructs and features. We went through a wide range of examples to understand how these fit the needs of practical data analysis. To build a concrete and consistent understanding of the R programming language and the behavior of data structures, we discussed several advanced topics such as R's evaluation model, metaprogramming, and object-oriented systems. With the above knowledge, we then explored a series of more practical topics such as working with databases, data manipulation techniques, high performance computing, web scraping techniques, dynamic documents, and interactive apps.

This books covers a variety of topics to expand a wide horizon on the possibility of what R and its extension packages can do. Now you should feel empowered and much more confident using R to solve data analysis problems with the right techniques. More importantly, I hope this book enables you to better work with data and go further with other useful topics such as visualization, specialized statistical modeling, and machine learning. If you are interested in going even deeper, I strongly recommend that you read *Advanced R* by Hadley Wickham.

Index